FIFTY KEY WORKS OF HISTORY AND HISTORIOGRAPHY

Fifty Key Works of History and Historiography introduces some of the most important works ever written by those who have sought to understand, capture, query and interpret the past. The works covered include texts from ancient times to the present day and from different cultural traditions ensuring a wide variety of schools, methods and ideas are introduced. Each of the fifty texts represents at least one of six broad categories:

- Early examples of historiography (e.g. Herodotus and Augustine)
- Non-western works (e.g. Shaddad and Fukuzawa)
- "Critical" historiography (e.g. Mabillon and Ranke)
- History of minorities, neglected groups or subjects (e.g. Said and Needham)
- Broad sweeps of history (e.g. Mumford and Hofstadter)
- Problematic or unconventional historiography (e.g. Foucault and White)

Each of the key works is introduced in a short essay written in a lively and engaging style which provides the ideal preparation for reading the text itself. Complete with a substantial introduction to the field, this book is the perfect starting point for anyone new to the study of history or historiography.

Kenneth R. Stunkel is Professor of History at Monmouth University, New Jersey, USA. His Ph.D in history is from the University of Maryland. Teaching and publication include classical civilization, South Asia (India), East Asia (China, and Japan), and European intellectual and cultural history. His recent books are *Ideas and Art in Asian Civilizations: India, China, and Japan* (2011), and *Understanding Lewis Mumford: A Guide for the Perplexed* (2004).

ALSO AVAILABLE FROM ROUTLEDGE

World History: The Basics
Peter N. Stearns
978-0-415-58275-9

Fifty Key Thinkers on History (Second Edition)
Edited by Marnie Hughes-Warrington
978-0-415-36651-9

The Modern Historiography Reader
Edited by Adam Budd
978-0-415-45887-0

Modern Historiography: An Introduction
Michael Bentley
978-0-415-20267-1

Companion to Historiography
Edited by Michael Bentley
978-0-415-28557-5

FIFTY KEY WORKS OF HISTORY AND HISTORIOGRAPHY

Kenneth R. Stunkel

Routledge
Taylor & Francis Group
LONDON AND NEW YORK

First published 2011
by Routledge
2 Park Square, Milton Park, Abingdon, Oxon, OX14 4RN

Simultaneously published in the USA and Canada
by Routledge
711 Third Avenue, New York, NY 10017

Routledge is an imprint of the Taylor & Francis Group, an informa business

© 2011 Kenneth R. Stunkel

The right of Kenneth R. Stunkel to be identified as author of this work has been asserted by him in accordance with sections 77 and 78 of the Copyright, Designs and Patents Act 1988.

All rights reserved. No part of this book may be reprinted or reproduced or utilised in any form or by any electronic, mechanical, or other means, now known or hereafter invented, including photocopying and recording, or in any information storage or retrieval system, without permission in writing from the publishers.

Trademark notice: Product or corporate names may be trademarks or registered trademarks, and are used only for identification and explanation without intent to infringe.

British Library Cataloguing in Publication Data
A catalogue record for this book is available from the British Library

Library of Congress Cataloging in Publication Data
Stunkel, Kenneth R.
  Fifty key works of history and historiography / by Kenneth R. Stunkel.
    p. cm.
  1. Historiography. 2. History–Bibliography. 3. Historiography–Bibliography. I. Title.
  D13.2.S88 2011
  016.909–dc22
                          2010046798

ISBN 13: 978-0-415-57331-3 (hbk)
ISBN 13: 978-0-415-57332-0 (pbk)
ISBN 13: 978-0-203-81665-3 (ebk)

Typeset in Bembo and Helvetica
by Taylor and Francis Books

CONTENTS

Introduction		xi
Greece		1
1	The Persian Wars (Herodotus, ca. 484–ca. 424 B.C.)	1
2	History of the Peloponnesian War (Thucydides, ca. 460–ca. 395 B.C.)	7
	Section Notes	13
Rome		14
3	Lives of the Caesars (Gaius Suetonius Tranqullus, ca. 69–ca. 140)	14
4	The Jugurthine War (Sallust, 86–34 B.C.)	19
	Section Notes	23
Judaism and Christianity		24
5	The Jewish War (Flavius Josephus, A.D. 37–ca. 100)	24
6	The City of God (Augustine of Hippo, A.D. 354–430)	30
	Section Notes	35
Byzantium		36
7	Secret History (Procopius, ca. 500–ca. 554)	36
	Section Notes	42

Islam 43

8 The Rare and Excellent History of Saladin (Baha' al-Din Ibn Shaddad, 1145–1235) 43
Section Note 48

Medieval Europe 49

9 The Anglo-Saxon Chronicle (Anonymous, early Christian Era to 1154) 49

10 The Life of Saint Louis (Jean de Joinville, 1225–1317) 54
Section Notes 58

Renaissance Europe 59

11 Discourse on the Forgery of the Alleged Donation of Constantine (Lorenzo Valla, 1406–1457) 59

12 Method for the Easy Comprehension of History (Jean Bodin, 1530–1596) 64
Section Notes 69

Reformation Europe 70

13 Historical and Critical Dictionary (Pierre Bayle, 1647–1706) 71

14 On diplomatics (Jean Mabillon, 1632–1707) 76
Section Notes 81

Eighteenth-century Europe 82

15 The Age of Louis XIV (Voltaire, or Françoise-Marie Arouet, 1694–1778) 83

16 The Decline and Fall of the Roman Empire (Edward Gibbon, 1737–1794) 88

17	Reflections on the Philosophy of the History of Mankind (Johann Gottfried Herder, 1744–1803)	94
	Section Notes	99

Nineteenth-century Europe 101

18	History of the Popes, their Church and State (Leopold von Ranke, 1795–1886)	101
19	Mohammed and Charlemagne (Henri Pirenne, 1862–1935)	109
20	Civilization of the Renaissance in Italy (Jacob Burckhardt, 1818–1897)	113
21	Popular Account of Discoveries at Nineveh (Austen Henry Layard, 1817–1894)	118
22	History of the Rise and Influence of the Spirit of Rationalism in Europe (William Lecky, 1838–1903)	123
23	The Life of Jesus Critically Examined (David Friedrich Strauss, 1808–1874)	127
24	Inaugural Lecture on the study of history (John Dalberg-Acton, 1834–1902)	133
25	The Provinces of the Roman Empire from Caesar to Diocletian (Theodor Mommsen, 1817–1903)	137
	Section Notes	142

China 143

26	Tai Chen on Mencius: Explorations in Words and Meanings (Tai Chen, 1724–1777)	144
27	Traditional Government in Imperial China: A Critical Analysis (Ch'ien Mu, 1895–1990)	148
	Section Notes	153

Japan 154

28 An Outline of a Theory of Civilization (Fukuzawa Yukichi, 1835–1901) 155

29 The Culture of the Meiji Era (Irokawa Daikichi, 1925–) 161
   Section Notes 167

India 168

30 Culture, Ideology, Hegemony: Intellectuals and Social Consciousness in Colonial India (K. N. Panikkar, 1936–) 169

31 Elementary Aspects of Peasant Insurgency in Colonial India (Ranajit Guha, 1922–) 173

Africa 179

32 The African Experience (Vincent Khapoya, 1944–) 179

33 Pan-African History: Political Figures from Africa and the Diaspora since 1787 (Hakim Adi and Marika Sherwood) 186

Twentieth-century Europe and America 191

34 The Protestant Ethic and the Spirit of Capitalism (Max Weber, 1864–1920) 192

35 The Great Chain of Being: A Study of the History of an Idea (Arthur O. Lovejoy, 1873–1962) 197

36 Technics and Civilization (Lewis Mumford, 1895–1990) 203

37 Religion and the Decline of Magic: Studies in Popular Beliefs in Sixteenth- and Seventeenth Century England (Keith Thomas, 1933–) 209

38 The Heavenly City of the Eighteenth Century Philosophers (Carl Lotus Becker, 1873–1945) 214

39	The Grand Titration: Science and Society in East and West (Joseph Needham, 1900–1995)	219
40	The Majority Finds Its Past: Placing Women in History (Gerda Lerner, 1920–)	225
41	The American Political Tradition and the Men Who Made It (Richard Hofstadter, 1916–1970)	230
42	Inventing Human Rights: A History (Lynn Hunt)	235
43	The Hour of Our Death (Philippe Ariès, 1914–1984)	241
44	Intellectual Origins of the English Revolution (Christopher Hill, 1912–2003)	247
45	From Slavery to Freedom: A History of African Americans (John Hope Franklin 1915–2009)	252
46	Orientalism: Western Conceptions of the Orient (Edward W. Said, 1935–2003)	256
47	The History of Sexuality, Volume 1: An Introduction (Michel Foucault, 1926–1984)	263
48	Young Man Luther: A Study in Psychoanalysis and History (Erik H. Erikson, 1902–1994)	267
49	Metahistory: The Historical Imagination in Nineteenth-Century Europe (Hayden White, 1928–)	272
50	The World of Odysseus (M. I. Finley, 1912–1986)	277
	Section Notes	282
	Index	283

INTRODUCTION TO FIFTY KEY WORKS OF HISTORY AND HISTORIOGRAPHY

Most societies have preferred, with more or less success, to avoid being swallowed by *Lethe*, the river of forgetfulness. For the human animal, it seems anything is preferable to complete amnesia, which accounts for early devices on behalf of remembrance like myth, legend, and oral tradition. Better a myth than nothing at all. Greek myths are not merely convenient vehicles to explain natural events; they also provide markers into the past, accessible stories about how things came to be what they are. While useful for understanding literature, art, and religion, however, such devices do not qualify as history.

For our purposes, history refers to human thought and activity in past time, their settings and consequences, and what can be known about them from surviving traces. Historiography refers to distinct bodies of historical inquiry and writing, for example, Greek. Medieval, Chinese, Islamic, and how such works have been researched, written, used, and passed on in different times and places. Any discussion of historical works and their authors cannot avoid how and why the work was done, justified, and disseminated. These fifty essays afford a glimpse of how the past has been queried, recovered, interpreted, understood, and explained from ancient times to the present. The emphasis is on works, what they say, and on what principles they were written, with supporting remarks as needed about careers and views of their authors.

This slender volume on such a big subject rests on three assumptions. The first is that historical knowledge has been achieved in a plurality of cultural settings. These include the West since the ancient world as well as several non-Western societies. The second is that whatever knowledge there is has authority because credible sources

INTRODUCTION

were used by critical minds. The third is that the scope of historical realities confirmed by usable knowledge has expanded into nearly every accessible crevice of the past. World literature teems with writers of history, while libraries are stuffed and overflowing with their articles, monographs, and books.[1] Innumerable past events, persons, objects, and settings have left traces inviting some form of historical study, which has been done from many theoretical and methodological perspectives. Varieties of historical inquiry have been increasing without a sign of leveling off.

Fifty "key" works—what and why

The practice of history has its own history (another meaning of historiography) with many players and points of view. Any attempt to cover that ground is a huge undertaking. Such an overview is not the task of this volume, which must not be confused with histories of historiography.[2] Commentary on a mere 50 works barely touches a vast subject crisscrossed by myriad ways and byways. It follows that an effort to be representative in these pluralistic times must inevitably neglect someone's preferences and expectations.[3] A second caution is about audiences, which for this volume are students, undergraduate and graduate, and possibly a slice of the general public endowed with curiosity, but not specialists or professionals in search of heavily footnoted scholarship, this introduction being an exception.

Since it is improbable that ten historians from various fields would agree on the "key" status of many works in a list of 50, why attempt the enterprise at all? A foremost reason is to explain and illustrate in one slim volume some variations of method, purpose, and style in major traditions of historiography. Clear perspectives are needed, however daunting the task, in an ocean of subject matter and a rainforest of historians and their works. A second reason is to survey in 50 works how objectivity and truth in history have been pursued, defended, and neglected from the ancient world to the present in several cultural traditions, which is *a principal aim* of this volume.

Because of so much historical literature within a diversity of interests, the scope of this book is limited by necessity. One limitation is the essays, for each must stay within range of 2000 words to keep the length of the book manageable and economical.[4] Multi-volume works, with a couple of exceptions, are avoided, since dealing with them effectively in a brief essay is usually unsatisfactory. It was difficult to locate foreign language works in English translation also

INTRODUCTION

available in accessible editions. The search, on balance, worked out, but influenced the choice of works.

The 50 works selected are described as "key" because they represent and illustrate, more or less, a rationale of six themes. Justification for each lies in plausible connections with the themes. They are: (1) early examples of method and style in historiography (e.g., Herodotus, Sallust, Augustine, Anglo-Saxon Chronicles); (2) select non-Western works for contrast with Western works (e.g., Shaddad, Fukuzawa, Pannikar, Ch'ien Mu); (3) issues of evidence, and the emergence and practice of critical historiography, by which is meant a self-conscious search for believable evidence needed to support generalizations about the past, and the exploitation of new kinds of evidence (e.g., Mabillon, Ranke, Mommsen, Thomas); (4) the expansion of historical subject matter, or genres of history—women, minorities, science, technology, ideas, broad interpretations (e.g., Pirenne, Lerner, Needham, Said); (5) works that take on generous chunks of the past (e.g., Lovejoy, Ariès, Mumford, Hofstadter); (6) problematic historiography, or eccentric works that rest uneasily in the familiar domain of history (e.g., Procopius, Herder, Foucault, White). Themes overlap in a number of works.

The present array of 50 works would of course be different if guided by other rationales, which could have been political, diplomatic, economic, ethnic, feminist, multicultural, postcolonial, regional, and so on. While there is no iron necessity about the choices, they are not merely random and arbitrary, but reflect the rationale as well as knowledge, experience, and judgment of the author others may legitimately dispute. Justification for selections is less evident at the beginning of the book than at the end. What matters is a reader's final satisfaction that light has been shed on historiography from several angles and in more than one tradition.

A thread connecting works, more so in some places than others, is the question of how evidence has been identified, evaluated, and used. If this is a Western "bias," it is freely admitted because systematic critical techniques arose most fully in Western historical works. But from a concern about standards of evidence, it does not follow that one size fits all or that only Europe did true and useful history. While the essays can be read, pondered, and discussed individually, students are served best by connecting works with themes and paging through an occasional primary work. An overview helps bring a single work into perspective, so it is advisable to start at the beginning of the volume rather than skip from one work to another. Here is further explanation of the themes.

Pioneer works

Works discussed in this volume span some 2500 years. Historical inquiry had beginnings and halting first steps. Those beginnings are themselves part of an imperfect historical record. When works from early centuries are studied, their deficiencies are obvious compared with contemporary works. Yet history practiced in the modern world owes a debt to earlier writers who sought knowledge of the past amidst distractions of the present with few prior examples for guidance. A book on 50 key works of historiography would be incomplete without Greek, Roman, Christian, and Medieval examples (including Islam) that attempted some form of historical narrative and explanation.

Non-Western perspectives

Works are included from China, India, Japan, Africa, and Islam. Two examples are provided for all except Islam. For our purposes, basic principles of Islamic historiography are sufficiently illustrated by Ibn Shaddad. In the current state of scholarship, much has been learned about the quest for historical knowledge in non-Western societies.[5] The works chosen have three roles. The first is to remind readers that civilizations other than those in the West sought to recover, understand, and make use of the past. The second is to show that elements of a critical outlook were not confined to Western historiography and that sensitivity to evidence in some form appeared in more than one place and time. The third is to show that within non-Western traditions of historical writing, just as in the West, there were differences about what counts as evidence and how historians should proceed with inquiry.

Critical historiography

Works are included to highlight critical attitudes and methods that distinguish history from invention, apologetics, whim, legend, and myth. Good history needs a dose of art and imaginative insight as well as empirical criticism to do its job, but without means to test and verify sources, the results are not history.[6] Techniques have been mastered over the centuries that compel the historical record to qualify as usable evidence for knowledge that can be pulled out of shape only so far. The development of reliable methods took place unevenly in several traditions of historiography, but did so most fully and visibly in nineteenth-century Europe. Critical history needs a scheme to place events in a succession of years (chronology); techniques for authenticating documents (diplomatics); knowledge of handwriting styles to read documents correctly (paleography); decipherment of languages in their various historical forms (philology); classification, dating, and reading of inscriptions (epigraphy) and coins (numismatics). An associated advance in technique and scope is systematic excavation and interpretation of ancient ruins (archeology). Archeology reminds us that documents are not the only road to historical knowledge. Sources like oral history have been exploited more recently, and French *annalists* opened further possibilities for tapping into local history with quantitative methods. There is an inescapable difference between facing the past with these tools at hand, even some of them, and doing so without any of them.

But technique is not enough. Historical material, chiefly documents of all kinds, must be collected and classified in accessible archives and libraries, state, public, private, or otherwise, and made available to historians through some mechanism of institutionalized services. Continuity of historiography needs a teaching tradition in schools and universities *to train* professional historians so inquiry and publication are not confined to curious laymen, literary people, or court and church functionaries. Finally, professional journals or other means of systematic dissemination are needed so specialized knowledge can be shared routinely among practicing historians. In the West, landmark examples are for Germany the *Historische Zeitschrift* (1856), for France the *Revue Historique* (1876), for England the *English Historical Revue* (1886), and for the USA the *American Historical Revue* (1895). Since the nineteenth century, journals devoted to history have proliferated. The more fully these conditions are realized, the more assurance we have that historical knowledge has a fair chance of accumulating.

Critical historiography does not imply history is objective like natural science, which can make predictions and eliminate competing hypotheses with experiments. Contrary to J.B. Bury's view that history is neither more nor less a science, it is not and cannot be an *exact science* even with doses of quantification.[7] Where there is knowledge, there must be a known object, but for history and physics, the objects are not identical. Those of natural science can be analyzed quantitatively. The facts (*factum*, to make or to do) upon which historical knowledge is based are about human thoughts, deeds, and artifacts, not phenomena of nature. Historians want to know how and why as well as what but must address non-quantitative ideas, motives, and feelings. What history and natural science have in common is a *scientific attitude*, an urge to find something out and convey it truthfully with a systematic method of inquiry.

What occurred in the past must be inferred from surviving evidence, but historians have means to establish that a record comes from the past and is what it seems to be. Any reconstruction of past events, beliefs, and thoughts has a degree of probability depending on the quantity and quality of evidence that survives critical examination. Much the same is true of historical sciences that reconstruct earth history and its life forms. Unlike natural science, written history necessarily has ties with literature. Despite advocacy of quantification as the portal to objectivity, history relies mostly on ordinary language. This is a good thing, for it explains the accessibility and long-time appeal of historical works. Communication of knowledge and understanding demand a union of readability and truthfulness, imagination and criticism.[8]

Genres of history

Until modern times, preservation of memory has included inscriptions, king lists, memoirs, chronologies, journals, chronicles noting exceptional events in this or that year, and occasionally more ambitious narrative efforts to codify some aspect of the past. For centuries, such writing served local, didactic, religious, dynastic, and moral purposes. Historical writing has long since expanded beyond politics, diplomacy, war, and their associated personalities. Since the twentieth century, historians have widened and deepened understanding of the past even further in both variety and complexity.

A purpose of the 50 works in this volume is to suggest the range of variety of historiography from the ancient world to the twentieth century. Now there are histories of science and technology, urban history, intellectual history, legal history, social history, cultural history, and economic history. In the second half of the twentieth century several kinds of "new history" surfaced about women, mental structures (French *annales*), and former colonial peoples. Some recent histories have featured beans, shoes, glamor, and food advertising. While additional types of evidence and principles of evaluation have been used by new sub-fields (i.e., oral evidence, quantification, psychoanalysis, anthropology), all are still beholden to earlier pioneers who demonstrated that believable history depends on shared principles of inquiry. The mere existence of so much diversity confirms the current range and power of historical study.[9]

Widening the lens of historiography

The nineteenth-century impetus of historical writing has not let up despite profoundly disruptive upheavals. Two world wars, the subsequent breakup of empires, Ottoman as well as European, a world depression, a number of lesser but costly international conflicts, a cold war between Western liberalism and Soviet communism have stimulated historical output to record, understand, and explain those events as archives worldwide have opened up. In the meantime, domains of history continue to proliferate and now comprise more perspectives and their literatures than any diligent person can survey in several lifetimes. Yet some historians have tried to coordinate and consolidate piles of facts, books, and articles to fashion shape and meaning from long stretches of past time.

In this volume some works exemplify breadth and a "big picture." Lovejoy's history of the chain of being from the ancient world to the nineteenth century explores a single idea. Chi'en Mu sweeps across the successes and failures of traditional China's many dynasties. Theodore Mommsen takes on all the provinces of the Roman Empire. Lewis Mumford expounds and analyses the history of technology and speculates about its meaning. That kind of synthesis and interpretation at the highest level is essential if world historiography is to be more than a growing, shifting heap of sand.

Problematic works

Some works are strange and off beat to a reader of standard history and its forms. They raise questions about a believable fit in the category of historiography, but invite representation because they have influenced historical debate and understanding. What does one do with an undocumented work written and kept secret (Procopius)? What is to be said about a work full of obscurities that overlaps strongly with philosophy and literature while proposing an influential standard of historical reality and meaning (Herder)? How does one assess a work about history that uses history, but essentially denies its objectivity and views it as a genre of literature (White)? What does one do with a purported history of sexuality that is mainly concerned to show that all social phenomena are governed by power relations (Foucault)? Students of historiography should be aware of

INTRODUCTION

such works, the problems they raise, and the uses to which they might be put.

An avalanche of historical writing

Historiography in the West underwent a transformation in the nineteenth century when an unprecedented audience for history flourished. There arose a conviction that human thought, society, creations, and institutions are best understood by doing history to describe and explain their origin and development, that knowledge of the present is contingent on knowing how and why change has taken place in successive eras. This "historicist" outlook was a result of propulsive change—political and social revolution in France, industrialization in Western Europe, philosophers who argued that historical development produced the world as we know it, and the claim of evolutionary biology that change is law of existence.[10] Historicism in this sense underlies earlier works, like those of Voltaire.[11] By the turn of the twentieth century the historicist way of thinking produced an overwhelming body of historical literature whose growth and complexity have not let up.

Yet this abundance and variety conceal an irony. Historical awareness is not a given. It does not come easily and may not stick. The attention of most people everywhere has been dominated by events unfolding in immediate experience, supplemented by myths, legends, traditions, and hearsay that may or may not contain fragments of historical truth. The idea that systematic history might be written based on testimony, travel, artifacts, and documents scrutinized by critical methods, with a view to understanding the condition, flow, causes, and consequences of past events, has not been a commonplace for humanity. Even today, with enormous resources available in books, journals, university departments, conferences, book clubs, and the Internet, average historical literacy probably is less healthy than it was in the nineteenth century. A further irony is that a world awash in historical literature faces postmodern claims that historical knowledge is flimsy or unlikely. A student of historiography should be aware of these claims and think about their consequences.

Postmodern challenge[12]

With respect to history, "postmodern theory of historiography is the denial that historical writing refers to an actual historical past." According to several theorists, "historiography does not differ from

xviii

INTRODUCTION

fiction but is a form of it."[13] The postmodern "challenge" more broadly understood is a mosaic of cultural relativism, social constructivism, and linguistic deconstructivism.[14] Postmodern reservations about historical knowledge peaked in the 1990s.[15] Going well beyond moderate skepticism of historians like Charles A. Beard, Carl Becker, and E.H. Carr, postmodern critics claim that statements about the past are so culture bound, strapped by limitations of language, and sullied by personal bias that objectivity by any standard is a wish rather than a fulfillment.[16] Addressed briefly here, as it must be, the issue is whether those strictures are fatal to historical knowledge.

Doubts about the objectivity of knowledge—historical, scientific, or otherwise—originated in a Western tradition of criticism and skepticism of which postmodern theory is a part. The names David Hume (knowledge of the world is probable), Friedrich Nietzsche (knowledge is interpretation), Sören Kierkegaard (a leap of faith transcends knowledge), and Robert Musil ("the man without qualities" who does not know up from down or front from back) are evidence that doubts about scientific and philosophical rationality predate postmodern writers. Carl Becker in the 1930s characterized the modern world as chaos without a center: "The fact is that we have no first premise. Since Whirl is King, we must start with the whirl, the mess of things presented in experience."[17] The climate of opinion for postmodern doubt could hardly be stated better.

Postmodern criticism is unfriendly to historical knowledge while usually assuming exemption from skeptical implications of its own principles. The serpent swallowing its tail is acknowledged by deconstructionist Jacques Derrida, for whom all texts, including his own, are "undecidable."[18] Postmodern criticism is therefore vulnerable to methods of analysis it turns on historical works.[19] As Derrida might say, texts are just texts, equal in their ambiguity. If that is the case, one relativistic view of knowledge is as good as another, a point of view incompatible with a premise of this book—that a real past can be recovered, more or less, and that historians have means to do it. While there is no one acceptable way to history, all traditions and forms of historiography are not equal. Some are more trustworthy and useful for understanding the past than others. The test is the presence or absence of evidence critically used for analysis, narrative, and generalization. Traditions of historiography from any time or place supported by standards of evidence and inquiry may be regarded as triumphs of humanity on behalf of shared knowledge and understanding.

In descending order of severity, three intertwined claims of the postmodern challenge are suggested here: (1) instead of knowledge about a real past, we have only subjective, socially conditioned interpretations; (2) cultural bias forecloses objectivity about any other culture; (3) no degree of objectivity in history is possible because texts of whatever kind have no reference outside themselves, and even within texts meanings are variable and ambiguous, at the mercy of reader response. These claims owe much to cultural anthropology, *avant garde* philosophy, and modern literary criticism. Some familiar names are Claude Lévi-Strauss, Richard Rorty, Jacques Derrida, Michel Foucault, and Roland Barthes.[20]

As for the first claim, it is self-defeating to think interpretations are equal because selection and evaluation of facts betray the historian's interests and values. Anyone inquiring into anything must select and evaluate, the physicist as well as the historian (add the postmodern critic). The consequences of no selection and evaluation are no focus and no knowledge. The only escape is to reject evidence and knowledge altogether, which leaves critics high and dry along with historians. A distinction between subjective and objective impinges on commonplace human experiences. Your headaches are subjective and therefore yours alone, clearly distinguishable from a public experience like a company of students viewing the Rosetta Stone and its three scripts at the British Museum. Apart from the familiar interplay of subjective and objective experiences in historical research and thought, a more subtle connection of the two is to be touched, changed, and even overwhelmed by the past when reading a text.[21] The past can seem more vivid, real, and objective than the immediate present.

A response to the second claim is that membership in a culture is no guarantee that it is understood, nor is comprehension of an alien culture necessarily blocked. This is a fish bowl approach to possibilities of awareness and understanding. An occidental student of Chinese civilization might know more than most Chinese, and a Chinese student of American history might know more than most Americans. Arthur Waley was a respected scholar and translator of Chinese and Japanese literature and art who never visited China or Japan. Any serious student of another civilization knows that imperfect knowledge of an "other" throws light on one's own cultural milieu because differences can be perceived and assessed. All historical writing is affected more or less by personal bias and cultural background, but an uncritical historian must be distinguished from one consciously seeking distance from those limitations in a critical spirit. A little common sense helps. Whatever a historian's personal tastes and cultural affiliation, if something is made up willfully, it is usually

INTRODUCTION

described as fiction. If fact is ignored or manipulated for political or religious causes, it is called propaganda or apologetics. Fudging these distinctions results in obscurantism and self-contradiction.

As for the third claim, if the meaning of texts is self-enclosed and uncertain with no connection to an author's intentions (we might ask, who would read a historian oblivious of his or her intentions?), the reservation applies with reflexive logic to postmodern texts. In other words, if texts (books, essays, monographs) are closed systems of ambiguous signs isolated from minds that conceived them, how can postmodern critics of history be sure they *know* anything? If the past is truly inaccessible because objectivity is an illusion, and if all such writing is no more than a literature of "tropes" and social fictions, historians must be resigned to exchanging subjective impressions or publishing their books as a genre of fiction. Practicing historians have been notably reluctant to embrace those options, which is also true of most postmodern critics.

A concluding point is that uncertainty and incompleteness do not foreclose objective knowledge. Uncertainty is a necessary condition for knowing anything at all, for without it there would be no need for questions and inquiries. Certainties are no stimulus to curiosity and finding things out. Incompleteness is a spur to add more and better knowledge, which can never be final because a complex world with a tangled past changes beneath our feet and defeats closure. But incomplete knowledge is still knowledge and better than no knowledge. Our contemporary dilemma is not a lack of historical knowledge, but making sense of its accumulated immensity while it continues to grow.

With that much said, postmodern criticism is a reminder that getting at historical truth has always faced obstacles of language, individual bias, and cultural exclusiveness, all better taken into account and consciously managed than overlooked. Furthermore, historians should be prodded to think often and deeply about the foundation of their discipline instead of taking it for granted while plowing ahead innocently with the next monograph. Finally, historians should restrain themselves from asserting more than can be delivered, which includes thinking past realities are palpable like kitchen crockery, or reducible to iron laws of nature driving the historical process in predictable directions.

Notes

1 See for example, John Cannon et al., *Blackwell Dictionary of Historians* (1988), which has 450 entries; Lucien Boia et al., *Great Historians from Antiquity to 1800* (1989), with 600 entries; and Lucien Boia et al., *Great*

INTRODUCTION

Historians of the Modern Age: An International Dictionary (1991), with 900 entries.
2 See James T. Shotwell, *An Introduction to the History of History* (rev. ed.; New York: Columbia University Press, 1939); James Westfall Thompson, *A History of Historical Writing*, 2 vols. (New York: Macmillan, 1942); Matthew Fitzsimmons et al., *The Development of Historiography* (Port Washington, New York: Kennikat Press, 1954); Harry Elmer Barnes, *A History of Historical Writing* (2nd rev. ed.; New York: Dover Publications, 1962); Donald R. Kelley, *Faces of History: Historical Inquiry from Herodotus to Herder* (New Haven, Connecticut: Yale University Press, 1998). The Thompson volumes stop at the end of the nineteenth century, but detail is excellent. For an anthology of twelve twentieth-century "schools" with commentary, see Anna Greene & Kathleen Troup (eds.), *The Houses of History: A Critical Reader in Twentieth Century History and Theory* (New York: New York University Press, 1999).
3 Latin America is not represented because its historiography is not non-Western; it is associated with Europe and America, for which there is already a sufficient number of works in this volume.
4 An effort has been made to avoid works of historians in Marnie-Hughes Warrington's *Fifty Key Thinkers on History* (2nd ed.; London: Routledge, 2009). With a few exceptions, her book constrained my choices. For example, she writes on Livy and Tacitus for Rome, so I turned to Suetonius and Sallust. She writes about historians and their thought. I write about works. Despite some overlap in historians, the two books might be considered complementary.
5 See Georg G. Iggers, Q. Edward Wang, and Supriya Mukherjee, *A Global History of Modern Historiography* (Edinburgh Gate, United Kingdom: Pearson Longman, 2008). The first chapter surveys historiography in the West, Middle East, India, East Asia (China, Korea, Japan), and mainland and island Southeast Asia.
6 H. Stuart Hughes defends narrative in history without a loss of empirical substance in *History as Art and as Science* (New York: Harper and Row, 1964), Chapter IV. Hayden White believes this conjunction of art with science is naïve and discredited. *Tropics of Discourse: Essays in Cultural Criticism* (Baltimore, Maryland: Johns Hopkins University Press, 1978). A temptation to dismiss Hughes as "out of date," however, merely begs the question.
7 In his inaugural address in 1902 as Regius Professor of Modern History at Cambridge University, Bury was firm: "It has not yet become superfluous to insist that history is a science, no less and no more, and some who admit it theoretically hesitate to enforce the consequences which it involves." In Fritz Stern (ed.), *The Varieties of History: From Voltaire to the Present* (2nd ed.; New York: Vintage Books, 1973), p. 210.
8 E.H. Carr, in perhaps the most widely read book on history and historiography, argues that history has more of science about it than literature. *What is History?* 40th anniversary edition, intro. Richard J. Evans (Basingstoke: Palgrave, 2001), pp. 51–60.
9 A convenient summary of where we are with history in its social, political, religious, cultural, gender, intellectual, and imperial guises can be

found in one short book: David Cannadine (ed.), *What is History Now?* (New York: Palgrave Macmillan, 2002).
10 Historicism has other meanings. See Dwight E. Lee and R.N. Beck, "The Meaning of Historicism," *American Historical Review* (April, 1954), and Calvin G. Rand, "Two Meanings of Historicism," *Journal of the History of Ideas* (October–December, 1964). Karl Popper wrote a book about it, and defines it as a claim that "historical prediction" is possible by uncovering fixed patterns in the past, which implies a doctrine of inexorable historical destiny. *The Poverty of Historicism* (New York: Harper Torch Books, 1957), p. 3. Georg G. Iggers takes it to mean professionalization of history and the view that historical inquiry can be "scientific." *Historiography in the Twentieth Century: From Scientific Objectivity to the Postmodern Challenge* (Hanover and London: Wesleyan University Press, 1997), p. 31.
11 See Donald R. Kelley, *Faces of History: Historical Inquiry from Herodotus to Herder* (New Haven, Connecticut: Yale University Press, 1998), pp. 263–269.
12 Postmodernism has no focused meaning as a movement. Ihad Hassan notes its "semantic instability: that is, no clear consensus about its meaning exists among scholars." He goes on to suggest it is a manifestation of "neo-*avant garde*" thinking and preferences, for example, chance, decreation, exhaustion, deconstruction. *The Postmodern Turn: Essays in Postmodern Theory and Culture* (Ohio: Ohio State University Press, 1987), pp. 87, 91. Stanford Lyman proposes that postmodern social theory, which has implications for everything else, has two theses: (1) the world makes no sense despite meanings people insist on finding in it, and (2) both self and society are social constructions. *Postmodernism and a Sociology of the Absurd* (Fayetteville: The University of Arkansas Press, 1997), p. 13.
13 Iggers, *Historiography in the Twentieth Century*, p. 118. The theorists referred to are Roland Barthes and Hayden White.
14 On the "crisis" of scientific history, see Georg G. Iggers, *New Directions in European Historiography* (Middletown, Connecticut: Wesleyan University Press, 1975), Chapter 1.
15 A straightforward distinction between historical knowledge and fiction is made by Chase F. Robinson, who reminds us that historians must be *trained*, while poets and novelists do not. *Islamic Historiography* (Cambridge: Cambridge University Press, 2003), pp. 83–84.
16 These rivulets of doubt come together in writings of Hayden White. See his chapters on "Historical Text as Literary Artifact" and "Fictions of Factual Representation" in *Tropics of Discourse*. Alan Sokal and Jean Bricmont, in *Fashionable Nonsense: Postmodern Intellectuals' Abuse of Science* (New York: Picador USA, 1998), critique a coterie of French writers who try to undermine knowledge in natural science. Their discussion is relevant to history as well.
17 Carl L. Becker, *The Heavenly City of the Eighteenth-Century Philosophers* (New Haven: Yale University Press, 1932), p. 16.
18 Jacques Derrida, *Positions*, trans. by Alan Bass (London: Athlone Press, 1981), pp. 36–37. For a critique of postmodern assumptions and principles, see

Kenneth R. Stunkel, "Rabindranath Tagore and the Aesthetics of Postmodernism," *International Journal of Politics, Culture, and Society* 17:2 (Winter 2003). See also Richard J. Evans, *In Defense of History* (New York: W.W. Norton, 1997), pp. 198–201.

19 This is the "self-excepting fallacy." Alan B. Spitzer, *Historical Truth and Lies about the Past: Reflections on Dewey, Dreyfus, de Man, and Reagan* (Chapel Hill: University of North Carolina Press, 1996), p. 3. Philosopher-logician Susan Haack remarks: "Radical critics ... conclude there are no objective epistemic standards and that there is nothing epistemologically special about science [read also "about history"]. My view is much less exciting. There are objective standards of better or worse evidence and better- and worse-conducted inquiry." *Manifesto of a Passionate Moderate: Unfashionable Essays* (Chicago and London: University of Chicago Press, 1998), pp. 104 ff.

20 Green and Troup, *The Houses of History*, Chapter 12. Roland Barthes, "The Discourse of History," *Comparative Criticism*, 3 (1981). Frank Ankersmit, "Historiography and Postmodernism," *History and Theory*, 28:1 (1989).

21 In his analyses of Voltaire, Hume, Robertson, and Gibbon, J.B. Black acknowledged long ago that history involves "pragmatism and subjectivism" and that seeing it from a present perspective merely tells us it cannot "be known absolutely," which is to say that historical knowledge, like all knowledge, comes to us with degrees of probability depending on the amount and quality of evidence. *The Art of History: A Study of Four Great Historians of the Eighteenth Century* (London: Methuen & Co., 1926), pp. 12–13. Frank Ankersmit suggests, in a twist on subjectivity, that "historians take more seriously ... how the past sometimes may be given to them in historical experience ... that they will feel directly addressed by the past and that this may then have its resonance in their whole being." *Sublime Historical Experience* (Stanford, California: Stanford University Press, 2005), p. 282.

GREECE

Themes 1 (early historiography), 3 (issues of critical historiography), 5 (breadth of inquiry)[1]

Extended historical narrative in prose was a Greek invention. Other cultures may have attempted it, but Greek civilization provides the first known examples. Herodotus wrote a prose epic dealing with causes and consequences of a war between Greece and Persia, a new genre of literature. He showed how broad historical narrative can encompass a major event and all the peoples within the historian's reach. In a sense, he wrote the first universal history.

While Herodotus was still alive, Thucydides wrote about the disastrous war between the Athenian Empire and the Spartan state. Unlike Herodotus, he insisted on a narrow focus of contemporary military and political history, a genre of history that was to be influential for centuries, and applied rigorous standards for testing sources and testimony. He is often called the first "scientific" historian.

Both Herodotus and Thucydides continued to be cited and imitated nearly to the end of the ancient world, the first as a model for dramatic story telling and eloquent rhetoric, the second for self-conscious truth telling and a detached study of human behavior under stress. Their achievement was newly appreciated and applied when surviving classical literature was recovered by humanists in the Italian Renaissance. The two Greek historians, after a long period buried in obscurity, entered the main stream of Western historiography.

1. THE PERSIAN WARS[2] (HERODOTUS, CA. 484–CA. 424 B.C.)

We know he lived until 430 because events of that year are mentioned in his history. He died probably before 424 because significant events datable to that year are not mentioned. His book was finished by the 420s and scholars generally agree that he wrote it in the last few years of an active life that involved a prodigious amount of travel

1

and first-hand observation. Otherwise, little is known about the man's life and character.

He produced a work far in advance of genealogies, king lists, chronicles, and the purely contemporary history later championed by Thucydides. He was the first to compose a work that unfolded a panoramic view of nearly a whole century. His narratives, descriptions, reports, and interpretations were supported by travel and oral traditions noted along the way. Openness to experience and exotic facts was a result in part of living in Halicarnassus in southern Asia Minor, a crossroads where Greek and Persian confronted one another in an atmosphere of commerce and philosophical speculation about the nature of the physical world.

Herodotus plunges a reader at once into questions of what can be known about the past and how it might be known. He was first to describe what he did as "history," from a Greek word that means knowing by inquiry. The ideas of "knowing" and "inquiry" are what set his book apart from what came before. He assumed things worth knowing can be recovered from the past. His reputation in antiquity endured despite charges of dishonesty, but admirers were taken more with the book's style and pleasure it gave than with its trustworthiness. Despite such reservations, recognition came in later times when the nine books were named after the nine Muses of Greek mythology, the first book being Clio, the muse of history. He was also first to write a work in extended prose, actually the first in any Indo-European language. Other long compositions of the ancient world like the Homeric *Iliad* and the Indian *Ramayana* are in verse. Needless to say, few historians since Herodotus have written in verse.

The Roman orator and statesman Cicero named him "the father of history" (*De legibus* 1.5) some 400 years after his death, but at the same time called him a great liar. Thucydides rejected his subject matter and methods and decided only contemporary political events can be examined and confirmed by oral evidence, which set the standard for historical writing in later antiquity. Plutarch (d. A.D. 120), biographer of notable Greeks and Romans, wrote an essay *On the Malice of Herodotus* that praises his style and faults his truthfulness.[3] Attacks on his accuracy came at a time when hardly anyone believed it was possible to study a vanished past. No one understood how Herodotus could know so much about remote lands and peoples without knowledge of their languages. His reports of strange customs seemed far-fetched to people who traveled little. As for the Persian wars, skepticism greeted his attempt to make sense of events he never witnessed.

So the matter stood for centuries. Then Herodotus received a new and favorable hearing in the fifteenth-century Renaissance. Translations from Greek into Latin, such as Lorenzo Valla's complete Herodotus (see essay 11 in this volume) joined hands with European travel abroad and a comparative study of customs. It turned out there were even stranger customs and beliefs than those rejected as fantastic in antiquity. In the Reformation era, when biblical studies got a tentative start, his knowledge of the "Orient" clarified biblical passages. In the seventeenth century, Johannes Scaliger and Isaac Newton used Herodotus to develop a master chronology for events in all times and places. He was thereby vindicated and ceased to be the father of lies. In modern times, his reputation has shone even brighter.

What led him to write *The Persian Wars*? First, to rescue for memory "the great and wonderful actions of the Greeks and Barbarians from losing their due mead of glory"; second, to record "what were their grounds of feud"; third, to explain why Persia was defeated (1.1). He believed himself in touch with realities of the past expressible as knowledge. His work has nothing in common with royal or sacred annals immune to criticism; it was capable of being expanded and corrected by others better informed. His idea of causation is drawn from language of Greek tragedy and myth, but the events explained retain their status as things that really happened.

By creating an epic in historical form, Herodotus gave the war meaning, purpose, and a concrete setting. He understood what was momentous about a confrontation between values of Greek and Persian civilizations. Because mainland Greeks successfully resisted two Persian invasions in 490 and 480, civilization in the West was ultimately shaped, at least in part, by ideals of Greek humanism, rationalism, and democracy. History in the West would have been different had the Greeks lost and been absorbed by Persia. The conflict is dramatized as a smaller free society of Greek city states standing against a vast slave society controlled by imperial despotism. But the narrative was not propaganda for the Greek cause, even though he favored Athens. He noted courage on both sides worthy of acknowledgement by posterity. Glory and excellence were for the Greek mind tickets to immortality. He offered tickets to the Persian as well, a spirit of impartiality necessary for balanced, dependable history.

To fill in background for what he thought was the greatest event of his time, he traveled untiringly in an exhaustive search for information. Given the rigor and insecurities of travel in the fifth century B.C., his range of geographical and cultural exposure was unusual, including many sites and cities in Greece as far south as Sparta and north as Thrace, ancient cities of Susa and Ectabana in Asia Minor, the Greek colony of Cyrene in Cyrenaica (Libya), Tyre in Phoenicia, cities around the Euxine (Black Sea) to the mouth of the Ister River (Danube), and, most famously, Egypt. He must have stood before ancient monuments long vanished or later crumbled into ruins. In a mere two pages he comments on no less than eight tribes (4.169–74).

These expeditions provided a geographical and cultural setting for the first six of nine books comprising the history. He might have written only about Persia and Greece, but chose to incorporate material from all points of the known world. It is fair to view his book as a "world history" that aimed for comprehensiveness and scope, a form of cultural history with anthropological overtones. Although the core subject is politics of empire and strategies of war, he anticipates the diversity of historical outlook that would emerge 2500 years later. He was not just the first recognizable historian but also the first ethnographer and student of comparative religion.

Descriptions of non-Greek customs and institutions, for example, the Scythians, cannot be found elsewhere. In his account of Egypt, a place of "wonders," speculations about summer rising of the Nile are reviewed, the crocodile is described, universal reverence for cats and dogs is discussed, medical specializations are noted, and embalming technique is covered in detail (2.19–24, 66–68, 84, 86–90). His surveys of such customs and beliefs across a huge geographical and cultural range, mocked in his time as fabrications, have been verified in many instances by modern history (especially oral history), anthropology, and archeology.

After taking the reader on a leisurely tour of the "world," with much detail about places, peoples, customs, plants, animals, and major events, the last three books address the war of Greeks with Persians down to 479. An endearing virtue is the fairness with which he treats non-Greek peoples (for him, the term *barbaros*, or barbarian, means only non-Greek), a quality of humanity and breadth of mind rare in all times and places. In his view, custom is king and every society has its own ways. Intolerance offends reason and forecloses access to knowledge. More to the point, a "cause" of the war is traced to the rule of Persian custom that a king must extend conquests of his predecessors. Xerxes says: "Persians, I shall not be the first to bring in among you a new custom … I have not ceased to consider by what means I might rival those who have preceded me … " (7.8).

Travel was one arm of his method. The other was collecting oral traditions where he found them. Like more obscure predecessors, he was a *logographer* (reporter of stories) who recorded tales and reports, improbable or not, without agonizing too much over their credibility. On balance, he tells what he has heard from various sources and invites the reader to decide what to believe or reject. On Egyptian gods he says, "I believe all men know equally little about the gods," but accepts that Greek gods have power to intervene and deliver setbacks to those who aim too high and demand too much. He repeats tall tales, but says clearly enough that Greeks believed "foolish tales" (2.3). He was a master of *logos* (things said) and says it is "my duty to report all that is said, but I am not obliged to believe it all alike—a remark which may be understood to apply to my whole History" (7.152). If he had been like Thucydides, beliefs and practices of many tribes and peoples of the period, however bizarre or exotic, would be lost to the historical record. Ethnographic observations are knowledge as much as narrative history based on sources. Herodotus supplied both.

Historiography of *The Persian Wars* adopts the form and tone of a tragic drama played out on a world stage. He refers throughout to *moira* (fate), *hubris* (arrogance), and *nemesis* (retribution), still another explanation of how and why the war happened. The historical process is viewed as an unfolding of events shaped by human greatness and folly, a vision shared with Greek tragic dramatists whose works showed flawed greatness defeated by excess. The greatness in this case was the immense Persian Empire and its omnipotent king. The flaw was royal haughtiness and the excess of wanting to control the world by absorbing the Greeks. In this worldview, rising higher than one deserves out of conceit and unreasonable ambition invites Fate to exact retribution to restore a balance: "See how god with his lightning always smites the bigger animals and will not suffer them to wax insolent, while those of a lesser bulk chafe him not. How likewise his bolts fall ever on the highest houses and the tallest trees?" (7.10).

The result of overreaching is inevitable suffering redeemed perhaps by a moment of self-knowledge. Herodotus records just such a flash of insight when the king confesses to a relative: "There came upon me ... a sudden pity, when I thought of the shortness of a man's life, and considered that of all this host, so numerous as it is, not one will be alive when a hundred years have gone by" (7.46). There is another lesson to be learned. Herodotus counsels a moderation the Persians lacked: "We have now had the great good luck to save both ourselves and all Greece by the repulse of this vast cloud of men; let us then be content and not press them too hard now that they have begun to fly. Be sure we have not done this by our own might. It is the work of gods and heroes, who were jealous that one man should be king at once of Europe and Asia ... " (8.109).

With all his good qualities, Herodotus disappoints modern expectations in several ways. He quotes speeches never made, a practice imitated by successors. He could not have recorded extended dialogues like the one between Xerxes and the exiled Greek Demaratus about the prowess of Spartans in battle (7.101–4). Chronology is unreliable, although in fairness, Greeks never devised a system for reckoning what happens in successive years. His sense of numbers—millions in the army of Xerxes—is often inflated if not absurd, which probably came from unreliable reports that invite skepticism about his sources. Being a pious man respectful of the gods, he credits divine meddling too much and frequently wraps his accounts in Greek theology.

He can be forgiven, however, the thinness of sources. There were few books and documents to be had, but he did use interviews, inscriptions from monuments, temple records, writings of predecessors like the geographer Hecateaus, and documents from the archives of major Greek city states like Sparta and Athens, all in addition to "stories" he pulled together in villages and towns. It is doubtful that Persian archives were opened to him.

History at its best touches thought and imagination. *The Persian Wars* is more than an assemblage of facts about players and events in a struggle between east and west in the classical age. It is an expansive, meandering tale of adventure and discovery composed by an urbane, informed, cosmopolitan guide. Herodotus tells a grand story with many players. He does it with style and a sense of narrative structure. As such, apart from its worth as a substantial record of remote times, it is a delight to read.

Works by Herodotus

Herodotus, *The Persian Wars*, 4 vols. Loeb Classical Library (Cambridge, Massachusetts: Harvard University Press; London: W. Heinemann, 1920).
Herodotus, *The Persian Wars*, trans. by George Rawlinson (New York: Random House, 1942).
Herodotus, W. Blanco (author), J. Roberts (editor), *The Histories: New Translation, Selections, Backgrounds, Commentaries* (New York: W.W. Norton, 1992).
Herodotus, R. B. Strassler (ed.), R. Thomas (intro.), A. Purvis (trans.). *The Landmark Herodotus: The Histories* (New York: Pantheon, 2007).

Works about Herodotus

Hart, John, *Herodotus and Greek History* (New York: St. Martin's Press, 1982).
Luraghi, Nino, *The Historian's Craft in the Age of Herodotus* (Oxford: Oxford University Press, 2007).
Meyers, John L., *Herodotus, Father of History* (Oxford: Oxford University Press, 1953).
Monigliano, Arnoldo, "The Place of Herodotus in the History of Historiography," *Studies in Historiography* (New York: Harper and Row, 1966).

Useful references

Dewald, Carolyn and John Marincola (eds.), *The Cambridge Companion to Herodotus* (Cambridge: Cambridge University Press, 2006).
Evans, James Allan, *Herodotus* (Boston: Twayne Publishing, 1982).

2. HISTORY OF THE PELOPONNESIAN WAR[4] (THUCYDIDES, CA. 460–CA. 395 B.C.)

Thucydides was a contemporary of Herodotus (see essay 1 in this volume) and about thirteen years his junior. In later antiquity *The Persian Wars* was better remembered, probably because Herodotus is entertaining and Thucydides is austere. Thucydides had his eye fixed on posterity: "The absence of romance [an oblique shot at Herodotus] in my history will, I fear, detract somewhat from its interest ... I have written my work, not as an essay which is to win the applause of the moment, but as a possession for all time." His attention to evidence had an overarching purpose, which was less to isolate and explain causes of a war and its human dislocations than to extract from its history enduring lessons for those "who desire an exact knowledge of the past as an aid to the interpretation of the future." He believed human nature never varies in its reactions to physical circumstances. The future, therefore, will resemble the past (i. 23, 24).

He was a wealthy Athenian aristocrat with roots in Thrace. He grew wealthier by investing in Thracian gold mines. Study with the skeptic Protagoras may have stiffened his critical frame of mind. Study with the orator Antiphon may have influenced his style of eloquence. He was twenty-five when the war broke out in 431 and was appointed general in 424 to relieve a besieged city in Thrace. Spartans had already occupied it by the time he arrived. He was blamed and exiled for twenty years, possibly a reason he was so little known, but also an advantage because he was free to travel and study the war from both sides. He returned to Athens when exile ended and dropped out of sight.

In Hellenistic and Roman times, the rhetorical style of his speeches was much imitated and may have contributed to the book's survival. As a "scientist" he had little impact, but was respected as a writer of secular history as late as the sixth century by the Byzantine historian Procopius (see essay 7 in this volume). Dionysius of Halicarnassus (d. 8 B.C.), rhetorician and historian, wrote treatises on him and concluded the *History* was wasted on a minor, inglorious war deserving of oblivion.

About three-fourths of the work is narrative and one-fourth is speeches. It covers twenty years of a complex struggle, actually two wars with an intervening truce, from 431 to 411 (the end came in 404). Athens, a sea power, and Sparta, a land power, both faced internal dissension among their respective allies and had military setbacks. The decisive outcome was Spartan victory and the end of Athenian authority in Greece. Book I discusses causes and preparations. The Trojan and Persian Wars are cited as minor upheavals compared to the Peloponnesian War, for never before had the entire Greek world been plunged into such a destructive struggle. Thereafter a few narrative and analytical high points include the demoralizing plague that struck Athens in the second year and killed Pericles in 429; the violent revolution in Corcyra driven by class hatred; the fortuitous event at Pylos that might have ended the war; defeat of the Spartans on the island of Sphacteria, where to universal surprise the legendary warriors did not fight to the death; brutal Athenian conquest of neutral Melos on the principle that strength trumps weakness; pathetic fate of the hapless town Plataea at the hands of Athenians; successes of the Spartan general Brasides; and the catastrophic Sicilian campaign that destroyed an Athenian fleet and army.

Among speeches not to be missed are:

- The funeral oration of Pericles that contrasts commercial, civic Athenian culture with Spartan agrarian, military culture: "The freedom which we enjoy in our government extends also to our ordinary life ... we provide plenty of means for the mind to refresh itself from business ... We cultivate refinement without extravagance and knowledge without effeminacy ... In generosity we are equally singular, acquiring our friends by conferring not by

receiving favours ... In short, I say as a city we are the school of Hellas ... " (ii. 37–42).
- An Athenian delegation to neutral Melos notifying a helpless populace that strength against weakness is the issue; " ... since you know as well as we do that right, as the world goes, is only in question between equals in power, while the strong do what they can and the weak suffer what they must" (v. 90).
- The brilliant demagogue Alcibiades casually arguing for invasion of Sicily (and before the Spartans, explaining how Athens can be ruined); " ... we cannot fix the exact point at which our empire shall stop; we have reached a position in which we must not be content with retaining but must scheme to extend it, for if we cease to rule others, we are in danger of being ruled ourselves" (vi. 19).

In addition to narrating what happened, he wanted to understand why events unfolded as they did. The difference from Herodotus lies in his program of selection and evaluation, a mark of disciplined, systematic historical inquiry. Where Herodotus is expansive and digressive, Thucydides is narrow and focused. While details of confrontation between democratic Athens and oligarchic Sparta are the nominal focus, his attention is on the dynamics of power politics wielded by leaders in a contest. There are a few pages on what Greece was like before the war, but otherwise no ethnic, anecdotal, or mythical digressions. He is scrupulous about geography relevant to the war but does not stray beyond it. Minor causes are distinguished from the major cause: "The real cause I consider to be one which was formally kept out of sight. The growth of the power of Athens, and the alarm which this inspired in Lacedaemon made war inevitable" (i. 24). Spartan alarm resulted in a land-based alliance system to counter the sea-based Athenian Empire. The contest between federations eventually reached a point of no return. He did strict contemporary history in a specific time and place because he had no good evidence for distant times or remote places.

Oral tradition is declared unreliable: "The way that most men deal with traditions, even the traditions of their own country, is to receive them all alike as they are delivered, without applying any critical test whatever" (i. 20). But he agreed with Herodotus that history relies on it. Documents have a minor role for both historians. His difference from Herodotus is a higher standard for trusting oral reports; he must be present at an event or his source must be. Only oral testimony by eyewitnesses open to question was acceptable. In addition, however, he consulted some documents and inscriptions such as Athenian militia peace treaties on tablets kept in the Acropolis, a letter of Aterpharnes to Sparta, a dispatch of Nicias. He says his "proofs ... may be safely relied upon." Tested evidence is a defense against the poet "displaying the exaggeration of his craft" and "compositions of the chroniclers that are attractive at truth's expense; the subjects they treat being out of the reach of evidence, and time having robbed most of them of historical value by enthroning them in the region of legend" (i. 21).

Philosophical theories, religious myths, oracles, and the like are excluded as evidence. The gods are absent as intervening forces, but superstition and piety can have consequences in nature. At Syracuse, Nicias would not withdraw vulnerable troops and fleet because of a lunar eclipse and thereby assured the destruction of his forces. Thucydides comments on his superstition: " ... Nicias, who was somewhat over-addicted to divination and practices of that kind, refused from that moment even to take the question of departure into consideration, until they had waited the thrice nine days prescribed by the soothsayers" (vii. 51).

Sources of this scientific rationalism were Ionian natural philosophy from Thales to Democritus and medical teachings of Hippocrates of Cos. Ionian philosophers speculated about the material basis for observable change, eliminating non-naturalistic intervention of Olympian gods. The Hippocratic School developed a procedure from observation of disease symptoms to a description of them (*semeiology*) to a classification of the illness (*prognosis*). An illness builds to a crisis and then resolves itself with death, invalidism, or recovery.

This method separates fact from legend and poetry. Not only is confirmed fact the irreducible standard, facts are connected with what preceded and followed them to understand prior conditions and resulting consequences of events. He sought regular patterns of human behavior in the factual material. Since physical nature includes human nature, the latter responds in a stable way to changes in the former. Human action in nature is his subject. It follows that society is part of nature as well and accessible to understanding like other natural phenomena. While Thucydides is best understood as a naturalist who applies psychological analysis to motives of political and military leaders, a sense of Greek tragic drama pervades the *History* as *hubris* (over reaching) and *nemesis* (retribution) overtake flawed greatness.

Armed with a naturalistic approach to historical method, he analyzed human behavior under stress. The Peloponnesian War brought out the worst in everyone: " ... the whole Hellenic world was convulsed ... The sufferings which revolution entailed upon the cities were many and terrible, such as have occurred and always will occur, as long as the nature of mankind remains the same ... In peace and prosperity states and individuals have better sentiments ... but war takes away the easy supply of daily wants, and so proves a rough master, that brings most men's characters to a level with their fortunes" (iii. 82). At Corcyra, northernmost of islands in the Ionian Sea, where Athens and Sparta were aligned against one another, rivalries of the disadvantaged and the privileged ceded political moderation to extremists. Mutual hatreds intensified and reached a crisis.

He notes symptoms of disintegration: "Reckless audacity came to be considered the courage of a loyal ally; prudent hesitation, specious cowardice; moderation was held to be a cloak for unmanliness ... Frantic violence became the attribute of manliness; cautious plotting, a justifiable means of self-defense. The advocate of extreme measures was always trustworthy" (iii. 82). Then he diagnoses the disease: "The cause of these evils was the lust for power rising from greed and ambition" (iii. 82). The crisis was resolved by Corcyra's ruin, the fate of more than one diseased state: "Thus every form of iniquity took root in the Hellenic world by reason of the troubles" (iii. 83). Here is the clue to his political philosophy, which sided with moderation over extremism.

Thucydides has been faulted on several debatable counts. First, his stress on politics squeezed out cultural glories of Athens. Yet he was aware of Athenian cultural achievements. The funeral speech of Pericles alludes to them as well as to a love of beauty and respect for intellect. Those matters were not his subject. He wanted to know why Athens was a political failure and brought ruin on herself, an inquiry best pursued in the community setting where issues of power were supreme. The war was not about culture but power politics. Excursions into drama, philosophy, and architecture would have added nothing to a narrative about power relations and their effects on people and society.

Second, his focus on causes was narrowly confined to immediate conflict between the two federations. He had no interest in underlying causes stretching back several decades. This is a just criticism. He isolated strictly those causes immediately touching the war. In this respect, Herodotus focuses with a wider angle and rises above direct clashes of Persian and Greek.

Third, his method of counting years and placing events is confusing. While this is true, it was not his fault. There was no unified Greek calendar. A lunar system was in use, but no agreement among city states as to which month marked the beginning of the year. Thucydides created his own system. Year 1 is 431, beginning of the war, and years thereafter are divided into summer and winter campaigns. When events were spread over several years, like the three year Sicilian campaign, it is admittedly easy to lose track of where one is in a summer–winter scheme.

Fourth, the speeches are suspect. Some critics accept that he transcribed accurately what was said. Others argue he made it up. There is a middle ground explained by Thucydides: "With reference to the speeches ... , some were delivered when the war began, others while it was going on; some I heard myself, others I got from various quarters; it was in all cases difficult to carry them word for word in one's memory, so my habit has been to make the speakers say what in my opinion was demanded of them by the various occasions, of course adhering as closely as possible to the general sense of what they really said" (i. 22). Allowing his intellectual integrity, substance of the speeches is probably trustworthy on his terms. The identical form they take is entirely his own. Their common function is to expose causes of the war, reveal the character of men, and isolate sources of political conflict.

With that much said, he is secure with posterity, which has been the case for 2400 years. His history remains an incomparable narrative of political upheaval and military leadership in time of war, one of the surviving treasures of the ancient world, studied and admired today as never before. He articulated modestly problems of evidence that were to haunt Voltaire (see essay 15 in this volume) centuries later:

> "And with reference to the narrative of events, far from permitting myself to derive it from the first source that came to hand, I did not even trust my own impressions, but it rests partly on what I saw myself, partly on what others saw for me, the accuracy of the report being always tried by the most severe and detailed tests possible. My conclusions have cost me some labour from the want of coincidence between accounts of the same occurrences by different eyewitnesses, arising sometimes from imperfect memory, sometimes from undue partiality for one side or the other."
>
> (1. 22)

Works by Thucydides

Strassler, Robert B. and Victor Davis Hanson (eds.), *The Landmark Thucydides: A Comprehensive Guide to the Peloponnesian War* (New York: Free Press, 1996).

The Complete Writings of Thucydides: The Peloponnesian War, trans. by Richard Crawley (New York: The Modern Library, 1951).

Thucydides, *History of the Peloponnesian War*, trans. by C. F. Smith (London and New York: Loeb Classical Library, various dates from 1923). Greek with English translation.

Thucydides, *The Peloponnesian War*, A New Translation, Backgrounds, Interpretations by Blanco, Walter and Jennifer Tobert Roberts (New York: Norton Critical Edition, 1998).

Works about Thucydides

Abbott, George F., *Thucydides, A Study in Historical Reality* (London: Routledge, 1925).

Cochrane, Charles N., *Thucydides and the Science of History* (New York: Russell & Russell, 1965).

Finley Jr., John H., *Thucydides* (Cambridge, Massachusetts: Harvard University Press, 1942).

Kagan, Donald, *Thucydides: The Reinvention of History* (New York: Viking, 2010).

Useful references

Monigliano, Arnoldo, *The Classical Foundations of Modern Historiography* (Berkeley, California: University of California Press, 1990).

———, "Historiography on Written Tradition and Historiography on Oral Tradition," *Studies in Historiography* (London: Weidenfeld and Nicolsen, 1966).

Scheville, Ferdinand, *Six Historians* (Chicago, Illinois: Chicago University Press, 1956). Chapter 1.

Section Notes

1 See pages 3–6 of the Introduction for an explanation of themes.
2 George Rawlinson's translation is cited in this essay. References to Herodotus in parentheses have two sets of numbers. The first indicates one of the nine Books. The second indicates the chapter (actually a paragraph) within a Book, which Rawlinson places at the top of each page.
3 See Herodotus: *The Histories*, ed. and trans. Walter Blanco and (ed.) Jennifer Roberts, pp. 271–76.
4 The unabridged Crawley translation of the text is used in this essay, from the Modern Library Edition, which has a fine introduction by the well-known classicist, John H. Finley.

ROME

Themes 1 (early historiography), 4 (genres of historiography)

Historical consciousness in the ancient world has two fountainheads—Greece and Rome. Roman historiography has two great names—Livy and Tacitus. Suetonius and Sallust are considered lesser figures, but one has to be careful with such a distinction. Written historical material from Roman civilization is not abundant, and must be supplemented by judicious use of other sources from epigraphy, numismatics, and archeology. Much has been lost, including big chunks of Tacitus and some books of Livy.

Major works of Suetonius and Sallust are intact and can be studied as a whole. The two authors clearly thought recovery and presentation of the past in some aspects was worth time and effort. Both shared the view that history can be morally elevating, and that it should be presented in a style both graceful and pleasing. The one was fascinated by personalities, the other by foreign policy and war. They also provide a substantial body of factual material, some admittedly hard to confirm, about persons and events without which our knowledge of Rome toward the end the Republic and in the early Empire would be the poorer. Both had access to valuable documents, but we have to guess what they may have looked at and how critical their use of them might have been. The rhetorical tradition that prevailed in Rome forbade citations that distracted from exciting narrative.

3. LIVES OF THE CAESARS[1] (GAIUS SUETONIUS TRANQULLUS, CA. 69–CA. 140)

Suetonius may have been a teacher of rhetoric in Rome, where he was born. It is known that he made friends and secured appointments in high places. Where he is mentioned by contemporaries, reports are favorable about the man and his writings. With the help of Pliny the Younger, he became a military tribune, a post he relinquished to a relative. Pliny also thought well enough of Suetonius to persuade

Emperor Hadrian (d. 138) to hire him as a secretary, an appointment that ended when he breached a point of etiquette with Hadrian's wife. After that incident, nothing more is heard of him and it is assumed he spent years of retirement writing his books. He was a prolific author on a variety of topics. Among lost works are *Lives of Famous Whores*, *Roman Manners and Customs*, *Physical Defects of Mankind*, *Methods of Reckoning Time*, and *On Cicero's Republic*. A few have survived in fragments. A work on famous literary men left portraits of Terence the playwright, Horace the master of odes, and Lucan the epic poet.

As a historian he preferred biography to record the past. An advantage of that approach was his relatively close proximity to the careers of his subjects when documents were available and memories of informants were fresh. Official positions gave him access to archives that probably supplied material for *Lives of the Caesars* (*De vita Caesarum*), published in A.D. 121, and surviving mostly intact. While he seems to have preferred documents over testimony and apparently handled a body of material that has vanished, it is well to remember that careful study of documents was not an established practice among most Roman historians. Citation of documents was considered a stylistic disadvantage and bad form in a literary climate dominated by rhetoric. But the absence of document citation in Suetonius, or any other Roman historian for that matter, does not prove they were not consulted and used.

Lives of the Caesars opens with Julius Caesar (d. 44 B.C.) and moves through the Julio-Claudian Dynasty's Augustus, Tiberius, Caligula, Claudius, and Nero, then through brief, fatal reigns of Galba, Otho, and Vitellius in the Civil War of 69, and ends with the Flavian Dynasty's Vespasian, Titus, and Domitian. The time span between Augustus and Domitian is about 127 years, 31 B.C. to A.D. 96, a respectable stretch of time linking twelve successive Roman rulers who presided collectively over half the famous Roman Peace (*Pax Romanum*) initiated by Augustus after his rivals, Marc Antony and Cleopatra, were bested in the civil war that followed the assassination of Julius Caesar.

The work brims with detail and incident, running some 300 pages in the Graves translation. Great events are mixed with trivia. The short biography of Titus gives more space to his dinner parties than to his generalship in the Judaean revolt and the fall of Jerusalem, perhaps the most tumultuous and bloody event of the first century (see essay 5 in this volume). Suetonius has been criticized justly for exaggeration, sensationalism, and gossip, but often and cautiously he prefaces a narrative with: "The story goes ... "

As though a skeptic himself, the word "superstition" (*superstitio*) is used to describe beliefs of the emperors, yet many pages are littered with portents, prodigies, prophecies, and premonitions he takes seriously. On the eve of Julius Caesar's assassination, portents abounded: "Unmistakable" signs forewarned Caesar of his assassination: " ... on his last night Caesar dreamed that he was soaring above the clouds, and then shaking hands with Juppiter (sic)" (Caesar 81). In the case of Galba, signs of his end appeared "in accurate detail" (Galba 18). In Vespasian's biography, Josephus, the Jewish historian, is an omen that his captor and liberator would become emperor (Vespasian 5).

But Suetonius delivers vivid portraits linked to an assorted mass of information about events and practices of the times that would otherwise be lost. Side by side with the scandals is material on acts of the Senate and imperial edicts that are invaluable. He was in a position to use archival documents, but apparently did not consult them systematically or critically. He was acquainted with Augustus's memoirs and cites his letters. Other informants are occasionally mentioned by name, but their truthfulness and accuracy are seemingly taken for granted.

His narratives have a semblance of materials patched together without much hope of identifying sources or their reliability. Yet it is fair to recall that footnoting was not a practice of ancient historiography, and telling a colorful, exciting tale was a high priority. The emperors are not wholly disconnected from business of the Empire by a garish façade of evils in Rome. Tiberius seems a hypocritical pervert, but was a successful general and efficient, strict administrator until his last years of isolation on Capris. Caligula comes off as a madman, Claudius an absent minded fool, and Nero a megalomaniac even though the Empire expanded and flourished during their regimes.

Considering the power they wielded over others, what the emperors were like as men is important knowledge even if imperfectly realized. Suetonius provides materials for biography in a loosely organized format even though he did not exploit their potential for characterizing the whole man. For each Caesar he traces ancestry (those passages for Julius Caesar are lost), relates birth, summarizes life before becoming emperor, provides a physical description of the man, and reviews doings on the throne. The good side of the man is sketched, followed by failures as a ruler and damaging flaws of character. What Suetonius does for Augustus applies as well to the other emperors: "Thus completes my account of Augustus' civil and military career, and how he governed his wide Empire in peace and war. Now follows a description of his private life, his character, and his domestic fortunes" (Augustus 61).

Service to the Empire comes first, then the man's character. Even Nero and Domitian, cruel and capricious as they were, emerge with some achievements and good points. The last years of Domitian's reign were marred by paranoid executions and murders of nearly everyone in sight—senators, officials, relatives, friends, servants. Yet early on he cared about welfare of the Empire, was conscientious about justice, beautified Rome with new buildings, exhibited good-will, and tried to improve public morals. Only Caligula seems beyond redemption. The onset of vice in Tiberius, Nero, and Domitian is described as gradual, although the inclination was always present.

By the first century B.C. Rome had become an empire ruled inadequately by ancient institutions of a republican city state. The violent transition from Republic to Empire was dominated by Julius Caesar (d. 44 B.C.), to whom he devotes some forty pages. As a politician he won wide support for his liberality at home and abroad: "Caesar thus became the one reliable source of help to all who were in legal difficulties, or in debt, or living beyond their means" (Caesar 27). His brilliance was universally acknowledged: "Caesar equaled, if he did not surpass, the greatest orators and generals the world had ever known" (Caesar 55). He defeated all his enemies and "was never defeated himself" in Gaul, Egypt, Asia Minor (the Pontus), North Africa, and Spain (Caesar 36, 37).

Suetonius works through numerous domestic reforms Caesar consummated or attempted, including revision of the calendar: "Yet other deeds and sayings of Caesar's may ... justify the conclusion that he deserved assassination" (Caesar 76). He set for himself a "golden throne in the Senate House," though "the Republic was nothing—a mere name without form or substance," expressed "scorn for the Constitution," and "lay under the odious suspicion of having tried to revive the title of King" (Caesar 76, 77, 79).

After Caligula's assassination at age 29, Claudius, his uncle, became emperor at age 50 under bizarre circumstances. When news of his nephew's much deserved murder reached him, "he slipped away in alarm to a near-by balcony, where he hid trembling behind the door curtains. A guardsman wandering vaguely through the Palace, noticed a pair of feet beneath the curtain, pulled their owner out for identification and recognized him. Claudius dropped on the floor and clasped the soldier's knees, but found himself acclaimed Emperor" (Claudius 10). Rome was in chaos and the Senate wanted to restore the Republic. The imperial succession was less than orderly and predictable. Immediate power was with the Praetorian Guard, which had no interest in restorations. It was in their camp that a frightened Claudius donned the purple.

Before his accession, he had been continually an object of derision and neglect because of a disability that made him appear stupid and comical: " ... he stumbled as he walked owing to the weakness of his knees ... he had several disagreeable traits. These included an uncontrollable laugh, a horrible habit, under the stress of anger of slobbering at the mouth and running at the nose, a stammer, and a persistent nervous tic ... " (Claudius 30). His "scatter-brainedness and shortsightedness" encouraged his wife Messalina to engage in sexual exploits that culminated in actually marrying one of her lovers publically, for which she was executed (Claudius 26, 39). His intellectual powers functioned nevertheless, for he wrote histories of Etruscans and Carthaginians in Greek which were honored in Alexandria by "a new wing to the Museum called 'The Claudian'" (Claudius 42).

The years 68–69 after Nero's suicide, helped along by a servant, saw no less than three emperors who suffered violent deaths. The lesson of their short careers was that emperors need not have originated in Rome when the Julio-Claudian line became extinct. Their biographies are proportionately short. Galba, noted for greed, gets eleven pages, Otho, afflicted with vanity, gets six, and Vitellius, famous for gluttony, gets nine.

Suetonius considered himself a scholar and serious historian. Evidently he tried to be impartial. In each of the lives more than one version of a source or informant is noted, but rarely do we learn what or who they are (Julius Caesar 86). Too often he reflects uncritically the bias or malice in his sources. On balance, he reports rather than moralizes; although he does cite Caligula is a "Monster" (Caligula 22). Mostly he keeps to himself, unlike the self-promotion of Josephus in *The Jewish War*. The attractiveness of his biographies lies in the dramatic power of incidents themselves, as in the account of Nero's death (Nero 49). His style in translation is straightforward and highly readable, mostly free of rhetorical distortions. His Latin style has the same qualities of directness and no nonsense, with facts and observations stitched together with economy of expression.

Works by Suetonius

Lives of the Caesars, trans. by Catherine Edwards (Oxford: Oxford University Press, 2009).
Lives of the Caesars, trans. by J. C. Rolfe, 2 vols. (Loeb Classical Library). Latin and English on facing pages. Volume 2 contains *Lives of Illustrious Men*.

The Twelve Caesars, trans. by James Rives (New York: Penguin Classics, 2007).
The Twelve Caesars, trans. by Robert Graves (Baltimore, Maryland: Penguin Books, 1957).

Works about Suetonius

Baldwin, Barry, *Biographer of the Caesars* (Amsterdam: A. M. Hakkert, 1983).
Hadas, Moses, *A History of Latin Literature* (New York: Columbia University Press, 1952), Chapter XVII.

Useful references

Scarre, Chris, *Chronicle of the Roman Emperors: The Reign-by-Reign Record of the Rulers of Imperial Rome* (London: Thames and Hudson, 1995). Lavishly illustrated.
Stuart, D.H., *Epochs of Greek and Roman Biography* (Berkeley, California: University of California Press, 1928).

4. THE JUGURTHINE WAR[2] (SALLUST, 86–34 B.C.)

Gaius Sallustius Crispis, known as Sallust, was a historian who rose to high positions in the Roman state. A commoner in origin, he was one of ten tribunes representing plebeians. He held office as one of two quaestors in charge of Rome's treasury, as a provincial governor in Africa, and as a praetor, or judicial authority. He was admitted to the Senate twice as a result of the quaestorships, the second of which was arranged by Julius Caesar. As governor in Africa for a year, in 46 after Numidia was annexed by the Republic during its civil war, he accumulated a fortune and lived sumptuously in Rome, his property embellished by a garden reputedly a wonder of the city.

He was accused in some quarters of sensual indulgence, but caution reminds us that malicious gossip and personal abuse were customary in Rome. In his book on the African war, he praises the wonders of mind over body: " ... exceptional deeds of the intellect are, like the soul, immortal. Ultimately, the advantages of the body and of fortune end as surely as they began, and all of them rise and fall, grow and decline, but the mind—incorruptible, everlasting, the ruler of the human race—moves and controls everything and yet is not itself controlled" (2:3). In politics he supported Caesar's reforms and condemned arrogant excesses of the aristocratic Senate. He married the divorced wife of statesman and orator Cicero, who opposed Caesar's policies.

After Caesar's assassination Sallust retired from public life to write history for the last nine years of his life. His first published work was on the Conspiracy of Catiline in 63, an attempt to incite revolt against the Republic. He wrote a history of Rome in five books for the period 78 to 67, most of which has been lost. *The Jugurthine War* (*Bellum Jugurthinum*), published in the year 41, had as its main purpose to expose the corruption of senatorial aristocrats whose greed and irresponsibility he believed were undermining the Republic. The Senate was the one permanent institution whose members served for life: "The war I am about to write is that which the Roman people waged with Jugurtha, king of the Numidians, first because it was great and fierce and of only sporadic success, then because that was the first time that the haughtiness of the nobility was confronted— and the latter struggle convulsed everything, divine and human alike, and advanced to such a point of derangement that only war and the devastation of Italy put an end to the citizen's passions" (5:2). The heart of convulsion was warfare between the Senate and citizens of Rome, whose power had been weakened during many previous years of war with Carthage and others.

After the destruction of Carthage in 146, which Sallust believed sent the Republic from virtuous stability into ruinous decline, Rome annexed its territory and Caesar made it a province, which amounted to the northern half of Tunisia, running 200 miles north and south, 100 miles east and west. It was adjacent to the kingdom of Numidia, an extensive territory that corresponded roughly to modern Algeria. Pragmatic Rome, occupied in warfare elsewhere, had no interest in further conquest beyond Carthage and cultivated client relations with Numidian rulers. Sallust was less interested in Jugurtha and the territorial settlement that followed his defeat than in whatever damage the twisted affair might have inflicted on the Senate and its nobles.

The war originated on the death of the Numidian king Micipsa. His three heirs, Hiempsal, Adherbal, and Jugurtha (the first two, natural sons, the third, an adopted nephew), "agreed, because of their differences, that the treasures should be divided and the boundaries of their individual commands established ... " The agreement quickly broke down because of Jugurtha (10–28). He seemed promising as a youth: "When Jugurtha first reached adolescence, he was powerfully strong, of becoming appearance, but, above all, forceful in intellect. He did not surrender himself to corruption by luxuriousness and idleness but ... rode horses, threw the javelin, competed with his contemporaries at running, and, though he outstripped them all in glory, was nevertheless dear to them all" (6). As Sallust's narrative unfolds, however, Jugurtha emerges as a man ambitious, unscrupulous, conniving, treacherous, and brutal. The war Sallust describes with such brilliance exposes a Republic governed by men divided into corrupt factions ready to let an upstart like Jugurtha rise to power through bribery and intrigue.

He seized Hiempsal's domain by force and his invading troops "delivered his head to Jugurtha." To win supporters and head off outrage in Rome, Jugurtha bribed senators. He had "no hope at all against their anger except in the avarice of the nobility and his own money ... he sent legates to Rome with a quantity of gold and silver, directing them first to satisfy his old friends with gifts, then to find new ones ... " When the legates distributed gifts, "such a change occurred that, from being an object of the greatest resentment, Jugurtha acquired access to the favor and good will of the nobility." Jugurtha then isolated Adherbal in his capital city of Cirta, who resisted with the help of Cirta's Italian residents. After more bribes to forestall Roman interference, Jugurtha took the city, tortured and executed Adherbal, and killed many Italians.

The fate of Italians obliged the Senate to declare war and send an army. Roman legions, however, were not sent to subdue or absorb Numidia but to pursue Jugurtha, who surrendered on suspiciously favorable terms. He was summoned to Rome for questioning, tried to murder a rival, distributed more bribes, was expelled from the city, went home and defeated a Roman force, demanded recognition as Numidia's ruler, and was refused by the Senate. Metallus, leader of the Senate's conservative faction and a good soldier, led an army into Numidia with little success. His subordinate, Marius, a commoner, discredited and replaced him, but then only succeeded in driving Jugurtha into guerilla warfare without a decisive victory.

Marius, a successful soldier-politician admired but not overly praised by Sallust, had weakened the Republic by securing command in Numidia without Senate approval: "But Marius ... had been made consul at the most eager desire of the plebs, and, after the people ordered Numidia as the province for him, that was the time when he regularly and defiantly hounded the nobility, to which he was already hostile: he sometimes lashed them individually, sometimes collectively, he said repeatedly that he had seized the consulship from them like spoils from the conquered ... " (84).

Since a military solution in Numidia was unlikely, a deal was made with Jugurtha's father-in-law, king of Mauretania, a domain just west of Numidia, who had joined forces with his beleaguered relative. Jugurtha was betrayed, handed over, and "led to Rome in chains" (114).

Central to these final negotiations was Sulla, Marius's quaestor from a faded aristocratic family (95). He rivaled Marius later as an instigator of the Republic's civil war, for which conditions had already been created in part by the war with Jugurtha: "For the nobility began to turn their rank, and the people their freedom, into matters of whim: every man for himself appropriated, looted, and seized. So the whole was split into two parties, and commonwealth, which had been neutral, was rent apart" (41).

Sallust the historian was universally respected. By many, he was compared with Thucydides and even given priority over Livy. Tacitus admired and imitated him. Among authors who praised his works, however, not one addressed his effectiveness as historian as opposed to his brilliance as stylist. His achievement for Latin language and literature is unquestioned. The terseness of style was an innovation, although anticipated by Caesar's *Commentaries*. The disadvantage of compression in the original is that Sallust often falls into ambiguity by leaving out too many words. Translators are obliged to supply more words in English than are in the Latin original.

Sallust's contribution to historiography is problematic but not negligible. As with Suetonius, historians are grateful to have his works. He abandoned a tradition of chronicle that recorded events year by year and pursued a new form—the historical monograph distinguished by dramatic, concise, and vivid narrative, although his battle scenes are mostly set pieces in the Hellenistic style, a defensible fault because military history is sure to be vague without maps and field dispatches. His model for style, if not for evidence, was the brevity and narrative power of Thucydides (see essay 2 in this volume).

He chose to write about particular events judged to be of special importance. His emphasis on personalities anticipated Tacitus and Suetonius (see essay 3 in this volume). Although his public career afforded access to written records, testimony of contemporaries, private papers, and experience with places he wrote about, there are no citations and few references mentioned in the text, a practice commonplace in ancient historiography. He is unaccountably poor with chronology and geography despite being familiar with Africa.

His contrived orations (those of Adherbal and Marius are notable) usually convey an impression of the speaker's character (24, 85). While Thucydides inspired his style, Sallust did not absorb from him a passion for empirical truth supported by evidence. If history is viewed as an amalgam of art and "science," he was mostly an artist. His weaknesses are fairly typical of much ancient, especially Hellenistic, historiography, whose rhetorical purpose was to tell an exciting tale with moral lessons rather than pursue issues of causation, development, and influence from documented fact. But Sallust's conventional moralizing accounts in part for his enduring reputation. St. Augustine was impressed, as were scholars in the Middle Ages, who preserved and studied his manuscripts.

Works by Sallust

Cataline's War, the Jugurthine War, Histories, trans. and ed. by A. J. Woodman (New York: Penguin Classics, 2008). There is a helpful index.

Sallust, Loeb Classical Library, trans. by J.C. Rolfe (Cambridge, Massachusetts: Harvard University Press, 1921). One volume containing all of Sallust surviving work with Latin and English on facing pages.

The Jugurthine War: Partly in the Original and Partly in Translation, trans. and ed. by H.E. Butler (Oxford: Clarendon Press, 1903).

This is a handy version of Sallust prepared for students of Latin. The Latin of each section is followed by an English translation.

Among the aids are a geneology of Numidian kings, a chronology of the war, definitions of military and bureaucratic terms, an introduction to Sallust's life and his times, a Latin vocabulary, supplementary notes for all the chapters, and a good map of Numidia, Rome's province, and major towns.

Works about Sallust

Laistner, M. L. W. *The Greater Roman Historians* (Berkeley, California: University of California Press, 1947), Chapter III.

Loeb Classical Library edition cited above, ix–xviii.

Sym, Ronald, *Sallust* (Berkeley, California: University of California Press, 1964), Chapters IV, V, XV for Sallust's purpose, credibility, and style.

Section Notes

1 This essay uses the translation by Robert Graves. Citations are for numbered passages in the text.
2 This essay uses the translation of A.J. Woodman.

JUDAISM AND CHRISTIANITY

Themes 1 (early historiography), 3 (issues of critical historiography), 4 (genres of historiography), 5 (breadth of inquiry)

Jews and Christians are woven into the fabric of Roman civilization, and in later centuries became the Judao-Christian tradition. Roman historians had little to say about either religious movement and apparently were not much interested. It remained for Jewish and Christian writers to explain who they were, what they wanted, and how they related to the Roman Empire. The most important Jewish historian by all reports is Josephus, the only surviving historian of the Jewish Revolt against Rome in 67 A.D. that dragged on with bloody effect until destruction of Jerusalem in the year 70. Although not discussed by Roman writers, the event was a religious and national catastrophe for Jews. Augustine takes the palm as spokesman for early Christianity. He undertook a wide-ranging interpretation of Roman decline to vindicate the new faith against the criticisms of pagan writers.

Josephus and Augustine were highly regarded in their time and thereafter for partisan reasons. For modern readers, they were pioneers in the historiography of religious belief, politics, and relations with Rome during the empire.

5. THE JEWISH WAR[1] (FLAVIUS JOSEPHUS, A.D. 37–CA. 100)

Knowledge of the author, Joseph ben Matthias, who took the Roman name Flavius Josephus, is confined to his books. Born into an aristocratic family of priests, his education, which included fluency in Greek and Latin as well as Hebrew and Aramaic, was preparation to become a historian. In 64 he traveled to Rome to secure release of imprisoned members of the priesthood, a mission that succeeded. On his return to Judea in 66, he became governor of Lower Galilee, and the next year commander of military forces in the city of Jotapata.

THE JEWISH WAR

Josephus tells us he was a resourceful governor and military leader who mobilized citizenry, fortified cities, and trained an army. After Jotopata fell to Rome, he surrendered after all but one of his fellow survivors committed suicide, was spared by Titus, offered his services as guide, interpreter, and apologist, and later became a Roman citizen. When the war ended he retired to Rome and wrote his history, probably between 75 and 79.

Josephus is the lone source for a ruinous insurgency of Judea against Rome between A.D. 66 and 70. Jerusalem was taken in 70 and the war ended with a siege at Masada, a fortress atop a high rocky plateau whose rebel defenders committed mass suicide in 73 rather than surrender, except for two old women who hid themselves (365–66). Consequences of the revolt were devastating. The commanding Roman general and future emperor, Titus, leveled Jerusalem and the Second Temple (built by King Herod in the first century B.C.), dismantled religious institutions, and dispersed surviving Jews. Judea lost whatever autonomy, indulgence, and privilege it had under previous Roman rule. The land was confiscated and farmed out. The uprising cost a huge number of lives, most of whom were Jews (337).

Non-Josephan information about the war is meager. It is nonexistent for the early stages. A few pages in Tacitus have survived and even less in Suetonius (see essay 3 in this volume). Other extended descriptions of the war are lost or exist in fragments. While there is some material in rabbinic literature, it is regarded as a small dose of fact laced with fantasy. Christian writers relied solely on Josephus for what mattered to them—prophetic destruction of the Temple.

Josephus wrote three other works to justify the Jewish people to contemporaries and to reconcile Jews to the Roman Empire: *History of the Ancient Jews, Jewish Antiquities* (from Creation to the revolt of 66), a *Vita (Autobiography)*, and *Against Apion*, his response to charges of an Alexandrian anti-semite. The first two works have alternative versions of the war and his involvement.[2] Among his readers were Romans, Greek-speaking Jews, early Christians, Church Fathers, and ecclesiastical historians. All but the *Antiquities*, written in Latin, were in Greek, but later translated into Latin while he lived. The war volume was written first in Aramaic, which he later translated into Greek. That all four works survive is a distinction (manuscripts surfaced between the ninth and eleventh centuries). The greatest historians of the Roman period, Polybius, Livy, and Tacitus, were not so lucky.

The Jewish War (Bellum Judaicum) is a complete work, originally in seven "books," some 381 pages in the Williamson translation, divided into 23 chapters and nine descriptive sections on matters such as "The Roman Army," Jerusalem and the "Temple," and "The Defense of Masada."[3] Full of incident, description, personalities, and colorful narrative, the work is delivered in readable, sometimes brilliant prose. He wrote in a Hellenistic style of historiography that stressed drama, spectacular events, bloody battles, and a high pitch of excitement: "The Temple hill, enveloped in flames from top to bottom appeared to be boiling up from its very roots; yet the sea of flames was nothing to the ocean of blood, or the companies of killers to the armies of killed: no where could the ground be seen between the corpses ... " (325) He composed long speeches for key participants, including himself. Virtue and vice, good and evil are adversaries. Supernatural portents and prophecies are evoked (327). He provides vivid descriptions of places, cities, and buildings, and informative accounts of Roman military training, equipment, and tactics (378 ff).

The volume opens with a declaration of its importance: "The war of the Jews against the Romans was the greatest of our time; greater too, perhaps, than any recorded struggle between cities or nations" (21). Before Emperor Nero killed himself in 68, his general, Vespasian, had subdued most of the Judean rural areas. In 69 he became the new emperor and left his son, Titus, to finish the job with his "amazing courage and strength" (270). He led armies with a "habit of victory and unfamiliarity with defeat, their constant campaigning and uninterrupted training, and the greatness of the Empire—above all that fact that always, in every place, by every man stood Titus" (279).

The war's background falls roughly into two phases: Jewish discontent with intrusive elements of Greek-based Hellenistic civilization, and resentment of Roman rule. Within each phase Jews could not agree among themselves on policy and divided into factions. When a Seleucid ruler (second century B.C.) interfered with religious customs, angry Jewish leaders "competed for supremacy because no prominent person could bear to be subject to his equals" (27). The outcome was successful military resistance and autocratic rule by a powerful Jewish family (most famous for Judas Maccabeus) that inflamed factionalism further until Roman conquest in 63.

Initially victorious Rome preferred client kings to direct rule. The most notable choice was Herod (reigned 40 and 4 B.C.), a Jew with strong Hellenistic sympathies. His political career, military successes, grim treatment of courtiers and relatives, and monumental building projects receive close attention (78–79). Josephus passes no moral judgment and represents him as an example of Jewish–Roman harmony before sectarianism broke the peace. Anti-Roman Zealots eventually prevailed by persuasion or force. Provoked by this instability, Rome absorbed Judea into its provincial system in A.D. 6. Zealots then focused internal tensions on Rome, building to the revolt of 66.

For Josephus, responsibility for the revolt and its consequences were not in doubt: "She [the country] was destroyed by internal dissensions, and the Romans who so unwillingly set fire to the Temple were brought in by the Jews' self-appointed rulers ... " (22). Reversals of the Jews against Rome are attributed to God's displeasure and punishment. Ordinary Judeans and the priesthood–aristocracy (Pharisees and Sadducees) are excused from hating Rome and rejecting occupation. A credulous people were manipulated and tyrannized by brutal anti-Roman factions that also battled one another for possession of the city and the Temple, slaughtering thousands of citizens and commencing destruction of the Temple completed later by the Romans: "Unhappy City! What have you suffered from the Romans to compare with this?" (264) Divine as well as human causation was instrumental. Jewish rebels and other sectarians caused the war in defiance of God's will: " ... it was God who condemned the whole nation ... " (301). But gangs, bandits, and partisans did their share: " ... the destruction of the people the partisans welcomed; it left more for them. The only people who, in their opinion, deserved to survive were those who had no use for peace and only lived to defeat the Romans" (282).

Jerusalem is described as an incomparably great city, with a circuit of nearly four miles, three nested walls, and high towers. Two spectacular monuments were King Herod's palace, which "no tongue could describe ... its magnificence and equipment were unsurpassable," and the Second Temple (built by King Herod), which "had everything that could amaze either mind or eye. Overlaid all round with stout plates of gold ... " (390, 394). For Josephus, the doomed city was a wonder of the ancient world. His account of physical splendors is accompanied by information about social, economic, and religious functions of the Temple, and sectarian politics over its meaning and uses. It was the most sacred place for Jews. During the Roman siege, citizens stored their wealth in its precincts and toward the end crowded into it by the thousands expecting God to protect them (326).

According to Josephus, Titus had no desire to ravage the city or raze the Temple. Both were useful to the empire intact. Radical Jews controlling Jerusalem forced his hand after several offers of peace and clemency: "The Romans were upheld by the combination of strength with experience, the Jews by reckless courage nourished by fear, and by their characteristic obstinacy amid disasters" (279). He praises Vespasian and Titus as prudent, merciful opponents unhappy with bloodshed, but driven to it by duplicitous extremists: "Faction reigned everywhere, the revolutionaries and jingoes with the boldness of youth silencing the old and sensible" (223).

Without discomfort, he managed to be pro-Jewish, pro-Roman, and pro-Hellenistic culture. He later became a Pharisee, the "leading sect," but doubted that traditional Judaism could prevail over Roman paganism. The empire and its might were undefeated realities. One intention of his writings was to help Jews fit in with that established fact without loss of self-respect, but also to pacify Roman authorities in hope of softening post-war policies. He sought in part to neutralize prejudice against Jews by representing major religious sects, Pharisees, Sadducees, and Essenes (he describes this semi-monastic sect in detail) as philosophical schools to blur contradictions between Judaism and Greco-Roman culture (375).

He describes himself as a great general. His army of Jewish recruits at Jotapata was organized on the Roman model: "Above all he [Josephus] trained them for war by stressing Roman discipline at every turn; they would be facing men whose physical prowess and unshakable determination had conquered almost the entire world." His characterization of recruits without discipline is not flattering: "He would feel certain of their soldierly qualities ... if they refrained from their besetting sins of theft, banditry, and looting, from defrauding their countrymen, and from regarding as personal gain the misfortunes of their closest friends" (168).

Josephus is an indispensable source for internal Jewish politics and relations of Rome to Judea from the time of the Maccabees to the end of the Jewish war. Scholars still mine his work for knowledge and insight. In the Preface he says: "To those who took part in the war or have ascertained the facts I have left no ground for complaint or criticism; it is for those who love the truth, not those who seek entertainment ... " (25). At the end of the work he reaffirms its truthfulness: "And here we bring our story to an end—the story which we promised to set down with the utmost accuracy. Its literary merits must be left to the judgment of the readers; as to its truth, I should not hesitate to make the confident assertion that from the first word to the last I have aimed at nothing else" (370).

The problem for modern historians is how far these claims can be trusted. Reliability is hard to test without corroboration from other writers who also took part and "ascertained the facts." Sources are not cited, and historians were expected to improve them rhetorically, so a fair assumption is that he did so. Battle descriptions are probably overwrought in the Hellenistic style. Judgments about people, politics, behavior, and especially statements about himself, are problematic. A warning sign is boundless self-regard, a major theme of the history. His greatness never slackens. In Galilee, he is an exemplary governor and general (182). His commitments are slippery. The transition from general defending Lower Galilee to client of Titus and negotiator for Rome in the siege of Jerusalem went smoothly (272, 285). He explains on the one hand why he stopped fighting the Romans but is silent on the other hand why he fought them in the first place. Was he a revolutionary like the "gangs?"

On balance, however, it is widely held that his narrative is credible in essentials, that he supplies an accurate account of events and their course, and that he made careful use of varied sources to be informative to a wide audience. First and foremost, he was an eyewitness with a foot in Jewish and Roman camps, a huge advantage. Self-criticism is rare but not absent. Here and there he admits emotion carried him away. Physical descriptions hold up well against topographical and archeological studies in Jerusalem (the Temple area, Herod's palace, and the third wall), Jericho, and other sites. The archeological findings have been supported by epigraphic and numismatic evidence.

A jarring curiosity about *The Jewish War* is comparative judgments of Jews and Romans. Josephus says other reports by "eyewitnesses have been falsified either to flatter the Romans or to vilify the Jews, eulogy or abuse being substituted for factual record" (21). Yet he is far from evenhanded. He wanted to save and elevate Jewish brethren and fend off the worst of Roman vengeance, but seldom makes them look as good as Romans.

On the Romans: "Did they [the rebels] not know that the might of Rome was invincible, and submission to her an everyday experience? ... God was on the Roman side" (284). On the Jews: "Somehow those days [the revolt] had become so productive of every kind of wickedness among the Jews as to leave no deed of shame uncommitted; and even if someone had used all his powers of invention he could not have thought of any vice that remained untried: so corrupt was the public and private life of the whole nation ... " (357).

Works by Josephus

The Jewish War and Other Selections from Flavius Josephus, trans. by H. St. Thackery and Ralph Marcus, edited and abridged with an Introduction by Moses I. Finley (New York: Washington Square Press, 1963).

The Jewish War, trans. by G. A. Williamson (New York: Penguin Books, 1959). This edition includes useful maps and a detailed table of contents.

The Works of Josephus, in the *Loeb Classical Library*, trans. by H. St. J. Thackery, Ralph Marcus, and Allen Wikgren. This scrupulous translation is extensively annotated.

Works about Josephus

Bilde, Per, *Flavius Josephus between Jerusalem and Rome: His Life, his Works and their Importance* (Sheffield: JSOT, 1998).

Cohen, Shaye J.D., *Josephus in Galilee and Rome: His Vita and Development as a Historian* (Leiden: E.J. Brill, 1979).

Hadas-Lebel, Mireille, *Flavius Josephus, Eyewitness to Rome's First Century Conquest of Judea* , trans. from the French by Richard Miller (New York: Macmillan, 1993).

6. THE CITY OF GOD[4] (AUGUSTINE OF HIPPO, A.D. 354–430)

He was born in North Africa in 354 of a Christian mother and a pagan father. Father rather than mother had the greater influence. Christianity had been officially recognized within the Empire for half a century, but paganism was still a powerful force even though forced underground. He was educated at Carthage, the leading African city, where he absorbed Latin literature and rhetoric. Later he became a professor of rhetoric at Carthage. He reveals in his *Confessions* a taste for pleasures of the flesh that lasted into his early thirties. In *The City* he alludes also to an early taste for pagan entertainment: "I myself, in my younger days, used to frequent the sacrilegious stage plays and comedies. I used to watch the demoniacal fanatics and listen to the choruses, and take delight in the obscene shows in honor of their gods and goddesses" (II.4). Such admissions gave the "saint" a comfortable human dimension.

His *Confessions* traces steps of experimentation with various philosophies and faiths until he finds in Christ the absolute certainty he was seeking. For some time he was a pagan in his father's footsteps, and then a brief convert to Manichaeism, which taught a dualism of good and evil derived from Zoroastrianism, a Persian faith. He studied with Bishop Ambrose in Milan as he struggled with his lust for women and pagan delights. By 387 his urges for sensual gratification were overcome, the rhetoric professorship was surrendered, and he was inducted into the Church by Ambrose. His gifts of intellect and service were recognized in 395 with the bishopric of Hippo in a Roman province. Augustine died in 430 while his city was under siege by Germanic Vandals bent conquering North Africa.

In *The City of God (Civitate Dei)*, his idea of rival cities in heaven and earth from the beginning of time in the last 12 books was considered sober history for the next 1,000 years. An idea so long consulted and revered was sure to leave traces well beyond its origin. He crystallized two opposed outlooks—the secular and the religious, the material and the spiritual: "Of all visible things, the universe is the greatest; of all invisible realities, the greatest is God" (XI.4). His mentor was Plotinus (d. A.D. 270), a late follower and interpreter of Plato, who argued that timeless truth and meaning lay in a reality beyond reason and the senses. The duality of two cities explained the past from the Assyrian Empire to the breakup of the Western Roman Empire.

By the fourth century of our era Augustine's dualism ended the Greco-Roman belief that relations of humans to each other and to nature can be understood by reason without supernatural intervention. With his two cities, Augustine shifted the center of gravity to a spiritual world accessible only to faith entailing dependence on powers beyond reason: "What we see ... is that two societies have issued from two kinds of love. Worldly society has flowered from a selfish love ... whereas the communion of saints is rooted in a love of God ... The latter relies on the Lord, whereas the other boasts that it can get along by itself" (XIV. 28). Once more: "In regard to mankind I have made a division. On the one side are those who live according to men; on the other, those who live according to God" (XV.1). The Greco-Roman belief in human self-sufficiency guided by reason eventually fell by the wayside, to be revived a thousand years later in the Renaissance. The two sides of this dualism have remained at odds over the relative weight of worldly and religious ways of life into modern times.

An event that inspired the work was Rome's invasion in 410 by Alaric the Goth. He allowed troops to loot the city, rape women, and pile up corpses even though he was a Christian. The event sent waves of shock and disbelief through an already crumbling Roman Empire in the west. Given its historic might and longevity, how could an army of barbarians wreak havoc on the legendary capital city? Widespread distress inspired two explanations: neglect of Rome's ancient pantheon of gods, thus forfeiting their protection, and weakening of Roman strength and spirit by Christian pacifism and otherworldliness: " ... why do the calumniators of Christian civilization affirm that disaster came upon Rome because she ceased to honor her deities?" (1.15). Critics believed Christianity's guilt and impotence was compounded because Alaric plundered Rome while the empire was ruled by a Christian emperor.

A resurgence of pagan sentiment and its hostility to Christianity mobilized Augustine's intellect and energies. A Roman official, also a Christian, invited him to answer charges that Christianity was responsible for the sack of Rome. At the time of Alaric's raid, Augustine was recognized as a leading churchman and theologian. Until the crisis of 410, his life had been devoted to finding his way to Christ and then defending his faith against heretics. Now he was galvanized to show that Christianity did not create Rome's troubles: "Let the pagans blame their own gods for all their woes, instead of repaying our Christ with ingratitude for all His good gifts" (III.31). Augustine's refutation of the charge that Christianity caused Rome's problems had consequence for historiography—a radical change in how the structure, chronology, and meaning of historical process was perceived.

The City of God decisively replaced the tradition of Greco-Roman historiography. The work was begun in 413 and completed in 426. The first ten books reject the claim that pagan gods were protectors of the Roman Empire, or even cared about it, and the charge that Christian life and teaching were responsible for the barbarian assault on Rome. The foundation and intention of *The City* are theological, but it contains a wealth of empirical detail about Greco-Roman belief in their gods before the advent of Christianity from lost sources, or from Augustine's early experience as a pagan believer: " ... I have gone to the books in which their own historians have recorded, for men's information, the things that happened in the past ... " (IV.1).

In the tenth book he makes a transition to his thesis of two cities, which is then fleshed out in the remaining 12 books. Throughout he contrasts the corruption, violence, and vice of the pagan Empire with the integrity, gentleness, and uprightness of the Church of Christ. He acknowledges that in his time the two realms co-exist and interpenetrate. Virtuous pagans belong in the Church. Self-serving, hypocritical, worldly churchmen belong in the Empire. Stylistically the book is often overblown and repetitive, but he confesses long-windedness attributable to a teacher of rhetoric lured by devices of language that might enhance persuasion. History was regarded as a branch of rhetoric and literature. The historian was expected to preserve important events, dramatize examples of good and evil, and provide a guide to life, all of which Augustine does and more.

His denunciation of Roman polytheism unfolds on several levels. First, the many gods of Rome did not prevent catastrophes inflicted before Christianity: "The chronicles are filled with wars waged before Rome was founded, and since it rose and grew to be an empire" (I.1).

Second, Roman gods were indifferent to moral lapses of worshippers, which was more crucial than "hunger, disease, war, plunder, imprisonment, massacre ... " (III.1). "Such misfortunes are not a source of evil, which comes from within rather, not from without: ... moral evils ... must be regarded as the only real and serious calamities" (IV.2). Not only did the gods fail to protect life and property, they offered no moral teaching or uniform standard of conduct, a fault admitted by eminent Romans, without which there could be no justice. There "was never a true republic, because in it true justice was never practiced" (II.21). Moreover, "in the absence of justice, what is sovereignty but organized brigandage?" (IV.4).

Third, the full extent of Roman polytheism, with hundreds of deities for every occasion, could have no moral significance, groaned under its own weight, and blunted serious commitment with their overlapping functions: "They do not see ... how many gods remain without worship, how many have no temples or altars built to them, and to how few of the heavenly bodies they thought of dedicating such things, and of offering special sacrifices." Viewing the supernatural chaos of Roman pagan religion, Augustine concludes: " ... what could the Romans lose if, with a wiser economy, they should worship one God" (IV.11).

Finally, though Rome had accepted Christianity, the conversion came too late and was half-hearted. Alaric's raid was a providential warning that the flame of pagan polytheism still produced heat if not light.

In *The City of God,* human purposes are replaced by God's purposes worked out in human activities and wills. It claims universal scope. Greco-Roman historians had relatively confined interests—the Persian Wars for Herodotus (although his setting for the wars has breadth), the Peloponnesian War for Thucydides, the founding and history of Rome for Livy (one city, but he covers centuries), Rome under the early Caesars for Tacitus. Augustine's setting is the world, which for him was Europe, Asia, and Africa. He reaches back in time to the origin of man in the Garden, identifies a mid-point with the appearance of Christ, and anticipates the end of history in a last judgment. Rather than a Greco-Roman cyclical view of history, a linear view took over with beginning, middle, and end.

A result was a transformation of chronology, a division of the past into two distinct periods, before Christ (B.C.) and after (A.D.), a scheme still with us. Augustine went further and divided past, present, and future into seven ages, modeled on the biblical schedule of creation: Adam to the flood, the flood to Abraham, Abraham to David, David to the Babylonian captivity of the Jews, Babylon to Christ, his own age of indeterminate length, and an eighth age, the Lord's Day (XXII.30). Thus periodization became a standard practice for indicating historical eras.

The Greco-Roman view was that history has an element of chance beyond explication—that is, some things are just fated to happen. The historian's best course is to be content with immediate experience rather than try to make sense of the past in its totality. Augustine sought unity by arguing that nothing happens by chance. All events are the work of divine Providence. Whatever happens or has happened is due to God's purposes. Thus the entire past can be understood and mobilized to explain the present and anticipate the future. Modern historians work on the assumption that whatever happened can be understood without fate or Providence if there is sufficient evidence. But credit for the idea of uniting past, present, and future goes to Augustine. For him, without the drama of human salvation, written in the language of original sin and redemptive grace, and played out in the two cities, there would be no history.

Works by Augustine

The City of God, trans. by Marcus Dods (New York: Modern Library, 1950).
The City of God, an abridgement from the trans. Gerald Walsh, Demetrius Zema, and Grace Monahan, ed. with intro. by Vernon J. Honan (New York: Image Books, 1958).
The City of God against the Pagans, 7 vols., trans. by George E. McCracken and others, Loeb Classical Library (Cambridge, Massachusetts: Harvard University Press, 1957–72).
The Confessions of St. Augustine, trans. by Edward B. Pusey (New York: Pocket Books, 1952).

Works about Augustine

Brooks, Edgar Harry, *The City of God and the Politics of Crisis* (London; New York: Oxford University Press, 1960).
Grimes, Tom, *City of God* (New York: W.W. Norton, 1995).
Hanby, Michael, *Augustine and Modernity* (London; New York: Routledge, 2003).
Matthews, Gareth, *Augustine* (London: Blackwell, 2005).

Useful references

Collingwood, R.G., *The Idea of History* (Oxford: Oxford University Press, 1946). See pp. 46–52.

Fitzgerald, Allan D.(ed.)., *Augustine through the Ages* (Grand Rapids: William B. Eardmans Publishing, 1999).

Section Notes

1 The translation used for this essay is by G.A. Williamson.
2 Cohen distinguishes these accounts in three of the works to show they have different motives, pp. 240–42.
3 Williamson provides a correlation of his "chapters" with the "books" of Whiston on page 407.
4 The Walsh, Zema, Monahan abridged translation is used for this essay. The original work is very long, over 800 pages in the Modern Library edition, seven volumes in the Loeb Classical Library edition. The abridgement retains the original twenty-two books but leaves out digressive chapters within the books unnecessary to follow Augustine's argument, although all of them are briefly summarized. The Image Books edition, which runs over 500 pages, is readily available.

BYZANTIUM

Themes 1 (early historiography), 6 (problematic historiography)

The Byzantine Empire centered at Constantinople arose as the eastern arm of the Roman Empire. After barbarian invasions and internal decay ended Rome's dominion in the west, the eastern empire survived for another thousand years until Constantinople was taken by the Ottoman Turks in 1453. Justinian was the most famous Byzantine ruler, associated with major achievements in law and architecture in the sixth century. His policies, character, and life at the Byzantine court were subjects of a remarkable document by Procopius, who knew the emperor, held office in his government, and was an eye witness of major events. He wrote about what he knew in public documents but also in one kept secret because of its sensational and seditious revelations about the emperor and his wife, Theodora. It is remarkable that the document has survived, but that fact may underscore its intrinsic interest to later generations of scholars and officials. The problem for historians remains—what to make of it?

7. SECRET HISTORY[1] (PROCOPIUS, CA. 500–CA. 554)

Best known of early Byzantine historians, also last and greatest historian in the classical tradition of the ancient world, Procopius came to Constantinople from Palestinian Caesarea (now modern Israel) in 527. Knowledge about his early life is skimpy, but it seems he had a good education, studied and practiced law, and was good with languages—Attic Greek, Latin, and Aramaic. For many years he was secretary, legal advisor, and confidant to Belisarius, the general commanding armies of the emperor. Thereafter he held other official posts in government for some 20 years, and even received the title *illustris* from the emperor. Despite prominence in Byzantine politics, military affairs, court life, and culture, it is unknown what happened to him later or when he died. His monument is seven volumes in the Loeb Classical Library.

Procopius is the main source for the first two-thirds of Emperor Justinian's reign from 527 to 565.[2] During that period the Eastern Roman Empire, which escaped disintegration of the Western Empire, expanded its domains by defeating barbarian regimes in Italy, North Africa, and Spain. Lands to the east were also taken from Persians. The empire doubled in size for a time and wallowed in wealth despite huge costs of almost continuous warfare, a luxurious court, and an extravagant building program. A remarkable woman, Theodora, consort to Justinian and co-equal with him in power, was active in politics, diplomacy, religious disputation, and intrigue.

The scandalous and irresistibly readable *Anecdota* ("unpublished," "not given out"), or *Secret History*, was unknown until long after his death. It is mentioned in a tenth-century encyclopedia. A unique work of ancient historiography, it consists of 30 short chapters in the Atwater translation. Written about 550, it was under wraps in the author's lifetime because public knowledge of its blistering contents would likely have led to his arrest for treason: " ... it was not possible, during the life of certain persons, to write the truth of what they did, as a historian should. If I had, their hordes of spies would have found out about it, and they would have put me to a most horrible death. I could not even trust my nearest relatives. That is why I was compelled to hide real explanations of many matters glossed over in my previous works" (3). After a denunciation of Theodora's intrigues, he reminds the reader "it is in this book ... that I necessarily tell the real truths and motives of events" (88).

The problem for modern historians is its usefulness as a source for Justinian's reign. Given the high reputation of Procopius's war volumes, the concealed volume deserves benefit of a doubt. Claims of the *Secret History* have been confirmed from other sources. Others cannot be verified and still others are obviously exaggerated or even ridiculous. After rejecting references to doubtful reports and appeals to the supernatural, the volume has information not available elsewhere about Byzantine state and society, including the bureaucracy, postal service, wages and prices, political factions in Constantinople, and even the status of prostitution. Irregular behavior of magistrates merits an entire chapter. The office of Quaestor, whose job was oversight of public finance and punishment of sexual offenses, blasphemy, and heresy, was especially prone to abuse: "And the Quaestor, when he condemned persons coming before him, confiscated as much as he pleased of their properties, and the Emperor shared with him each time in the lawlessly gained riches of other people. For the subordinates of these magistrates neither produced accusers nor offered witnesses when these cases came to trial, but during all this time the accused were put to death, and their properties seized without due trial and examination" (99).

The *Secret History* is best viewed in light of the public histories, which have three notable features. First, they are secular works in an age preoccupied with theology and church history. Second, the models were Greek, He turned to the best—Herodotus, Thucydides, and Polybius—for examples of style and narrative form, especially the use of entertaining digressions from Herodotus and contrived speeches from Thucydides. Translators say his Greek prose has a persuasive classical ring. The reason for this influence is that Greek literature flowed into the Eastern Empire for centuries. Greek works were readily available and competitive with Christian works. Third, the Byzantine Church did not control historical writing like the Roman Church in the Western Empire, and emperors were consistent patrons of historians, the most important of whom were laymen rather than churchmen.

From the fourth to the seventh centuries there were some 40 historians who produced 54 volumes, about 40 percent of which have survived in 200 manuscript copies.[3] The two most widely read of the lot with the most surviving manuscripts are Eusebius (255–339), father of church history and the universal Christian chronicle, and Procopius. All the early Byzantine historians were more interested in Greek literary style than research, despite the existence of libraries and archives in Constantinople, Alexandria, Antioch, and other cities among the 950 of the empire. Consequently they did little research and relied on what they already knew or could easily find out. The advantage of Procopius is that he was a participant in events he describes. He was close to the top general of the time, knew many public officials, and had audiences with Justinian.

With Belisarius, he was on campaigns in Africa, Italy, and Syria. He saw Rome under siege by Goths in 538 and accompanied victorious Belisarius when he entered the Gothic capital of Ravenna in 540. He witnessed in 533 the uprising of a faction hostile to the emperor in Constantinople that was crushed in the Hippodrome (the great circus) by Belisarius and his troops, reputedly killing 30,000 demonstrators. In 541–42 he survived the great plague in Constantinople, which he describes with a precision reminiscent of Thucydides, noting that thousands died each day, their bodies stacked in the streets. He was contemporary with other great events of the age, which included Justinian's codification of Roman law, his efforts to reunify the Roman Empire and reconcile Greek and Roman branches of Christianity, and a grand building program that resulted in Hagia Sophia (Holy

Wisdom). Its lofty dome secured to four piers by pendentive arches and mystical interior bathed in light are described vividly by Procopius in his volume on Justinian's buildings.

He was a sharp, intelligent historian with experience, industry, and style. His multi-volume *Wars of Justinian*, essentially military histories, recount attempts to reclaim lost portions of the Roman Empire in the east from Persia, in Italy from the Ostrogoths, in North Africa from the Vandals, and as far west as Spain and Gaul. His patron general, Belisarius, one of the best military leaders of the Roman world, does not always get high marks, although enough good things are said to preserve the lucrative connection while downplaying the role and importance of Justinian, neglect the emperor apparently endured without complaint. These public historical works are admired for their logical structure, copious detail, arresting narrative, and confirmed accuracy, except when Procopius strays now and then from direct experience of events. In the *Secret History*, his chief criticism of Belasarius is that jealousy of his wayward wife's infidelities distracted him from duty and impaired his judgment (13).

Although a Christian, he associates the pagan idea of fate, or nemesis, with divine Providence to explain the historical process. The rule of God, or Fortune, is irresistible and incomprehensible. All one can do is yield to it: "Indeed, it is not by the plans of men, but by the hand of God that the affairs of men are directed; and this men call Fate, not knowing the reason for what things they see occur; and what seems to be without cause is easy to call the accident of chance. Still this is a matter every mortal will have to decide for himself according to his taste" (25). No doubt a tinge of heresy lies in this suggestion that God's will is a matter of chance, but what Procopius apparently meant is that God controls the inscrutable unfolding of Fate, with the proviso that demons were responsible if things went badly. If things went well, then God's hand behind the movement of Fate was responsible.

Despite attacks on Justinian and Theodora in the *Secret History*, including Balisarius's openly unfaithful wife, Antonina, there are facts readily known to others he could not suppress, so the two rulers are not always depicted without a redeeming virtue: "It was easy for Justinian to look after everything, not only because of his calmness of temper, but because he hardly ever slept ... and because he was not chary with his audiences. For great opportunity was given to people, however obscure and unknown, not only to be admitted to the tyrant's presence, but to converse with him, and in private" (76). Procopius was not as negative as the *Secret History* suggests. In all the histories there are about 130 character sketches, about two-thirds of which are positive. He did not care much for the human race, but he did admire individual men.

But his anger, bitterness, and disillusionment can be read in the chapter titles: "How Theodora, Most Depraved of All Courtesans, Won His [i.e., Justinian's] Love"; "How the Defender of the Faith Ruined His Subjects"; "That Justinian and Theodora Were Actually Fiends in Human Form"; "How All Roman Citizens Became Slaves"; "How Justinian Killed a Trillion (*sic*) People." And so on, with a personal assessment of Justinian that would have singed his royal ears: "This Emperor ... was deceitful, devious, false, hypocritical, two-faced, cruel, skilled in dissembling his thought, never moved to tears by either joy or pain ... " (43). While his account of Justinian's disastrous policies may be true, it does not follow that the emperor intended the worst rather than the best outcomes. Rulers can make mistakes with good intentions.

Not content to heap charges of gross immorality on the empress and destructive incompetence on the emperor, he says they are creatures from another realm exercising unnatural, wicked powers: "Wherefore to me, and many others of us, these two seemed not to be human beings, but veritable demons, and what the poets call vampires, who laid their heads together to see how they could most easily and quickly destroy the race and deeds of man; and assuming human bodies, became man-demons, and so convulsed the world. And one could find evidence of this in many things, but especially in the superhuman power with which they worked their will" (63).

The basis of this claim is that spectacular evil he attributes to the royal pair was possible only for non-human agencies: "Robbery, enslavement, torture, war, massacre, injustice, and persecution" are not the only evidence of fiendishness, but corruption of nature as well: " ... but to destroy all men and bring calamity to the whole of the inhabited earth remained for these two to accomplish whom Fate aided in their schemes of corrupting all mankind. For by earthquakes, pestilences, and floods of river waters at this time came further ruin ... Thus not by human, but by some other kind of power they accomplished their dreadful designs" (64).

It is not clear if he intends to brand Justinian and Theodora as demons incarnate or merely as agents of the Devil (there is no word in Greek for "devil," so the best option is "ruler of demons"). After composing this clandestine work, he produced a volume on *Buildings of Justinian* replete with praise for the very emperor he attacks in the *Secret History*. In both cases, his reputation for impartiality is diminished, although inflated praise for the emperor was commonplace in Byzantine circles.

The *Secret History* was written in a despotic world strapped by religious constraints both theological and legal. A historian was enclosed by beliefs, practices, and institutions over which he had no control. Rulers who wielded virtually absolute power over everyone were not usually inclined to smile on harsh criticism, much less verbal abuse. Justinian designated himself "sacred." Those who approached him at court were obliged to kiss the hem of his purple robe. Getting what one wanted from such a person required flattery rather than exposure of their poor behavior and policy making. Keeping objections and charges to oneself was the wiser course for a historian wishing to avoid unpleasant consequences.

A tradition of senatorial resistance to absolutism fueled his resentment of imperial autocracy. He was part of the senatorial class numbering some 2,000 members. The resort to demonism comes from his Christian perspective. Great evils and misfortunes were routinely attributed to demonic forces. A more profound motive was rooted in classical historiography, which usually sought to praise virtue and condemn vice. In his view, responsibilities of emperor and empress demanded a high level of virtue. Failure invited criticism if not public condemnation.

In fairness to the rulers, Procopius was never close enough to appreciate that power and resources were unequal to effective management of a vast, populous, turbulent empire. Justinian was not responsible for the rigid, corrupt bureaucracy he inherited or the burdensome tax system devised by his predecessors. Procopius is reluctant to give Justinian credit for attempting brave reforms even when he needed funds to pursue the unrealistic ambition of reunifying the empire. Theodora was likely debauched in her youth, but in maturity she seems to have been a wise counselor, unusually tolerant, and even came to the defense of prostitutes. She was virtually co-emperor with Justinian and acquitted herself as well as might be expected of a woman within limitations of the age. Nevertheless, Procopius tars her with the brush he uses on Justinian. For perspective on the age of Justinian, *Secret History* has legitimate uses, but requires correction against testimony of other sources and must be used with caution. Despite weaknesses, later historians of Byzantium were glad to have it.[4]

Works by Procopius

The Secret History, trans. from the Greek by Richard Atwater, forward by Arthur E.R. Boak (Ann Arbor, Michigan: University of Michigan Press, 1963).

The Secret History, trans. from the Greek by G.A. Williamson and Peter Sarris; intro. and notes by Peter Sarris (New York: Penguin Books, 2007).
Wars of Justinian, The Secret History, and Buildings of Justinian, 7 volumes, trans. from the Greek by H.B. Dewing (Cambridge, Massachusetts: Harvard University Press, *The Loeb Classical Library*, 1914–40). Greek with English translation. *Secret History* is volume 6.

Works about Procopius

Cameron, Averil, *Procopius and the Sixth Century* (Berkeley, California: University of California Press, 1985).
Damus, Joseph, *Seven Medieval Historians* (Chicago: Nelson Hall, 1982), Chapter 1.
Kaldellis, Anthony, *Procopius of Caesaria: Tyranny, History and Philosophy at the End of Antiquity* (Philadelphia, Pennsylvania: University of Pennsylvania Press, 2004).
Treadgold, Warren, *The Early Byzantine Historians* (New York: Palgrave Macmillan, 2007), Chapter 6.

Useful references

Browning, Robert, *Justinian and Theodora* (New York: Praeger, 1971).

Section Notes

1 The translation cited in this essay is by Richard Atwater.
2 Sources other than Procopius for sixth-century Byzantium are listed and commented on in Browning, pp. 261–64.
3 For a summary of early Byzantine historians as a group, their histories, the tradition of historiography, and a chronological table of the historians and their works, see Treadgold, pp. 350–384.
4 Gibbon was skeptical but considered the *Secret History* a valuable source. Condemning the emperor and his consort as demons "must doubtless sully the reputation, and detract from the credit, of Procopius: yet, after the venom of his malignity has been suffered to exhale, the residue of the *anecdote*, even the most disgraceful facts, some of which had been tenderly hinted in his public history, are established by their internal evidence, or the authentic monuments of the time." *The Decline and Fall of the Roman Empire* (the 1990 Great Books of the Western World edition), Chapter 40, I: 649. Voltaire viewed the *Secret History* as "a satire prompted by motives of revenge, and although revenge may sometimes speak the truth, this satire, which contradicts his own official history of the reign, seems to be false in several instances." *The Age of Louis XIV*, trans. by Martyn P. Pollack (1958), p. 255.

ISLAM

Themes 1 (early historiography), 2 (non-Western historiography), 3 (issues of critical historiography)

Islamic civilization exhibits a long succession of writers who produced histories of cities, countries, and reigns for a thousand years, especially during the Middle Ages. In a huge literature, the great division is between earlier Arabic works through the medieval period and later ones in other languages, like Ottoman. Basic principles governing the composition and transmission of histories remained the same, with a few exceptions, and were dictated by tradition. Islamic historiography is heavily endowed with works of chronology and biography. Chronology was needed to establish a succession of events and rulers since Mohammed. Biographical material was commonly designed to present edifying examples of the ideal Islamic believer. A couple of writers attempted universal history, Ibn Khaldun in the fifteenth century and Muhammed al Tabari in the tenth century being two notable examples.

Despite a deep shadow of religious doctrine and surveillance cast over historical writing, Muslim authors knew the difference between truth and falsehood in testimony and contrived tests to detect it. Shaddad respected modest first-hand reports without exaggeration. The work chosen for this section illustrates principles that guided most Islamic historical writing. For this section, we stay with the Arabic phase of historiography for issues and style Muslim historians thought most essential and appropriate. The relationship between historical writing and religion was very tight. The consequences of that bond are dramatically evident in Shaddad's approach to the career of a celebrated Muslim leader during the medieval crusades.

8. THE RARE AND EXCELLENT HISTORY OF SALADIN[1] (BAHA' AL-DIN IBN SHADDAD, 1145–1235)

Ibn Shaddad died shortly before the Mongols ravaged Baghdad in 1258, which brought Islam's long era of greatness in Western Asia to a close and ended the exclusive Arabian phase of historiography. His work reflects a mature stage of the Islamic tradition of historical writing in Arabic. A convenient short account of his life was written by a schoolmate, who was also author of a respected biographical dictionary. Ibn Shaddad was born in Mosul, now Kurdish Iraq. Before moving to Baghdad, his studies included the Koran, the tradition of Mohammed's sayings and doings (*hadith*), and Muslim law (*sharia*). In Baghdad he studied at a well-known *madrassa*, a mosque school, where he subsequently became a professor of Islamic law. After four years he returned to Mosul and continued as a professor.

In 1188 he set out for Mecca on the obligatory pilgrimage required by Islam's "five pillars" of belief and practice. On the way home via Damascus to visit Jerusalem, recently recaptured by Muslims from Crusaders, he was summoned by Saladin, sultan of Egypt and Syria, who was engaged in a bloody campaign against Franks and other European crusaders to recapture Jerusalem, which he succeeded in doing: "The sultan left Acre and besieged Kawkab ... It came about that I returned from the Hajj [pilgrimage to Mecca] via Syria to visit Jerusalem and its sites ... News of my arrival came to the ears of the sultan ... He summoned me to him and went to great lengths to show me honour and respect. When I took my leave to depart for Jerusalem, one of his retinue came out to me and delivered his command that I should return and present myself at his service upon my return from Jerusalem" (80).

Ibn Shaddad had met and impressed Saladin twice before on diplomatic missions. On this third occasion, he presented the sultan with a treatise he had composed titled *The Virtues of the Jihad*, and thereafter took up duties as judge of the army, diplomat, and confidant. The content of his biography is therefore first hand for Saladin and mostly first hand for many events described. On Saladin's death in 1193, Ibn Shaddad continued for a while to serve his successors and family. He wrote a number of treatises on legal matters relating to *hadith*, but the most enduring work is his biography of Saladin.

As a result of lofty connections, he was wealthy enough to build colleges for the study of *hadith* and law. He died frail and sickly at age 89. Having no children, although married twice, his house was bequeathed to others for religious study and devotions. He was a conspicuously pious man. In the Prologue to his work on Saladin he declares "there is no god but God alone, who has no partner, a testimony which quenches hearts' burning thirst," and that "lord Muhammad is His servant and prophet ... " (13).

The biography was composed between 1198 and 1216. It reflects long-established conventions of Islamic historiography, although writing of a historical nature was slow to materialize. The first biography of Mohammed, for example, appeared in the first half of the ninth century, almost 200 years after his death. Despite the range of Muslim conquests, Greco-Roman historiography was unknown. No Greek or Roman historian was translated into Arabic. The impulse to write history came initially from genealogy to trace the lineage and traditions of ancestors. After the conquest of Persia, which had a tradition of narratives about kings, the Muslims began to write about the words and deeds of rulers. The Persian influence is attested by the five best Islamic historians of the ninth century, four of whom were Persian, although writing in Arabic.

As Islam expanded through conquest, so did the Arabic language, which became standard everywhere and displaced other languages and dialects. Because Arabic is the language of the Koran, which was taken to be the literal speech of Allah, scripture was immune to criticism. Records were subject to question for their accuracy in the chain of authorities, but any historical content in the Koran was off limits. The classical period of Arabic literature, including history, was from 750 to 1000. The post-classical period was from 1000 to 1258, when Saladin was active. History emerged gradually under the wings of theology, law, and philology, but never became a separate discipline. It was always a second rate subject dominated by lawyers. Ibn Shaddad is a good example of the lawyer-historian glorifying a ruler.

Ibn Shaddad illustrates the classical Muslim idea of what history was for, which was to conserve a special kind of knowledge rather than freely search the past by systematic, critical inquiry. History preserved a tradition of significant events and persons. Knowledge at its best was embodied in the pious, great men of the past. Two kinds of "reports" were established, the *hadith*, or actions and words of Mohammed, and the *khabar*, which could be any kind of report or account. Both were prefaced with an *isnad*, which refers to a chain of authority leading back to an original source or observer—i.e., so and so said, according to so and so, and on back to a starting point.

With a *hadith* the chain of reports had to be as complete and trustworthy as possible because they touched on Mohammed. With the *khabar*, there might be only one or a few. Reports were compared where possible to establish the most reliable links to the past. The tradition of *isnad* required attention to what was honestly reported rather than fabricated or exaggerated. A repertory of qualifications was developed to evaluate a source as acceptable, doubtful, or false.

Such judgments included an idea of corroboration between sources. Ibn Shaddad says: "I have decided to give a short account of what personal experience has dictated or of what I have been told, the source of which is close to complete reliability" (14). Furthermore: "I have only recorded what I witnessed or what trustworthy sources told me which I have checked" (38).

The basic forms of history were chronography (a sequential dating of events and people), biographies, and prosopography (group biographies, such as lawyers or clerics). All three might be utilized together. The voluminous history of al-Tabari (d. 923) runs from the "creation" to the year 915. Chronology was straightforward because it started with Mohammed's flight to Medina in 622. Thus Saladin's death is recorded by Ibn Shaddad as Wednesday 27 Safar 589, which translates as 3 March 1193 (244). By comparison, Christian chronological systems were varied and chaotic. Ibn Shaddad's account of Saladin is not biography in the Western sense. Apart from date and place of birth and some information about his family, nothing is reported about early experiences and development from childhood to manhood. The objective was to present Saladin as a model for all pious Muslims to admire and emulate, which is accomplished by a wealth of anecdotes about his personal qualities and public life. The text is divided into two parts: Saladin's character and demeanor, and his military campaigns in episodic but chronological order, although the ups and downs and back and forth of battles and negotiations with Crusaders is hard to follow and sometimes bewildering. Saladin is consistently described as an ideal Muslim guided by Allah.

He was devoted to scripture: "Whenever he heard the Koran, his heart was touched and his eyes would fill with tears on most occasions" (20). He was compassionate: "Saladin was just, gentle, and merciful, a supporter of the weak against the strong" (22). He was a dauntless warrior: "Saladin was one of the great heroes, mighty in spirit, strong in courage and of great firmness, terrified of nothing" (26). Holy war (Jihad) against the infidel was his obsession: "The Jihad, his love and passion for it, had taken a mighty hold on his heart and all his being, so much so that he talked of nothing else, thought of nothing but the means to pursue it, was concerned only with its manpower and had a fondness only for those who spoke of it and encouraged it" (28).

His chivalrous manner won the respect even of Crusaders: "He was a paragon of chivalry, generous, extremely modest and had a welcoming face for any guests that arrived ... He received graciously anyone who came to him on a mission, even if he were an infidel"

(35, also 139–40). He was solicitous of those around him: "In his kindness of heart he would ask one of our number about his health, what treatment he was having, his diet and drinks, and how his affairs progressed ... Nothing but good was ever mentioned about anyone in his presence. He disliked gossip, not wishing to hear anything but good of a person" (38).

When King Richard I of England (the Lion Heart) arrived, Ibn Shaddad said "God curse him," but went on to defend him in a spirit of fairness: "The king of England was a mighty warrior of great courage and strong in purpose. He had much experience of fighting and was intrepid in battle, and yet he was in their eyes below the king of France in royal status, although being richer and more renowned for martial skill and courage" (146).

Virtually all Islamic historical writing occurred in the shadow of theology. Whatever happened was due to the will of Allah, the unfolding of His providence. There was no issue of causation, but the historian could nevertheless record words and deeds of His human instruments: "The Muslims rejoiced at God's victory over the enemy through their won hands" (143). Battle with the infidel was always a struggle of the true faith with a false faith. How Muslims prevailed at the battle of Hattin (on the western side of the Sea of Galilee) in July 1187, a prelude to Saladin's recapture of Jerusalem, is a typical account of Muslim exploits:

> The conflict continued at close quarters, each horseman clashing with his opponent, until victory (for the Muslims) and for the infidels the onset of disaster were imminent ... Eventually, there came Saturday morning, on which the blessing was vouchsafed. Both sides sought their positions and each realized that whichever was broken would be driven off and eliminated. The Muslims were well aware that behind them was Jordan and before them enemy territory and that there was nothing to save them but God Almighty. God had already ordained and prepared the believer's victory and he duly brought it about according to what he had predestined.
>
> (73)

If there were a Muslim setback on the battlefield, the explanation was that God denied victory but made recompense later. At Ramla, "the Franks charged them [the Muslims] and God decreed their defeat ... It was a major defeat which God mended with the famous battle of Hattin (to God be the praise)" (54, also 151). If there were no recompense, the response was, "God knows best" (165). A priority for using the past as a source of moral and religious exemplification, with Allah presiding over whatever happened, did not encourage historical explanation.

Works by Ibn Shaddad

The Rare and Excellent History of Saladin, trans. from Arabic by D.S. Richards (Burlington, Vermont: Aldershot, 2001).

Works about Ibn Shaddad

Gabrieli, Francesco and E. J. Costello, *Arab Historians of the Crusades* (London: Routledge and Kegan, 1984).
Khalidi, Tarif. *Arabic Historical Thought in the Classical Period* (New York: Cambridge University Press, 1994).
Robinson, Chase F., *Islamic Historiography* (Cambridge: Cambridge University Press, 2003).

Useful references

Duri, A. A., *The Rise of Historical Writing among the Arabs*, ed. and trans. by L.I. Conrad (Princeton, New Jersey: Princeton University Press, 1983).
Houtsma, M. Th. et al. (ed), *Encyclopedia of Islam* (Leiden: E.J. Brill, 1987).
Rosenthal, Franz, *A History of Muslim Historiography* (Leiden: E.J. Brill, 1968).

Section Note

1 His name in Arabic is Salah al-Dunya wa'l-Din, which means "the goodness of this world and religion," or Salah al-Din in its shortened form, which Europeans rendered as Saladin.

MEDIEVAL EUROPE

Themes 1 (early historiography), 3 (issues of critical historiography), 4 (genres of history)

Historiography in medieval Europe (ca. eleventh to the fourteenth centuries) was less important and got less attention than philosophy and theology. Those who wrote history were uncertain what models from classical antiquity they should follow, but produced nevertheless a variety of works of uneven quality in England, France, and even in Sicily, many in vernacular languages rather than Latin. This diversity was not accompanied by any fundamental changes in principles of traditional historiography. The safest route was the chronicle, a year-by-year account of events bearing on multiple human activities, The Anglo-Saxon Chronicle being a prime example, usually compilations of facts ordered chronologically and keyed to the reigns of popes and secular rulers. As with classical works, the best histories were those whose authors were eye witnesses of events they write about. An example is the first-hand memoir by Joinville about St. Louis.

9. THE ANGLO-SAXON CHRONICLE[1] (ANONYMOUS, EARLY CHRISTIAN ERA TO 1154)

In England the chronicle emerged as a fusion of annals (Latin *annus*, or year) drawn from several monasteries. An *annal* records selected facts about events and persons in a succession of years without providing narrative connections or causal relations. Instead there is simply a bare record of facts jotted down from year to year pretty much according to a scribe's discretion and judgment, overseen no doubt by his superior. A monastery abbot was obliged at Easter to build a calendar for the coming year to note Sundays, feast days, saint's days, and other religious observances. In the margins or in spaces left blank a scribe recorded events and might include other material like popular songs, folklore, and phenomena of nature. The oldest surviving annals come from the sixth-century monastery at Lindisfarne, a tidal island opposite Northumberland in north east England.

The practice of keeping annals spread to other English monasteries and was carried by missionaries to the European continent in the seventh century. In the eighth century, Charlemagne, founder of the Holy Roman Empire, ordered monasteries to keep annals as part of his program to encourage learning and culture. In time, such brief, atomistic notices accumulated and were combined into narrow but recognizable chronicles, which are more elaborate historical records retaining a chronology of events but with a semblance of continuity and style. In England, enlightened Alfred the Great (871–91) also encouraged learning and specifically promoted the use of English instead of Latin, but went a step further. He had a chronicle compiled from available monastic annals, which were then distributed to monasteries throughout his domain, where they were expanded, amended, and updated.

As a collection of annals stitched into continuity, the resulting *Anglo-Saxon Chronicle* exists in nine handwritten manuscripts containing events from early Christian times to 1154 (200 pages plus notes in the Whitelock edition). Year one records two events: "Octavian reigned 66 years and in the 52nd year of his reign Christ was born" (6). Year 1154 ends with installation of an abbot:

> "That same day that Abbot Martin of Petersborough was to have gone there [London], he fell ill, and died on 2 January, and the monks within the day chose another from among themselves, whose name is William of Walterville, a good cleric and a good man, and well loved by the king and by all good men ... and soon the abbot-elect ... went shortly to Lincoln and was there consecrated abbot before he came home, and was then received with great ceremony at Peterborough with a great procession ... and has now made a fine beginning, Christ grant him to end thus."
>
> (203)

The *Chronicle* is mostly about royal and religious doings, although other kinds of events appear and there is even poetry from time to time (164–65). The text itself is the finest surviving example of Old English prose, as *Beowulf* is the exemplar of poetry in Old English. The nine manuscripts are the best source for Rome's departure from England to nearly a century after the Norman invasion in 1066. Here is the entry for 410 from a lost annal: "In this year Rome was destroyed by the Goths, eleven hundred and ten years after it was built. Then after that the kings of the Romans no longer reigned in

Britain. Altogether they had reigned there 470 years since Gaius Julius first came to the land" (9). Coverage includes reference to kings, popes, bishops, wars, famine, epidemics, invasions, celestial eclipses (solar eclipses are noted for 664, 733, and 809), commerce, law, agriculture, and religion not available in other sources. Announcements of prominent deaths are commonplace. For 885, " ... Charles, king of the Franks, died. He was killed by a boar, and a year previously his brother ... had died. They were both sons of Louis, who had died the year of the eclipse of the sun" (51). In 1087 there was plague and famine:

> " ... it became a very severe and pestilential year in this country. Such disease came on people that very nearly every other person was ill with the worst of diseases—high fever—and that so severely that many people died of the disease. Afterwards because of the great storms as we described them above, there came so great a famine over all England that many hundreds of people died a miserable death because of the famine. Alas, how miserable and pitiable a time was then."
>
> (162)

The *Chronicle* is a thorn bush of difficulties that plague much early historical evidence and its interpretation. The nine manuscripts are all copies from previous unknown versions produced at different times at the abbeys of Abingdon, Peterborough, Winchester, and Worcester. The content was taken from earlier year-by-year annals that are lost. There are different recensions as well, for example, an original Abingdon, a shorter version, and a longer version. The earliest text is from Alfred the Great's reign, possibly the Winchester chronicle of 892 (the scribe wrote DCCCXCII in the margin), incorporating annals that have not survived. The latest is from Peterborough Abbey in 1116, which shifts from Old to Middle English toward the end, the earliest known example of the language at that stage. Problems of philology, paleography, and diplomatics arise because there are multiple copies written in two versions of early English by different hands from different places over some three centuries. English sometimes alternates with Latin and there are cases of the two languages mixing in the same sentence. Toward the end of the Norman period, French words make an appearance.

Chronology is inconsistent and based on different systems of reckoning. The chronology of Venerable Bede's *Ecclesiastical History* was used, but dates are often wrong or contradictory. A source of the problem was when the year begins, since no uniform convention was recognized. Some entries start the year at Christmas, others in March or September. There are dislocations between manuscripts where scribes have the wrong date, left it out, or post-dated an entry. Between the eighth and ninth centuries there are dislocations of two to three years. Scholars consulting the *Chronicle* must sort out these discrepancies, but not always to a trustworthy conclusion. The death of King Alfred is recorded in 901, but the right year, whether 899 or 900, is uncertain: "He was king over the whole English people except for that part which was under Danish rule, and he had held the kingdom for one and half years less than thirty" (58).

The nine manuscripts reflect local biases interjected by scribes, which surely included responsible abbots, so reports are sometimes at odds. Some scribes are preoccupied with affairs in the north of England, others with the south. Events of importance known from other sources that should have been reported are left out. On the other hand, scribes may be taken as frequent "eyewitnesses" of the events they record. In many passages disparate events of varying importance crowd the entry. Thus for 952:

> "In this year ships of the vikings (*sic*) arrived in Dorset and ravaged in Portland. The same year London was burnt down. And in the same year two ealdormen died ... That same year two abbesses died ... Odda, emperor of the Romans, went to the land of the Greeks, and he then encountered a great army of the Saracens coming up from the sea, wishing to make a raid on the Christian people; and then the emperor fought against them and a great slaughter was made on both sides, and the emperor had control of the field, and yet he was much harassed there before he left."
> (81)

Entries vary in length from a single event briefly announced to more extended narrative. For 823 one lonely sentence tells us: "In this year Ceolwulf was deprived of his kingdom" (40). England was much troubled by Danish invasions and raids about the turn of the millennium. The *Chronicle* provides abundant details about these violent encounters. In 1010: " ... the Danish army came to Northampton and at once burnt that town and as much around it as they pleased, and from there went across the Thames into Wessex, and so towards Canning march, and burnt all of it" (90). In 1011:

> " ... the king and his councilors sent to the army and asked for peace, and promised them tribute and provisions on condition

that they should stop their ravaging. They had then overrun: (i) East Anglia, (ii) Essex, (iii) Middlesex, (iv) Oxfordshire, (v) Cambridgeshire, (vi) Hertfordshire, (vii), Buckinghamshire, (viii) Bedfordshire, (ix) half Huntingdonshire, (x) much of Northhamptonshire ... All those disasters befell us through bad policy, in that they were never offered tribute in time nor fought against, but when they had done most to our injury, peace and truce were made with them."

(91)

The 1066 return of Halley's Comet (every 75–76 years), which appears on the famous Bayeaux Tapestry, was viewed as a bad omen for King Harold at the historic Battle of Hastings, where he was defeated and lost his kingdom to William, Duke of Normandy, the "Conqueror." The *Chronicle* notes both events:

"Then over all England there was seen a sign in the skies such as had never been seen before. Some said it was a star 'comet' which some call the long-haired star; and it first appeared on the eve of the Great Litany, that is 24 April, and so shone all the week ... And King Harold ... assembled a naval force and a land force larger than any king had assembled before in this country, because he had been told that William the Bastard meant to come here and conquer this country. This was exactly what happened afterwards."

(140–41)

Without *The Anglo-Saxon Chronicle* and Venerable Bede's *Ecclesiastical History*, the history of England from Roman times to the conquest of William the Conqueror in the eleventh century would have very little content. The *Chronicle* was a major source used by three major Anglo-Norman historians, John of Worcester, William of Malmesbury, and Henry of Huntingdon. Still later historians either consulted it directly or took material from predecessors who used it, thereby pouring it into the mainstream of English historiography. With all its imperfections, the work is indispensable.

The Chronicle

The Anglo-Saxon Chronicle, trans. and intro. by George Garmonsway (rev. ed.; New York: E. P. Dutton, 1954). Side by side translations.

The Anglo-Saxon Chronicles, trans. by Anne Savage (London: Phoebe Phillips/ Heineman, 1982).
The Anglo-Saxon Chronicle, trans. and ed. by Michael J. Swanton (London: J. M. Dent, 1996).
The Anglo-Saxon Chronicle, a revised translation, ed. and intro. by Dorothy Whitelock with David Douglas and Susie I. Tucker (New Brunswick, New Jersey: Rutgers University Press, 1961).

Useful references

Blair, Peter H., *An Introduction to Anglo-Saxon England* (3rd ed.; Cambridge: Cambridge University Press, 2003).
Stenton, F. M., *Anglo-Saxon England* (3rd ed.; Oxford: Oxford University Press, 1971).
Thompson, James W., *A History of Historical Writing*, with collaboration of Bernard J. Holm, 2 vols. (New York: Macmillan, 1942), I: 160–62.

10. THE LIFE OF SAINT LOUIS[2] (JEAN DE JOINVILLE, 1225–1317)

Joinville was born in a noble family from Champagne, a province in the northeast of France. He received a noble's education at the court of Theobald IV, count of Champagne, and on the death of his father became *seneschal* of the province, an office responsible for local administration for the crown. Theobald introduced him to King Louis, who received him with affection and confidence. Joinville decided to accompany Louis when he organized the seventh crusade to free the Holy Land from Muslims. Always close to the king, he became an observant, intelligent eye witness who could follow events from a position of advantage.

The *Life of Saint Louis* (*La vie de saint Louis*) was begun in 1305 and probably completed in 1309, 39 years after the death of the king: "In the name of God Almighty, I, John of Joinville, *seneschal* of Champagne am dictating the life of our saintly King Louis: what I saw and heard during the six years I was in his company on pilgrimage overseas, and after our return" (19). The original manuscript given to the son, Louis X, has not survived. On hand are an older copy and two later ones, one of which has many changes and additions. The older one is likely close to the original. It is a single volume of 391 pages in double columns. Each paragraph begins with a gilded letter. The first page is embellished with gold illumination and a painting of Joinville handing Louis X the memoire of his father.

The older manuscript showed up in the library inventory of Charles V of France in 1373. An analysis of the illumination suggests it was 20 years older than the original, which would put it about 1320. Over time it ended up in Brussels, was lost, and then recovered in 1746. Presently it resides in the National Library of France.

The work is divided into two parts—Louis's "holy words and pious teachings," and his deeds. He "loved God [Jesus] with all his heart and emulated his deeds," and "put his own life at risk on several occasions because of his love for his people" (20). He "so loved honesty that he would not even lie to the Saracens regarding an agreement he had made with them … " (21). His eating habits were so modest that he consumed whatever the cook placed before him. Piety was everything to the king. The most valued trait of any person was unquestioned faith in God. Near misfortunes, like a wind blowing the king's ship aground near Cyprus, were seen as warnings from above. Joinville interprets the lesson: "This is how we should make use of this God-given warning: if we think there is anything in our hearts or in our conduct that might be displeasing to God we should rid ourselves of it without delay … " (41).

Joinville is instructive about the force of religious belief. For Louis, doubts about the faith, however minor, were intolerable: "The king strove with all his ability to teach me to believe firmly in the Christian law given to us by God … He said we should believe the articles of faith so firmly that neither death nor any ill that might befall our bodies should induce us to go against them in either word or deed" (43). Any temptation to stray from faith is prompted by the Devil, and authority is sufficient to confirm faith's articles: "The king said that faith and belief were things we should be fully confident about, even if our only assurance lay in what we had been told" (45). Being "told" included mother and father as well as priests. There must have been more than few whose religious conviction fell short of royal expectations: "The king so loved God and his sweet Mother that he severely punished all those he could ascertain had spoken basely of them and had sworn blasphemous oaths" (685).

Debate about matters of faith was dangerous:

> "He [the king] told me there was once a great debate between clerics and Jews at the monastery of Cluny … There was an old knight present … and he asked the abbot to let him open the debate. Reluctantly, the abbot said yes. The knight got up, leaning on his crutch, and said that the most eminent of the clerics and the most eminent of the Jewish masters should approach

him ... He asked the Jew one question ... : 'Master, do you believe that the Virgin Mary, who bore God in her womb and in her arms, was a virgin when she gave birth, and is the Mother of God?' The Jew replied that he did not believe any of this. And the knight said to him he had acted most foolishly when, neither believing in nor loving the Virgin, he had come inside her monastery ... Then he raised his crutch and struck the Jew with it across he ear, bringing him to the ground. The Jews all turned and fled ... Thus ended the disputation ... When a layman hears the Christian law slandered, he should defend it only with his sword, which he should thrust right into the offender's guts as far as it will go."

The abbot told the knight he had behaved "foolishly." The knight said it was the abbot who was foolish to arrange a debate with many faithful Christians present "who before the disputation ended would have left shaken in their faith ... " (51, 52, 53).

Joinville recounts how Louis came to "take the cross" and embark on his crusade:

" ... it so happened that God's will was that the king should be taken seriously ill at Paris. It was said that he was so unwell that one of the women attending him wanted to draw the sheet over his face, saying he was dead. But another woman ... would not allow her to do this. She said that his soul was still in his body. As the king listened to these two women argue, Our Lord worked in him and restored him immediately to health ... He asked for someone to give him the cross, and they did."

(106, 107)

This seventh crusade from 1248 to 1254 (the first was organized by the Catholic pope in 1095) ended in disaster. Egypt was the goal. Louis believed it would serve as a base for attacks on Jerusalem and provide food and other resources for his army. The expedition arrived at Damietta, a port city at the intersection of the Nile River and the Mediterranean Sea, a key to controlling the Nile and invading Egypt. As with the king taking the cross, Joinville's straightforward descriptions alternate with supernatural explanations: "Three times the Saracens sent carrier pigeons to the sultan to let him know that the king had arrived, but they received no message in return because the sultan was in the grip of his sickness. Because of this they thought the sultan was dead and they abandoned Damietta" (163). On the other hand: "We should acknowledge that God Almighty granted us great grace when he protected us from death and danger in the course of our landing, since we arrived on foot to attack out mounted enemies. And Our Lord granted us Great grace in delivering Damietta to us, which city we might not otherwise have been able to take except by starvation ... " (165).

Initial successes in battle were costly: "After the two battles already recounted, grave troubles began to afflict our camp. After nine days the bodies of our people who had been killed at Mansurah came to the surface of the water ... There was such a great number that the entire river was full of corpses from one bank to the other ... " (289). Louis's army was defeated and he was captured by the Saracens. Joinville was also captured and helped with ransom negotiations that freed Louis. Thereafter the chronicle recounts what befell Louis's crusaders at Acre, Caesaria, Sidon, and Jaffa in the Kingdom of Palestine.

Disappointment with the Egyptian venture convinced Joinville that participation in Louis's eighth crusade in 1270 would be a mistake. He declined, believing the crusade useless. He was persuaded that staying home to serve God was a better choice: "I told them that if I wanted to act in accordance with God's will I would stay here in order to help and protect my people" (734). As it turned out, the second crusade also ended badly, and Louis died near Tunis (Tunisia) at age 56. The abortive crusades served him posthumously with canonization as Saint Louis, the only king so honored. Joinville was a major witness at the hearings for his zealous devotion to Catholicism.

Joinville's work is a memoir as well as a chronicle. On one level, it recounts the seventh crusade, but does far more than that. Unlike a dry, matter of fact, year-by-year record of events in the usual style of chronicle, Joinville provides a portrait of the Christian king's character and deeds, describes his own long association with Louis as friend and counselor, and comments on the meaning of crusades. Bent on praising Louis as a model Christian king worthy of emulation by other monarchs, the writing is at once devotional, apologetic, and didactic. While attempts at explanation usually rely on the supernatural, descriptions supply much instructive detail.

The eyewitness concludes with reference to a secondary source:

> " ... I have set down here a great number of deeds of our saintly king that I saw and heard myself, as well as a good number of his deeds that I found in a book in the French language ... so that those who hear this book might believe firmly what it says about

those things I did truly see and hear myself. I cannot state whether the other things written down here are true since I neither saw nor heard them."

(768)

Where Joinville ends and the "book" begins is not clear.

Works by Joinville

Joinville and Villehardouin: Chronicles of the Crusades, trans., intro. and notes by Caroline Smith (New York: Penguin Books, 2008). There is also a helpful glossary of terms.

Joinville and Villhardouin: Chronicles of the Crusades, trans. by M.R.B. Shaw (New York: Penguin Books, 1963).

Useful references

Houseley, Norman, *Contesting the Crusades* (Oxford, England: Blackwell Publishing, 2006).

Jordan, W.C., *Louis IX and the Challenge of the Crusade: A Study in Rulership* (Princeton, New Jersey: Princeton University Press, 1979).

Runciman, Steven, *A History of the Crusades*, 3 vols. (Cambridge: Cambridge University Press, 1951–54). See volume 2.

Strayer, J.R., "The Crusades of Louis IX," in K. M. Sutton (ed.), *A History of the Crusades*, 6 vols. (2nd ed.; Madison: University of Wisconsin Press, 1969–89), 2: 487–518.

Section Notes

1 The translation cited in this essay is that of Susie I. Tucker in the edition of Dorothy Whitelock and David Douglas, which shows detailed correlations between the nine manuscripts.

2 This essay uses the translation from old French by Caroline Smith. The paragraphs of Joinville's text are numbered and used here for citation.

RENAISSANCE EUROPE

Themes 3 (issues of critical historiography), 4 (genres of history)

In the fifteenth and sixteenth centuries the recovery by humanist scholars in Italy of most surviving Greek and Latin literature from the classical era launched an intense period of editing, commentary, teaching, disputation, and publication that was mostly secular. The result was advances in the writing of critical history and the emergence of fresh genres of historiography.

The study of classical literature in original works stimulated the development of philology to understand the changing forms of language, whether Greek or Latin. There was also much attention to passages in classical texts that dealt with method, which were pulled out for discussion and interpretation. On the one hand, inquiry was into artistic methods, including communication, or rhetoric, and on the other, in scientific methods, which had its focus on the writings of Aristotle.

This revival of classical antiquity and recovery of Greek and Roman historians inspired historical inquiry. Histories of cities, especially Florence, were written. A history of Italy was produced. Proceedings of the 1564 Council of Trent, which set a firm direction for the Roman Church in the age of Reformation, were recorded and analyzed in a single work. Inevitably the widespread dialogue about method spilled over into historiography, which was newly respected as an instructive art. Philological method was turned on the analysis of specific texts, illustrated by Lorenzo Valla in the fifteenth century. A broader conception of method was explored by Jean Bodin in the sixteenth century, who wanted history to become more believable and coherent and thereby more useful.

11. DISCOURSE ON THE FORGERY OF THE ALLEGED DONATION OF CONSTANTINE[1] (LORENZO VALLA, 1406–1457)

Valla exposed as a forgery the Donation of Constantine (*De falso credita et ementita Constantini donatione*), a mid-eighth century document that claimed the Roman emperor Constantine gave Pope Sylvester II temporal authority over the western Roman Empire 500 years before. He did so allegedly out of gratitude that Sylvester cured him of leprosy. The Donation was used thereafter to justify papal claims to secular as well as religious authority.

Valla's knowledge and skills were respected but he was feared and even hated by many as a ruthless, scathing personality. The dangerous implications of his critical works, especially those treating scripture as a historical document, were resisted into the seventeenth century. He mocked the Latin of Jerome's Vulgate, the Church's official version of scripture, and compared his translation of the New Testament unfavorably with the original Greek text. He was an ordained priest who doubted the value of monastic life, which made his life and writings even more controversial.

He had trouble finding and keeping a position and wandered from city to city teaching rhetoric and Latin. He held a professorship in Pavia for a time but had to move on after attacking the Latin style of a well-known jurist. He eventually found a protector in the court of Alfonso V in Naples. Alfonso was at odds with the Pope over land in the Papal States and encouraged Valla to dismantle the Donation, who was already hostile to temporal claims of the papacy. After 1447 his fortunes changed and he was welcomed by a new pope, Nicholas V, who made him apostolic secretary.

Valla was part of a fifteenth-century surge of historical consciousness, a growing sense of the past accompanied by awareness of critical evidence and possibilities of causal explanation. At the forefront of textual criticism, he was a man to be reckoned with: "I have published many books ... in almost every branch of learning. Inasmuch as there are those who are shocked that in these I disagree with certain great writers already approved by long usage, and charge me with rashness and sacrilege, what must we suppose some of them will do now! For I am writing against not only the dead, but the living also ... not merely private individuals, but the authorities. And what authorities! Even the supreme pontiff ... " (21).

He was a Renaissance humanist, which had meanings specific to a revival of Greco-Roman literature. In fifteenth-century Italy men called "humanists" recovered, edited, and printed most works surviving from classical antiquity. They founded a system of education and inquiry, *studia humanitatis*, based on grammar, rhetoric, poetry, moral philosophy, and history in classical literature as opposed to the medieval faculties of theology, law, and medicine that dominated universities. The wider significance of their achievement was the diffusion of classical ideas and values into the mainstream of Western civilization from original sources. The Latin prose of Marcus Tullius Cicero (d. 43 B.C.) was the model most widely imitated. Medieval scholastic Latin was scorned and regarded as barbarous. Humanists had at their disposal authentic Latin texts that spanned centuries, so changes in the language were easily confirmed by alert scholars. Classical Greek texts also became available after the fall of Constantinople to the Ottoman Turks in 1453 when Greek scholars fled to Italy and set up private schools for instruction.

Valla was the most celebrated beneficiary of this scholarship. For internal and external criticism of Latin documents he had no equal in the fifteenth century. His treatise on Latin, *Elegancies of the Latin Language* (*De elegantiis latinae linguae*), was widely read and demonstrated his mastery of the language. His reputation was boosted by another celebrated work, *On Pleasure* (*De Voluptate*), which defended Epicurus against the Stoics, arguing that satisfaction of appetites is a good thing. He also corrected many Latin texts, a best-known effort being Livy's history of Rome. One of his staunchest admirers was the humanist Erasmus of Rotterdam, who respected and used his biblical criticism.

As a Latin philologist, Valla was aware of the language in its historical forms. A union of philology with history was a long-range consequence of unmasking a document long held to be authentic. Medieval scholars did not understand that the meaning of a document is linked to its historical setting. Valla established that relationship by demonstrating that Latin has a history, a step toward unshackling historical study from tradition and ecclesiastical authority. He directed minds to a past that differed from the present by proving through textual criticism successive changes in Latin diction and grammar. His attack, however, was comprehensive. It included not just grammar and vocabulary but also law, chronology, and geography. His task was lightened because the *Donation* was a crude invention rather than a true forgery. A skilled forger must have a sense of the past so as not to commit all the naïve errors Valla uncovered, such as anachronisms—that is, names, places, and linguistic expressions non-existent at the time a document was falsified.

Valla knows how easy the *Donation*'s author has made it for him, and complements incisive analysis with contemptuous abuse:

> "Does not this fable-fabricator seem to blunder, not through imprudence, but deliberately and of set purpose, and so as to offer handles for catching him. In the same passage he says both that the Lord's resurrection is represented by the tiara, and that it

is an imitation of Caesar's power; two things which differ most widely from each other ... I find no words ... merciless enough with which to stab this most abandoned scoundrel; so full of insanity are all the words he vomits forth."

(123)

The *Donation* would have been illegal for both emperor and pontiff:

"But before I come to the refutation of the instrument of the Donation, which is their one defense, not only false but even stupid, the right order demands that I go further back. And first, I shall show that Constantine and Sylvester were not such men that the former would choose to give, would have the legal right to give, or would have it in his power to give those lands to another, or that the latter would be willing to accept them or could legally have done so ... I shall show that in fact the latter did not receive nor the former give possession of what is said to have been granted, but that it always remained under the swat and empire of the Caesars ... "

(27)

The idea that an emperor would give away his entire patrimony was for Valla an absurd improbability:

"Is there any one of you who, had he been in Constantine's place, would have thought that he must set about giving to another out of pure generosity the city of Rome, his fatherland, the head of the world, the queen of states, the most powerful, the noblest and the most opulent of peoples, the victor of the nations ... and betaking himself thence to an humble little town, Byzantium ... giving the whole West; depriving himself of one of the two eyes of his empire? That anyone in possession of his senses would do this, I cannot be brought to believe."

(29)

An abundance of anachronisms give the author away: "How in the world ... could one speak of Constantinople as one of the patriarchal sees, when it was not yet a patriarchate, not a see, nor a Christian city, not named Constantinople, not founded, not planned!" (93).

On "churches" for Peter and Paul: "O you scoundrel! Were there in Rome churches, that is, temples, dedicated to Peter and Paul? Who had constructed them? Who would have dared to build them, when, as history tells us, the Christians had never had anything but secret and secluded meeting places" (97).

On confused terminology: " ... let us talk to this sycophant about barbarisms; for by the stupidity of his language his monstrous impudence is made clear, and his lie" (105). After correcting the *Donation* author on diadems, robes, and shoulder bands, he notes a phrase in which "imperial sceptres" are conferred: "What a turn of speech! ... What are these imperial sceptres? There is one sceptre, not several; if indeed the Emperor carried a sceptre at all. Will now the potiff carry a sceptre in his hand? Why not give him a sword also, and helmet and javelin?" (109). The *Donation* uses the term "satrap," which refers to a Persian province, as though it were Roman: "O thou scoundrel, thou villain! ... How do you want to have satraps come in here? Numskull, blockhead! Do the Caesars speak thus; are Roman decrees usually drafted thus? Whoever heard of satraps being mentioned in the councils of the Romans?" (85).

His knowledge of Latin and its historical conventions was the irresistible weapon of choice:

> "Nor will I here pass over the fact that 'given' is usually written on letters, but not on other documents, except among ignorant people. For letters are said either to be given one (illi) or to be given to one (ad illum); in the former case they [they are given to] one who carries them, a courier for instance, and puts them into the hand of the man to whom they are sent; in the latter case [they are given] to one in the sense that they are to be delivered to him by the bearer, that is [they are given to] the one to whom they are sent. But the 'privilege,' as they call it, of Constantine, as it was not to be delivered to anyone, so also it ought not to be said to be 'given.' And so it should be apparent that he who spoke thus lied, and did not know how to imitate what Constantine would probably have said and done."
>
> (139)

Valla's distaste for papal territorial ambitions surfaces frequently in his critique: "Thus it is a fact that the worse the supreme pontiff is, the more he exerts himself to defend this Donation" (161). But the *Donation* was a symptom of deeper corruption, which Valla indicates without equivocation, going well beyond demolishing a spurious document:

> "Can we justify the principle of papal power when we perceive it to be the cause of such great crimes and such great and varied

evils? ... in my time no one in the supreme pontificate has been either a faithful or a prudent steward ... And the Pope himself makes war on peaceable people, and sows discord among states and princes. The Pope thirsts for the goods of others and drinks up his own."

(179)

Thus aggressive historical criticism was mixed with an open assault on power politics in the Roman church.

Works by Valla

Discourse on the Forgery of the Alleged Donation of Constantine, trans. by Christopher B. Coleman (New Haven, Connecticut: Yale University Press, 1922). The Latin original and English translation are on facing pages.

Works about Valla

Bullard, Melissa Meriam, "The Renaissance Project of Knowing: Lorenzo Valla and Salvatore Camporeale's Contributions to the Querelle between Rhetoric and Philosophy," *Journal of the History of Ideas*, 66.4 (2005).
Copenhaver, Brian P., "Valla Our Contemporary: Philosophy and Philology," *Journal of the History of Ideas*, 66.4 (2005).

Useful references

Moss, A., *Renaissance Truth and the Latin Language Turn* (Oxford: Oxford University Press, 2003).
Nauti, Lodi, *In Defense of Commonsense: Lorenzo Valla's Humanist Critique of Scholastic Philosophy* (Cambridge, Massachusetts: Harvard University Press, 2009).

12. METHOD FOR THE EASY COMPREHENSION OF HISTORY[2] (JEAN BODIN, 1530–1596)

His father was an affluent master tailor, his mother of Spanish-Jewish descent. While still a youth he joined the Carmelite order and lived for a time in a monastery. It is not clear, but he may have fallen under suspicion for heresy after a two-year visit to Paris. Subsequently he was released from monastic vows. In 1550 he commenced law studies at the University of Toulouse. Along the way he learned Hebrew, Greek, German, and Italian. In 1559 he published a treatise on education which defended and recommended humanist studies in public schools to strengthen the state in both politics and religion. Social order and political stability, he argued, relied on one educational system for all. Having studied constitutions of the west European states, he was prominent in political and legal affairs as an authority on constitutional law. He died of the plague and was buried in Laon.

The background for his writing is the chaotic, disruptive age he lived in, punctuated by religious war in France between Huguenots (French Calvinists) and Catholics and uncertainties about the scope of royal power. Political arrangements of the era were unable to moderate religious passions and afford battered European or French populations with a semblance of peaceful stability. Bodin sought a pathway to order without which nothing else could be accomplished. He wanted an end to religious violence, the bloodiest event being a Catholic massacre of Huguenots on St. Bartholomew's Day in 1572. Although he supported Catholicism as the one true faith in France, he was critical of the Papacy and toward the end of his life published a work that urged toleration of different faiths, the famous *Sevenfold Conversation*. He was accused by some of being a secret Calvinist and even an atheist.

His works on political theory, notably *La République* (which refers to a "state"), sum up political and legal thought of Renaissance France. Social order depended on a clarification of sovereignty, the legitimate seat of state power. He defined sovereignty as "supreme power over citizens and subjects unrestrained by law," and denied the existence of a "mixed" state. The choices were monarchy with popular assemblies as nonbinding advisors, aristocracy with assemblies binding on the monarch, or democracy with final power invested in assemblies. His preference was the first, "since the royal power is natural, that is, instituted by God ... " (282). He believed a proper study of history, freed of medieval limitations and associations with rhetoric, would aid government "since history for the most part deals with the state and with changes taking place within it ... " (153).

His political theory was at odds with itself and its objectives probably undoable. The political solution to disunity and violence was unquestioned power invested in a sovereign, but he wished also to preserve the integrity of ancient constitutional laws. The solution to religious war was prudent toleration under a sovereign of more than one tradition of belief, including Judaism and Islam, but he also wanted a single religion to help unite the state. A reformed view of history did not help resolve these dilemmas.

Renaissance historians shared a growing consciousness that change had indeed taken place, that past and present are not the same.

However ordinary or obscure, everything was granted a past and therefore a history of development. The perceived nature of history underwent change as well. A new climate of opinion (see essay 38 in this volume) held that its purpose was to explain why things happened as they did, not merely to persuade or give pleasure in the ancient and still popular tradition of rhetoric.

Behind this desire for causal explanation was a sharper awareness of evidence. Medieval historiography accepted authority uncritically. Whatever was in print must be true. If there were no sources, it was acceptable to invent stories and fabricate documents. These practices fell into disrepute among Renaissance scholars, who critiqued documents and exposed fictions, religious or secular, passed off as fact (see essay 13 in this volume). In Italy the humanist movement, inspired by recovery and study of surviving Greco-Roman historical works, elevated history as an independent "art" (*ars historica*) rather than a branch of rhetoric, an ideal developed most fully in France, with Bodin the preeminent figure.

He aimed to show how various traditions of law could be reconciled by applying the right method of writing and reading history, which he defined as "the true narration of things" (15). The shift from rhetoric to method moved history forward as a discipline governed by rules of evidence: "I have made up my mind that it is practically an impossibility for the man who writes to give pleasure, to impart the truth of the matter also ... " (55). Thucydides was his admired example (see essay 2 in this volume). From truthful, impartial history lessons useful to the present would emerge. Virtue would be strengthened by exposure to good and ill effects of human motives and actions.

His book on the methodology of history, *Methodus ad facilem historiarum cognitionem*, appeared when he was thirty-six. It was a departure from fifteenth-century Italian understanding of history as style and presentation in narrative form. The idea of *methodus* was fashionable at the time. The word was used in titles of treatises on "arts" (*ars anatomica*, *ars grammatica*, and so on) that had nothing to do with method. Bodin's method is inconsistently critical of rhetoric and does not claim to be a science, but it differed from the humanist idea of method, which was confined mostly to analyzing methods in classical literature with no specific application to philosophy or science. Shortly after his death from plague in Laon, fruitful method would become a momentous issue in science and philosophy with Galileo and Descartes.

Bodin aimed to expand and control fact within a framework of general principles. In addition to his substituting his version of a disciplined method for pleasing rhetoric, readers of history are advised how best to approach it as a body of internal procedures and standards. With respect to sources, for example, a distinction between primary and secondary documents emerges, which rhetoricians had never bothered with. He also attempted to formulate a framework of universal history with chronological divisions, recognizing that different chunks of historical time have their own character and directions of change.

The work consists of a dedication, a preamble, and ten chapters—what history is, the order for reading works, arrangement of material, choosing historians, assessing histories, types of government, a critique of "four monarchies" theory (Assyrian, Persian, Greek, Roman) and a golden age, a universal chronology, a test for origins of people, and his order for collecting histories, altogether 380 pages. Chapter 10 is his 15-page "bibliography" of 282 texts. Chapter headings summarize his "method," although "easy comprehension" is hard to come by in the absence of straightforward exposition unencumbered by a blizzard of names. The sum of his learning and industry is immense but exhausting to follow, especially in the chapter on how to choose historians (e.g., 54–55). The work is marred by an earnest accumulation of tedious detail that was probably a drag on later influence. Bodin is more successful outlining his purposes than lucidly working them out. Thus he wants to start with the general, universal history, and then flesh it out with details, but relations of the two and transitions between them are rarely clear or easy to digest.

Three kinds of history are distinguished—human affairs, physical nature, and the divine: "So of the three types of history, let us for the moment abandon the divine to the theologians, the natural to the philosophers, while we concentrate long and intently upon human actions and the rules governing them" (15–17). In human affairs, history can be particular, confining itself to words and deeds of one man or one people, or universal, dealing with numerous men or states. To bring order out of profusion, "let us place before ourselves a general chart for all periods, not too detailed and therefore easy to study, in which are contained the origins of the world, the floods, the earliest beginnings of the states and of the religions which have been more famous, and their ends, if indeed they have come to an end" (21).

Sorting good history from the bad requires empirical knowledge of geography and climate. The world and human nature are not everywhere the same:

" ... it seems necessary to speak about the correct evaluation of histories ... the disagreement among historians is such that some not only disagree with others but even contradict themselves, either from zeal or anger or error, we must make some generalizations as to the nature of all peoples or at least of the better known, so that we can test the truth of histories by just standards and make correct decisions about individual instances."
(85)

One such "generalization" is that invasions and conquests have moved from north to south. The reason is that climate has shaped cultures and human behavior:

"Let us therefore adopt this theory, that all who inhabit the area from the forty-fifth parallel to the seventy-fifth toward the north grow increasingly warm within, while the southerners, since they have more warmth from the sun, have less from themselves. In winter the heat is collected within, but in summer it flows out. Whereby it happens in winter we are more animated and robust, in summer more languid ... This, then, is the reason why Scythians have always made violent attacks southward; ... the greatest empires have spread southward, rarely from the south toward the north."
(92–93)

Climate shapes human character and government, which in turn shape history. People living in the north should be ruled by force, those in the south by religion.

Bodin's contribution to rescuing historical truth from rhetoric and its preoccupation with style and form was not without ambiguity. He escaped medieval ways without fully entering the modern world. He was a transitional influence on the changing face of historiography. He wants method to assure truthfulness and detachment, but it does not save him from intellectual dead ends of the age, notably the application of numerology, expressions of the numbers 7 and 9, to historical explanation and understanding (225). The idea of microcosm–macrocosm, involving the theory of four humors corresponding to four elements of earth, air, fire, and water, both with astrological correspondences to heavenly bodies, is retained as a descriptive and explanatory principle (121). He also believed, as did most everyone, in demons, witches, sorcerers, and Satan. Late in life he wrote a guide for the interrogation of witches and recommended burning at the stake.

Despite faults and limitations, he made a conscious effort amidst a bewildering profusion of historical works to formulate rules for order, system, evidence, and credibility while defending history as a practical guide for his troubled world.

Works by Bodin

Method for the Easy Comprehension of History, trans. by Beatrice Reynolds (New York: Columbia University Press, 1966). See her introduction.
The Six Books of the Commonwealth, Les Six livres de la République, 1576, trans. by M.J. Tooley (Oxford: Blackwell, 1955).

Works about Bodin

Brown, John L, *The Methodus ad facilem historiarum cognitionem of Jean Bodin* (Washington: Catholic University Press, 1939).
Franklin, Julian H., *Jean Bodin and the Sixteenth Century Revolution in the Methodology of Law and History* (New York: Columbia University Press, 1963).
Grafton, Anthony, *What Was History? The Art of History in Early Modern Europe* (Cambridge: Cambridge University Press, 2009).
Kelley, Donald R., *Faces of History: Historical Inquiry from Herodotus to Herder* (New Haven, Connecticut: Yale University Press, 1998), pp. 197–200.

Useful references

Burke, Peter, *The Renaissance Sense of the Past* (New York: St. Martin's Press, 1969).
Gilbert, Neil W., *Renaissance Concepts of Method* (New York: Columbia University Press, 1960), pp. 79–80.
Huppert, George, *The Idea of Perfect History: Historical Erudition and Historical Philosophy in Renaissance France* (Urbana: University of Illinois Press, 1970).

Section Notes

1 The translation by Christopher Coleman is used for this essay.
2 The translation of Beatrice Reynolds is used in this essay.

REFORMATION EUROPE

Themes 3 (issues of critical historiography), 4 (genres of history), 6 (problematic historiography)

Religious controversy in the sixteenth century accelerated the momentum of historical inquiry in the West. Protestant and Catholic scholars each put themselves to work proving the truth of their version of Christianity by establishing from history alleged falsehoods of the other side.

In the second half of the sixteenth century, Protestant scholars set out to discredit the Papacy in the massive *Magdeburg Centuries*, which dealt with the history of Christianity over thirteen hundred years to the end of the thirteenth century. A Catholic scholar replied toward the end of the century with the *Ecclesiastical Annals* to discredit Protestant doctrines and defend papal authority and Church tradition. Neither side convinced the other, but the tasks of refutation and counter refutation, done less by theological argument than by appeals to original historical documents, strengthened critical historiography, and there were genuine efforts to write history based on documents apart from religious bias.

This spirit of criticism and confidence that history could yield truth continued into the seventeenth century with Pierre Bayle and the Maurist monk Mabillon. The irony is that ferociously intolerant and violent Reformation controversies promoted objective criticism in history by stressing primary sources. Bayle's writings were not histories in a strict sense, but by making extensive use of historical documents he developed a powerful, influential case for the detection of error, the other side of getting at a truth. Mabillon did not intend a revolution in historiography, but wished merely to put monastic documents in order and confirm their authenticity. Yet he established fundamentals of critical method in history that could be separated from religious issues and applied to other aspects of the past.

13. HISTORICAL AND CRITICAL DICTIONARY[1] (PIERRE BAYLE, 1647–1706)

Bayle's *Dictionary* was composed in a climate of opinion influenced by Sextus Empiricus, whose writings were based on teachings of Pyrrho, the first notable Greek skeptic. For a century since the skeptical *Essays* of Michel de Montaigne (d. 1592), Pyrrhonism rolled across Europe in the hands of Catholic and Protestant apologists who used its ten principles of doubt to demolish other's claims to religious primacy and authority. Bayle was a leading Pyrrhonist who took seriously the original meaning of *skeptikos*, the word for "inquiry," which he pursued doggedly in the *Dictionary*. Pyrrhonism among theologians and philosophers was abstract. Bayle's skeptical historical method was concrete and focused on particulars. Before his work appeared, historical writing was dominated by a tradition of rhetoric, whose method was to transmit uncritically what others had said in fine language rather than convince by an appeal to believable evidence. Bayle understood the difference and chose the latter course while training his skepticism on errors in documents.

The fire in Bayle's mind was ignited by the fate of French Calvinists, known as Huguenots. In 1598 the French king Henry IV issued the Edict of Nantes, which extended limited toleration and protections, including self-defense, to Frenchmen converted to the Calvinist version of Protestantism. Although France was officially a Catholic state, toleration was intended to strengthen the monarchy by promoting harmony between Catholic and Protestant. In the seventeenth century the tables were turned. Increasingly the Huguenots were regarded by the crown as a seditious influence, a state within the state. Gradually their privileges were undermined until the Edict of Nantes was fully revoked in 1685 and toleration ceased.

The upshot for Huguenots was exclusion and persecution. Bayle's brothers and father died as a result of maltreatment He ended up in Holland, one place in Europe where thought was not controlled or repressed. There he launched a ferocious assault on Catholic absolutism in France, but the subtext was skepticism about all systems of thought that claimed certain truths. Everywhere he saw dubious science, contradictory philosophies, dogmatic theologies, and bad history. He says in the article Pyrrho: " … the inconstancy of human opinions and passions is so great it might be said that man is a small republic that often changes its magistrates" (209).

Bayle's *Dictionnaire historique et critique*, appeared in 1697 and went through several editions. The last one in 16 volumes was published in

1820–24. While this massive work no longer has a wide audience other than scholars and students, every historian, philosopher, and literary person of note in the eighteenth century consulted it. For *philosophes* of the Enlightenment like Voltaire and Diderot, Bayle was the *philosophe* of Rotterdam who provided an arsenal of arguments and knowledge useful in battles against oppressions and rigidities of the Old Regime in Europe, especially in France. Other admirers were David Hume, Scottish skeptic and historian, and the German philosopher-mathematician Leibniz. When Thomas Jefferson donated his library to inaugurate the Library of Congress, Bayle's dictionary was among the first 100 key books.

The word *"Dictionary"* barely suggests what Bayle was doing, even though the organization of 2000 articles is biographical and alphabetic, from "Aaron" to "Zuylichem." Famous persons are left out and obscure ones are put in. Many of the entries are brief and the real substance is found in extended footnotes, often in footnotes to the footnotes. The key words are "historical" and "critical." In a letter to a cousin in 1692 he explained that his purpose was to compile an inventory of errors committed by theologians, philosophers, and historians. Popular belief was a major target as well. Not content with errors, he added delusions, crimes, superstitions, and deceptions, a full indictment of humanity at its worst. His war on superstition included a treatise on comets in which he assailed the common belief that such phenomena were supernatural portents sent by God.

Bayle was obsessed with error, whether deliberate or inadvertent, and undertook to doubt and dissect virtually every idea, claim, and doctrine afloat in his time. Nothing or no one was spared, including himself. Whether the subject was metaphysical, theological, or scientific, his vast learning, logical intelligence, appeal to history, and forceful style left no apparently secure monuments to human belief unscathed. He identified unerringly the weaknesses in ideas of the seventeenth century's leading minds. He was a systematic enemy of all fanciful thinking, which he believed was indissolubly and unhappily associated with religious belief.

He concluded that truths could not be established with certainty by reason, the "natural light," which rebuffed arguments to the contrary by the French mathematician and philosopher Renée Descartes. It follows, he argued, that "religious truth and belief are confined to revelation." With reason unable to establish unshakable truth, the only refuge is faith, the "supernatural light." There is, however, no consensus in theology, reason, or experience about content or imperatives of revelation or precise objects of faith: "God, deity, eternity, omnipotence, infinity, these are only words thrown into the air, and nothing more to us. These are not things subject to human understanding ... If all that we say and profess about God were judged rigorously, it would be nothing but vanity and ignorance" (285). A consequence of reasoning that denied revelation common standards of belief and conduct was a defense of broad religious toleration that even included atheists, a view clearly directed at persecutions of the French monarchy.

While Bayle left reason shipwrecked as a vehicle for certainty, he decided it has uses for managing historical knowledge with degrees of probability. While that insight was taking root in his mind, about which he was ambivalent, he collected examples of historical error from documents that fell under his watchful eye. While skepticism was deep and far reaching, despite some appearances to the contrary, it had limits. Here and there he challenged the credentials of any kind of evidence, but finally drew a line by using historical evidence to defuse and demolish errors of pretentious adversaries.

His historical method has four interwoven threads. The first is exposure at a Jesuit school in Toulouse, during a brief conversion to Catholicism, to scholastic logic and dialectic. The lesson he absorbed was one of thoroughness and clarity when advancing and defending arguments, which accounts in part for the prodigious length of footnotes in his *Dictionary*. Uses of scholastic method were transferred to historical method.

The second is the methodology of Descartes. While rejecting his claim to know certain truth, he adopted the strategy of "systematic doubt" and two of his rules of reasoning—that only "clear and distinct ideas" amount to knowledge, and that every step of a demonstration must be verified. For Bayle, clear and distinct ideas were to be found in history, not in theology, philosophy, or science. Facts must be verified against their sources, and the best sources are the earliest ones. An irony is that Descartes was contemptuous of history as an inquiry remote from the rigor and certainties of mathematical reasoning, yet Bayle partially transferred his geometrical method to the credibility of historical records. If ideas must be clear and distinct, they must also square with experience (145).

The third thread is the Protestant doctrine of individual examination, which appealed to an "inner light" of understanding independent of scripture, dogma, and tradition. Bayle's inner light was the bedrock of his intellectual integrity and impartiality as he fired off criticism at all and sundry. In the face of so much bad judgment, he trusted his own. In doing so, he could say he was a servant of God's will in defense of truth.

The fourth thread is systematic exposure of error and falsehood in historical documents. He distinguished between credulous and critical historians. The former accept what they find in previous writings and traditions and simply pass errors up the line. The latter insist on being informed by a source after subjecting it to critical examination. Majority opinion on an issue is no test and turns out to be wrong. Popular errors are the most numerous. Minority opinion can be trusted because skepticism is leveled at sources. He conceded that all error is not harmful, only that "taught by persons whose relations to the populace furnish them with the opportunity of gaining authority and forming a party ... An error ought to be carefully followed, watched, and restrained when a man of venerable character, a pastor, a professor of theology, spreads it ... " (396).

He dismantled the strongest arguments of prominent adversaries on their own principles. Circular reasoning was laid bare. Biblical and church traditions could not be defended by appealing to history and history then confirmed by appealing back to those traditions. His principle for assessing the credibility of witnesses was their proportional distance from an event—the closer the better. Documents must be examined to detect error due to copying and recopying. Faults of memory in an author must be identified. Bias because of passion and corruption must be rooted out. A fact that survived these criteria could be trusted as probable enough to refute error and assume the status of an indirect truth. He did not discover truth in the record, but the record could be forced to yield limited fruits by uncovering distortions, misjudgments, and outright lies.

Bayle's achievement was to develop a technique of falsification by applying Descartes's systematic doubt to documents, whose facts could be justified only as clear and distinct ideas. A systematic questioning of alleged facts to uncover error might border on certitude. While positive truths may be elusive in history, there is no doubt that error can be identified. This standard of factuality was severe and uncompromising. No one could be let off the hook, so impartiality was essential. He was as tough on Protestantism in general, and Calvinism in particular, his own "faith," as he was on Catholicism. He uncovered and published a wealth of mistakes in the popular *History of Calvinism* by Pére Maimbourg. This ideal of historical accuracy did for history what Galileo had done previously for natural science.

Bayle transcended national and sectarian ties to write for an informed public in his journal, *Nouvelle de la République des lettres* (*News of the Republic of Letters*). Armed with a method and principles, he took the past in its entirety as his field of inquiry and did something genuinely new. While he described history pessimistically as a record of "crimes and misfortunes," a sequence of moral and physical evils, it is nevertheless accessible to an inquiring mind: "Scholars who never leave their study acquire the most knowledge about these two matters because in reading history they make all the centuries and all the countries of the world pass in review before their eyes" (147).

In Bayle's writings, all those laboriously corrected facts bearing on human malfeasance, ignorance, credulity, and adversity remained mostly isolated from one another. Little effort was made to organize them into patterns of explanation and meaning, into truths of a higher order than a pile of credible facts. Instead of pearls strung together in a coherent necklace, Bayle poured them separately and without collective form into a roomy box, his diffuse but critical dictionary. With this reservation acknowledged, anyone who ploughs through a fair sample of his work must be convinced, despite his bewildering, almost universal skepticism, that he did more than enough for the cause of history in one amazingly productive lifetime.

Works by Bayle

Dictionary, Historical and Critical, 5 vols. (London, 1734–38). A complete English translation.
Dictionnaire historique et critique, ed. A.J.Q. Beuchot, 16 vols. (Paris, 1820–24). The last complete edition.
Historical and Critical Dictionary: Selections, translation from the French with introduction and notes by Richard Popkin, with the assistance of Craig Brush (New York: Bobbs Merrill Company, 1965).
Oeuvres diverses, 4 vols. (The Hague, 1727).
Selections from Bayle's Dictionary, trans. from the French and eds. E.A. Beller and M. du P. Lee, Jr. (Princeton: Princeton University Press, 1952).

Works about Bayle

Brush, Craig B., *Montaigne and Bayle: Variations on the Theme of Skepticism* (The Hague: Martinus Nijhoff, 1966).
Labrousee, Elizabeth, "La Méthod critique chez Pierre Bayle et l'Histoire," *Revue Internationale de philosophie,* XLII (1957); 1–17. An important work that merits translation.
Robinson, Howard, *Bayle the Skeptic* (New York: Columbia University Press, 1932).
Sandburg, Karl, *At the Crossroads of Faith and Reason* (Tucson, Arizona: University of Arizona Press, 1966).

Stunkel, Kenneth R, "Montaigne, Bayle, and Hume: Historical Dynamics of Skepticism," *The European Legacy*, 3:4 (1998): 43–64.

Whelan, Ruth, *The Anatomy of Superstition: A Study of the Historical Theory and Practice of Pierre Bayle* (Oxford: The Voltaire Foundation at the Taylor Institution, 1989).

Useful references

Hazard, Paul, *The European Mind, 1680–1715*, trans. by J. Lewis May (London: Hollis and Carter, 1953). See Chapter V.

14. ON DIPLOMATICS[2] (JEAN MABILLON, 1632–1707)

For centuries historians appealed to many kinds of documents without knowing for sure any of them were authentic. Knowledge of how to test authenticity and truthfulness (known as external and internal criticism) was the work of seventeenth-century scholar-monks working in the serene confines of French abbeys. Among them, Mabillon stood out as a revolutionary figure. The greatest scholar of his day, he put objective historical analysis decisively on the map.

A precocious student from childhood, he nursed early monastic ambitions. After study at the University of Rheims, he was ordained in the Benedictine Congregation of St. Maur, which included several abbeys that accepted historical inquiry as a legitimate practice alongside prayer and contemplation. His talent for documentary analysis and historical exposition unfolded at two prominent abbeys near and in Paris—St. Denise and St. Germain-des-Prés. The latter, where he spent the remainder of his life, and where he was buried, was known throughout Europe for its learned men and their scholarly work. Collaboration with that circle gave him access to sources and scholars in Italy and southern Germany as well as in France.

Participation in major projects of the abbey developed his analytical powers. These undertakings included an edition of works by St. Bernard (1090–1153), recognized by peers as a brilliant achievement, and a multi-volume lives of Benedictine saints. The work's critical methods are explained in prefaces and appendices. A few years before his death, he produced a third set of scrupulous volumes, *Annals of the Benedictine Order*. The volumes on saints aroused disapproval because he dethroned more than a few due to insufficient or defective evidence. He responded firmly and modestly to complaints and was vindicated. His landmark work on diplomatics, for which previous undertakings were a training ground, arose from disputes over the authenticity of ancient charters legitimizing the Abbey of St. Denise, doubts he sought to resolve by systematic analysis of documents relating to the abbey's origin and its succession of abbots (171 f).

As a Maurist of high repute Mabillon had access to archives of the order's several abbeys and other sources in Europe. At the time Europe was awash in documents, but there were no agreed upon methods for establishing with confidence either authenticity or truthfulness. This was not a trivial matter: "Those who attempt to diminish the authority and trustworthiness of ancient documents and records do harm to the study of literature and ... attack and undermine constitutional law, not to mention legal privilege" (164). The latter admonition included legal rights and status of monastic institutions.

Historical study was heavily monastic and ecclesiastical in the sixteenth and seventeenth centuries. Critical methods were formulated in a contentious religious environment. During the sixteenth century Reformation and Counter Reformation, history was a weapon used by Protestants and Catholics to demolish one another's claims to priority and authority of belief and practice. Both parties ransacked archives in Europe to find incriminating evidence against the rival faith. In neither case were historical materials submitted to objective analysis, and many documents were tampered with or fabricated outright. Reigning purposes were aggressively polemical and partisan. An unintended consequence was the public accumulation of an unprecedented array of materials that could be assessed impartially by others.

An "age of erudition" followed from about 1600 to 1750. Scholars continued to discover and publish long neglected documents from a variety of sources, principally monastic, ecclesiastical, and royal. Differences between these *érudits,* a designation that applies to Mabillon, and their predecessors were development of critical standards for authenticating documents and a desire to get facts right. The three great names were French—Pierre Bayle (see essay 18 in this volume), Bernard de Montfoucon, and Jean Mabillon.

Montfoucon was an authority on the paleography (handwriting, penmanship) of Greek documents. Mabillon founded Latin paleography and laid a foundation for critical historiography by showing how documents can be authenticated and dated. No one before Mabillon had been able to do that credibly with documents from different time periods. He perfected and codified principles of criticism begun by Lorenzo Valla (see essay 13 in this volume) capable of revealing the honesty of documents. This science he named *diplomatics*, from the word "diploma," referring to a folded piece of paper, but now meaning letters, decrees, charters, and other kinds of documents.

De re diplomatica libri VI (On *The Study of Documents in Six Books*) formulated principles of external criticism that enabled scholars to validate documents with confidence. Latin paleography, the interpretation of handwriting and written symbols in ancient documents, was a major instrument, based on the fact that alphabetic letters take on different forms from one century to the next and must be interpreted to be read correctly. Scribes made the task of reading more difficult with editorial changes, which require further interpretation. Mabillon also pioneered internal criticism, or systematic analysis and judgment of truthfulness in content. Mabillon's style reflects a scientific spirit. Unlike Lorenzo Valla, he was sober, measured, fair minded, and objective rather than distractingly polemical and political.

While Bayle excelled at detecting individual factual errors with high probability, Mabillon moved on to discover positive truths about the status of entire documents with high probability. Philosophers and theologians still argued that true knowledge has the property of absolute certainty. By that standard, history was viewed as falling short of logic and mathematics. Mabillon's methods and principles shifted the balance by dignifying history as a reliable source of knowledge, however tentative, rather than a mere repository of moral lessons and rhetorical pleasures. He viewed history as an empirical science that does not and cannot aspire to "metaphysical" certainty.

He believed also that trustworthy history study requires intuition and experience in addition to tested empirical methods, and that a strong alliance of the three results in "moral certainty": " ... Beyond a doubt a moral certitude cannot be acquired without long and constant observation of all the coincidences and circumstances which can lead to attaining the truth. In exactly this way the authenticity of spuriousness of ancient documents can be demonstrated" (170). In other words, historical demonstrations are of a different order than logical or mathematical ones, but without loss of soundness or persuasiveness.

The six books of *De re diplomatica* expound principles of textual analysis and apply them to many ancient examples. Books I and II explain tests by which charters can be judged true or false. In Book I, types of charters are defined and discussed with the conclusion that a document's age does not count against it since royal charters were issued in the fifth century. Five kinds of materials used for documents are reviewed, with attention to differences in ink and types of writing. In Book II he addresses the language of documents, showing, like Valla before him, that antiquity and change over the centuries are imprinted in grammar and vocabulary. Five parts of medieval charters are dissected, especially seals, signatures, and different chronologies.

The remaining books provide examples of how diplomatic proof works. Book III looks at an alleged privilege granted to the monastery of Maximin by the Merovingian king Dagobert (seventh century) and finds the document wanting for ten reasons, including a host of anachronisms in the language: "Certainly what I have just mentioned clearly shows that this document of Dagobert either is spurious, or that it is not so undoubtedly genuine that it can or should be presented as a genuine and legitimate example of the other documents" (186). Book V is a compendium of handwriting samples to illustrate paleography, and Book VI offers some 200 documents copied from originals with notes explaining why they may be taken as authentic.

Suspicious documents abound, many forged or altered in antiquity and the middle ages. No category is exempt: "Neither historical works, nor writings of the Fathers, nor decretal letters, nor the records of Councils, nor the lives of the Saints—out of reverence I will not mention Scripture ... " (168–69). Diplomatic analysis to find truth about documents is not possible without a fund of experience. The method of discovery is not abstract: " ... cleverness of mind and reason alone cannot be substituted for it." This kind of judgment requires time poring over a variety of documents: " ... those who wish to learn the art of criticizing ancient documents must consider themselves experts only after careful and thorough preparation. For it is difficult for someone without experience in this field to give an authoritative judgment about one single document ... " (170).

If a forgery is detected by comparing it with an authentic document, the question arises as to how one knows for sure the "archetype" is truly authentic and not the work of a forger. Mabillon is fully aware of this argument and how far such skepticism can go to demolish confidence in any document (168). His response is that all features of an authentic document are judged by an expert to be in order. The claim that a forger could get all of them right in a document is hypothetical and improbable. The claim that all documents in every archive could be forgeries is equally improbable and skepticism out of control: "No one ever attempted to do this unless he was a complete novice who had no experience at all with antiquities" (170).

Experience is the ultimate guide:

> "If you should ask why I regard some documents as genuine and reject others, I reply that I consider the former to be genuine because the type of script, the style, and everything else convinces me that they are genuine, and the fact that there is nothing in them contrary to historical fact; on the other hand, I judge the forgeries to be such because one of these conditions is not fulfilled. If you should further ask why I consider one type of script and one style as genuine as against another, I shall reply that I have learned this from experience and from comparing many such documents of different dates and from different places ... All who are experienced in this matter agree that this art cannot be learned except through constant comparison of manuscripts which give a certain indication of their dates with others that do not."
>
> (167)

Proof lies in his detailed analysis of examples, as with a document attributed to Charlemagne (187 f). Burden is on the skeptic to prove an accepted archetype is not genuine by refuting all of its characteristics.

Mabillon was not fooled even by authenticity: "It often happens that the authors of documents are completely wrong when they mention past events; on the other hand, forgers tend to be more accurate. Not only can errors creep into documents, even originals, when any event in the distant past is mentioned, but also copyists who are careless can deceive or be deceived in the case of fairly recent events" (192). Historical criticism must be vigilant.

Works by Mabillon

Gay, Peter and Victor J. Wexler (eds.), *Historians at Work* (New York: Harper and Row, 1972), Chapter 8. A translation of selections from Books 1 and 2 of *De re diolomatica libri VI*.

Treatise on Monastic Studies, 1691, trans. with intro. by John Paul McDonald (Lanham, Maryland: University of America Press, 2004). Mabillon responds to Trappist criticisms that scholarship displaces piety and contemplation and defends historical inquiry.

NOTE: Most commentary on Mabillon is in French. One example can be mentioned here: Ph. Denis, "Dom Mabillon et sa méthode historique," *Revue Mabillon*, VI (1910–11).

Works about Mabillon

Catholic Encyclopedia online, article on Mabillon by Leslie A. St. L. Tore (http://oce.catholic.com/index.php?title=Jean_Mabillon).

Knowles, David, "Jean Mabillon," *Journal of Ecclesiastical History*, X;1 (1959), pp. 459–471.

Lord Acton, *Historical Essays and Studies* (London: Macmillan, 1908).

Thomson, James W., *A History of Historical Writing*, 2 vols. (New York: Macmillan, 1942): 1; 15–23. Good for background and bibliography.

Useful references

Kelley, Donald R., *Faces of History: Historical Inquiry from Herodotus to Herder* (New Haven, Connecticut: Yale University Press, 1998), Chapter 8.

Section Notes

1 The text used is the translation of selections assembled by Richard Popkin.
2 This essay uses selections from Books I, II, III, VI and the Supplement of 1704 translated by Richard Wertis, in Gay and Wexler, *Historians at Work*, II, Chapter 8. Despite historic importance of the work, and its undiminished authority for historians, there is no complete English translation from the original Latin, and it has not been reprinted since the eighteenth century.

EIGHTEENTH-CENTURY EUROPE

Themes 3 (issues of critical historiography), 5 (breadth of inquiry), 6 (problematic historiography)

Historical writing in the Enlightenment had rationalistic and often polemical objectives in major centers like Britain, France, and some of the German states. With those biases noted, historians sought to expand the range of inquiry and displayed a critical attitude toward available evidence. This was possible because thought and inquiry were conducted with less interference from state and church authorities than in the past, a sign that society was becoming more secularized. More fundamental was the emergence of a common language of proof accepted and used across national boundaries, a consequence of universally acknowledged advances in science since the seventeenth century.

History was widely read and appreciated more than ever before. Gibbon and Voltaire considered its truths provisional and probable. History for them was a guide to truth, not a source of certainties, which justified calling them "philosophical" historians, but Gibbon also believed history is a "science of causes and effects." The study of history beyond the confines of Europe widened the scope of human experience, which suited perfectly a writer like Voltaire with his belief that experience is the touchstone of knowledge.

Eighteenth-century confidence from about mid-century that linear progress was consistent reality in human history alternated with a cyclical version of the past in which periods of authority, faith, and superstition alternated with periods of freedom, rationality, and science. A historical lineup illustrating these alternating opposites were Greece and Rome (reason), the Middle Ages (faith), the Renaissance (reason), the Reformation (faith), and Voltaire's age of Louis XIV (reason). Both Gibbon and Voltaire were conscientious about sources, the former far more than the latter. Voltaire was a not memorable researcher, but he held aloft an ideal of evidence and covered as much ground as he could on behalf of enlightened achievement, an objective he proclaims for the work on Louis XIV and his age.

Gibbon swept up sources with such conscientiousness that his work still rings with authority.

Herder is problematic but deserves a hearing among historians. He comes over as a rambling philosopher and man of letters, but he nevertheless had a serious impact on historical consciousness and thinking by rejecting the Enlightenment's abstract argument that men are everywhere the same and best guided by reason. Thus he was the particularistic counterpoint to the Enlightenment's love of generality and sounded a shot over the bow of the Old Regime's Neo-Classical ideals that signaled the Romantic movement and cultural nationalism in the next century.

15. THE AGE OF LOUIS XIV[1] (VOLTAIRE, OR FRANÇOISE-MARIE AROUET, 1694–1778)

Voltaire was a rationalist whose long life confronted intolerance, cruelty, and superstition with learning, wit, and style in a stream of articles, stories, books, and correspondence. His effectiveness in France is attested by occasions of arrest, imprisonment, and exile. Certain of his works were burned by the royal hangman as a threat to public morals. At age 65 he purchased an estate called Ferney on the French–Swiss border so he could flee to Geneva if the French police came after him. He became something of a European hero and his greatness just before death was acknowledged in a Paris celebration.

He was renowned as a prolific historian and less successfully as epic poet and tragic dramatist. He published 23 historical works between 1727 and 1777. As historiographer, he produced another 14 or so to explain what history is, how it should be done, and how it might be used. His work embodied a novel, even revolutionary belief—that history can be as absorbing and important as natural science.

Three notable works are an account of Charles XII of Sweden (1731), focused on warmongering deeds of a charismatic ruler that finally buckled against Peter the Great of Russia. A universal history, *Essay on Customs* (1756), reached beyond Greco-Roman civilization and Europe to include India, China, and other non-European areas. The work he valued most, *The Age of Louis XIV* (*Siècle de Louis XIV*, 1751), attempted a comprehensive picture of an era that includes politics, economics, religion, science, and the arts while extolling the role of Louis as an indispensable catalyst of high achievement: "It is not merely the life of Louis XIV, that we propose to write; we have a wider aim in view. We shall endeavor to depict for posterity, not the actions of a single man, but the spirit of men in the most enlightened age the world has ever seen" (1). His argument is that Louis's reign from 1643 to 1715 was momentous for all of Europe as well as France.

Edward Gibbon's view that Voltaire skimmed gracefully over the past is not quite just. While he fell short of Gibbon's standard for locating and citing sources, he did something new. By mid-century, he articulated a fresh view of what history can be and might accomplish. It need not be a dead recitation of facts in the form of a chronicle or a dreary tale of politics and war: "There are plenty of books filled with the most minute particulars of military operations and details of human passions and misery. The aim of this history is to depict the chief characteristics of such revolutions, clear away the innumerable small events that obscure the great ones, and finally ... to depict the spirit that informed them" (103). Standards of selection and evaluation changed. Piles of fact and documents strung together as a chronicle are not useful history. Rather its life blood is ideas that changed states and countries.

On that premise, Louis's century outstripped Greeks and Romans: " ... Europe taken as whole is vastly superior to the whole of the Roman Empire." The nations of Europe "cultivate arts unknown to the Greeks and Romans; and of those nations, there is none that has shone more brilliantly in every sphere for nearly a century, than the nation moulded (*sic*) to a great extent by Louis XIV" (338). Voltaire distinguished four great ages in human history, Classical-Hellenistic Greece, the Rome of Augustus, and the Renaissance of the Medici, capped by the reign of Louis XIV. These ages are prominent for reason, science, philosophy, and enlightened government, compared to ages sandwiched in between dominated by superstition, dogma, fanaticism, and selfish authority. Enlightenment, the rule of reason, therefore alternates in history with unreason. This cyclical "philosophy of history" abandons a progressive linear view of history, and accepts that periods of light will not last and succumb to periods of darkness.

Begun 20 years before its publication, his original plan for the history was a pyramid, with political and military affairs at the bottom, social, economic, and religious issues in the middle, science, literature, philosophy, and art at the top. Unlike chronicles, organization of the volume was topical and analytical rather than chronological, a distinct innovation. Over time, however, the pyramid vanished and it became a different kind of book, with science, literature, and the arts no longer the focus. Although civilization is his announced target, politics and war are acknowledged as central to history.

The analytical structure was retained. An opening chapter summarizes the state of Europe before Louis. Thirty-three out of 39 chapters relate political, diplomatic, economic, administrative, military affairs with Louis as the centerpiece: "He was young, rich, well-served, blindly obeyed, and eager to distinguish himself by foreign conquests" (77). For 30 years territorial conquests glorified France and the throne, which Voltaire appears to revel in patriotically, until a coalition rose against him in the War of the Spanish Succession. Voltaire then unfolds a sad story of French decline, demonstrating a mastery of tangled dynastic politics, with many vividly sketched players—the king's generals and administrators, especially the brilliant finance minister Colbert, and opponents like the Duke of Marlborough, Prince Eugene of Austria, and John de Witt of Holland (Chapters XVIII and IX).

Out of 460 pages, only four chapters are given to science, philosophy, and the arts. Thereafter four chapters take up religious controversies swirling around Jansenism's theology of predestination, Quietism, a "cult of the interior soul," and French Calvinism (the Huguenots), beleaguered by monarchy and the Catholic (Gallican) Church after Louis rescinded the 1685 Edict of Nantes that had extended toleration to the Protestant minority. Louis was bent on strengthening central powers of the monarchy, which included religious unity, but he was no fanatical extremist. He even insisted on a performance of Molière's satirical play *Tartuffe* about a religious hypocrite: "The king wished to see this masterpiece before it was even finished. He afterward defended it against those false bigots who wished to move heaven and earth to suppress it," although it will continue to live ... "so long as there is good taste and a hypocrite in France" (272).

The volume concludes with a chapter on "Chinese ceremonies," the subject of a dispute between Papacy and Jesuit missionaries in China about tolerating ancestor worship and other non-Christian beliefs on behalf of conversion to Catholicism. Thus he breaks out of Europe to talk about Confucian China as a model of religious toleration, compared with French intolerance for Huguenots, until dogmatic Christians arrived with their exclusive message: " ... this mania for proselytizing is a disorder confined exclusively to our climes, and has always been unknown in Asia proper" (460).

Anecdotal reporting is suspect as a concession to popular taste for gossip. Voltaire has two chapters devoted to anecdotes and explains his reason: "Anecdotes are the gleanings left over from the vast harvest field of history ... the public is interested in them when they concern illustrious personages ... The most useful and valuable anecdotes are those left in the secret writings of great princes, their natural candour (sic) thus revealing itself in permanent records" (255). His anecdotes are a social history of monarch and aristocracy. The 1664 "fête of Versailles" is described eloquently as a king-centered spectacle, Louis as patron of the arts, that "charmed the mind" in "a delightful abode" (270–71). Decades later the once feisty, glory-seeking Louis expressed contrition on his death bed and advised modesty to his successor: "You will soon be monarch of a great kingdom ... Endeavor to preserve peace with your neighbors. I have been too fond of war; do not imitate me. Take counsel in all things and always seek to know the best and follow it. Let your first thoughts be devoted to helping your people, and do what I have had the misfortune not to be able to do myself ... " (307–8).

The Age of Louis XIV illustrates Voltaire's ideals as historian. History sits on three legs—literature, scholarship, and philosophy. First, it must be readable and give pleasure. Style matters and is not mere embellishment. History can be a proud branch of literature without loss of integrity. Second, criticism of sources is essential. They must be genuine (not forged) and authentic (truthful about what they report). And third, good history to be useful must express a unifying vision, written *en philosophe*, with critical reason presiding over the landscape of human creations, institutions, and behavior.

Confidence in reason persuaded him that science, philosophy, and history freed of censorship and religious dogma would promote a materially better, rationally organized, morally kinder world. History provided instructive contrasts between other times and his own. The enlightened reign of a Louis XIV eclipsed that of a mediocre Louis XV. He believed with other *philosophes* of the Enlightenment that human nature is constant. Only custom differs from one time and place to another, the way people live and beliefs they hold. The subject matter of history is not how people change, but what their customs are and how they change for better or worse.

While affirming that history cannot be an exact science, he formulated pioneer guidelines to keep historians on track with a distinction between fact (what happened) and fable (what is made up). Application of these principles makes *The Age of Louis XIV* arguably the first "modern" historical work. The central rule is: "Historical truths must first be proved before they can be submitted" (255). Facts are distinguished from their management.

Facts must be rejected that violate natural law. No miracles, no portents like comets credited as messengers from God. Mythical explanation is unacceptable. History did not begin with Adam and Eve. Events that violate commonsense require exceptional evidence. Witness reliability must be tested by comparing reports. First hand reports come before second hand ones. Bias of witnesses must be taken into account. Facts selected must relate to public events and not be included for their own sake or for sensational effects. Although difficult to handle, individual character can and should be part of history, but only if it can be shown to shape events by objective acts.

Management of fact converts heaps of data into instructive, readable narrative that highlights turning points of states and civilizations and the progress of humanity. Facts irrelevant to these larger purposes can be left in archives. He scorned indiscriminate scholarship of seventeenth-century érudites (see essay 14 in this volume). Their facts had no grand focus, philosophical purpose, or narrative coherence. On the other hand, Voltaire's history of Louis XIV's century sought to uphold standards of accuracy within a narrative to trace progress and enlightenment. Voltaire applied these critical standards to past historical literature. He was not pleased, for example, with Livy's account of early Roman history.

Still, ideals and possibilities were not fully realized. Despite insistence that good history must avoid a bare succession of facts and events typical of chronicle, the first six chapters, even in their dress of graceful prose, have a chronicle-like feel. While he is credited with reading hundreds of books, poring over unpublished mémoires, and consulting archives to which he had access at Versailles and other places as royal historiographer, there are no citations and no way to check his sources. Given his passion for truthfulness and accuracy, however, it is reasonable to assume that his narrative was "researched" and that standards of reliability were mostly applied according to his guidelines.

Although civilization was announced originally as his true subject in *The Age of Louis XIV*, best represented by science, philosophy, and art, their allotted space, a mere 29 pages, and hasty exposition are a disappointment, further marred in his account of art by a narrow neoclassical bias. Persuaded that history must be useful and teach lessons to inform the present, Voltaire does not press himself to find explanations for events and has almost no sense of historical development and continuity. Nevertheless, he gave mind and creativity a place in history and thereby expanded its scope, and he modestly succeeded in illuminating "the manners of men" (103). A virtue not to be forgotten or underrated, he wrote history in a clear and vigorous style that attracts readers rather than driving them away.

Works by Voltaire

Essay on Universal History, the Manners and Spirit of Nations from the Reign of Charlamaign to the Age of Lewis XIV, trans. by Nugent (2nd ed. rev.; Dublin: S. Cotter, 1759). This is volume 1, unfortunately, and unaccountably, the only English translation of *Essai sur les moeurs et l'esprit de Nations* available.

The Age of Louis XIV, trans. by Martyn P. Pollack (London: J.M. Dent; New York: E.P. Dutton, 1958).

Voltaire's History of Charles XII, King of Sweden, trans. by Winifred Todhunter (New York: E.P. Dutton, 1908).

Works about Voltaire

Brumfit, John.H., *Voltaire, Historian* (London: Oxford University Press, 1958).

Leigh, John, *Voltaire: A Sense of History* (Oxford: Voltaire Foundation, 2004).

Mazlish, Bruce, *The Riddle of History: The Great Speculators from Vico to Freud* (New York: Harper and Row, 1966), Chapter 3.

Pierse, Siofra, *Voltaire Historiographer: Narrative Paradigms* (Oxford: Voltaire Foundation, 2008).

Useful references

Sakmann, Paul, "The Problem of Historical Method and of Philosophy of History in Voltaire," *History and Theory*, 2 (1971): 24–59.

16. THE DECLINE AND FALL OF THE ROMAN EMPIRE[2] (EDWARD GIBBON, 1737–1794)

Gibbon has been corrected but never replaced. His reputation as a premier historian in the Western tradition is secure. *The Decline and Fall* was recognized in his own time as a masterpiece. Since then, the work has steadily grown in stature. Its strength lies in memorable writing sustained over hundreds of pages dealing with many centuries of events without loss, for the most part, of scholarly persuasion. The work's integrity comes from a vast quantity of notes that sweeps up virtually all usable evidence available to the author.

Independent means provided him with ample leisure to travel, research, read, and write. He was supported in his labors by well-placed, wealthy friends in France, Switzerland, and England who respected his character and abilities. A deceased friend in Lausanne, Switzerland left him a mansion, including servants, where last chapters of the *Decline and Fall* were written. He was intellectually gifted with a fine memory and intense powers of concentration. He was obsessive about reading serious books, surely a necessity for embarking on a history of some 1500 years. Elected to the English Parliament, he attended faithfully: "The eight sessions I sat in parliament were a school of civil prudence, the first and most essential virtue of a historian" (*Autobiography*, in Roper, 41). He was convivial, dined out almost nightly, and admits to occasional dissipation. The chief burden in his life was ill health, mainly from a crippling affliction in private parts that killed him at 57.

Five years of reading in Lausanne, where he was exiled by his father for converting to Catholicism, resulted in a precocious *Essay on the Study of Literature*, written in French at age 22, which hints at his idea of what history should do. The history of empires, he believed, has brought distress to humanity while the history of knowledge has brought fulfillment, and it is desirable that historians should be philosophers. In1757 he met Voltaire in Lausanne, whose writings eventually supplied most of his ideas about political, social, and religious matters with a heavy dose of skepticism and irony. Like Voltaire he despised tyranny, superstition, fanaticism, and persecution. Even some of his views on why Rome declined and fell came from Voltaire's *Essay on Customs* and Montesquieu's 1713 book on the grandeur and decadence of Rome. After returning to Protestantism, a trip to Rome and a tour of its ruins inspired him to undertake a project that would unite philosophy, art, and history. Philosophy would yield perspective and art would give form to scattered evidence.

At first his chosen subject was the decay of Rome as a city. This scheme was expanded to include the Western Empire's decline and eventual collapse in the late fifth century A.D. from its pinnacle under the Antonines from Nerva (d. 98) to Marcus Aurelius (d. 180). Then he added the long career of the Eastern Empire to the loss of Constantinople to Ottoman Turks in 1453, and concluded with the fate of Rome the city until the reign of Pope Sixtus V (1585–90). His theme was imposing—the slide of an entire civilization into oblivion, "a revolution which will ever be remembered and is still felt by the nations of the earth" (I, 1). Disintegration of the Western Empire is a haunting episode in world history. Inquiry continues unabated about the course of its fall and reasons for its collapse.

The original text was in six volumes. In 1776 he published the first 16 chapters and composed the final lines of the seventy-first chapter in 1787. The scope and quality of the work are remarkable by any standard. In the Great Books edition, the first 40 chapters are in volume one at 671 closely printed pages followed by 227 pages of notes. The second volume has chapters 41–71 at 598 pages followed by 296 pages of notes. The imposing size of Gibbon's history at 1792 pages gives us pause because 523 of the total, or about a third of the whole, are his scrupulous notes. There was no precedent for a vast narrative in memorable prose resting on such a broad foundation of explicit evidence. For Voltaire, details were unfortunate or even calamitous, interfering with readability, style, and an exposition of big ideas to hold a reader's attention. Gibbon addressed big ideas without a loss of detail.

In the six-volume edition, the work divides into two parts. The first includes volumes I–IV, which covers about 500 years from the end of the first century A.D. to the death of Emperor Heraclius in 641. The high point of the empire, "the fairest part of the earth and the most civilized portion of mankind," was from 98 to 180 under Nerva, Trajan, Hadrian, Antoninus Pius, and Marcus Aureliius (I, 1). The slide downward began when Aurelius's demented son Commodus succeeded him. Gibbon begins with three chapters on the extent of the empire, its military organization, and the structure of the Roman constitution in A.D. 98.

The second part covers ten centuries in two volumes, a lopsided apportionment of space that suggests his distaste for Byzantine history, although he deserves credit for a competent job at a time when prejudice against Byzantine studies ran high. Moreover, in these sparse pages there are outstanding episodes such as Fourth Crusade in 1204 and the taking of Constantinople by Mahmud II. He notes in Chapter 65 the irony about Constantinople is that a weapon of defense known to Europe, gunpowder used in cannon, was available but exported to the Ottomans rather than to the Byzantines. Cannon fire breached the ancient walls: "If we contrast the rapid progress of this mischievous discovery with the slow and laborious advances of reason, science, and the arts of peace, a philosopher ... will laugh or weep at the folly of mankind" (II, 510).

At the end he notes "four principal causes of the ruin of Rome, which continued to operate over a period of some thousand years." They were "injuries of time and nature, hostile attacks of the barbarians and Christians, use and abuse of the materials, and domestic quarrels of the Romans" (II, 591). The decline and fall was not, as he says elsewhere, just a "triumph of barbarism and religion." The fifteenth and sixteenth chapters of the first volume are notable for their secular account of Christianity and the rise of the Church. Gibbon puts aside supernatural agencies and theology. He describes the rise and success of Christianity as a result of "secondary causes," in other words, as a historical rather than a miraculous phenomenon, which provoked uproar among the faithful: "The theologian may indulge the pleasing task of describing Religion as she descended from Heaven ... A more melancholy duty is imposed on the historian. He must discover the inevitable mixture of error and corruption which she contracted in a long residence upon earth, among a weak and degenerate race of beings" (1, 179). Distress was aroused further by noting "a melancholy truth" about Roman persecution of Christians: " ... the Christians, in the course of their intestine dissensions, have inflicted far greater adversities on each other than they had experienced from the zeal of infidels" (I, 233).

As a philosophical historian, he notes in Chapter 2 with ill-concealed irony that religious pluralism resulted in social and doctrinal harmony: "The various modes of worship, which prevailed in the Roman world, were all considered by the people, as equally true; by the philosopher, as equally false; and by the magistrate, as equally useful. And thus toleration produced not only mutual indulgence, but even religious concord" (I, 12).

His mastery of French opened the way to sources in that language and to materials translated from other languages into French, including some from German. Accomplished in Latin, he read extensively not only in classical literature but also in ecclesiastical history, the Church Fathers, Roman law, and publications of the Benedictines. Available works on Byzantium, the Middle East, China, and India were tracked down. His Greek was sufficient to read Xenophon, which opened up Byzantine sources. He consulted principles of paleography in Mabillon's *On Diplomatics* and Montfaucon's *Greek Paleography*, although that kind of knowledge was not applied to a critical assessment of documents (see essay 14 of this volume).

Notes for the history suggest that no significant piece of evidence from the seventeenth and eighteenth centuries was overlooked. A compulsive reader, he assembled and pored over sources tirelessly in a library that grew to some 6000 volumes between 1785 and 1787. Reputedly he spent £3000 on books and other materials. He sought out and consulted inscriptions and coins, thereby integrating epigraphy and numismatics into his web of evidence. One wonders how time was secured to write multiple drafts of the history on top of collecting, reading, and note taking while suffering from chronic swelling of his scrotum.

Gibbon used scholarship produced by European érudits in the seventeenth and early eighteenth centuries, whose work he respected. He admired especially Pierre Bayle (see essay 13 in this volume), whose erudition in an age of learning was legendary and second to none. From Bayle he also acquired a knack for combining malice with scholarship. One of his major sources was Ludovico Muratori's *Annals of Italy (Annali d' Italia)*, which appeared shortly after 1751 in 18 volumes and took the story of Italy from the birth of Christ in the late first century B.C. to the eighteenth century. Gibbon called this work "My guide and master in the history of Italy" (quoted in Thompson, II, 51). He relied also on Louis-Sébastien Le Nain de Tillemont's histories of the Church (16 volumes) and the Roman emperors (six volumes) in the first six centuries, "whose inimitable accuracy almost assumes the character of genius ... " (*Autobiography*, in Roper, 37). Despite labor and diligence in locating and digesting sources, he was aware of the historian's limitations: " ... while he is conscious of his own imperfections, he must often accuse the deficiency of his materials" (Chapter 71).

The evidence he accumulated is transparent in the sense that it can be faulted and revised. One seldom knows where philosophical historians like Montesquieu, Hume, and Voltaire got their material or what they thought of it. Gibbon provided copious footnotes that display his sources up front, often with flashes of wit and irony. Books and other documents are supplemented by inscriptions, coins, medals, maps, and other materials he hunted down in Europe and England. With that said, he added nothing to techniques of source criticism developed by the Maurists (see essay 14 in this volume) or those pursued by German scholars in his own time. He rarely compares sources with one another or asks with analytical follow-up why one is to be trusted more than another. While using them much as they were found, at least knowable sources were at hand and the reader is told what they are. This feature of his book was praised by early reviewers. But reviewers then and since have voiced reservations: that he is too indulgent of pagans, who were intolerant as well as Christians, that no evidence supports his view that Christians were indifferent to the empire, and that Christianity as a cause of decline was less fundamental than economic and military decay.

His enduring contribution to historiography was to blend the fact-based ideal of antiquarians (*érudits*) with some aspects of the philosophical approach taken by Baron Montesquieu, David Hume, and Voltaire (see essay 15 of this volume). Doing history *en philosophe* meant omission of divine Providence in search of earthly causes for historical change. The goal was a wiser, better world, while conceiving history as something grander and more illuminating than facts and politics. The shortcoming of philosophical historians was inattention or even indifference to sources. Ideas were paramount for them—civilization, progress, and general movement of the past. While sharing that vision, Gibbon did not ignore or obscure the particular, nor did he reduce history to a convenient arsenal of examples to combat superstition and fanaticism. He demonstrated that philosophical history on a grand theme might be done without neglecting available evidence.

Works by Gibbon[3]

The Decline and Fall of the Roman Empire, Robert McHenry, Editor in Chief, 2 vols. Great Books of the Western World, Mortimer J. Adler, Editor in Chief (2nd ed.; Chicago, Illinois: Encyclopedia Britannica, Inc., 1990).

The Decline and Fall of the Roman Empire, Complete and Unabridged in Three Volumes (New York: Modern Library, 1990).

The Decline and Fall of the Roman Empire and Other Selections from the Writings of Edward Gibbon, Abridged, ed. Hugh R. Trevor-Roper (New York: Washington Square Press, 1963). Roper includes Gibbon's Autobiography.

The Portable Gibbon: The Decline and Fall of the Roman Empire, Abridged, ed. Dero A. Saunders (New York: Penguin Books, 1977).

Works about Gibbon

Bowerstock, Glen, *Gibbon's Historical Imagination* (Stanford: Stanford University Press, 1988).

Monigliano, Arnoldo, "Gibbon's Contribution to Historical Method," *Studies in Historiography* (New York: Harper and Row, 1966).

Plumb, J. H., "Gibbon and History," *History Today*, 14:2 (November, 1969): 737–743.

Porter, Roy, *Edward Gibbon: Making History* (London: Widenfeld and Nicolson, 1988).

Swain, Joseph W., *Edward Gibbon the Historian* (New York: St. Martin's Press, 1966).

Womersley, David P., *The Transformation of the Decline and Fall of the Roman Empire* (Cambridge: Cambridge University Press, 1988).

Useful references

Craddock, Patricia B., *Edward Gibbon: A Reference Guide* (Boston, Massachusetts: G. K. Hall, 1987).

Gay, Peter, *Style in History* (New York: McGraw Hill, 1974), Chapter 1.

Ghosh, Peter R., "Gibbon Observed," *Journal of Roman Studies*, 81 (1991): 132–156.

Keynes, Geoffrey (ed.), The Library of Edward Gibbon: A Catalogue (2nd ed.; Godalming: St. Paul's Bibliographies, 1980).

17. REFLECTIONS ON THE PHILOSOPHY OF THE HISTORY OF MANKIND[4] (JOHANN GOTTFRIED HERDER, 1744–1803)

Herder was born in East Prussia, brought up as a Lutheran, and attended Köningsberg University, where he was influenced by Immanuel Kant's lectures on how climate and geography have influenced human development and historical change. He became a pastor and held a number of religious offices, ending up in Weimar, capital of the duchy Saxe-Weimar-Eisinach, as chaplain to the duke and his court. His religious convictions were elastic, even ambivalent. After a sermon disturbing to the duke, Goethe was surprised he did not abdicate. Herder also took on duties as superintendant of the duchy's schools, which were widely known for their excellence.

There was no "Germany" in his time, only a jumble of mostly small principalities ruled by princes, dukes, and bishops. Pressures and influence came from France, cultural arbiter of the time, even after the revolution of 1789, which German literary figures and intellectuals like Herder bitterly resented and sought to neutralize by recovering a distinctly German culture. He was a dogged critic of the French Enlightenment, with its cosmopolitan rationalism and neoclassical aesthetic based on uniform rules for poetry and art that assumed a uniformity of human nature.

He was friends with poet and polymath Wolfgang Goethe, who recommended him for office to the duke, even securing a house for him and his wife, Caroline, when they moved to Weimar. Along with other literary figures of the time, notably Goethe, Christoph Wieland, and the poet Friedrich Schiller, he was the fourth luminary to burnish Weimar's reputation as a German "Athens" at a time when Germans had no central capital like Paris or Vienna for art and scholarship.

In his writing, he dwells at length on wholeness of personality, but personal integration in a harmonious group eluded him. By report he was a divided man, given to fits of petulance, hungering for praise, often resentful and suspicious, and tiresomely pedantic. Caroline attempted to provide domestic stability while he juggled ritual and ceremonial tasks as chaplain while toiling at a host of writing projects. A psycho-historian might be inclined to attribute his passion for cultural groups unified by language and custom, spontaneously expressing themselves in simple folk poetry and song, a poignant outreach of an unhappy, complicated life.

He wrote some history, which included a treatise on the origin of language in 1772, *One More Philosophy of History* in 1774, and *Reflections*, published in four parts between 1784 and 1791, but was mainly a prolific author of literary criticism, folklore, philosophy, theology, aesthetics, and linguistics. He produced a mountain of ideas, themes, and speculations, codified in some 33 volumes.

Reflections starts off: "If our philosophy of the history of man would in any measure deserve that name, it must begin from Heaven. For as our place of abode, Earth, is of itself nothing, but derives its figure and constitution, its faculty of forming organized beings, and preserving them when formed, from those heavenly powers, that pervade the whole universe." This is a fair sample of the prose that sprawls over 632 pages. It bears the stamp of romantic texture and diction for which Herder was a forerunner. It has a diffuse quality that comes from loosely disciplined enthusiasm for all forms of human expression, which makes him hard to read both in German and English translation. He neglected logical organization or systematic exposition. He never questions his own views. But within the intellectual-historical rainforest he created, *Reflections on the Philosophy of the History of Mankind* (*Ideen zur Philosophie der Geschichte der Menschheit*) is by wide consent a seminal document for historical consciousness in the nineteenth century and beyond.

Although not a historian by vocation, Herder conveys a definite notion of what history is and how it should be done, which he believed could rival natural science in explanatory power:

> The whole history of mankind is a pure natural history of human powers, actions, and propensities, modified by time and place. This principle is not more simple, than it is luminous and useful, in treating of the history of nations ... the examining mind must exert all its acumen on every historical event, as on a natural phenomenon. Thus in the narration of history it will seek the strictest truth; in forming its conceptions and judgments, the most complete connexion: and never attempt to explain a thing which is, or happens, by a thing which is not.

Faithful application of this principle aims to see through fantasies, mythical invention, and the supernatural to "simply what is: and as soon as this is seen, the causes why it could not be otherwise will commonly appear ... History is the science of what is, not of what possibly may be according to the hidden designs of fate" (214–15). Once more, he seems to anticipate Leopold von Ranke in aspiration if not in technique.

In Churchill's complete translation, *Reflections* divides into 20 books without notes or references. The early books, one through six, are freighted with eccentric, dated material on cosmology, geography, and biology better passed over, which Manuel decided to do in his abridgement. Nevertheless, those chapters show the extent of Herder's reading and his awareness of what science at the time had to say about the physical setting of societies. He postulates a sequence of frameworks that emerge successively from one another—the solar system, the earth, continents, plants, animals, and men in their varied physical and social environments. The current stage of human development is still physical. The next stage is spiritual. Books VII and VIII contain essentials of his thought, which are then applied to discussions of various peoples, cultures, and historical eras.

As an early historicist, he believed present artifacts must be explained by their development through time in unique societies: "... the Muse of Time, History, herself sings with a hundred voices, speaks with a hundred tongues" (107). Unlike the philosopher Hegel, the object of "development" was not an abstract whole detached from individuality and detail. Historical change is focused on organic nations steeped in their own traditions. These ideas nourished Romanticism, the broad European movement of cultural innovation and resistance to the Enlightenment whose writers and thinkers turned to feeling, intuition, and faith instead of reason, preferred local to universal truths, and preferred the Middle Ages and the Reformation to classical antiquity.

History forms individual consciousness within communities. For Herder, the group shapes historical identity, which he calls the *Volk*. World history is the genesis and unfolding of these groups, each with its distinctive spirit, or *volksgeist*. Cohesion of the group is supplied by a fabric of symbols woven from poetry and religion. A plurality of groups uniquely fashioned by history cannot be fused into one deliberately. One *Volk* is not reducible to another: "The historian of mankind must with eyes as impartial of the creator of the human race, or the genius of the Earth, and judge altogether uninfluenced by the passions ... Nature's year is long: the blossoms of her plants are as various as the plant themselves" (161). In this spirit of cultural pluralism, Herder extended to all peoples, however minor or obscure, a unique dignity, anticipating Ranke's view that all past societies are equal in the eyes of God (see essay 18 in this volume).

He also believed the garden of human cultures already contains whatever is possible: "What is the principal law, that we have observed in all the occurrences of history? In my opinion it is this: *that every where on our Earth whatever could be has been, according to the situation and wants of the place, the circumstances and occasions of the times, and the native or generated character of the people*" (159; Herder's emphasis).

Three terms of historical understanding are the individual, the *Volk*, and humanity, although the latter is more indistinct than the first two. The idea of "humanity" simply means that all human beings are formed culturally in a unique nation with religion as a common denominator and thereafter cultivate in varied ways literature, arts, and sciences. The individual is denied expression or identity without membership in a *Volk*, or a "nation," which is distinguished from a "state." States are artificial and centralized. Nations are spontaneously formed and free in expression. It is not possible to rise above a specific *volksgeist* to speak all languages, belong to all religions, and embrace all myths. In short, cosmopolitanism, the ideal of a one-world culture, language, or aesthetic ideal without limitations of time and space, is unattainable and cannot define humanity. A *Volk* gets vitality and meaning from being itself. The consequence of this argument is radical pluralism. There can be no one ideal society or good life for all, contrary to Plato, Augustine, Voltaire, and Marx. There is no reason, he argued, that all nations cannot live in peace, a conviction that led him to condemn and attack Immanuel Kant's view that human vices, a lust for power and control of scarce resources, result in progress through competition and struggle.

Change is inevitable, but no single pattern or law is at work. Each *Volk* develops and flourishes within its own environment: "The cultivation of a people is the flower of its existence; its display is pleasing indeed, but transitory … But every kind of human knowledge has its particular circle that is its nature, time, place, and periods of life" (216). Homer and the Greek tragedians had their day, but can never reappear again. While membership in a *Volk* is what gives meaning and direction to individual lives, it also imposes limits. What was possible for classical Greece was not an option for the Hebrews. A further limit is the inevitability of decay and exhaustion that overtook the brilliance of Greece and the grandeur of Rome.

All nations are not equally cultivated or elevated. Group uniqueness does not excuse, for example, the neglect of women:

> There is no circumstance … which so decisively shows the character of a man, or a nation, as the treatment of women. Most nations, that acquire subsistence with difficulty, degrade the female sex to domestic animals, and impose on them all the labors of the hut … this contempt of the woman prevails in all uncultivated nations, though it appears among every people, and in every particular region in a different form.
>
> (63)

Therefore it is a mistake to take Herder's pluralism as an endorsement of the doctrine, "whatever is, is right." Men are guilty of "stupid brutality," while women have "delicate civility," superior habits of cleanliness, "and gentle endurance" (54–65). It follows that judgments are admissible that transcend any particular *Volk*.

A *Volk* grows and decays organically like any individual organism, but retains integrity only if change comes from within. Mixture of one *volksgeist* with another, whether from borrowing or forced intervention from the outside, weakens the spirit of a people, corrupts their power of expression, and reduces the healthy plurality of nations: "Thus nations modify themselves according to time, place, and their internal character; each bears in itself the standard of its perfection, totally independent of all comparison with the others" (98). The lesson is to leave peoples alone to fulfill their group destinies and take pleasure in the variety and originality of their creations.

Herder was not alone in pointing up the historical uniqueness of societies and peoples (his teacher Johann Hamann did so) but it was his focus on traditions and customs that bind people as a "nation" that influenced proto-nationalism in Europe (see Book VIII). Herder was not a political nationalist. He inspired surges of cultural nationalism in central, eastern and southern Europe before 1848, which involved promotion of indigenous languages (grammars, dictionaries), local traditions of law, and ethnic historical origins, preliminaries of political nationalism among restive groups ruled by the empires of Austria, Russia, and the Ottomans.

His thought reached into the late twentieth century and underlies the contemporary movement known as "multiculturalism." His respect for so-called primitives and heathens preceded the founding of anthropology. As a pioneer defender of the "other," he exposed new genres of history by widening the landscape for curiosity, appreciation, and inquiry. He crystallized the idea of historicism, that what exists now emerged from the past in unrepeatable form.

Herder's romantic historiography countered abstractions of the Enlightenment, particularly the one that held men are the same everywhere. An interpretation of mankind on the principle of uniformity was rejected and in its place Herder defended differences, variety, and particular ways that cannot be duplicated outside the "nation" in which they originate.

Works by Herder

Another Philosophy of History and Selected Political Writings, trans. with introduction and notes by Ionnis D. Evrigenis and Daniel Pellerin (Indianapolis/Cambridge, 2004).

J.G. Herder on Social and Political Culture, trans. and ed. with introduction by F.M. Barnard (London: Cambridge University Press, 1969).

Outlines of a Philosophy of the History of Man, trans. from German *Ideen zur Philosophie der Geschichte der Menschheit* by T. Churchill (New York; Bergman Publishers, [1966?]).[5] First published in 1800.

Reflections on the Philosophy of History of Mankind, abridged, with an introduction by Frank E. Manuel (Chicago, Illinois: University of Chicago Press, 1968).

Works about Herder

Berlin, Isaiah, *Vico and Herder: Two Studies in the History of Ideas* (New York: Viking Press, 1976).

Lovejoy, Arthur O., "Herder and the Enlightenment Philosophy of History," in A.O. Lovejoy, *Essays in the History of Ideas* (Baltimore, Maryland: Johns Hopkins University Press, 1948).

Useful references

Barnard, Frederick M., *Herder's Social and Political Thought* (Oxford, United Kingdom: Oxford University Press, 1965).

Section Notes

1 The translation used in this essay is by Martyn P. Pollack.

2 The edition of Gibbon cited in this essay is volumes 37 and 38 of Great Books of the Western World, edited by Robert McHenry. This edition has a chronology added to the text that helps the reader keep track of where Gibbon is in time. Both text and notes are complete. Notes come at the end. There are 14 helpful maps, seven at the end of each volume.

3 *The Decline and Fall* is available in a number of abridgements, some longer, some shorter. Examples are those of D.M. Low at 924 pages (1960); Hugh Trevor-Roper at 456 pages, which includes the *Autobiography*, and part of the *Vindication* responding to critics of chapters 15 and 16 of the history (cited above); Frank Bourne at 735 pages (1963); Moses Hadas at 314 pages (1962); and Dero Saunders at 691 pages (cited above). The Saunders abridgement is an edited first half of the *History* from the Antonines to the end of the Empire in the West, except for the last chapter. Some chapters and Gibbon's footnotes are omitted. For the reader truly short of time, the Hadas abridgement is recommended. It retains the original's 71 chapters and thereby provides a sense of the work's structure and scope while supplying many of Gibbon's notable judgments and generalizations.

4 The version used in this essay is *Reflections on the Philosophy of the History of Mankind*, abridged by Frank E. Manuel. The abridgement has eight of the 20 books in Churchill's 1800 translation. Although truncated—books on

Eskimos, Africans, American Indians, Asia, Germanic and Slavic nations, and European barbarian kingdoms are omitted—the remainder is more readily available than Churchill's volume. Manuel has edited the text to remove Churchill's antiquated spelling and punctuation.

5 Unfortunately this is the only complete English version of Herder's *Outline*, which is consulted but not used for this essay because it is relatively inaccessible to the general reader. The translation as a whole has not been republished.

NINETEENTH-CENTURY EUROPE

Themes 3 (issues of critical historiography), 4 (genres of history), 5 (breadth of inquiry), 6 (problematic historiography)

The nineteenth century was in every respect an age of history. Historians abounded. Their works were published and translated from one language to another. Universities rushed to establish chairs for the most prominent men. Their works were read avidly by a receptive public. A number of historians, especially in France, became significant political figures. Governments in Britain and Prussia tapped historians for public duties. The range of historical study expanded, especially economic history, although politics, diplomacy, and war continued to rule despite the example of Voltaire. Cultural and intellectual history made their appearance. Full-dress biblical criticism also emerged. As historians and their fields multiplied and nation states were formed (Belgium, Italy, Germany), availability of sources expanded as doors of archives opened across Europe. Prominent historians toward the end of the century attempted assessments of what history is as a discipline and what it had accomplished.

Hovering over the sheer volume of historical research and publication was an aggressive attention to matters of evidence and its evaluation. German scholars were most responsible for defining, codifying, applying, and disseminating precise rules of evidence. Their influence was visible everywhere. By the end of the century Europe was literally awash in historical books and treatises from every major country and from many ethnic groups in the Austrian and Russian empires. The view arose that nothing human could be understood without knowing its history.

18. HISTORY OF THE POPES, THEIR CHURCH AND STATE[1] (LEOPOLD VON RANKE, 1795–1886)

Ranke was born in Thuringia, part of the kingdom of Saxony acquired by Prussia during the Napoleonic wars. His father was a lawyer and the family, noted for its pastors, devoutly Lutheran, which accounts for Ranke's long-term fascination with Martin Luther's historical influence. His early education was shared by home study and attendance at a respected, private Protestant school. Thereafter he went to universities in Leipzig and Halle, where he sharpened his talent for philology and knowledge of classical literature. For a time he taught classics at a gymnasium in Frankfort. That experience edged him in the direction of historical studies. He admired the *Roman History* of Barthold Niebuhr and his pioneer efforts to unfold the past with empirical rigor and disciplined objectivity. In later years, he kept a bust of Niebuhr in his study. Ranke married and enjoyed a stable, affectionate family life. He was a handsome man and a good speaker with much charm, all of which helped with access to private libraries and state archives.

His first book, *A History of Latin and Teutonic Nations*, was written in Frankfort and published at age 29. The volume included an added section that expounded his philosophy of historiography, which was to reconstruct without moral judgment specific periods of the past from facts embedded in original sources. He was suspicious that authors of secondary works merely repeated one another's information and errors. The cure for such uncritical history was eye witness narratives and original documents.

In 1825 the Prussian minister of education appointed him to a beginning professorship at the University of Berlin, which became a tenured full professorship in 1837. In 1841 he was appointed Prussian historiographer. During that interval he attracted the attention of Prince Klemens von Metternich of Austria, the most powerful man in Europe at the time. He opened the doors of archives nearly everywhere except for the Vatican, and Ranke was launched on an unprecedented career of research and publication that encompassed the political development of most European countries and made him a byword for "historian" in the nineteenth century.

His university seminars institutionalized the Rankean code of staying with facts from primary sources. He sent into the world a considerable number of fine historians who continued his methods of inquiry and instruction. At the age of 91, despite serious eye problems, Ranke was at work on a multi-volume world history as the capstone of his career. Before he died he had completed nine volumes that left the tale in the fifteenth century.

The most influential part of Ranke's vast corpus of writing dealt with major European powers in the sixteenth, seventeenth, and eighteenth centuries, to which must be added a remarkable history, by a Lutheran no less, of popes and the Papal States in the last four centuries (*Die romischen Papste in den letze vier Jahrhunderten*).[2] His strategy was to research and write about states most important to the development and character of European civilization. Usually beginning with origins, his narrative strategy expanded until it reached a crucial point of historical change. With France it was the reign of Louis XIV, with Germany the Reformation era, with England the two revolutions in the seventeenth century, and with the popes, formation of the Papal States.

In the introduction to *History of the Popes* he explains where he got his sources and how the project was mapped out. The text is a formidable three volumes comprising 914 pages of narrative, each volume divided into "books," 274 pages of archival documents, and a number of illustrations. This level of effort was typical of Ranke, a prolific, versatile, innovative historian whose career of scholarship, publication, and teaching spanned more than 60 years and dominated much of his century.

But why did he choose papal history?

> Not its particular relation to ourselves; for it no longer exercises any essential influence, nor does it create in us solicitude of any kind ... Popery can now inspire us with no other interest than what results from the development of its history and its former influence ... we shall find it affected, quite as deeply as any other government, and to the very essence of its being, by the various destinies to which the nations of Europe have been subjected ... as one nation or another has gained ascendency; as the fabric of social life has been disturbed; so also has the papal power been affected: its maxims, its objects, and its pretensions have undergone essential changes ...
>
> (I, x–xi)

With this said, how does the papal history reflect his profile as a historian?

First, he wrote reliable history from primary documents without losing the narrative ideal of a story told dramatically in the service of truth. As a stylist, his work is readable, even in translation, with short sentences and paragraphs, colorful diction, narrative thrust, alertness to dramatic effects, and a sense of development in time, all necessary to history as art to supplement and enliven scholarship. His portraits could be grim, as with the early career of Pius IV in a battle for Siena: "His shrewdness was not inferior to his daring; his undertakings were invariably successful, but he was altogether without pity; many a wretched peasant, who was attempting to carry provisions into Sienna, did he destroy with his iron staff. Scarcely was there a tree far and near on which he had not caused some one of them to be hanged" (I, 218).

Second, credibility meant reliance on archival materials—letters, diaries, mémoires, official records, eyewitness accounts—examined and used with a critical eye, rejection of gratuitous moral judgments, and resistance to finding prophetic lessons in the past. Without such methods and discipline, he believed there was no hope of doing real history. As he says in a preface to his first book in 1824: "It merely wants to show how, essentially, things happened" ("Es will bliss zeigan, wie es eigentlich gewesen ist").[3] In an appendix of the same work, he critiques published authorities he used to write it, concluding that earlier published histories are unreliable sources to be used with a critical eye. The fault is that earlier writers simply plundered one another's books without asking where and how their authors obtained the information. He trusted only the printed page—no hearsay, gossip, stories, speculations, or unsure oral testimony. In archives of Rome, Venice, Berlin, and Vienna, he excavated a mass of documents never before used by historians to write about papal history.

While critical methods were not his invention, he codified and applied them to a greater range of subjects and time periods. Classical philologists working with Greek and Roman texts since the Renaissance, *erudites* like Mabillon testing for document authenticity (see Chapter 14 of this volume), and a circle of German scholars at the University of Gottingen in 1788 pioneered techniques of external criticism, that is, authentication of documents by dating paper and ink, seals, and handwriting, and internal criticism, or testing the competence of an author as a witness or reporter. Previous scholars also worked in archives, but Ranke topped all of them as a relentless tenant in such holdings armed with techniques of verification.

The concluding appendix of his papal history displays 165 primary documents, suggesting tireless diligence tracking down and confirming usable evidence. Especially valuable were private collections and libraries opened to him: "The reigning kinsmen of the pontiff ... usually bequeathed as an heir-loom to the princely houses they founded a large part of the state papers accumulated during their administration ... In the palaces which they erected, a few rooms ... were always reserved for books and manuscripts ... Thus, to a certain extent the private collections of Rome may be regarded as public ones ... " (I, viii).

Third, the political career of nations was his subject of choice because he viewed them as major historical players since the Renaissance. The popes he took as cunning, ambitious politicians rivaling kings and princes. This focus on politics intensified while doing research in Vienna, where he got so much friendly help from Prince Metternich, a major architect of the political settlement that followed the Napoleonic wars. While politics of nations was Ranke's focus, he could dramatize individual men and women, relished ideas, analyzed financial and administrative issues, and pushed well beyond separate nations and peoples into the neglected domain of international relations. All of these topics are orchestrated and balanced in the papal history.

The first volume begins with Christianity in the Roman Empire and ends in the sixteenth century with the reigns of Gregory XIII, associated with calendar reform, and Sixtus V, who wrested control of the Papal States from the nobility, reinvigorated papal government, and completed the dome of St. Peter's Basilica according to Michelangelo's plan. Ten popes are discussed in some detail. There is a chapter contrasting the fourteenth and fifteenth centuries, and chapters on conflicts with Protestants and Jesuits, effects of the Inquisition, ambitions and policies of popes, and intellectual currents. On popes in the high Renaissance, he explains with irony that Julius II tore down the old St. Peter's, "every portion crowded with monuments that had received the veneration of ages," and erected "a temple" with "a purpose exclusively artistic." Julius's influence was less religious than aesthetic: "Men frequented the Vatican less to kneel in devotion on the threshold of the apostles than to admire those great works of ancient art that enriched the dwelling of the pontiff—the Belvedere Apollo and the Laocoon" (I, 50).

Renaissance worldliness that overtook the Papacy is highlighted in his portrait of the Medici pope, Leo X:

> Machiavelli composed more than one of his works expressly for him. His halls, galleries, and chapels were filled by Raphael with the rich ideal of human beauty, and with the purest expression of life in its most varied forms. He was a passionate lover of music, a more scientific practice of which was just was just then becoming diffused throughout Italy; the sounds of music were daily heard floating through the palace, Leo himself humming the airs that were performed.
>
> (I, 51)

Volume two begins with the state of Protestantism in 1563 and ends with failure of the Counter Reformation in Germany during the Thirty Years War. Ranke gives close attention to nine popes. Material in the volume is arranged in three "books." The first traces early phases of the Catholic Counter Reformation in the face of Protestant successes. Ranke occasionally exposes his Lutheran bias:

> To the most remote and neglected corner of Europe Protestant doctrines had extended their life-inspiring power. How immeasurable an empire had they conquered within the space of forty years ... This is all the more extraordinary because the Protestant creed was by no means a mere negation of the papacy—a simple renunciation. It was in the highest degree positive, a renovation of Christian sentiments and principles that govern human life even to the most profound recesses of the soul.
>
> (II, 13–14)

The second book reviews Catholic political and doctrinal tensions between 1589 and 1607. He reflects on a division of powers and ideas in Europe that resisted an overarching absolutism: "At no time ... has either a power or doctrine, least of all a political doctrine, gained pre-eminence in Europe to the extent of obtaining an absolute and undivided sovereignty ... A firm resistance has at all times arisen against every opinion that has labored to obtain exclusive domination, and this antagonism proceeding from the inexhaustible depths of human life ... has invariably called new and vigorous energies into action" (II, 132).

The third and longest book explores papal ambitions in Poland, Sweden, Russia, and Switzerland from 1590 to 1617, Catholic successes with the outbreak of war from 1617 to 1623, and emergence of a balance between Protestant and Catholic confessions in the Thirty Years War: " ... let it suffice that we have made ourselves aware of the means by which the mighty advance of Catholicism, which was on the point of taking possession of Germany ... forever, was at once arrested in its course; was opposed, when preparing to annihilate the Protestant faith at its sources, by a victorious resistance" (II, 389).

The final volume carries the narrative from mid-seventeenth century to the early nineteenth century just after Napoleon's defeat in Russia. A long decline of the Papacy's spiritual, territorial, and political fortunes culminated under Napoleon, who incorporated the Papal States into his empire when Pius VII refused to support the Continental System, and arrested the pope when he excommunicated the French emperor. These disasters were reversed with the support of three non-Catholic powers—Sweden, England, and Prussia, and Pius returned to Rome with the Papal States restored: "And now that the Pope had once more acquired a free and independent position among the sovereigns of Europe, he could devote his undisturbed attention to the revival and recovery of spiritual obedience" (III, 165).

Of the rulers and popes discussed in this volume, one of the most vivid portraits is that of Sweden's Christina, who assumed power in 1644 and was declared by a contemporary to have seen and read everything:

> The Queen of Sweden was ... a wonderful production of nature and fortune: so young a woman, yet free from all vanity; she never sought to conceal that one of her shoulders was higher than the other; she had been told that her principal beauty was the rich profusion of her hair, yet she did not bestow upon it the most ordinary attention ... To all the more minute cares of life she was a complete stranger ... She was a very bold horsewoman ... she scarcely waited to be in her saddle before she started at speed ... She studied Tacitus and Plato, and not infrequently expounded the meaning of those authors more clearly than philologists by profession ... She threw the fresh spirit of a native perspicacity and quickness into all her undertakings.
>
> (III, 61)

The history ends with Ranke's conviction that divine providence guides the movement of history to bring oneness out of division: "High above all conflict ... there will yet arise from the ocean of error, the unity of a conviction ... the pure and simple consciousness of the ever-during and all-pervading presence of God" (III, 174).

Criticisms of Ranke's historiography are well taken without being fatal. His stature as researcher is well established. Even detractors concede he wrote good history on a wider canvas than anyone else. If faultless objectivity eluded him, he set high standards for detecting falsehood and mining documents for the best knowledge available even if confined to archival documents. The papal history is replete with critical observations about sources, and nearly every page has footnotes citing or commenting on them.

He was aware that stressing particulars is a narrow road to the complexity of what happened. He also understood that staying with archival documents generated by governments and ruling classes has obvious limits. A focus on politics and policy neglected social and economic developments, but he was not totally remiss. As for his obsession with particulars, they bestowed in his mind dignity on the past while he also looked for points of universal interest, causes in the midst of descriptions, and viewed multiple sides of an issue. Every nation, he argued, has unique institutions and traditions derived from unrepeatable historical experiences. From a study of governments he concluded that no one system is best for all peoples. This respect for uniqueness echoes Johann Herder (see essay 17 in this volume), for whom uniqueness derived from language, folklore, and custom. For Ranke it was defined by law, government, and authority of the state, secular forces that shaped papal policies and aspirations, and the lives of millions, for 400 years. Finally, his belief that "scientific" inquiry from original sources could expose what really happened was a step up from historians who merely cited one another or used dubious sources.

Works by Ranke

A History of England, Principally in the Seventeenth Century (New York: AMS Press, 1966).

History of the Latin and Teutonic Nations from 1494 to 1514, trans. by Philip A. Ashworth (London: Kessinger Publishing, 2004).

History of the Popes: Their Church and State, trans. by E. Fowler, 3 vols. (New York: Colonial Press, 1901).

History of the Reformation in Germany, ed. Robert A. Johnson, trans. by Sarah Austin (London: Kessinger Publishing, 2007).

Works about Ranke

Iggers, Georg G., *The German Conception of History: The National Tradition of Historical Thought from Herder to the Present* (Middletown, Connecticut: Wesleyan University Press, 1968).

Iggers, Georg G. and Powell, J.M. (eds.), *Leopold von Ranke and the Shaping of the Historical Discipline* (Syracuse UP: Syracuse University Press, 1990).

Iggers, George G. and Konrad von Moltke (eds.), *Leopold von Ranke. The Theory and Practice of History*, with new translations by Wilma A. Iggers and Konrad von Moltke (Indianapolis: Bobbs-Merrill, 1973).

Krieger, Leonard, *Ranke: The Meaning of History* (Chicago, Illinois: Chicago University Press, 1977).

Useful references

Butterfield, Herbert, *Man in His Past: The Study of the History of Historical Scholarship* (Cambridge: Cambridge University Press, 1955), Chapter IV.

Gay, Peter, *Style in History* (New York: McGraw Hill, 1974), Chapter 2.

19. MOHAMMED AND CHARLEMAGNE[4] (HENRI PIRENNE, 1862–1935)

Born and educated in Belgium, Pirenne was the country's most noted historian from the end of World War I until his death. He was celebrated especially for a multi-volume history of Belgium that made him a national icon. Educated at the University of Liège, where he earned a doctorate, he went on to study in universities at Leipzig, Berlin, and Paris. In 1886 he was appointed professor of medieval and Belgian history at the University of Ghent and remained there until his retirement in 1930. His chief interest was medieval civilization and its origins.

His life included non-academic adventure. He joined a campaign of passive resistance when Germany occupied Belgium in World War I by refusing Germans access to his university, for which he was imprisoned and where he wrote a *History of Europe* without notes. He became a sharp critic of German nationalism, but without rejecting past achievements of German scholarship. One of his influential friendships was with historian Karl Lamprecht, which ended with Lamprecht's proposal that Belgium cooperate with Germany to nurture its long-term war objectives.

The war left Pirenne disillusioned like so many other European intellectuals. He abandoned an earlier confidence in human progress and perfectibility with two consequences—chance was accepted as a force in historical change and the decisive role of exceptional individuals was acknowledged. He was also convinced that geographical and economic circumstances are major players in historical failure and success. The fulcrum of his medieval studies was an influential theory about decline of Rome's empire in the west and its replacement by an economically backward, culturally thin, and decentralized feudal regime in Western Europe that constituted the beginning of the Middle Ages.

An enduring question for historians is why the Roman Empire in the west faltered and disintegrated. For Edward Gibbon, the main culprits were barbarians infiltrating from without and a new, otherworldly religion displacing paganism from within (see essay 16 in this volume). Other explanations have included epidemic disease, technological stagnation because of slavery, lead poisoning, imperial incompetence, overexpansion, too much complexity, moral decay, barbarization of the military, currency debasement, or a combination of these and other factors. The end of the Empire in the west is dated conventionally from 476 when the last Roman emperor was replaced by a German chieftain.

For Pirenne, the Empire rolled on from then without serious interruption. He offered a provocative interpretation and explanation—the Pirenne Thesis—that the Empire was sound from the fifth century to the eighth: " ... despite its losses, the Empire was still the only world power ... The foreign policy of the Empire embraced all the peoples of Europe, and completely dominated the policy of the Germanic State. Until the 8th century, the only positive element in history was the influence of the Empire" (73). His thesis can be summarized in a nutshell with three compartments.

First, the Empire's vigor and wealth was due to its Mediterranean orientation. The grandeur of Rome faced water rather than land. The most important provinces—for example, Syria, Egypt, Africa, and Spain—were connected with the sea. This orientation included lands around the Black Sea, which is an extension of the Mediterranean. Frontiers on the Danube, the Euphrates and the Sahara were of far less economic and social importance. It was on Mediterranean waters that a vast traffic of people, goods, resources, and culture circulated between east and west: "Thanks to the Mediterranean, then, the Empire constituted, in the most obvious fashion, an economic unity. It was one great territory, with tolls but no custom houses. And it enjoyed the enormous advantage of a common monetary unit, the gold *solidas* of Constantine ... which was current everywhere" (19). The strategic importance of the Mediterranean is indicated by the panic that swept through Rome when Vandals took the great naval base of Carthage in Africa in 439, but the crisis was ended by a truce in 442.

Second, invasions by Germanic barbarians that commenced in the fifth century, who were pushed against Roman borders by the Huns, destroyed imperial unity but not the empire itself. Where the Emperor was no longer sovereign, he still reigned in principle. Barbarian tribes did not have a culture superior to that of Rome, which they promptly adopted in its main outlines: " ... if the barbarians had wished to destroy the Empire, they had only to agree among themselves, and they must have succeeded. But they did not wish to destroy it" (31). In effect, they were Romanized and did not break the continuity of Roman civilization: " ... the Empire continued to defend itself for two hundred years ... It had its fortresses, against which the barbarians were powerless, its strategic routes, a military art whose tradition was many centuries old, a consummate diplomacy which understood how division might be created among enemies of the Empire, or how they might be bought ... and further, its aggressors were incapable of agreeing among themselves. Above all, the Empire had the Mediterranean ... " (21).

Pirenne works his way through key features unchanged by barbarian presence—the Latin language, writing on papyrus, currency, consumption of similar foodstuff, religion, social classes, law, art, taxes, economic organization, and bureaucratic administration: "From whatever standpoint we regard it ... the period inaugurated by the establishment of the Barbarians within the Empire introduced no absolute historical innovation ... Far from seeking to replace the Empire by anything new, they established themselves within it, and although their settlement was accompanied by a process of serious degradation, they did not introduce a new scheme of government" (140).

Third, the explosive rise of Islam after 632 was fundamentally different from the barbarian invasions: "In the case of the Germans, the conqueror spontaneously approached the conquered. With the Arabs it was the other way about; the conquered had to approach the conqueror, and they could do so only by serving Allah ... and by reading the Koran, like the conquerors; and therefore by learning the language ... " (151). In record time Muslim armies took Arabia, Mesopotamia, Palestine, Egypt, Africa, and Spain. The effect was to close down Roman access to the Mediterranean and its former ports:

> Thus, it may be asserted that navigation with the Orient ceased about 650 as regards the regions situated eastward of Sicily, while in the second half of the 7th century it came to an end in the whole of the Western Mediterranean. By the beginning of the 8th century it had completely disappeared ... The Mediterranean was henceforth at the mercy of the Saracen pirates. In the ninth century they seized the islands, destroyed the ports ... The great port of Marseilles, which had formerly been the principal emporium of Western trade with the Levant, was empty.
>
> (166)

Except for some Jews, merchants all but vanished. Goods like papyrus, wine, and spices that once reached Gaul in the west became rare. The economic impact of losing the Mediterranean, except for coastal areas around Byzantium in the east, led to governmental, social, cultural, and material decline: "The classic tradition was shattered, because Islam destroyed the ancient unity of the Mediterranean" (185).

The future lay in the west with Gaul, Germany, and the Franks, whose center of gravity, blocked by Islam in the south, shifted northward away from the Mediterranean: "Before the 8th century what existed was the continuation of the Mediterranean economy. After the 8th century there was a complete break with this economy. The sea was closed. Commerce had disappeared. We perceive an Empire whose only wealth was the soil ... " (236). Charlemagne (Charles the Great) rose to power in this impoverished environment, worked out a liaison with the Roman Church, which had turned away from Byzantium, undertook mass conversion to Christianity of the lands under his sway, viewed his kingdom as a continuation of the Roman Empire, and held the Muslims back in the south without regaining access to the sea:

> The Empire of Charlemagne was the critical point of rupture by Islam of the European equilibrium. That he was able to realize the Empire was due ... to the fact that separation of East from West had limited the authority of the Pope to Western Europe; and ... to the fact that the conquest of Spain and Africa by Islam had made the king of the Franks the master of the Christian occident. It is therefore strictly correct to say that without Mohammed Charlemagne would have been inconceivable.
>
> (234)

Symptomatic of transformation by 800, when Charlemagne was crowned in the presence of the Pope, were the disappearance of cities, beginnings of feudal vassal-master relationships, markets replaced by local production and consumption, and Latin no longer a spoken language except in corrupted form among the clergy. The Middle Ages were launched.

The scope of the Pirenne Thesis is to explain the end of the classical world and the beginning of the Middle Ages, with analysis of what happened in between. Dissenters, critics, and revisionists quickly moved in, but the thesis lives on with modifications in light of fresh knowledge. Pirenne relied exclusively on written sources. Since his time, archeology has been able to test parts of the thesis, such as the decline of commerce and disappearance of specific trade items. The general thrust of criticism suggests that Pirenne underestimated decline of the Roman Empire to the eighth century, which was a condition fostering the rise of Islam, and overestimated the impact of Muslim invasions. Most telling, the breakdown of trade in the Mediterranean was less complete than he believed, judging by artifacts from archeological sites in the west.

Works by Pirenne

A History of Europe: From the End of the Roman World to the Beginnings of the Western States, trans. from the French by Bernard Miall (London: George Allen and Unwin, 1939). First published in 1936.

Medieval Cities: Their Origins and the Revival of Trade, trans. from the French by Frank D. Halsey (Princeton, New Jersey: Princeton University Press, 1952).

Mohammed and Charlemagne, trans. from the French by Bernard Miall (New York: Meridian Books, 1957). From the 1935 original.

Works about Pirenne

Brown, Elizabeth, A.R., "Henri Pirenne: A Biographical and Intellectual Study," *History and Theory*, 15:1 (1976): 66–76.

Cate, James L., "Henri Pirenne, 1862–1935," in S. William Halperin (ed.), *Some 20th Century Historians: Essays on Eminent Europeans* (Chicago, Illinois: University of Chicago Press, 1961).

Lyon, Bryce, *Henri Pirenne: A Biographical and Intellectual Study* (Ghent: E. Story-Scientia, 1974).

Useful references

Havighurst, Alfred F. (ed.), *The Pirenne Thesis: Analysis, Criticism, and Revision* (Boston, Massachusetts: Heath, 1958). See the essay by Norman H. Baynes.

Hodges, Richard and David Whitehouse, *Mohammed, Charlemagne, and the Origins of Europe: Archeology and the Pirenne Thesis* (London: Duckworth, 1983).

20. CIVILIZATION OF THE RENAISSANCE IN ITALY[5] (JACOB BURCKHARDT, 1818–1897)

Burckhardt was the son of a clergyman, studied theology for a time, and lost his faith before he was 20. History soon filled whatever void there was. His student days included time in Basel, Berlin, and Bonn to study history and art history, the latter an emerging field in which he became a major player with a book on Renaissance architecture. For most of his career he was content to be professor of art history and civilization at the University of Basel. He turned down offers of professorships at Tübingen and Berlin, the latter vacated by Leopold von Ranke on his retirement, with whom he had studied earlier.

In 1853 he published *The Age of Constantine the Great*, which examines the decay of Rome's empire and the success of Christianity.

The next couple of years were spent traveling in Italy to amass observations and materials for a renowned travel book, *The Cicerone: A Guide to Works of Art in Italy*, which displays unsurpassed knowledge of painting, sculpture, and architecture. It was his first trip to Italy at age 19, however, that first aroused an enduring affection for things Italian. He was unimpressed by the cultural depth of his time: "The age in which we live is loud enough in proclaiming the worth of culture, and especially of the culture of antiquity. But the enthusiastic devotion to it, the recognition that the need of it is the first and greatest of all needs, is nowhere to be found in such a degree as among the Florentines of the fifteenth and the early part of the sixteenth centuries" (161).

Although published 150 years ago, Burckhardt's account of the Renaissance, like Gibbon's work on the decline and fall of Rome, has not been rendered obsolete by later scholarship. The book is still widely read and regarded as authoritative and innovative. Its immediate significance is a focus on cultural history as a discipline within Western historiography. He explained that "sources" include the life of a people at all levels and not just what is found in books, and called for subject matter and perspectives beyond politics and warfare.

In the title, *Die Kultur der Renaissance in Italien*, the word "Kultur" does not quite mean "civilization" as the idea was understood in his time. It implies a breadth of approach that includes aesthetic, intellectual, and psychological as well as material, political, institutional, and social developments. In German idealist thought of the period, a distinction was drawn between *kultur* and *zivilization*, the former referring to "higher" activities of mind and spirit, the latter to "lesser" issues of material life, institutions and politics. It is not clear that Burckhardt was influenced by that school of thought. His intention was to bring a historical period, the Italian Renaissance between 1350 and 1550, into focus as a whole, although he confesses frankly the problems of doing so: "It is the most serious difficulty of the history of civilization that a great intellectual process must be broken up into single and often into what seem arbitrary categories, in order to be in any way intelligible" (3). The fragmented Italian peninsula was nevertheless a scene of unique, fundamental change that involved many intertwined features without which "the Renaissance would not have been the process of world-wide significance which it is, if its elements could be easily separated from one another" (128).

It is commonly believed and taught that recovery of classical learning and art is central to the Renaissance. Burckhardt argues it was only one of many developments: "We must insist upon it, as one of the chief propositions of this book, that it was not the revival of antiquity alone, but its union with the genius of the Italian people which achieved the conquest of the western world" (Ibid.). The essence of that conquest, proposed no less as inception of the modern world, was an enhancement of individual consciousness and a thirst for greatness at all levels of society and culture. In that sense, " ... the Italian Renaissance must be called the leader of modern ages" (416).

The text is divided into six parts: The State as a Work of Art, The Development of the Individual, The Revival of Antiquity, The Discovery of the World and of Man, Society and Festivals, Morality and Religion. Each part has from three to 11 sub-sections, such as War as a Work of Art, Personality, Propagators of Antiquity, The Natural Sciences in Italy, Equality of Men and Women, and General Spirit of Doubt. The style in translation from the German is lucid, eloquent without flourishes, and carries the reader along with confident ease. Scholarship is integrated into the text with frequent and specific allusions to sources, but without footnotes. Burckhardt displays measureless knowledge and experience throughout. He examined and mastered innumerable chronicles, treatises, histories, letters, poems, plays, and other documents. With regard to one instance of brutal conspiracy, he puts a reader in the chair with him by saying: "The way in which all of this is narrated by Caracciola and Porzio makes one's hair stand on end" (31).

He organizes a steady procession of despots, popes, cardinals, poets, scholars, artists, and others. His grasp of Italian poetry and drama is applied to the unique unfolding of "inward life" (229 ff). Unexpected but illuminating facts emerge on every page: "A constant invitation to parody was offered by the 'Divine Comedy,' and Lorenzo il Magnifico wrote the most admirable travesty in the style of the 'Inferno' (Simposio or I Beoni)" (119). Provocative judgments are delivered and justified without hesitation. Among Italian cities, for example, Florence and Venice were "of deep significance for the history of the human race" (51). Florence, made famous by its historians, Bruni, Varchi, Machiavelli, "deserves the name of the first modern State in the world" (61). Venice "at the end of the fifteenth century was the jewel-casket of the world" (51). It was "the birthplace of statistical science" and the state's "supreme objects were the enjoyment of life and power, the increase of inherited advantages, the creation of the most lucrative of industry, and the opening of new channels of commerce" (57–58).

For Burckhardt, "individualism" was pervasive during the Renaissance because conditions were right. Elsewhere in Europe the corporate institutions of feudalism held on even as centralized monarchies were being formed in England, France, Spain, and the Holy Roman Empire, while "Italy had shaken it off almost entirely" (4). The Papacy was strong enough to prevent Italian unity but not to achieve it. Between the great monarchies and the Papacy lay the rest of Italy: ... "a multitude of political units—republics and despots—in part of long standing, in part of recent origin, whose existence was founded simply on their power to maintain it. In them for the first time we detect the modern political spirit of Europe ... " (Ibid.). In this loose assemblage of Italian states, the idea of being a citizen of the world appeared first rather than in Voltaire's France or Pierre Bayle's Holland: "The cosmopolitanism which grew up in the most gifted circles is in itself a high stage of individualism" (103).

In this arena of competing despotisms, whose rulers struggled to survive and improve their advantages, the individual flourished. While servitude under the despots is a fact, it is also a fact that "political impotence does not hinder the different tendencies and manifestations of private life from thriving in the fullest vigour and variety ... a municipal freedom which did not cease to be considerable, and a Church, which unlike that of the Byzantine or of the Mohammedan world, was not identical with the State—all these conditions undoubtedly favoured the growth of individual thought, for which the necessary leisure was furnished by the cessation of party conflicts" (102). Religious indifference and unbelief were evident and tolerated so long as the Church, as opposed to its officers, was not attacked directly.

Whatever the excesses and shortcomings of tyrannies in Italy, ruled by men undeterred by religious or moral scruples, "a new fact appears in history—the State as the outcome of reflection and calculation, the State as a work of art" (4). The "artists" who fashioned states like sculptors working marble were men like Sigismondo Malatesta of Rimini, whose "unscrupulouness, impiety, military skill, and high culture have been seldom combined in one individual ... " (28). Relations of these despotisms to one another and to foreign governments were also a result of "reflection and careful adaptation" (71). Foreign relations were calculated works of art.

Warfare also became a work of art. Italy first used mercenary troops and exploited the new technology of firearms and advanced military engineering: "In Italy, earlier than elsewhere, there existed a comprehensive science and art of military affairs" (78). Generalship was valued for its own sake as a source of fame and power as well as conquest. The mercenary Condottiere who led troops were self-serving, practical, rational, and "unsentimental," respectful only of demonstrated personal merit. Individualism was promoted by despots and Condottiere who valued it in the men who served them, all of whom were gripped by a "desire to obtain the greatest satisfaction from a possibly very brief period of power and influence" (101).

These passions overwhelmed the Papacy with "simony, nepotism, prodigality, brigandage, and profligacy" (95). More was to be feared for Papal stability from the character of Popes than from the aggression of rival states. Cardinals paid huge sums for their hats, and were then murdered by some pontiffs so their assets could be confiscated: " ... all means of compulsion, whether temporal or spiritual were used without scruple for the most questionable ends, and to these all the other objects of the Apostolic See were made subordinate" (84). The result was nearly its extinction in the hands of Alexander VI and his menacing son, Cesare Borgia, a military-political prodigy who sought to protect Papal States at all costs, and feared by the Pope himself. As a sign of the times, Burckhardt includes their joint deaths as the result of carelessly ingesting a poisonous sweetmeat intended for a Cardinal (91). Salvation for the Papacy came with the Reformation.

Burckhardt sees everywhere "frightful evidence of boundless ambition and thirst after greatness, regardless of means or consequences ... a burning desire to achieve something great and memorable" (114–15). Recognition through personal effort alone required a freedom of individual action that was not confined to despots, Popes, and generals, for artists, poets, architects, scholars, and engineers were similarly motivated. He notes "the increase in the number of complete men during the fifteenth century ... When this impulse to the highest individual development ... had mastered all the elements of the culture of the age, then arose the 'all-sided man'—'*l'uomo universale*'—who belonged to Italy alone" (104). Leon Battista Alberti, athlete, horseman, scholar, musician, architect, painter, sculptor, poet, author, is a model of fully developed individualism that "entered into the whole life around him" (106–7). The ideal courtier (Cortigiano) described by Baldassare Castiglione, and lived by Alberti, "was regarded by the civilization of that age as the choicest flower" (287).

Women shared in this drive for personal achievement and distinction: "For, with education, the individuality of women in the upper classes was developed in the same way as that of men ... There was no question of 'women's rights' or female emancipation, simply because the thing itself was a matter of course" (103–4).

Burckhardt's argument that Renaissance individualism inaugurated the modern world is rivaled by other candidates for priority—notably the Reformation, which shattered Christian unity in the West, the "new science" of Copernicus, Kepler, Galileo, and Newton that replaced a teleological cosmology adapted to Christian theology with one based on self-sufficient mathematical laws, and the critical program of the Enlightenment that aimed to secularize thought and society. But no better argument for the Renaissance has been made than Burckhardt's. His attempt to widen historical perspective around a unifying theme was anticipated by Voltaire (see essay 15 in this volume), but without a corresponding depth of scholarship, integration of insight with narrative, and firm powers of judgment.

Works by Burckhardt

On History and Historians, trans. by Harry Zohn, intro. by H.R. Trevor-Roper (New York: Harper and Row, 1958).

The Architecture of the Italian Renaissance, rev. and ed. by Peter Murray, trans. by James Palmes (Chicago: University of Chicago Press, 1985).

The Civilization of the Renaissance in Italy, trans. from the German by S.G.C. Middlemore, intro. by Hajo Holborn (New York: The Modern Library, 1954). *Die Cultur der Renaissance in Italien* was first published in 1860.

Works about Burckhardt

Hinde, John R., *Jacob Burckhardt and the Crisis of Modernity* (Montreal & Kingston: McGill-Queens University Press, 2000).

Gilbert, Felix, *History: Politics or Culture. Reflections on Ranke and Burckhardt* (Princeton, New Jersey: Princeton University Press, 1990).

Useful references

Gossman, Lionel, *Basel in the Age of Burckhardt: A Study in Unseasonable Ideas* (Chicago, Illinois: University of Chicago Press, 2000).

21. POPULAR ACCOUNT OF DISCOVERIES AT NINEVEH (AUSTEN HENRY LAYARD, 1817–1894)

Layard dominated the "heroic" phase of nineteenth century Assyrian archeology. He was a many-sided man—adventurer, diplomat, connoisseur of art, lively writer, Member of Parliament, and tireless archeologist. An imaginative amateur seized with a passion for lost civilizations, he learned what he needed to know along the way. He was born in Paris and grew up in Florence amidst art treasures.

He spoke fluent French and Italian. As a youth he dreamed of traveling to the Middle East in search of vanished peoples. He schooled himself in surveying, map making and started learning rudiments of Middle Eastern languages. In 1836 he became a lawyer and went to work in a solicitor's office, a stuffy profession that did not last long for such a restless man. By 1840 he was in Mesopotamia at Mosul on the Tigris River with a companion climbing over drab earthen mounds that concealed ancient Nineveh. Resources amounted to little more than back packs.

The 1840s brought Assyria to light with intoxicating speed. While Layard tunneled into the giant mounds, Henry Rawlinson was learning to read ancient Mesopotamian languages written in the wedge-like script called cuneiform. The discoveries came faster than European scholars could absorb them. The unearthing of Assyria pushed the history and achievements of Mesopotamian civilization back centuries before the Greeks and biblical times. Before Layard's efforts, Assyria was barely known. Artifacts were few. The British Museum had "the principal, and indeed almost only, collection of Assyrian antiquities in Europe. A case scarcely three feet square enclosed all that remained, not only of the great city, Nineveh, but of Babylon itself! Other museums in Europe contained a few cylinders and gems ... but they were not classified, nor could it be determined to what exact epoch they belonged. Of Assyrian art nothing was known. The architecture of Nineveh and Babylon was a matter of speculation ... " (xi).

Assyrian civilization lasted from the twelfth century to 609 B.C. and was one of the last great Mesopotamian empires. Conquests of Assyrian kings were notably cruel and ruthless. Their temperament and behavior are suggested visually by brutal war and hunting scenes in surviving bas reliefs. Kings built magnificent palaces decorated with sculptural scenes of the highest quality. Discovery of a royal library at Nineveh unearthed thousands of baked clay cuneiform tablets that supplied source material for what is known about Mesopotamian civilization in general and the Assyrians in particular.

Moving northward along the Tigris River from Ashur, the first capital and an Assyrian god, were successive capitals of Nimrud, Nineveh, and Khorsabad. Layard excavated at the Assyrian city of Nimrud from 1845 to 1847 and 1849 to 1851. Nimrud is located in upper Mesopotamia near the conjunction of the Tigris and Greater Zab Rivers. He worked later at Nineveh, whose site is across the Tigris from Mosul. The publications that flowed from Layard's eight years of excavation included hundreds of drawings he made on the spot.

In the absence of photography, his skill executing detailed sketches from life not only preserved items that later decayed or were lost but offered his reading public a feast of visual marvels from remote antiquity.

Layard's popular account, with the word "Nineveh" in its title, actually relates excavations mostly at Nimrud. The word "popular" is a bit misleading. Thirteen chapters are packed with detail about sites, excavations, finds, preservation, shipment abroad, physical, political, other obstacles faced by Layard, and some 72 finely drawn illustrations. He discusses the cuneiform script in an introduction. His narrative explains that archeology in Mesopotamia was a perilous business. The region was part of the Ottoman Empire, and Turkish rule was widely resented. For a while Layard's efforts were thwarted by the corrupt, devious governor of Mosul, who was later dismissed and imprisoned for his misdeeds. Layard started working at Nimrud during an uprising against the tyrant. The countryside was volatile, badly policed, and unsafe for travelers. Food and shelter were mediocre. In summer the heat, well over a hundred degrees, sapped strength, will, and undermined health.

Yet the uninviting landscape touched Layard as philosopher and discoverer:

> ... the stern shapeless mound rising like a hill from the scorched plain, the fragments of pottery, and the stupendous mass of brickwork occasionally laid bare by the winter rains ... The scene around is worthy of the ruin he is contemplating; desolation meets desolation: a feeling of awe succumbs to wonder; for there is nothing to relieve the mind, to lead to hope, or to tell what has gone by. These huge mounds of Assyria made a deeper impression upon me, gave rise to more serious thoughts and more earnest reflection than the temples of Balbec and the theatres of Ionia.
>
> (5)

He was adept at making friends and won the support of a local sheikh, who provided him with hospitality and a small workforce: "I had slept little during the night. The hovel in which we had taken shelter, and its inmates, did not invite slumber; but such scenes and companions were not new to me; they could have been forgotten, had my brain been less excited. Hopes, long cherished, were now to be realized, or were to end in disappointment. Visions of palaces under-ground, of gigantic monsters, of sculptured figures, and endless inscriptions floated before me" (15). These dreams were pursued in rickety accommodations shared with scorpions and other vermin.

Morning came and the ruins of Nimrud beckoned:

> The lofty cone and broad mound of Nimroud (*sic*) broke like a distant mountain on the morning sky ... The eye wandered over a parched and barren waste, across which occasionally swept the whirlwind, dragging with it a cloud of sand ... Twenty minutes brought us to the principal mound ... Broken pottery and fragments of bricks, both inscribed with the cuneiform character, were strewn on all sides. The Arabs watched my motions as I wandered to and fro, and observed with surprise the objects I had collected. They joined ... in the search, and brought me handfuls of rubbish, amongst which I found with joy the fragment of a bas-relief ... Convinced from this discovery that sculptured remains must still exist in some part of the mound, I sought for a place where excavation might commence with a prospect of success. Awad [Layard's Arab helper] led me to a piece of alabaster which appeared above the soil. We could not remove it, and on digging downward, it proved to be the upper part of a large slab. I ordered all the men to work around it, and they shortly uncovered a second slab. Continuing in the same line, we came upon a third; and in the course of the morning, discovered ten more, the whole forming a square, with a slab missing at one corner. It was evident that we had entered a chamber and that the gap was its entrance.
>
> (16)

The slabs that marked off chambers and halls were composed of relatively soft alabaster and gypsum, abundant types of stone in Mesopotamia perfect for carving images and inscriptions.

In this way, digging channels and shafts into the mounds, always cautious to find the right path and preserve what was found, Layard identified palaces and other dwellings decorated with magnificent bas-reliefs of court scenes, hunting forays, and sieges of cities, with massive sculptured figures of winged lions and bulls with human heads at the doorways: "The palaces and temples appear to have been at the same time public monuments, in which were preserved the records or archives of the nation, carved in stone. In them were represented in sculpture the exploits of the kings, and the forms of the divinities; whilst the history of the people, and invocations to their gods, were inscribed in written characters upon the walls" (343). Layard's imagination was stirred by the winged lions and bulls: "I need to contemplate for hours these mysterious emblems, and muse over their intent and history. What more noble forms could have ushered the people into the temple of their gods? What more sublime images could have been borrowed from nature, by men who sought, unaided by the light of revealed religion, to embody their wisdom, power, and ubiquity of a Supreme Being? They could find no better type of intellect and knowledge than the head of the man; of strength, than the body of the lion; of ubiquity, than the wings of the bird" (52).

Much of the sculpture Layard recovered went to England. Moving it was a feat with intimations of disaster. The works had to be extracted safely from the ruins, moved by cart to the Tigris, loaded on makeshift rafts for a six-hundred-mile trip down the river to Basra, and reloaded on an ocean going ship. Something might have gone wrong each step of the way, as with a contemporary French effort to move antiquities that was overtaken by bandits, the boats plundered and destroyed, and antiquities lost in the Tigris: "With the help of levers of wood, and by digging away the wall of sun-dried bricks, I was able to move the sculptures into the centre of the trenches ... They were then packed and transported from the mound upon rude buffalo carts ... to the river, where they were placed upon a raft constructed of inflated skins and beams of poplar wood ... The sculptures sent home ... formed the first collection exhibited to the public in the British Museum" (101).

While digging into mounds along the Tigris, his humanity was challenged to become a champion of Arab women: "When I first employed the Arabs, the women were sorely ill-treated, and subjected to great hardships. I endeavored to introduce some reform into their domestic arrangements, and punished severely those who inflicted corporal chastisement on their wives. In a short time the number of domestic quarrels was greatly reduced, and the women, who were at first afraid to complain of their husbands, now boldly appealed to me for protection" (235). The same women were afraid of what would befall them when his protective hand was removed.

Layard's place in historiography is secure. He unveiled a lost civilization and made it possible to write a history of Assyria from inscriptions, inscribed clay tablets, and varied archeological remains where before there had been nothing but material fragments and speculation.

Works by Layard

Discoveries among the Ruins of Nineveh and Babylon (New York: Harper, 1856).
Inscriptions in the Cuneiform Character from Assyrian Monuments (London: Harrison and Sons, 1851).

Monuments of Nineveh: From Drawings Made on the Spot (London: John Murray, 1853).
Popular Account of Discoveries at Nineveh (London: John Murray, 1851).

Works about Layard

Brackman, Arnold C., *The Luck of Nineveh: Archeology's Great Adventure* (New York: McGraw Hill, 1978).
Kubie, Nora B, *Road to Nineveh: The Adventures and Excavations of Sir Austen Henry Layard* (Garden City, New York: Doubleday, 1964).
Larsen, Mogens T., *The Conquest of Assyria* (London: Routledge, 1996).

Useful references

Gadd, C.J., *The Stones of Assyria* (London: Chatto and Windus, 1936), pp. 4–12.
Reade, Julian, *Assyrian Sculpture* (London: British Museum, 1983).

22. HISTORY OF THE RISE AND INFLUENCE OF THE SPIRIT OF RATIONALISM IN EUROPE[6] (WILLIAM LECKY, 1838–1903)

Lecky was born near Dublin and educated at Cheltenham College, which he disliked intensely, and Trinity College, Dublin, where he took a B.A. in 1859 and an M.A. in 1863. He was much admired in school as an orator. A poor student indifferent to academic routine, he was inclined to read widely on his own, which included history, philosophy, science, theology, and the arts. Initially he studied to become a priest in Ireland's Protestant Church, but changed his mind and turned to history. In 1871 he married a lady-in-waiting to Queen Sophia of the Netherlands and enjoyed a long, contented union. Trinity later honored him with an LL.D and a statue after his death. Honorary degrees were also forthcoming from Oxford and Cambridge in acknowledgment of his stature as a historian. In 1902 he was appointed to the Order of Merit, which had just been established by the king.

Lecky's father, a wealthy landowner, left an inheritance that made him self-sufficient. He was able to indulge three passions—travel, reading, and writing. Italy was his favorite place, attested by a sophisticated knowledge of Italian art and architecture in *The Spirit of Rationalism*, but he also sought intellectual refuge in "half the libraries of Europe." He developed an acute sensitivity to literary style and took great pains to perfect it in his works. Lecky believed the average person has no idea how difficult it is to write memorably and well—how false starts must be resisted, how a careless choice of words can clarify or ruin a meaning, how an unfolding text might embody or muddle a thought. He wrote with modest eloquence and could frame an apt saying as well: "Calumny is the homage which dogmatism has ever paid to conscience" (II: 263).

Successful in politics as well as authorship, he represented Dublin University in Parliament. He had a lifelong interest in Irish history, culture, and public affairs, and several volumes of his English history in the eighteenth century are a history Ireland later published separately. Lecky was a moderate liberal who believed in progress, reason, and achievements of the nineteenth century. He was suspicious of democracy, whose great danger was to stress equality over liberty, the worst outcome being the tyranny of majority vote. He anticipated the corruption of public life in unstable democracies by demagogues who climb to power through popular suffrage. He rejected socialism as a primitive type of society; control of property by the state is despotism.

Two early books on Irish leaders of public opinion and religious tendencies of the time failed to take off. His first undisputed success was the book on rationalism, which he finished at the remarkable age of 27. It made him famous and long continued to be influential, with no less than 20 printings. *The Rise of Rationalism* develops two themes: superstition in decline as a result of rational, scientific inquiry, and emergence of a secular industrial spirit at the expense of clergy and military aristocracies. Progress in Europe, by which he means liberty and prosperity, became possible because a constricting theological view of the world was gradually nullified.

Three chapters of volume 1 address decline of the miraculous with respect to magic, witchcraft, and miracles. The fourth chapter isolates conditions that favor persecution, the most important being a claim to "exclusive salvation" that denies "the spirit of truth ... that frame of mind in which men who acknowledge their own fallibility, and who desire above all things to discover what is true, should adjudicate between conflicting arguments ... For the object of the persecutor is to suppress one portion of the elements of a discussion ... to prevent that freedom of enquiry which is the sole method we possess of arriving at truth" (II: 89–90).

The three chapters of volume 2 discuss the history of persecution; secularization of politics, which occurs by removing religion from government, "expelling theology successively from all its political strongholds," thus diminishing its hold on the mind (II: 135); and influences of the "industrial spirit" upon rationalism: "For the love of wealth and the love of knowledge are the two main agents of human progress ... although the former is a far less noble passion than the latter ... It has produced all trade, all industry, and all material luxuries of civilization, and has ... proved the most powerful incentive to intellectual pursuits" (II: 278).

The guiding question for Lecky is how to explain a respect for reason in his own age that would have been incomprehensible and blasphemous in a previous age. He rests his case on "climates of opinion," a phrase taken from the seventeenth-century writer Joseph Glanville (see essay 38 in this volume): " ... the success of any opinion depended much less upon the force of its arguments, or upon the ability of its advocates, than upon the predisposition of society to receive it, and that predisposition resulted from the intellectual type of the age" (I: x). Lecky wants to understand and explain how a theological climate of opinion surrendered to one that is rational. The consequences for liberty were momentous for Europe, including the eventual formal abolition of slavery and torture.

With regard to witchcraft and magic, the major influence on popular opinion was the dominant religion:

> The Church of Rome proclaimed in every way that was in her power the reality and continued existence of the crime. She strained every nerve to stimulate the persecution. She taught by all her organs that to spare a witch was a direct insult to the Almighty, and to her ceaseless exertions is to be attributed by far the greater proportion of the blood that was shed ... Ecclesiastical tribunals condemned thousands to death, and countless bishops exerted all their influence to multiply the victims.
>
> (I: 32)

After centuries of persecutions for witchcraft, beliefs changed: " ... men came gradually to disbelieve in witchcraft, because they came gradually to look upon it as absurd; and that this new tone of thought appeared, first of all, in those who were least subject to theological influences, and soon spread through the educated laity, and last of all took possession of the clergy" (I: 37).

The shift in opinion was a process of secularization, a departure from the unworldly to the worldly. Lecky is impressed by the attraction of Renaissance artists to sensual beauty, including the nude body, rather than ascetic spirituality of the Middle Ages: "There can be no doubt that the secularization of art was due to the general tone of thought that had been produced in Europe" (I: 252). The focus of probabilities changed: "In the middle ages, and in the sixteenth and the beginning of the seventeenth century, the measure of probability was essentially theological. Men seemed to breathe an atmosphere that was entirely unsecular ... The predisposition to believe in the miraculous was so great, that it constructed ... this vast and complicated system of witchcraft" (I: 101).

Lecky illustrates this climate of belief with Jean Bodin in the sixteenth century (see essay 12 in this volume). After citing him as "the ablest man who had then arisen in France," he points out that Bodin's arguments for witchcraft rest solidly on unquestioning appeals to authority, "which the author deemed on this subject so unanimous and so conclusive, that it was scarcely possible for any sane man to resist it" (I: 107–8). The one thinker who broke free of this belief late in the same century was Michel de Montaigne: "The bent and character of his mind led him to believe that witchcraft was grossly improbable. He was the first great representative of the modern secular and rationalistic spirit" (I: 114).

Miracles of the Church suffered much the same fate as the climate of opinion changed:

> When it began, Christianity was regarded as a system entirely beyond the range and scope of human reason; it was impious to question; it was impious to examine; it was impious to discriminate ... Miracles of every order and degree of magnitude were flashing forth incessantly from all its parts. They excited no skepticism and surprise. The miraculous element pervaded all literature, explained all difficulties, consecrated all doctrines. Every unusual phenomenon was immediately referred to a supernatural agency ...

After witchcraft "passed into the region of fables," miracles became objects of disbelief: "The countless miracles that were once associated with every holy relic and with every village shrine have rapidly and silently disappeared. Year by year the incredulity became more manifest even where the theological profession was unchanged" (I: 194–95). Lecky reviews with graceful aplomb the new sciences of astronomy, physics, chemistry, and geology, even biblical criticism, and their damaging effects on supernatural belief. What science and its standards of objectivity have done is to foster "a gradual substitution of the conception of law for that of supernatural intervention" (I: 286).

In nineteenth-century historiography, Lecky focused history in directions other than traditional politics and diplomacy. His book on rationalism illustrated the power of ideas to a large, appreciative audience, including other historians. He was scrupulous about sources, asked important questions, marshaled effectively a huge fund of knowledge, and wrote with clarity and verve. Is there more one could ask of a historian?

Works by Lecky

A History of England during the Eighteenth Century, 8 vols. (London: Longmans, Green, 1879–90). The title should read *A History of England and Ireland*.

A History of the Rise and Influence of the Spirit of Rationalism in Europe, intro. by C. Wright Mills (New York: G. Braziller, 1955). First published in 1866 in two volumes.

Democracy and Liberty, 2 vols. (London: Longmans, Green, 1896).

History of European Morals from Augustus to Charlemagne, 2 vols. (London: Longmans, Green, 1869).

Works about Lecky

Auchmuty, James J., *Lecky: A Biographical and Critical Essay* (London: Longmans, Green, 1945).

van Dedem, Elizabeth, *A Memoir of the Rt. Hon. W. E. H. Lecky, M. P. O. M.* (London: Longmans, Green, 1910). A remembrance by Lecky's wife.

Useful references

Bowles, John, *Politics and Opinion in the Nineteenth Century: An Historical Introduction* (New York: Oxford University Press, 1954), pp. 241–247.

Thompson, James Westfall, *A History of Historical Writing: The Eighteenth and Nineteenth Centuries*, vol. 2 (New York: Macmillan, 1942), pp. 333–335.

23. THE LIFE OF JESUS CRITICALLY EXAMINED[7] (DAVID FRIEDRICH STRAUSS, 1808–1874)

Strauss was born in the German state of Wurttemburg. By age 12 he was immersed in classical studies and textual criticism at an evangelical seminary, attended the University of Tübingen to study theology in 1825, and in 1830 took a post teaching Latin, Hebrew, and history at two other seminaries. His brief, versatile teaching career also included logic, metaphysics, and history of ethics. He gave up those jobs in 1835 to finish *The Life of Jesus* which had been underway the previous five years and was completed at the precocious age of 27. The time and energy given to such intensive scholarship in due time probably cost him his marriage and family.

A scandal was ignited when the first edition of Strauss's book appeared in 1835. Its colossal proportions and detailed scholarship stripped the miraculous from Jesus's ministry, denied that he was divine, showed that a credible "biography" from birth to death is impossible, and set historical criticism of the gospel narratives on a modern path. A hundred years later the result was neglect of the historical Jesus for the Christ of faith and the Church. Theologians like Rudolph Bultmann argued that Jesus and Christianity must be "demythologized" to thrive in the modern world. Albert Schweitzer remarked that the quest for the historical Jesus had gone through two phases—pre-Strauss and post-Strauss.

Invited on the strength of published work to a professorship at the University of Zurich, he was forced to withdraw because of the uproar over his *Life of Jesus*. A public referendum was held that rejected his appointment, but the university pensioned him for life because he had already accepted the offer. Thereafter he never secured a position and became an independent writer undeterred by ecclesiastical and academic constraints and helped along in journalism by his straightforward prose style. He aroused such anger and hostility because his inquiries tore away a thick curtain of mostly unquestioning reverence for Jesus, the central figure of Christianity depicted in the Gospels as a supernatural being with miracle-working powers.

The Life of Jesus passed through four editions. The issue in all four is the historicity of Jesus's early life and later ministry as related in the Gospels. The first edition was the most radical and uncompromising, essentially a view of the Gospels as narratives reliant on myth. Editions two and three responded to criticisms and made compromises that diminished the shock of his initial conclusions. The fourth edition retained some reservations made in two and three but returned to core elements of the first edition. One reviewer of this formidable work condemned it as straight from hell. Every story, event, and pronouncement in the Gospels is examined with care, including, for example, how long Jesus hung on the cross and the nature of the spear thrust into his side (697 ff). The work is heavy with references and discussions of previous scholarship. The Old Testament is quoted throughout in Hebrew and the New Testament in Greek.

Strauss had plenty of help from other scholars. Early nineteenth-century German philologists and historians, notably at the University of Tübingen, accelerated critical scrutiny of the gospels, and laid groundwork for Strauss to analyze of them as myth and legend rather than history. Major figures like Johann Eichhorn, Heinrich Paulus, and Ferdinand Bauer sought naturalistic explanations for miraculous occurrences in the Gospels. They considered "the miraculous in the sacred history as a drapery which needs only to be drawn aside, in order to disclose the pure historic form" (50). Strauss used their work but differed from them by introducing the idea of myth in place of either guaranteed supernatural truth or purely naturalistic explanations. He argued also that myth and history interpenetrate.

Major leaps for New Testament criticism came in the late eighteenth and early nineteenth centuries. Lower Criticism sought to clarify what a document said before alterations were made by scribes and others either by mistake or intent. Higher Criticism aimed to identify when and where a document originated, who wrote it and for whom, what sources were used, what influences affected its composition, and what its intended message was. The two types of criticism established that sacred texts are vulnerable to change, which includes dubious authorship and textual corruption over time by careless copyists, and interpolations of group and individual bias.

Strauss was a preeminent higher critic. He demonstrated more fully than anyone else that sacred documents are vulnerable to historical analysis no different from that applied by Valla to *The Donation of Constantine* (see essay 11 in this volume). The gospel narratives are compared to reveal inconsistencies, omissions, contradictions, obscurities, and improbabilities. When narratives are shared, as in the three synoptic gospels, they may not appear in all three, vary in detail, or contradict one another. Stories that appear in John are absent from the other three, and so on.

In the midst of relieving the Gospels of their supernatural content, Strauss remained a Christian and even aspired to teach and write about theology, although his view of Jesus was remote from that of orthodox believers. Following the philosopher Georg Hegel, he viewed Christianity as a phase of the Absolute unfolding itself in time. The Hegelian doctrine was that the real is rational, the rational real, so he argues that supernatural claims in scripture must be judged by the universal standard of natural law.

He explains that God relates to the world as a whole through established regularities long known to the modern mind, not through piecemeal interventions and marvels: "The supernaturalists indeed claim an exception from this type on behalf of biblical history; a presupposition which is inadmissible from our point of view, according to which the same laws ... are supreme in every sphere of being and action, and therefore every narrative which offends against these laws, is to be recognized as so far unhistorical" (80). Wherever the miraculous appears in a document, it may be taken as borrowed from tradition or as a myth formed in the minds of believers from elements of tradition.

He lays out standards for detecting mythical, or unhistorical, elements, examines the birth, childhood, and early events in Jesus's life, his public life, and his passion, death, and resurrection. He concludes that all three phases are riddled with myths and legends introduced by New Testament authors to win converts and justify Jesus as the promised Messiah. If a miraculous event has a probable naturalistic explanation, he assesses the extent to which it might be historical, and usually reaches a negative conclusion. For example, the dead might have been raised by Jesus because they were not really dead and the incident subsequently became a myth.

While rejecting mythical and miraculous elements in the Gospels, Strauss also doubts their historic form and content: "That is to say, what is the precise boundary line between the historical and the unhistorical?—the most difficult question in the whole province of criticism" (90). He was not optimistic that such precision can be attained: "The boundary line between the historical and unhistorical, in records, in which as in our Gospels the latter element is incorporated, will ever remain fluctuating and unsusceptible of precise attainment" (91).

Nevertheless, there are credible standards of judgment. First, any example of the miraculous "is not history" and must be regarded as "fiction, the product of the particular mental tendency of a certain community ... That an account is not historical—that the matter related could not have taken place in the manner described is evident ... when the narration is irreconcilable with the known and universal laws which govern the course of events" (87–88). So much for apparitions, voices from heaven, miracles, and prophecies. Second, an account is historical if: " ... it is not inconsistent with itself, nor in contradiction with itself ... when one account affirms what another denies" (88). In the Gospels, myth not only trumps historical fact, it does so inconsistently from one narrative to the next.

Legends are another matter. They emerge from long traditions in which miraculous occurrences were expected. The idea of a Messiah had been elaborated long before the appearance of Jesus. Legends of a Messiah were embedded in people's minds: "Thus many of the legends respecting him had not to be newly invented; they already existed in the popular hope of the Messiah, having been mostly derived with modifications from the Old Testament, and had merely to be transferred to Jesus, and accommodated to his character and doctrines" (84). Strauss does not ask why messianic expectations were associated with Jesus and not with anyone else. The transfiguration of Jesus, "the sun-like splendor of the countenance ... , and the bright luster of his clothes," before his entrance into Jerusalem illustrates a multiple legendary origin: " ... to the Hebrew imagination, the beautiful, the majestic, is the luminous ... But especially in the Messiah himself, it was expected that there would be a splendour which would correspond to that of Moses ... " (543–44).

He explains the formation and nature of myth and its applications to religious belief in three parts. First, the evangelical myth, "a narrative relating directly or indirectly to Jesus, which may be considered not as the expression of a fact, but as the product of an idea of his earliest followers, such a narrative being mythical in proportion as it exhibits this character". Second, the pure myth, which has two sources: " ... the Messianic ideas and expectations that preceded Jesus in minds of Jews in Palestine, and the impression made on them, with respect to Messianic lore, by his personality, words, and actions." Third, the historical myth: " ... a definite individual fact which has been seized upon by religious enthusiasm, and twined around with mythical conceptions culled from the idea of the Christ. The fact is perhaps a saying of Jesus such as that concerning 'fishers of men', or the barren fig tree which now appear in the Gospels transmuted into marvelous histories" (86–87).

He compares biblical stories with Indian and Greek myths: " ... the biblical history *might* be true, sooner than the Indian or Grecian fables; not in the least on this account it *must* be true, and can contain nothing fictitious" (76). At issue are miracles associated with Jesus's birth, for example, angelic voices (unheard in Jerusalem) and the star leading magi to the manger (south rather than east to west), miracles performed by Jesus, which include cures (ten lepers and a paralytic unable to walk), control of nature (converting water into wine and walking on water), exorcisms (restoring speech to a mute man possessed by a demon), raising Lazarus from the dead after four days, and miracles within him such as the "transfiguration" in a blaze of light and ascension on the mountain. All of these marvels are for Strauss "an ascending ladder of miracles ... a gradation in inconceivability" (486).

Thus, historicity of the Gospels is dismissed. The content is judged as esthetic and theological poetry whose purpose was to attract Jewish and Greek audiences. Obviously the Evangelists, gospel authors, succeeded without providing indisputable historical evidence for the life and teachings of Jesus. The gospel narratives, laced as they are with miracles and apocalyptic expectations of the world's end, express a human desire to break free of history and the world into a realm of timeless being. No where is this desire more evident than in accounts of resurrection and ascension to paradise.

Strauss concludes "that in all the evangelical accounts of these first tidings of the Resurrection, we have before us nothing more than traditional reports." The Resurrection was a mythical expectation in the minds of believers, not a literal historical fact (718). Moreover, the Ascension of Jesus to heaven on a cloud was an extension by gospel writers of the legend that the Messiah would descend on a cloud: " ... as Jesus will at some future time return from heaven in the clouds, so he must surely have departed thither in the same manner" (755). Once again, myth formed in a collective mind by tradition is at work rather than fact or fabrication.

Strauss has been criticized for insufficient attention to the manuscript tradition of the Gospels, but the reservation is beside the mark because his focus was on internal rather than external criticism. His consistent method was analysis of gospel stories from both mythical and naturalistic perspectives. While supernaturalism is rejected, so is naked rationalism. He accounts for supernaturalism as a collective psychology of uncritical belief and expectation wedded to tradition, which is all that could be expected of the world Jesus lived in.

Works by Strauss

Controversies on the Justification of my Writing on the Life of Jesus (*Streitschriften zur Verteidigung miener Schrift über das Leben Jesu*), 1837. Not available in translation.

The Christ of Belief and the Jesus of History (*Der Christus des Glaubens und der Jesus der Geschichte*), 1865. Not available in translation.

The Life of Jesus Critically Examined, trans. from the fourth German edition by George Eliot, ed. and intro. by Peter C. Hodgson (Philadelphia: Fortress Press, 1972). The fourth edition appeared in 1840 and was translated in 1846. The German title: *Leben Jesu* (*kritisch bearbeitet*).

Works about Strauss

Barth, Karl, *Protestant Thought from Rousseau to Ritschl*, trans. from German by Brian Cozens (New York: Harper, 1959). Eleven chapters are translated. Original title: *Die protestantische Theologie im 19. Jahrhundert*.

Schweitzer, Albert, *The Quest for the Historical Jesus: A Critical Study of its Progress from Reimarus to Wrede* (London: A. and C. Black, 1910).

Willey, Basil, *Nineteenth Century Studies: Coleridge to Matthew Arnold* (New York: Harper Torchbook, 1966), Chapter 8.

Useful references

Sanders, E.P., *The Historical Figure of Jesus* (London: Allen Lane, The Penguin Press, 1993).

Schillebeeckx, Edward, *Jesus: An Experiment in Christology*, trans. from Dutch by Hubert Hoskins (New York Vintage Books, 1981).

Thompson, James Westfall, *A History of Historical Writing: The Eighteenth and Nineteenth Centuries*, Vol. 2 (New York: Macmillan, 1942), pp. 561–62, where a number of sources on Strauss are cited in an extensive note.

24. INAUGURAL LECTURE ON THE STUDY OF HISTORY[8] (JOHN DALBERG-ACTON, 1834–1902)

Acton was appointed Regius Professor of Modern History at Cambridge University in 1895, England's most coveted academic post. He marked the event with a lecture on the unity of modern history: " ... I describe as modern history that which began four hundred years ago, which is marked off by an evident and intelligible line from the time immediately preceding, and displays in its course specific and distinctive characteristics of its own ... it founded a new order of things, under a law of innovation, sapping the ancient reign of continuity" (27). For 30 years before the Cambridge honor, his career was a paradox—a Catholic out of favor with the hierarchy, an admired scholar without academic position until late in life, a historian with idiosyncratic views on how history should be done, a man renowned but unconnected to any school of historiography.

Born in Naples, his German-English parentage and cosmopolitan circle of relatives provided residences, travel, and connections in Italy, England, France, and Germany. His father was a Baronet with lands in Shropshire. When the title was passed on, Acton sat in the House of Lords as the Eighth Baronet. Denied entrance to English universities because of his religion, and dissatisfied with standards at his English school, higher education was pursued at the University of Munich under the guidance of Ignaz von Döllinger, an eminent Catholic priest, intellectual, historian, and political liberal, who attracted him to scholarship and history: "History compels us to fasten on abiding issues and rescues us from the temporary and transient" (26).

He lived in a cultural atmosphere dominated by widespread historical activity and perspectives that extended and deepened knowledge of religion, ideas, institutions, politics, and diplomacy. Great historians of Germany (Ranke, Mommsen), England (Carlyle, Macaulay), and France (Michelet, Renan) cultivated new realms of human experience. Modern history as a theme for his lecture looked from present into the past and into the future: " ... it is a narrative told of ourselves, the record of a life which is our own, of efforts not yet abandoned to repose, of problems that still entangle the feet and vex the hearts of men" (32).

The problematic value of Acton's 27-page *Inaugural Lecture* is a broad hint of what history had accomplished and was expected to accomplish on the brink of a new century: " ... if we lower our standard in history, we cannot uphold it in Church or State" (52). The lecture was delivered near the close of a century marked by prodigious historical research and publication: "Every country opens its archives and invites us to penetrate the mysteries of State" (31). With no lack of material for exploring the past, " ... there is more fear of drowning than of drought" (39). The address is not history but rather an assessment of history.

Acton may be taken as a touchstone for the place of history in European civilization at the end of the nineteenth century. Hailed as the most learned man of his time, he was fluent in English, French, German, and Italian. He knew Greek and Latin as well. A colleague believed he might have written all 12 volumes of the *Cambridge Modern History* by himself. As a youth he began accumulating what eventually became a vast, annotated library of some 60,000 volumes. But amidst the erudition he was also a deep thinker who believed the study of history "makes us wiser, without producing books, and gives us the gift of historical thinking, which is better than historical learning" (32).

He intended to write a history of liberty, but wrote neither that book nor any other. He excelled at lectures and essays, which have a place in historiography like those of Thomas Carlyle. Acton developed as an example of the burden historical learning can become for historical writing. He left behind a trove of notes but no plans. Research was constant but writing neglected because materials were too imperfect for him. A speculation is that failure to write was a consequence of knowing too much, although he published in the *English Historical Review*, which he founded. His Cambridge appointment included an invitation to plan and edit the *Cambridge Modern History*, to which he devoted the last five working years of his life, but never completed his own intended contributions. The first of 12 volumes was not even out when he died.

He viewed advances in historical knowledge and understanding as a defining feature of the modern world. As historian he was also a historicist, although he thought the word itself "depressing," for whom knowledge of the past was indispensable to inform and shape the present: "In this epoch of full-grown history men have not acquiesced in the given conditions of their lives. Taking little for granted they have sought to know the ground they stand on, and the road they travel, and the reason why. Over them, therefore, the historian has obtained an increasing ascendency" (29). Yet historicism was bothersome because it implied that history is the sole reference point for understanding and judgment about the human condition. Acton believed there is a reality outside history. Moreover, his idea of liberalism pointed to the future.

Learning is a necessary but not a sufficient condition for historical writing: "For our purpose, the main thing to learn is not the art of accumulating material, but the sublimer art of investigating it, of discerning truth from falsehood and certainty from doubt. It is by solidity of criticism more than by the plenitude of erudition that the study of history strengthens and straightens and extends the mind" (39). The model of such investigation is science. Scientists have been indispensable to history, as Ranke demonstrated: "For they can show how to test proof, how to secure fullness and soundness in induction, and how to restrain and to employ with safety hypotheses and analogy. It is they who hold the secret of the mysterious property of the mind by which error ministers to truth, and truth slowly but irrevocably prevails" (45). It turns out in human experience that " ... history made and history making are scientifically inseparable and separately unmeaning" (25).

His oft quoted maxim that "power tends to corrupt and absolute power corrupts absolutely" emerged from lifelong resistance to any unrestrained, centralized authority, which he believed, on historical grounds, squashes conscience and eclipses liberty. The objection applied to the papacy as well as to civil government. As a believing Catholic, he saw no conflict between liberty, science, and religion, including evolution and higher Biblical criticism, a view that brought him into tension and conflict with ecclesiastical authorities.

His impartiality as editor was expressed as a guideline that no author's religion or politics should mar a single page: " ... a historian is seen at his best when he does not appear" (36). While the historian is best kept out of sight in some respects, ethical judgment is not among them. The past teems with evils that invite exposure and condemnation. History itself is noncommittal about acts of murder, treachery, wanton cruelty, and bad motive: Only a historian can fill the gap: " ... to learn from undisguised and genuine records to look with remorse upon the past ... " (52).

Ranke, who professed impartiality in his dictum that all eras are equal in the eyes of God, was Acton's "master" (35): "Ranke is the representative of the age which instituted the modern study of history. He taught it to be critical, to be colourless, and to be new. We meet him at every step, and he has done more for us than any other man" (42). Yet Acton did not consider him impartial, but only removed indifferently from the people and nations he studied on the false premise that facts speak for themselves. True impartiality is taking the measure of institutions and men on universal moral grounds, a principle that set Acton apart from most historians of his time. The worst of crimes is murder, which applies not just to individuals but to institutions like the Inquisition. The impartial historian, even if a devoted Catholic, does not evade the judgment, which confers meaning on the facts (41–42).

Doing history rightly means a judicious union of science, sympathy, and morality. Science and sympathy alone are not good enough. The first detaches the historian morally from his material even while assuring fidelity to fact, which was Ranke's fault. The second permits engagement with the past through imagination, intuition, and feeling, but falls into a trap of relativism by granting equality to whatever happened, the fault of the Romantic school of historiography. The third stands outside history as a consistent judge of what happened in history. Indeed, morality in that sense is what Acton meant by "liberalism." The movement of history since the sixteenth century has established a broad arena of liberty: "And this constancy of progress in the direction of organized and assured freedom, is the characteristic fact of modern history, and its tribute to the theory of Providence" (35).

The reference to Providence explains in part his hostility to papal authoritarianism as contrary to divine purpose: " ... the wisdom of divine rule appears not in the perfection but in the improvement of the world and that achieved liberty is the one ethical result that rests on converging and combined conditions of advancing civilization" (36). What he means to say is that liberty is a historical expression of morality, which is in the hands of Providence.

Acton's advice to hearers and readers of the *Inaugural Lecture* came from a store of principles that guided his career:

> ... see that your judgments are your own, and do not shrink from disagreement; no trusting without testing; be more severe

to ideas than to actions; do not overlook the strength of the bad cause or the weakness of the good; never be surprised by the crumbling of an idol or the disclosure of a skeleton; judge talent at its best and character at its worst; suspect power more than vice, and study problems in preference to periods.

(48)

An ironic piece of advice was: "Learn as much by writing as by reading" (47).

Works by Acton

Essays on Freedom and Power, ed. and intro. by Gertrude Himmelfarb (New York: Meridean Books, 1955).
Lectures on Modern History (London: Macmillan, 1906).

Works about Acton

Brinton, Crane, "Acton's Philosophy of History," *Harvard Theological Review* (June 1919).
Butterfield, Herbert, *Man on His Past: The Study of the History of Historical Scholarship* (Cambridge: Cambridge University Press, 1955), Chapter III.
Himmelfarb, Gertrude, *Lord Acton: A Study in Conscience and Politics* (Chicago, Illinois: University of Chicago Press, 1952). Her introduction is also useful.
Kochan, Lionel, *Acton on History* (Port Washington, New York: Keenikat Press, 1954). The introduction is a compact though detailed account of his life and work.

Useful references

Gooch, G.P., *History and Historians in the Nineteenth Century* (Boston, Massachusetts: Beacon Press, 1959), Chapter XIX. First published in 1913.

25. THE PROVINCES OF THE ROMAN EMPIRE FROM CAESAR TO DIOCLETIAN (THEODOR MOMMSEN, 1817–1903)

Born in Schleswig, he was at first a student of law and gradually became a historian. The combination fueled his versatility. Law and classics were studied at the University of Kiel, capped by a doctorate in 1843. For a time, he edited a liberal newspaper and was active as a journalist. His publications landed a professorship in law at the University of Leipzig, a position from which he was expelled for liberal political views during the revolutions of 1848. He took positions at the University of Zurich in 1852, where he wrote on Roman constitutional and criminal law, and the University of Breslau in 1854, where he started the *Corpus of Latin Inscriptions* and wrote the *Roman History*.

Mommsen accepted a professorship of ancient history at the University of Berlin in 1861. As a liberal in newly unified Germany, he opposed policies of Otto von Bismarck, who sued for slander. Mommsen was tried and acquitted in 1882. His academic career was rounded off as permanent secretary of the Prussian Academy of Arts and Sciences and election to the Prussian Parliament (the Reichstag) as a member of the liberal faction. In 1902 he was awarded the Nobel Prize for Literature, edging out Leo Tolstoy, whose views were too radical for the committee. In the midst of these achievements, he married and fathered a brood of children.

A prodigious scholar and writer, Mommsen was known as a man who wasted no time. Up in the morning by five, he read, researched, wrote, and taught through the day. He mastered half a dozen fields, which included law, history, numismatics (study of coins), epigraphy (study of inscriptions), archeology, and early Italian philology, and made enduring contributions to all of them. He was comfortable with classical and a number of modern languages. His publications exceeded some 1500. In 1887 over a thousand were collected into a bibliography. In one three-year period (1844–47), while in Italy collecting inscriptions, he published 90 articles. One contemporary remarked that it would take him 400 years just to copy all that Mommsen had written.

Mommsen's *History of Rome* in three volumes was one of the most admired works of nineteenth-century historiography, and held its own ever since as a powerful account of the Roman Republic down to 46 B.C. His strategy as historian was to avoid moralizing and understand events in their contemporary setting. Thus Julius Caesar's behavior and policies, which Mommsen was accused of overestimating, might be unworthy in another place or time, but in his own time he was the best available man, the least of evils, who understood what was needed to rescue Rome from civil strife. The same operative principle governs exposition in his work on provinces.

Although the *Roman History* was considered the best available, it was faulted for lacking notes and references, which missed the point. With that book, Mommsen wrote for a general readership. *Provinces of the Roman Empire* is a different matter. Notes are frequent and extensive, and the text is unrelenting in substantive detail: "Charms of detail, pictures of feeling, sketches of character, it has none to offer; it is allowable for the artist, but not for the historian, to reproduce the features of Arminius [a German chieftain who destroyed three Roman legions in A.D. 9] With self-denial this book has been written; and with self-denial let it be read" (I:7). What both works have in common, especially the one on provinces, is a fresh dimension of evidence.

Mommsen reoriented and transformed historiography of the ancient world by an extensive use of coins, inscriptions, and archeology in addition to literary sources and works of art. In *Provinces of the Roman Empire*, his opinion of written sources is skeptical: "Anyone who has recourse to the so-called authorities for the history of this period—even the better among them—finds difficulty in controlling his indignation at the telling of what deserved to be suppressed, and at the suppression of what there was need to tell" (I:3). In response to the problem of weak sources, he produced two landmark solutions.

The *Corpus of Latin Inscriptions*, a monument of nineteenth-century scholarship, catalogues inscriptions from sources throughout the Mediterranean world. The 15 volumes contain 130,000 inscriptions, most of them edited by Mommsen, who did the first five volumes himself. Instructions to agents searching for inscriptions were to see first-hand the original stones bearing inscriptions, or original manuscripts in which the inscriptions appeared, to establish dates, and to suggest how incomplete inscriptions might be completed. He also introduced the method of "autopsy." Inscriptions already used in publications were to be confirmed against the originals. Under his guidance, an epigraphic journal was founded in 1872 to continue the work of collecting and evaluating inscriptions. His *History of Coinage*, published in 1860, is an encyclopedia of coins from Greco-Asiatic times to Rome, then to Italy, then to the Mediterranean world. With his help a journal of numismatics was founded.

Provinces of the Roman Empire routinely uses evidence from coins, inscriptions, and archeology in addition to conventional sources (I:78–80, 280, 376–77; II:70–71, 300–301, 365). With these new sources at hand, the horizon of evidence for ancient history was vastly expanded and gave Mommsen's works their special authority.

In *Roman Public Law*, written while he was absorbed in the *Corpus*, he expounds the system and history of Roman government and administration and advances an interpretation that explains the time span "from Caesar to Diocletian" in the work on provinces. The first emperor, Augustus, developed a system of "dyarchy" in which he ruled but consulted and respected the Senate. Diocletion (reigned 284–305) rejected the moderate principle of dyarchy and ruled absolutely. After him, the history of the empire took a different course and would require from the historian a different kind of book.

Provinces of the Roman Empire corrects narrow focus on events in the city of Rome. Action of the empire was elsewhere: "We must take into account ... the vast extension of the sphere of rule, and the shifting of the vital development from the centre to the circumference. The history of the city of Rome widens out into that of the country of Italy, and the latter into that of the Mediterranean world" (I:2–3). The scope of the work includes, in volume 1, northern frontiers of Italy, Spain, Gaul (roughly modern France), Roman Germany and the free Germans, Britain, lands of the Danube, Greek Europe, Asia Minor, and in volume 2, the Euphrates frontier and Parthia (a kingdom in northeastern Iran), Syria, Judaea and the Jews, Egypt, and Africa. Eight customized maps (the titles are in German) provide a visual panorama of the provinces. Mommsen supplies overwhelming evidence that most provinces prospered in peace with decent administration and submitted willingly to lenient Roman rule: "It is the agricultural towns of Africa, in the homes of the vine-dressers on the Moselle, in the flourishing townships of the Lycian mountains, and on the margin of the Syrian desert that the work of the imperial period is to be sought and to be found" (I:5).

The case of Athens is an example of Roman tolerance and flexibility in provincial administration. Athenian negative response to Roman policy and conquests during the late Republic merited extermination, but the city was spared:

> No Greek city from the standpoint of Roman policy erred so gravely against Rome ... its demeanour (*sic*) ... would, had its case been that of any other commonwealth, have inevitably led to it being razed. But from the Philhellenic standpoint, doubtless, Athens was the masterpiece of the world ... Athens was never placed under the fasces [a bundle of rods with an ax in the middle symbolic of a magistrate's authority] of the Roman governor, and never paid tribute to Rome ...
>
> (I:279)

The case of Judaea was the opposite. An uprising of Jewish radicals in the first century A.D. inflicted catastrophe on the Jewish population, their country, and their religion (see essay 5 in this volume). The destructive outcome of radical Jewish defiance of the empire was not initially what the Romans wanted and savage intervention came near the end of the war: "Thus the insurgents had entirely free sway in Jerusalem from the summer of 66 till the spring of 70. What the combination of religious and national fanaticism ... in those four years of terror brought upon the nation, had its horrors intensified by the fact that the foreigners were only onlookers in the matter, and all the evil was inflicted directly by Jews upon Jews" (II:232).

Out of patience, a Roman army under the future emperor Titus destroyed Jerusalem and the Second Temple "with all the treasures accumulated in it for six centuries." Rome's policy of toleration was modified: "The policy pursued by earlier Hellenistic states, and taken over from them by the Romans—which reached in reality far beyond mere toleration towards foreign ways and foreign faith, and recognized the Jews in their collective character as a national and religious community—had become impossible" (II:235).

The extent of Mommsen's fame is suggested by an anecdote from Mark Twain, American humorist and novelist, who was a guest of honor at a heavily attended banquet for distinguished men. Apparently everyone was seated, but then ceremonial trumpets sounded again and a slight, bespectacled figure was seen on his way down the aisle. As he walked forward everyone on his flanks rose in successive waves and a hushed murmur was heard: "it's Mommsen." No one else received such a welcome.

Works by Mommsen

A History of Rome under the Emperors, ed. by Barbara and Alexander Demandt, trans. by Clare Krojzi (London: Routledge, 1996). This "fourth volume" was reconstructed from lecture notes.

Corpus Inscriptionum Latinarum, 16 vols. (Berlin Academy, 1867–1959.) Fifteen volumes appeared in Mommsen's lifetime, five of which he compiled.

The History of Rome (Römische Geschichte): An Account of Events and Persons from the Conquest of Carthage to the End of the Republic, a new edition by Dero A. Saunders and John H. Collins (New York: Meridian Books, 1958). Published originally in 1854, 1855, 1856 and translated by W.P. Dickson.

The Provinces of the Roman Empire from Caesar to Diocletian, 2 vols., trans. from the German by William P. Dickson (London: Macmillan, 1909). First published in 1885.

Works about Mommsen

Fowler, Warde W., "Theodor Mommsen: His Life and Work," in *Roman Essays and Interpretations* (Oxford: Oxford University Press, 1920).

Gooch, George P., *History and Historians in the Nineteenth Century* (2nd ed.; Boston, Massachusetts: Beaconds Press 1959). Published originally in 1913 by Longmans, Green and Co.

Kelsey, Francis W., "Theodore Mommsen," *The Classical Journal*, 14:4 (January 1919).

Useful references

Thompson, James W. *A History of Historical Writing: The Eighteenth and Nineteenth Centuries*, vol. 2 (Berkeley: University of California Press, 1942), pp. 502–508.

Section Notes

1 In Adam Budd (ed.), *The Modern Historiography Reader: Western Sources* (London and New York: Routledge, 2009), pp. 1174–77.
2 The text referred to in this essay is *History of the Popes, their Church and State*, 3 vols., trans. from the German by E. Fowler (New York: Colonial Press, 1901).
3 Iggers and von Moltke, *Leopold von Ranke*, pp. 135–38. In 1822, Wilhelm von Humboldt, founder of the University of Berlin, said: "The Historians task is to present what actually happened. The more purely and completely he achieves this, the more perfectly has he solved his problem. A simple presentation is at the same time the primary, indispensable condition of his work and the highest achievement he will be able to attain." "On The historian's task," in Adam Budd (ed), *The Modern Historiography Reader* (London and New York, 2009), p. 168. Ranke's introduction to *History of the Popes* is in Budd's anthology. Ibid., pp. 174 ff.
4 This essay is using the Miall translation.
5 The Middlemore translation is used in this essay.
6 This essay cites the Braziller edition, which has Lecky's two volumes under one cover with the original pagination.
7 The translation of *Leben Jesu* used in this essay is by George Eliot (Mary Ann Evans).
8 This essay uses the text in *Lord Acton, Essays on Freedom and Power*. There are nine others, including "History of Freedom in Antiquity" and "History of Freedom in Christianity."

CHINA

Themes 2 (non-Western historiography), 3 (issues of critical historiography), 4 (genres of history), 5 (breadth of inquiry), 6 (problematic historiography)

The function of history in traditional China was to serve the empire in association with Confucian ideals that valued continuity with past models of good government and personal decorum. Writing and transmitting history was central to Chinese culture almost continuously for 2800 years. With unification of the country in 221 B.C., inaugurating an imperial period of successive dynasties that lasted until 1911, a new dynasty took on responsibility to write the history of the previous dynasty based on an elaborate model established by Ssu Ma-ch'ien, a historian of the former Han Dynasty (second century B.C.). The compilation of dynastic histories was managed by state officials successful in the imperial examination system.

The result was hundreds of volumes, much of it compiled from a variety of sources. Some translation has been done into Western languages but the immense corpus has barely felt the bite of modern scholarship. A draft history of the Ch'ing Dynasty is still in the works by scholars in Taiwan. These dynastic histories were supplemented by local gazettes assembled by magistrates who recorded local events, and there was some isolated writing of history by private individuals. There was no general reading public for historical works. Those who did the writing and the reading were members of the literati class who had succeeded in at least the first of three stages of examination.

Despite limitations, Chinese scholars accumulated an unmatched, extensive, continuous record of their past. History, literature, and philosophy were intertwined. In the eighteenth century a school of Confucian thought emerged that stressed analysis and evidence. Chinese historians were not given to footnotes or other documentation. The idea was to assimilate learning from many sources and write freely from an organized store of knowledge and wisdom. This section offers two Chinese scholars, a problematic one narrowly focused on textual issues, the second on the entire sweep of dynastic China over 2000 years.

26. TAI CHEN ON MENCIUS: EXPLORATIONS IN WORDS AND MEANINGS[1] (TAI CHEN, 1724–1777)

By all reports, Tai Chen was an intellectual prodigy whose devotion to learning was meticulous and obsessive. Born into relative poverty, he died without improving much on material conditions of life. His economic destiny was to drift from one minor post to another, often relying on loans, temporary patronage of admirers, and jobs as a tutor. Impoverishment dogged him even though he succeeded in the first two of three stages in the imperial examination system. Things were so bad one year he could feed his family only by soliciting scraps daily from a local noodle shop. Lacking political and social ambition, his mind was usually on things other than material gain and personal advancement, a major reason he failed to achieve distinction in Chinese officialdom.

Failure to achieve the third and highest degree ("presented scholar," or *chin shih*) in the triennial examinations after six tries closed the door on appointment to high office. Even when the emperor gave him the top degree by decree for his services and reputation, which included him among a handful of candidates who succeeded in the prestigious palace examination, chances for sustained appointment were slim because there were too many graduates vying for appointments. All who collaborated with him were impressed by superior industry, scholarship, and depth of thought. He was a technical expert on phonology, the study of pronunciation in ancient texts, and accomplished at philology, the study of language in historical sources. He wrote and edited some 50 works, 35 of which still exist in print. The difference between his learning and that of many contemporaries was an insistence on documentary truth and a "scientific" attitude toward revered texts. An innovative student of Confucian classics, he was also proficient in mathematics and astronomy, which may have intensified his sense of evidence.

The issue for this essay is the connection between Tai Chen's philological inquiries and historiography. *Explorations on Words and Meanings in Mencius* (*Meng Tzu tsu-I shu cheng*) illustrates dissent within Confucian ranks about the status and interpretation of classical texts written before China's unification in 221 B.C. For 2000 years history and philosophy were interwoven. Moral standards embedded in philosophical literature were applied to judge concrete historical examples of virtue and malfeasance.

Tai Chen's book is divided into 43 "articles," each of which asks a question and provides a response. The articles address the meaning of key ideas that had, according to Tai Chen, lost their way in speculation—that is, Principle, Heavenly Way, Nature, Potential, Way (Tao), Humanity, Righteousness, Propriety, Wisdom, Sincerity, and Weighing (knowledge of what is important and unimportant). Historical philology is his technique and focus: "Erroneous words do not just end with words; they change and influence the minds of men. A mind that is beclouded must do injury to the conduct of affairs and government" (66).

All educated Chinese in dynastic China found models and inspiration in the past: "By acquainting themselves with the words and deeds of the ancients, students are able to make up for their own deficiencies" (80). Whatever the issue at hand, the past was viewed as a repository of all that was excellent and good, evil and reprehensible. The purpose of historical study was to confirm and inform moral judgment. On the other hand, if the foundations of moral judgment were shaky, that is, if the Confucian classics were imperfectly understood, then history could not be read or written properly. These issues would have been merely academic if Confucianism had not been for centuries the official ideology of imperial China.

A huge body of literature had accumulated since the Han Dynasty (200 B.C.–A.D. 200) on the Confucian canon—that is, books on history, poetry, ceremonies, divination, and moral philosophy that included teachings of Confucius (ca. 551–479 B.C.) and an entire work by Mencius (ca. 372–289 B.C.), his most important follower. These "classics" were part of a literary tradition whose magnitude is suggested by the ambitious Ch'ing Dynasty project called the *Complete Library of the Four Treasuries*, which encompassed classics, history, philosophy, and belles-lettres (poetry), and eventually assembled 36,000 volumes. Tai was briefly one of numerous compilers working on that monumental project.

These texts belonged to a long tradition of historical literature. Included were 24 dynastic histories amounting collectively to hundreds of volumes. There were also innumerable local and private histories, factual with little comment, compiled by members of the literati class. Custom required each dynasty to compile a history of the previous one. The histories were assembled by committees of scholars whose method was scissors and paste without attempts at synthesis or interpretation to nail down causation or sequences of development. Historical change from the Chinese perspective, mainly one dynasty replacing another, was explained as a Mandate of Heaven replacing a corrupt dynasty with a virtuous one. Not only was the idea of sequential historical development absent, there was no idea of progress. But with these limitations, Chinese civilization was notable in world history for scope and longevity of historical consciousness.

All texts of whatever kind were considered part of a historical tradition. If thought and action were to be justified by reference to the past, every classical text was taken to have historical parentage and meanings a scholar was obliged to master before offering a fresh point of view. An educated man required extensive knowledge of the four "treasuries" to assist self-cultivation and to formulate public policy. History and philosophy were intimately knotted together in ways difficult for the Western mind to grasp. Tai Chen was nearly at the tail end of an overwhelming legacy of historical and literary texts bound together by a virtually air tight tradition.

His book examines ideas and words in the Neo-Confucian tradition, the intellectual scaffolding of Chinese ideology since the Sung Dynasty (960–1279). The most prominent representative was Chu Hsi (d. 1200), whose commentaries on the classics were laced with metaphysical speculations influenced by Taoism and Buddhism. The relatively straightforward teachings of Confucius had focused on moral qualities of the best kind of man and how they might be achieved by regulating desires and actions through example and study to achieve consistently good conduct and wise public service. Tai claims Mencius, a later Confucian, never departed from those teachings.

Yet in later centuries, Taoist and Buddhist ideas were absorbed so that desires were viewed as a bad thing to be eliminated and that submergence in a non-human *One* is the proper goal of life. Also entangled with early Confucianism were cosmological ideas, particularly yin-yang (female-male complementary opposites that alternate with one another) and the Five Elements (water, fire, metal, wood, and earth) that move in a cycle. These two kinds of movement accounted for change in nature and were organized into an elaborate system of correlations with things, ideas, and relationships in human experience.

The words Tai Chen was most concerned to explore are "principle" (*li*), to which Neo-Confucian writers attributed an existence independent of the material world (*ch'i*), and its relationship to nature (*hsing*), including human nature. This was done by arguing for two kinds of reality, principle and matter. The former gives form and meaning to the latter. Everything in the world takes its specific character from principle. All principles come from and have unity in a dominant reality called the Supreme Ultimate, which is independent of matter and would exist without it. He sought to explain why this view is a mistake, that principle hardly appears in the classics, and where it does, it is embedded firmly in the material world: "Thus

Mencius used what was known to prove what was not known. He attributed the desire to hear, see, smell, and taste to the ear, eye, nose, mouth, and the appreciation of moral principles to the heart-and-mind. All those desires and preferences are within the bounds [of one's natural tendencies] and are not outside them" (78).

Disembodied independence of principle was due, he argued, to a damaging importation of Taoist and Buddhist ideas. For Tai Chen, the dualism meant that principle was separate from the "minds and hearts" of men. His philological analysis shows that such distinctions were alien to Mencius, whose book was essential in the imperial examinations. Neo-Confucians like Chu Hsi, whose commentaries on the classics were also required for the imperial examinations, wanted to give Confucian ethics and the idea of a "superior man" of high moral character a cosmic, metaphysical framework. In doing so, the connection between principle and human desires was sundered: "Everything in our lives arises from desires. Without desires there would be no action. Only when there is desire can there be action. When man's action arises at what is most correct and immutably so, that can be called accordance with principle. If there is no desire and no action, what is there that can be called principle?" (173).

Tai Chen was known as a "Master of Investigations Based on Evidence." At the center of a movement that rejected speculative tendencies of Sung Dynasty Neo-Confucianism, he sought a close relationship with ancient texts by means of critical analysis and understood the principle of verification. Within the narrow confines of textual analysis, he demonstrated a connection between evidence in a text and historical truth, reminding one a bit of Lorenzo Valla (see essay 11 in this volume). He anticipated modern science by arguing that no one's private opinion can be called *li*. No individual has his own facts, which are a reality all men face equally. The implications for doing history are clear. Subjective feelings and intuitions do not lead to truth. Rather they give people in power justification for imposing their narrow views on the helpless and the weak. In the meantime, we learn nothing of value about the world, past or present.

He provided a narrow kind of evidence by urging that texts be respected for what they really say, but his methods and assumptions were not applied to traditional ways of conceiving and writing history, nor did they result in a revision of questions and judgments in the imperial examinations. The weight and inertia of tradition were too much for his work to overcome even though others shared his views on evidence. If his approach to knowledge and critical method had been taken more seriously by the establishment, readiness to respect and promote science might have been improved at a crucial moment in China's history.

Works by Tai Chen

Tai Chen on Mencius: Explorations in Words and Meanings, trans. and intro. by Ann-ping Chin and Mansfield Freeman (New Haven, Connecticut: Yale University Press, 1990).

Wang-Tsit Chan (trans. and compiler), *A Source Book in Chinese Philosophy* (Princeton, New Jersey: Princeton University Press, 1963). See Chapter 38. A partial alternate translation of Tai Chen's book.

Works about Tai Chen

Elman, Benjamin A., *From Philosophy to Philology: Intellectual and Social Aspects of Change in Late Imperial China* (rev. ed.; Los Angeles, California: University of California Press, 2000).

Hummel, Arthur W., *Eminent Chinese of the Ch'ing Period, 1644–1912*, 2 vols. (Washington: United States Government Printing Office, 1944), II: 695–700.

Needham, Joseph and Wang Ling, *Science and Civilization in China, vol. 2, History of Scientific Thought* (Cambridge: Cambridge University Press, 1956), pp. 513–515.

Yu-lan, Fung, *A History of Chinese Philosophy*, trans. and intro. by Derk Bodde, 2 vols. (Princeton, New Jersey: Princeton University Press, 1953), 2: 651–672.

Useful references

Huang, Chin-hsing, *Philosophy, Philology, and Politics in Eighteenth Century China: Li Fu and Li Wang School under the Ch'ing* (Cambridge: Cambridge University Press, 1996).

Iggers, Georg G. and Q. Edward Wang, *A Global History of Modern Historiography* (Edinburgh Gate, UK: Pearson Education Ltd, 2008).

Pulleyblank, E.G., "Chinese Historical Criticism," in Beasley and Pulleyblank (eds.), *Historians of China and Japan* (Oxford: Oxford University Press, 1961). See chapters 9 and 10 on the historiography of Liu Chih-chi and Chang Hsüeh-ch'ing. Liu stressed methodology, Chang sought to expand the role of ideas in history.

27. TRADITIONAL GOVERNMENT IN IMPERIAL CHINA: A CRITICAL ANALYSIS[2] (CH'IEN MU, 1895–1990)

Ch'ien grew up in the village of Wusih in Kiangsu Province during the last years of the Ch'ing Dynasty, which collapsed in 1912. The family was poor and his father died early on. His mother could not get him into the village school until age 12. An able, diligent student, he impressed his teachers. Encouraged but still poor, the family, with difficulty, saw him through Middle School. His omnivorous reading in Chinese literature and history was done at home.

He soon became a teacher in 1912 without attending college. In the 1920s he taught history in Chinese colleges on the strength of his knowledge and talent and did so in the midst of civil war. He experienced nearly four decades of contemporary Chinese history in the Republic under Chiang Kai-shek, many of them fraught with danger, until the latter was expelled from the mainland by the communists in 1949. At the time, Ch'ien made his way to Hong Kong, where he co-founded New Asia College, and in 1967 relocated to Taiwan. In due time, as his reputation peaked, he was awarded honorary doctorates by Yale University and the University of Hong Kong.

Ch'ien authored nine books on Chinese history and philosophy and many articles, no less than 99 between 1924 and 1962. He opposed the New Culture Movement that flourished in the 1910s and 1920s after the Chinese Republic failed to solve China's problems. Leaders of the movement rejected Confucian ideas and culture as backward and antiquated. They argued for a new China founded on Western standards, such as egalitarianism and democracy, rationalism and modern science, similar in spirit to Fukuzawa Yukichi's diagnosis and prescription for traditional Japan (see essay 28 in this volume). Ch'ien holds that traditional China and the Confucian way were an enduring if mixed success worthy of study by modernizing societies, a notable departure from the common Western view that China was static, backward, and reactionary for centuries.

China's political development differed from that of ancient Greece and Rome. Greece was dominated by the city state, small in territorial scope and population, with a common culture, thus lending itself to democratic government. Rome's empire presided over a diversity of ethnic groups behind a façade of Republican forms developed in a city state. China was huge in extent, as it is now, with a relatively homogeneous population living in thousands of villages. An electoral system was out of the question. The practical route of government was "imperial succession through inheritance as an unavoidable institutional device" (2).

The traditional system of government was complex and sophisticated, with a balance between autocracy represented by the emperor and his entourage and ethically oriented Confucian officials who were selected on merit by an examination system. Sometimes the relationship would shift too much to one side, but the usual outcome was for it to swing back into balance. Over many centuries the Chinese system was refined and improved. Its greatest achievement was relative stability of China's civilization from the T'ang (618–907) to the Ch'ing (1644–1912), which involved many adjustments in government organization and bureaucratic practice, including relations of the emperor to the imperial system. Ch'ien responds to a common belief that Chinese imperial government was static and autocratic for centuries until finally overthrown: "Those who have not studied Chinese history often have the impression that China did not change for two thousand years and those who know little about traditional Chinese government tend to dismiss it as unenlightened despotism. These widely held opinions are patently false" (35). Although without notes and with only a short bibliography of English works, his book provides a wealth of detail, including innumerable technical terms in Chinese with Romanized versions, that suggest a wide grasp of primary sources.

Out of some 26 dynasties that arose after the unification of China in 221 B.C. by the warlike state of Ch'in, five of the greatest are subjects of Ch'ien's analysis—the Han, T'ang, Sung, Ming, and Ch'ing, which account together for more than 1500 years of Chinese history: " ... an analysis of Han institutions will best reveal the pattern of traditional government in China, though this pattern was always in flux. Two key elements in this pattern proved decisive for Chinese history. The first was the relationship between the Imperial House and the central government, and the second that between the central government and various units of local administration" (1). Labels changed, but the mutual relationship endured.

The imperial household related to government through a Chancellor. The Emperor and the Chancellor each had a Secretariat with different functions. The Emperor's broke down into six "Masters" for clothing, food, head gear, feasts, baths, and writing. The Chancellor's was comprised of 13 "Bureaus" for appointment and employment of officials, their promotion and dismissal, revenue for the imperial household, government memorials, litigation under civil law, weights, measures, and other standards, transportation of troops, bandit suppression, criminal executions, military service and weapons, granaries, coinage and state iron and salt monopolies, and maintenance of records. Obviously the Chancellor had more control over administrative affairs than the Emperor: "Actual power in the Han Dynasty ... legally resided not in the Imperial House but in the office of the Chancellor. He acted as the real head of the new central government ... The entire tradition of political institutions in China had been characterized strongly by this early separation of powers" (5).

In later imperial history this pattern of separation continued with variations. Of the issues discussed by Ch'ien—government organization, fiscal policy, military affairs, the examination system—we shall concentrate on recruitment of officials by examination. The ideal was recruitment of the most talented, learned, and virtuous men in the empire to run the government. The system that developed had ups and downs, strengths and weaknesses, successes and disappointments, but stabilized the Chinese empire for centuries:

> Nowadays it is fashionable for Chinese to look back with disdain on the traditional examination system noting the many abuses it became prone to. But we must not overlook the amazing soundness of its underlying theoretical assumptions. We should not take a modern institution such as popular election for public office as a basis for criticizing a system that functioned effectively for over a thousand years. Even in modern Western-democratic countries, election affects only a minority of government officials. The vast majority are chosen through a civil service examination system that can be traced back to the great Chinese tradition.
> (52)

In Han times after 140 B.C. recruiting officials was a major task of government. Instead of criteria based on heredity or wealth, the standard was merit: "The solution adopted by the Chinese involved one of the very first historical attempts to guarantee succession to administrative power based upon objective standards ... To determine whether the prospective bureaucrat was familiar with the knowledge deemed necessary for office an extensive examination system was eventually set up" (13). The emphasis was on recommendation reinforced by examination. Men who cleared both hurdles administered economic, legal, diplomatic, and military business of the empire:

> This system can hardly be called an aristocracy. Although some among the Court Gentlemen were sons of the nobility, they constituted on a small minority of the total numbers. Nor can it be called government by the military, for Court Gentlemen were certainly not from military backgrounds. Again, it was not a bourgeois plutocracy either, for none of the Court Gentlemen

owed their appointments to commerce or finance. This can only be called government by scholars or the literati.

(17)

In the T'ang Dynasty, recommendation as the chief means of identifying candidates was displaced by competitive examination. By this time a Ministry of Rites supervised examinations while a Ministry of Personnel assigned posts and decided on promotion or demotion. Standards of objectivity became more rigorous. Abilities of candidates were classified into nine grades under the watchful eye of "referees" tracking men from their own districts. In principle, unlike the Han system, the door was thrown open to a wider field of candidates who could apply and present their credentials. Those excluded included merchants and artisans, who worked for profit, and criminals. On the other side, officials were not allowed to participate in business. Devotion to public service was the standard, not making money.

In the Sung Dynasty, candidates came increasingly from families of lesser wealth than in the T'ang: " ... the great family traditions had completely disappeared. Village boys, students from humble homes, candidates from remote areas suddenly were able to hold degrees but were necessarily at a loss in practical administration and devoid of personal culture" (78). Procedures were stiffened: "To prevent favoritism and assure anonymity, candidates' names on the examination papers were covered up, and the papers were identified by numbers. Examination results became the sole criteria for success and even scholars most respected by the examiners might fail" (79). The content was commentary on Confucian principles like benevolence and righteousness. An emergent weakness was too many degree holders for too few positions.

In the Ming Dynasty, changes in the system outstripped any made previously. Clear status groups emerged. Of the three degree levels, district, provincial, and metropolitan, only the third group might achieve high public office. The second group was confined to minor posts, and the third group could hope for none at all. The second change was the notorious eight-legged essay, "the greatest destroyer of human talent ... devoid of imagination and thought" (112). The content of the essay was poetry and rhymed prose in a highly structured format, a misguided way to enforce rigor. Any deviation from the rules meant failure.

In the Ch'ing Dynasty, a lofty ideal was corrupted: "The original intention of the examination system was to allow the various government positions to be filled by the best-qualified people chosen from the general public. The Ch'ing emperors ... had absolutely no intention of sharing political power with the people; consequently, the examination system degenerated into a mere propaganda device" (135). While up to 80 percent of candidates were Chinese, almost none could hold office, while Manchus, whatever their abilities or qualifications, occupied the highest positions.

Ch'ien argues that "spiritual" support stood behind the examination system despite its problems. Even the modern reformer Sun Yat-sen wanted to reestablish it early in the twentieth century, but collapse of the Ch'ing Dynasty discredited it and removed the option. As for Chinese tradition in general, Ch'ien counsels that political systems cannot work without attention to "traditions of a country," and advises against a "down with the past" approach to reform (142).

Works by Ch'ien Mu

Traditional Government in Imperial China: A Critical Analysis, trans. by Chun-tu Hsueh and George Totten, with Wallace Johnson, Conrad Schirokauer, Romeyn Taylor, and Ramon Woon (Hong Kong: The Chinese University Press; New York: St. Martin's Press, 1982).

Works about Ch'ien Mu

Dennerline, Jerry, Qian Mu and the World of Seven Mansions (New Haven, Connecticut: Yale University Press, 1988).

Useful references

Ip, Hung-yuk, Tze-ki Hon, and Ch'iu-chun-Lee, "The Plurality of Chinese Modernity: A Review of Recent Scholarship on the May Fourth Movement," *Modern China*, 29:4 (2003): 490–509.

Section Notes

1 This essay uses the translation of Ann-ping Chen and Mansfield Freeman. Two critical theorists widely separated in time with important views about how history should be done were Liu Chih-chi (661–721) and Chang Hsüeh-ch'eng (1738–1801). Unfortunately their works, Liu's *Generalities on History (Shih-t'ung)* and Chang's *General Principles of Literature and History (Wen shih T'ung-i)*, are not available in English translation.
2 In quotations from this work, I have omitted Romanized names and terms as well as accompanying Chinese characters.

JAPAN

Themes 2 (non-Western historiography), 3 (issues of critical historiography), 4 (genres of history), 5 (breadth of inquiry)

In this section two Japanese historians from different eras connected with events of the Meiji Restoration, 1868 to 1912, exhibit skepticism about settled habits of historiography in Japan that set off internal self-searching and debate about the proper object and purpose of historical inquiry.

The Restoration, named after the emperor Meiji, abandoned the quasi-feudal Tokugawa Shogunate that ruled Japan for some 250 years and embarked on a rapid career of modernization. Japanese historiography ever since has been preoccupied with how it was done and what it meant. No voice in that transformative era can rival the public presence, provocative thought, and influence of Fukuzawa Yukichi (family name first) in opposing a national historiography influenced by imperial China in style, terminology, and purpose. The role of historical study had long been preservation and dissemination of a self-congratulating mythical Japanese and a program of good behavior according to a Confucian standard of ethics. The onset of modernization after collapse of traditional institutions and their supporting rationales called for a reassessment of Japan's place and direction in history. Fukuzawa undertook a revised historiography that rejected traditional thinking about the past and provided a fresh vision of the future within a Western frame of reference.

Irokawa Daikichi is a second voice looking back on the Meiji era more than a hundred years later. He attempts to explain why the "emperor system" corrupted and deflected aspirations of ordinary Japanese people to achieve "people's rights." His viewpoint and handling of evidence, which he terms "people's history," were sharply at odds with dominant trends in Japanese historiography. After World War I Marxism was an influential trend as historians sought to understand and explain Japan's new mass urban, industrial culture. What the "emperor system" and Marxism had in common was lack of interest in common people living obscurely in the countryside. Irokawa's departure from that pattern and his study of grass root practices and attitudes became popular in Japan and challenged previous as well as contemporary trends in historiography.

28. AN OUTLINE OF A THEORY OF CIVILIZATION (FUKUZAWA YUKICHI, 1835–1901)

In 1875 Fukuzawa published *Bummeiron no gairyaku,* his mature reflections on the nature of civilization and its implications for Japan. At the time his country was in the midst of shaking off feudal ways and embracing reforms on behalf of rapid modernization. Reformers were still debating what and how much of Western ways to adopt. There is hardly a more dramatic, revolutionary example of change in a country than the Japanese experience in the second half of the nineteenth century.

After 250 years of self-imposed seclusion from the rest of the world, a rigidly stratified feudal regime suddenly collapsed, the emperor Meiji was restored to authority over the ruling Tokugawa clan, and a band of "enlightened" reformers set out to make Japan a modern state equal to Western nations in power and prosperity. Fukuzawa estimates these reformers at about ten percent of five million samurai who ruled the country, and on balance they were "men with brains and no money" (*Outline,* 70).

In less than two generations they succeeded in modernizing the economy, education, civil law, the military, and the political system. The fabric of society was rewoven. Commoners were recognized as citizens and formerly ruling, sword-carrying samurai were deprived of their traditional status and powers. Victory in a major war with China in 1894 made Japan the preeminent Asian power. Victory over Russia in 1905 made her a world power. At the heart of this transformation was not just a response to diplomatic and military challenges of Western powers that threatened Japanese autonomy, but a swift reassessment of Japan's relationship to history.

The agent of that reassessment was Fukuzawa Yukichi, public intellectual, teacher, scholar, translator, author, journalist, and tireless student of Western civilization, several of whose publications, some 22 volumes, were best sellers. He was not part of government, but leaders of Japan's modernization read his works and counted themselves as participants in *keimo* (Enlightenment), the reform movement for which he was a major spokesman.

In *Theory of Civilization* the dominant theme of its ten chapters is the primacy of Western civilization, the only source in the world from which Japan might acquire means to "enlightenment" and "independence." He says

> those who are to give thought to their country's progress in civilization must necessarily take European civilization as the basis of discussion, and must weigh the pros and cons of the problem in light of it. My own criterion throughout this book will be that of Western civilization, and it will be in terms of it that I describe something as good or bad, in terms of it that I find some things beneficial or harmful. Therefore let scholars make no mistake about my orientation
>
> (*Outline*, 15)

What circumstances led him to a point of view that magnified the West and diminished Japanese traditional culture?

According to his *Autobiography,* he was born a low level samurai in a small town in Kyushu, the southernmost of Japan's four main islands. Although samurai were the ruling group, his clan was rigidly stratified and class differences were strongly enforced. If on a journey, a lower samurai was obliged to prostrate himself by the roadside if he encountered an upper samurai. Being near the bottom rung of samurai status, his family was impoverished and often treated with contempt by their betters. The annual rice stipend was a meager 65 bushels a year, which his father had to convert into money by negotiating with merchants, a task considered demeaning in the samurai code. Because of these oppressive circumstances, he learned to despise a society and government that blocked social mobility for men of talent and enterprise. No matter how brilliant, he had no chance of rising in the samurai pecking order and was often treated by upper-level clan members as no better than a commoner. In due time he exploited the advantage of two perspectives at his disposal, one facing backward to the feudal past, the other looking forward to modernization on a Western model. His first 30 years were spent in the social and cultural straightjacket of old Japan, the remainder of his years in an emerging modern Japan. He did not lament passing of the former and was heartened by success of the latter.

In 1854 Commodore Perry arrived in Japan from the USA with threatening warships to demand a treaty arrangement and sparked government interest in Western gunnery to defend the country. At age 19, Fukuzawa seized a rare chance to study Western arms in Nagasaki with countrymen who knew Dutch. Under Tokugawa seclusion policy, the Dutch were the only Westerners allowed to trade with Japan and were the only available window on the West. A handful of men had immersed themselves in "Dutch learning." He went on from there to a school in Osaka to study Dutch and read books about unfamiliar knowledge. The clan sent him to the capital at Edo, soon to be renamed Tokyo, to start a school for Dutch studies that in due time became Keio University. He soon decided that his Dutch was inadequate for the times and undertook to master English, which he took to be a world language.

In 1860 he visited San Francisco. In 1862 he was translator for a delegation and went to France, England, Holland, Germany, Russia, and Portugal. Out of his vivid experiences and copious notes came *Conditions in the West* in 1866, which sold 250,000 copies in several editions. A key insight from these foreign missions was that the West had not always been in the forefront of civilization. The leap to power, prosperity, and enlightenment came after *Ca.* 1800 in about two generations. Standing on shoulders of the West, a similar leap was within Japan's grasp.

Thereafter Fukuzawa unleashed a steady stream of writings, including several on the status of women, praised civilization in the West, and faulted customs, institutions, and beliefs of old Japan. He concluded that his country lagged behind on every front that mattered and had nothing to recommend it except beautiful scenery. Power, prosperity, and enlightenment were centered in the West: "The Confucian civilization of the East seems to me to lack two things possessed by Western civilization: science in the material sphere and a sense of 'independence' in the spiritual sphere."[1] Ongoing achievement in Japan, understood in the Western sense as progress, would not be possible without hard work supported by advanced knowledge and individual initiative, both of which Japan lacked. In *An Encouragement of Learning*, he defined the role of a scholar in critical times: " ... I find that Japanese civilization will advance only after we sweep away the old spirit that permeates the minds of people ... Some persons must take the initiative in doing things to show the people where their aims should lie. We cannot look to the farmers, the merchants, or the scholars of Japanese or Chinese learning to personify these aims. The scholars of Western learning must fill this role" (*Encouragement*, 24).

The *keimo* scholars and reformers were acutely influenced by two European historical works, Françoise Guizot's *History of Civilization in Europe* (1829–32), and Thomas Buckle's *History of Civilization in England* (1857–61), both subsequently translated into Japanese.[2] For both authors, Western civilization is characterized by progress, that is, steady improvement in knowledge, institutions, and morality. Buckle argued there could be no history without the natural sciences and thought he was writing scientific history. The two Western historians were instrumental in transmitting a spirit of positivism (confidence in science) to Japan. The eighth chapter of *Theory of Civilization* is a deft summary of European development from the fall of Rome, based substantially on Guizot and Buckle.

Fukuzawa believed Japan's traditional historiography, dominated by Confucian texts and teaching heavily freighted with ethical bias, obstructed progress. History was viewed as a repository of timeless moral examples both good and bad. The reason for studying the past was application of those lessons to the present as a guide or warning to those in authority. Confucian historiography did not attempt to connect events in a chain of causation or development. Events stood alone and got their significance from the moral status of rulers and officials. Fukuzawa was persuaded there could be no advancement toward enlightenment with such a narrow understanding of the past.

He argued that history alone could explain why the West was advanced and Japan was backward. Japanese historiography was not up to the job because of its claim that ethical behavior is what matters while knowledge of things (i.e., nature and society) is irrelevant. He explained that a ruler's goodness could not result in progress without a "spirit of the times" (*jisei*) cognizant of natural law and ordinary people as well as rulers. His analogy is a ship with an engine capable of one speed. With such an engine, a navigator (the ruler) cannot make the ship go faster and exceed the mechanical limit no matter how virtuous he is. Design and power of the engine must improve.

Without a progressive climate of opinion receptive to discovery a ruler is mostly helpless to push the status quo in a direction of progress. A society may remain static for centuries no matter how upright the rulers are. Then some precipitating event may change the general way of thinking and initiate a new *jisei*, which in Japan's case was the arrival of Commodore Perry's fleet. China's *jisei*, on the other hand, had remained retrograde even in dangerous, changing times, which explained failures to adapt and successfully resist foreign intrusion. Japan's weakness lay in too much sameness of opinion:

> The point of difference between Western and other civilizations is that Western society does not have a uniformity of opinions; various opinions exist side by side without fusing into one ... There are proponents of monarchy, theocracy, aristocracy, and

democracy. Each goes its own way ... Although they vie with one another, no single one of them ever completely wins out ... Once they start living side by side, despite their mutual hostility, they each recognize the others' rights and allow them to go their ways ... each makes its own contribution to one area of civilization ... until finally, taken together, the end result is one civilization. This is how autonomy and freedom have been developed in the West.
(*Outline*, 126)

What about diverse "opinions" of Shinto, Buddhism, and Confucianism, the three traditional strands of Japanese belief and thought? The crux of the matter is intelligence and knowledge versus morality and virtue. Both are needed, but, traditional Japanese thought stressed the latter at the expense of the former. Knowledge did not refer to science and technology but rather to virtuous behavior. A perfect example is the position of women: "Anyone who feels private virtue suffices to respond to all situations should be satisfied with the decorous behavior of women today ... But why, then, are these women not employed in the public sector of society? This is proof that private virtue alone is insufficient for dealing with human affairs ... private virtue is less important than human attainment" (Ibid., 81). Morality applies to a single person. Intelligence, by discovering new truths of nature, can move an entire nation or the whole world.

Apart from this distinction, a division between rulers and ruled further impeded the development of intelligence. The rulers controlled learning and never allowed any branch of Japanese thought to become independent of government, a situation that prevailed throughout Japanese history. This "imbalance of power" effectively limited the scope of knowledge and the play of intelligence for centuries: "We have sunk to the depths of stagnation. This is why there were so few people in this country who accomplished any great works during 250 years of Tokugawa rule" (Ibid., 160).

Fukuzawa's enthusiasm for the West was not unqualified. He saw plenty of injustice, arrogance, exploitation, and stupidity. He understood that virtue had problems against triumphs of intelligence and that Japanese virtue had much to recommend it in comparison: "The ugly aspects of human life are certainly no different from what we find among Japanese. Sometimes they are even worse. But even with such social injustice there is still a pervading spirit of individuality and nothing hinders the expansion of the human spirit" (Ibid., 161). An ethos of independence drives the West. Such a thing has never existed in isolated Japan.

Fukuzawa's comparative analysis of Japan and the West in historical perspective was intended to identify and clear away obstacles to modernization. Understandably he slides over positive features of Japan's historical development. Foremost is the experience of borrowing from China that moved Japan in the sixth century from a neolithic culture to the status of a civilization with a written language, advanced political institutions, and sophisticated art. When the time came, the Japanese were historically ready to acknowledge that people on the outside could do things better that were worth imitating.

Confucianism was conservative as he describes it, but the tradition stood for two valuable traits—personal discipline and the importance of learning, even though study was confined to literary and ethical texts. Members of the warrior samurai class were able to recognize the superiority and necessity of Western military technology and organization.

Finally, the politically powerless and socially despised townsmen who provided goods and services to the daimyo ("great lords") and their samurai retainers developed a commercialized economy based on money rather than agricultural produce, which facilitated a transition to modern economic institutions and practices. Only one of these potential advantages was found in China—disciplined learning—whose unresponsive Confucian tradition turned out to be a major disadvantage in promoting rapid change. In the race to modernize before independence of movement was lost, Japan succeeded while China faltered.

Steeped in historical awareness, Fukuzawa knew that Japan's transformation would be halting as each faction sniped at the weaknesses of rivals: "Since the vast stream of history has been flowing down from the distant past, tumbling millions of humans in its path, and sweeping them along in one direction, it is no wonder that we are unable to check the flow all at once" (Ibid., 170). His weakness was to champion critical thought and autonomy of the individual while later supporting the authority of a central government, creation of a modern military establishment, and pursuit of territorial ambitions abroad, all of which pressed down heavily on his ideal of doubt from within and dignity of the person. He ended as a great but ambiguous figure as Japan leaped into modernity.

Works by Fukuzawa

An Outline of a Theory of Civilization, trans. by David A. Dilworth and G. Cameron Hurst, III (Tokyo: Sophia University, 1973).

Encouragement of Learning, trans. by David A. Dilworth (Tokyo: Sophia University, 1969).
The Autobiography of Yukichi Fukuzawa, rev. trans. by Eiichi Kiyooka (New York: Columbia University Press, 2007).

Works about Fukuzawa

Blacker, Caemen *The Japanese Enlightenment: A Study of the Writings of Fukuzawa Yukichi* (Cambridge: Cambridge University Press, 1964).
Craig, Albert M., *Civilization and Enlightenment: The Early Thought of Fukuzawa Yukichi* (Cambridge, Massachusetts: Harvard University Press, 2009).
Hopper, Helen M., *Fukuzawa Yūkichi: From Samurai to Capitalist* (New York: Pearson Longman, 2004).
Tamaki, Norio, *Yukichi Fukuzawa, 1835–1901: The Spirit of Enterprise in Modern Japan* (New York: Palgrave Macmillan, 2001).

Useful references

Keene, Donald, *The Japanese Discovery of Europe, 1720–1830* (rev. ed.; Stanford: Stanford University Press, 1969).
Mehl, Margaret, *History and the State in Nineteenth Century Japan* (Basingstoke, United Kingdom, 1998).
Sansom, George B., *The Western World and Japan: A Study in the Interaction of European and Asiatic Cultures* (New York: Knopf, 1950).

29. THE CULTURE OF THE MEIJI ERA (IROKAWA DAIKICHI, 1925–)

Irokawa was born in 1925 and graduated from the Department of National History at the University of Tokyo in 1948, just a few years after his country surrendered unconditionally after massive wartime destruction, including detonation of two atomic bombs over Japanese cities. Subsequently he became Professor of Japanese History at Tokyo University of Economics and has been a major force in Japanese history. He served in the Imperial Navy and developed an intense skepticism about Japanese pre-war thought. The nation's authoritarian rulers and their record of militarism and repression shaped him as a radical.

He came to view Japanese history after 1868 as an evolving social and political system imposed from the top down with little regard for the lives, needs, and "culture" of ordinary people. Especially culpable in his eyes was the "emperor system" claimed as a "spiritual structure" that came to prevail after Japan was launched on a program of modernization: "Meiji liberated the natural talents of the Japanese people ... On the other hand, it also gave birth to desperate farming villages, to shockingly uncivilized conditions among the urban poor, and to the emperor system ... Its poison invaded the body of the masses to form a deeply rooted slave mentality" (19). The spirit of doubt and criticism he cultivated also included as a target the slavish acceptance of Western culture, which he believed had penetrated the hinterland and damaged Japanese consciousness.

He rejected the prevailing fashion of Marxism:

> I wrote this work ... in the fall of 1969 when the concept of 'people's history' had yet to win acceptance among Japanese historians. The hold of Marxism was still so strong then that it fettered most of us and stifled scholarly creativity. Most of us were trying to explain our nation's past from the material base of society by studying land ownership and other economic relationships, or else through a thesis of class conflict ... between ruling elites and opposition leaders.
>
> (vii)

Such a relatively abstract approach did not open the door to an understanding of the dilemma Japan's masses faced in the Meiji era—that is, modernization by elites from the top down versus "people's rights" discussed and defined in remote rural communities:

> During the last ten or fifteen years I have pursued massive quantities of historical documents, but in no period of Japanese history have I encountered evidence of the same kind of enthusiasm for study and learning that existed in mountain farming villages in the 1880s ... We should not be surprised, then, to come across a mountain village in Musashi where there was a local study society founded by the mayor, who was himself a People's Rights activist, and that it included many prominent citizens ...
>
> (107)

In addition to Japanese authors like Fukuzawa Yukichi, village storehouses have yielded translations of Western writers on constitutional law and natural rights. Rural debaters and reformers were well informed about alternative political theory and practice as the Meiji government consolidated the emperor's position and power in the state.

Irokawa's view, modernization for Japan in the Meiji era was a two-edged sword. One edge of the blade freed the nation from external threats by achieving industrial and military power. The other edge fell on the majority of Japanese people, who were obliged to pay a heavy price of subservience for success. He extends due regard to Fukuzawa Yukichi (see essay 28 in this volume) as a modernist champion of doubt from within, free controversy, individual enlightenment, self-reliance, and Western learning, which made him a hero among ordinary Japanese. The evidence is copies of Fukuzawa's books discovered in village storehouses.

But Irokawa argues that rural admirers were betrayed when he supported as forward looking Meiji policies that constrained their minds and bodies:

> Fukuzawa was against the early establishment of a national assembly and opposed any overthrow of the autocratic government ... He regarded the Meiji regime as a 'progressive government' and advocated harmony between government and people. He proposed that Japan cut its ties with Asia, pressed for the build-up of a navy and army designed for continental expansion, and urged a quick increase of national wealth by favoring the privileged capitalists ... I think it is because of this that today, a century later, we still have not been able to work out a conclusive appraisal of Fukuzawa.
>
> (68)

Societies to study and debate how people's rights might be embodied in a constitution resulted in the drafting of many such documents by people outside the mainstream of power. Many of these draft constitutions have survived:

> Further evidence of the ardor and seriousness with which local People's Rights societies dedicated themselves to the drafting of constitutions can be seen in the case of the Kumamoto Sōai (Mutual Love) Society in Kyushu. Members held all-night sessions for ten consecutive days before they were able to reach a consensus ... It is a matter of the most profound regret that modern Japan was not able to adopt a constitution that emanated from the spirit of the people and embodied their enthusiasm and wisdom.
>
> (108)

Visible advocates of change at the village level were the literate "intellectuals." They were "the lowest link in the chain of official power" who stood between government and the masses: "Therefore, these men were always exposed to pressures from both sides, and they were in danger of being split up, especially during this period of radical change. Their historical consciousness became all the more acute, for they sensed the potential to play a crucial role in shaping the future" (151). While paying much attention to the interests, ideas, and activities of this middle tier of spokesmen for the common people, Irokawa reaches down to the silent members of society to understand their feelings and wishes: "But then how can we expect to be able to get at the consciousness of the 'inarticulate masses'"? If we want to grasp the consciousness as a whole and not in fragments, we have to examine it in the abnormal forms in which it is revealed in popular actions during a time of upheaval. "On some occasions we may be able to come across traces of that consciousness, through cries, appeals, and protests, at other times, through detailed official records and reports and through the testimony of bystanders and eyewitnesses" (152).

Just such an upheaval presented itself in the Chichiba District uprising near Tokyo in 1884 (154–72). Somewhere between 5000 and 8000 people marched on Tokyo in opposition to the Meiji government. About 100 to 150 were organizers, the articulate minority. All of them were dismissed by the government as thieves and hooligans, but the truth was otherwise. The ages of participants were between 17 and 77. They were mostly middle-level and lower-level farmers, but the rebels included in smaller numbers landlords, merchants, laborers, business proprietors, carpenters, plasterers, and others in humble vocations. On the march for people's rights and justice, they were armed with swords, spears, guns, some cannon, and pitchforks. One old man was armed with a cane.

Their collective grievances, long repressed behind a mask of resignation and passivity, were heavy taxation, property confiscation, debt, and merciless harassment by creditors, which burdened them with unbearable hardship. Creditors were supported by the government to extract money for capital formation, since the Meiji government did not take out foreign loans to build industry and military. The agricultural sector provided the bulk of revenue. The rebels had relied in good faith on "conventional morality" to get them through—hard work, thrift, honesty, patience, and responsibility for debt—but none of those traditional virtues made a difference: "How did they overcome this deeply rooted passive attitude and undergo a transformation so as to confront governmental power proudly? The answer is that they pursued conventional morality, the basis of their own inner morality and self-discipline, and then broke through its limitations. Only after they had presented petitions time after time with diligence and sincerity, and had gone through self-reflection on their own shortcomings, did they finally reach the point at which they could endure no longer" (178).

Creditors in the Tokugawa era had responded to conventional morality and made allowances for gradual payment of debt with extensions of time. Not the Meiji collectors. Hence the intensity of frustration and anger among people cornered by severe poverty as Meiji officials and their agents squeezed a dried orange for non-existent juice. The uprising was crushed by government forces, thousands of the "hooligans" were declared guilty out of hand, and their leaders were executed or imprisoned. The movement for people's rights among rural people, which had counterparts with coal miners and women exploited in the silk industry, was a brief refusal "to starve in silence." With this defeat, what was in their minds? "These farmers believed that their poverty and distress stemmed from their own or their parent's crime of not being able to endure the self-discipline enjoined by a stern conventional morality, and this helpless resignation made their plight more serious" (223). In short, they blamed themselves.

What Irokawa calls "consciousness in the lower depths" survived and was expressed in poetry, songs, and diaries from tenant formers, miners, soldiers, factory workers, and prostitutes, which contain "the strong reality of the people's consciousness of that day" (227–29). But this consciousness came to include demeaning signs of submission as well as flashes of resistance to state authority. In time, consciousness of Japan's masses about people's rights was dimmed and diverted by indoctrination into the system of national polity (*kokutai*), which was undergirded by investment of reverence and state power in the emperor. The entire educational system was reworked to stress an ethics of loyalty and submission to the emperor, a divine being descended from the Sun Goddess.

The Meiji state needed a comprehensive framework for inculcating mass discipline and compliance. Tradition had its limitations. Grasping the Japanese mode of thought "ends up in intellectual fragments— Buddhist, Confucian, shamanistic, and Western bits and pieces ... What was called traditional thought provided no true legacy for the future since it was never 'traditionalized' and so succumbed easily to the onslaught of Westernization in the Meiji period ... Japan lacked an organizing intellectual principle—a spiritual axis like Christianity where authority was closely symbolized by an absolute providence ...

" (261). The result was a vacuum waiting to be filled. The strongest contenders were the contrived "emperor system" and "family-state" to foster unity, group consciousness, and supply a spiritual axis on the national level. Folk morality cultivated in the village family—humility, obedience, diligence, discipline—was reinterpreted as state loyalty and patriotism.

Irokawa argues that popular consciousness was not wholly captured and subdued by this strategy: "It seems to me that the notion of *kokutai* never penetrated the inner life of the people deeply enough to have become a spiritual axis ... If the leaders had actually achieved their goal, there would have been no need for Japan to become a police state ... " (272). Diverting family sentiments and loyalty to emperor and state, with which he was identified, necessitated regular shocks in the form of war: "At a moment of national crisis, the idea of the family-state took its first hold on the masses. Then the state had to sustain the fiction by providing additional war shocks at appropriate intervals to tighten the loosening bonds around the national psyche" (293).

Irokawa's research, thought, and writing are focused on "people's history" (*minshushi*), an attempt to recover the substance and meaning of a deeper current of Japanese sensibility than that found among people living in cities. His effort was ground breaking. The "culture" referred to is that of ordinary men and women largely neglected by Japanese historiography until recent times. Instead of the usual focus on elites, whether political, economic, social, or intellectual, he turns to "people's history." Therefore his idea of "culture" is not achievements of philosophy, art, and literature that attracted a cultural historian like Jacob Burckhardt (see essay 20 in this volume), but rather values and activities of obscure people in humble settings explored more in line with the French *Annales* School. Accordingly he was much indebted to fellow scholars who deviated like him from historical fashions of the day and turned to insights of folklore, popular Japanese religion, sociology, geography, and anthropology.

Works by Irokawa

The Culture of the Meiji Era (Meiji no bunka), trans. edited by Marius B. Jansen; trans. by Ronald Morse, Nobura Hiraga, Stephen Vlastos, Eiji Yutani, Carol Gluck (Princeton, New Jersey: Princeton University Press, 1985).

Works about Irokawa

For a biographical sketch, see *The Culture of the Meji Era*, pp. ix–xiii.

Short Biographies of Eminent Japanese in Ancient and Modern Times, 2 vols. (1890). This work, published in Tokyo, is anonymous. See volume 2.

Gluck, Carol, "The People in History: Recent Trends in Japanese Historiography," *Journal of Asian Studies* 38:1 (November 1978).

Useful references

Botsman, Daniel, *Punishment and Power in the Making of Modern Japan* (Princeton, New Jersey: Princeton University Press, 2004).

Bowen, Roger, *Rebellion and Democracy in Meiji Japan: A Study of Commoners in the Popular Rights Movement* (Berkeley, California: University of California Press, 1980).

Gluck, Carol, *Japan's Modern Myths: Ideology in the Late Meiji Period* (Princeton, New Jersey: Princeton University Press, 1985).

Section Notes

1 Quoted in Blacker, *The Japanese Enlightenment*, p. 10.
2 Guizot's unfinished volumes were translated from French into English by William Hazlitt in 1846.

INDIA

Themes 2 (non-Western historiography), 3 (issues of critical historiography), 4 (genres of history)

For some time India was thought not to have an indigenous historical tradition because timelessness rather than time was more important to its dominant Hindu culture. History came to India, it was long claimed, only through British occupation and rule. British persuasion was that India had no history worth discussing anyway, being a *mélange* of competing petty courtier politics and sectarian religions. The chief impetus to historical writing was the growth of Indian national consciousness in the nineteenth century. Indian historiography arose from precursors in the nationalist schools that flourished before Independence. They had a firm sense of evidence and ranged over the entire 3500-year spectrum of Indian history.

India now has its own ample historiography that includes the main branches of history—political, diplomatic, social, economic, cultural, colonial, postcolonial, and so on. There are many distinguished Indian historians of various methodological and ideological persuasions who have contributed knowledge about traditional and modern India from indigenous sources, which includes archives as well as epigraphic, numismatic, and archeological material. They have written about India in ancient times, the relations of Hinduism and Islam, dynamics and consequences of the British Empire in India from its inception, the movement for independence, and much besides.

This section offers two historians who represent the postcolonial genre of historiography, a major focus of Indian scholarship, but from different conceptual perspectives. Pannikar writes from the Marxist viewpoint that history is driven by class struggle, Guha from that of recently established subaltern studies in the 1980s about beliefs and activities of Indians caught in subordinate positions by imperialism. Focus is distinctive in both cases, but the works are detached in spirit and sensitive to evidence in support of findings and conclusions.

30. CULTURE, IDEOLOGY, HEGEMONY: INTELLECTUALS AND SOCIAL CONSCIOUSNESS IN COLONIAL INDIA (K. N. PANIKKAR, 1936–)

Panikkar was born in the progressive state of Kerala in Southern India and educated at Government Victoria College. He went on from there to the University of Rajasthan for a doctorate. He taught at a number of Indian universities and serves as Dean of Social Sciences at Jawaharlal Nehru University in New Delhi. He has been a Visiting Professor or a Fellow at institutions in Paris, Berlin, and London. His chosen specialty is the cultural and intellectual history of India, fields in which he is a leading authority.

One of his themes is the uniqueness of cultural identity even if nations share the same types of political and economic organization. A second is the damage wrought to cultural identity by a policy of exclusion instead of inclusion, for national identity is tied to a varied cultural past, which Panikkar expresses in the plural as "pasts." His reputation as author and academic has been supplemented by political activism on behalf of human rights in India, which has not always endeared him to the Hindu national government because of even-handedness with Muslims and other minorities and rejection of caste as a standard for identity.

He is a progressive secularist in a country with ongoing religious and communal tensions. Critics on the far right of the Hindu social and political spectrum are especially annoyed when he reminds them of a difference between religious mythology and history. He is blunt about the status of Hinduism in the nineteenth century: "Undoubtedly, Hinduism was beset with idolatry, polytheism, and superstition" (4). He qualifies this observation with a reminder that reform and change were in the air through the latter half of the eighteenth century and was stifled by the time the British East India Company locked up India in the mid-nineteenth century.

While an undergraduate, he worked for the Malabar Student Federation, affiliated with the Communist Party of India. A party leader, also a relative, became his mentor, imparting the Marxist analysis of poverty, inequality, and injustice as a result of class struggle. The word "ideology" in the title of his book is classically Marxist in meanings and overtones: "Ideologies being material and not ideal in their origin and existence, changes in the influence of the dominant ideology are related to changes in the material conditions of existence. The nature, direction and momentum of these changes as well as the ideological forms in which men become conscious of these changes, constitute the basis for the creation or adoption of an alternative system of beliefs" (176).

Culture, Ideology, Hegemony is about the conflict of colonialism, modernism, and tradition in the minds and ideals of nineteenth-century Indian intellectuals, Hindu and Muslim. It attempts to explain why they failed to understand their situation in a Western colonial empire and were unable to implement reforms on a Western or a traditional Indian model: "Who constituted intellectuals in colonial India? How did they come into being ... and what function did they perform in the given social and political situation? ... Basically they were nonconformists, critical of existing social conditions and performing the social function of generation or adoption and propagation of ideas with a view to ushering in socio-political progress ... " (63).

The eight interlocking essays, delivered at various institutions, are carefully and heavily documented. Often half a page is given to notes. It is doubtful that any author or thinker of importance in Indian intellectual life is overlooked, including views of some westerners. With the help of colleagues and students, Panikkar ransacked libraries, archives, and private collections for books, journals, newspapers, tracts, and pamphlets. Outside of India he searched the India Office Library in London, the London School of Oriental and African Studies Library, the British Museum Library, Oxford's Bodleian Library, the National Library in Paris, and other collections. After an overview of his subject, Panikkar discusses cultural trends in pre-colonial India, conceptual and historiographic issues, the relation of culture to ideology, the quest for alternative meanings in British India, cultivation of new cultural interests, the relation of medicine to cultural hegemony, and the ideological background of marriage reform in Malabar.

Nineteenth-century intellectuals viewed culture in a way at cross purposes with their colonial masters. For Panikkar, the explanation of failure by well meaning, intelligent men is clear: "Marxist historiography has primarily attempted to demonstrate how politico-economic structures warped intellectual development in nineteenth-century India. Though tending towards reductionism and determinism at times, it does define ... why intellectuals in the nineteenth century had to face certain defeat and tragedy in their socio-cultural efforts" (62). A major reason was an ideological mistake: "The political perspective and activities in colonial India were based on the ideal of gradual realization of a bourgeois-democratic order" (94). The missing insight was what happened in the material base of existence—the British expropriated the fruits of Indian labor in a capitalist framework.

Initially the British were welcomed as a cleansing, stabilizing force:

> The decline of the Mughal empire and the consequent emergence of autonomous states resulting in the absence of a strong political and military power over large parts of the country provided a golden opportunity for freebooters, both European and Indian, who plundered and ravaged the countryside ... the country lay prostrate and helpless. Minor chieftains who were unable to defend themselves applied for military and political protection to the East India Company ... the changes brought about by the British—the rule of law, security to life and property, and opportunity to acquire the arts and sciences of Europe, appeared 'truly astonishing.'
>
> (20–21)

The British presence was viewed as providential: "The notion of divine dispensation–British rule was willed by God—enabled intellectuals to welcome and legitimize the colonial presence ... That British rule could be an instrument not so much of exploitation and oppression, but of socio-political transformation, was an articulation of this consciousness" (24).

The future of India lay not in teachings of the ancient Vedas but in the modern ideas of Thomas Paine, John Stuart Mill, and Herbert Spencer: "European rationalist and humanist thought, scientific knowledge, economic development and political institutions were conceived by Indian intellectuals as progressive characteristics of the west" (59). The prominent reformer Rammohun Roy, in "a famous letter on education addressed to Lord Amherst," compared Indian to Western knowledge unfavorably: "If Indian minds continued to be enclosed within the indigenous system, Rammohun argued, the country would remain in darkness. The only way out according to him, was to internalize western knowledge and thus embark on a path of progress" (147).

What Indians did not understand was that such ideas, filtered through colonialism, did not have the same strength and meaning in India that they had in Europe: "While these progressive attributes of Western society were looked upon with admiration and approval and compared with conditions in India, there was no appreciation of the social and intellectual forces which made these advances possible ... no attempt was made to test their adaptability in the context of the existing indigenous cultural and intellectual traditions" (59–60).

Panikkar argues that Intellectuals were misled by early advantages of British rule. Ideological misdirection lay in the belief that Western science and "enlightenment" would conquer poverty and superstition and revitalize the country. Western knowledge was the answer: "The formula was very simple: familiarity with European history, institutions and languages, and the concomitant influence of the European ideas of liberty, rationalism, and humanism acted as the 'open sesame' which made Indians critical of their own institutions and consequently led them to embark upon a career of reform" (3–4; see essay 28 in this volume).

Then British contempt for traditional Indian institutions and ways sidetracked intellectuals attracted by Western ideas and models and forced them into a posture of ambivalence, particularly about language, religion, and education: "Therefore the subjected increasingly took to the defence of indigenous institutions and traditional culture. Resurrection of the past, identification of modernity in tradition, an enquiry to establish the superiority of traditional knowledge and achievements ... were the chief characteristics of the response. Intellectual transformation was inevitably curbed by this historical necessity ... " (101).

A fresh look at tradition was necessitated by the inability of European medicine, introduced for the benefit of Europeans, to reach more than a few Indians because of inadequate staffing and infrastructure. The result was a resurgence of traditional medical practices: "The increasing influence of colonial culture ... underlined the possible loss of the cultural heritage ... intellectuals were caught in a paradox; to discard the old and create a new cultural milieu, or, to preserve and retrieve the traditional cultural space so that the past is not swept off the ground ... efforts to reconcile this paradox led to a critical inquiry into both the past as well as the present" (145).

Reform for many intellectuals centered on mass education stressing science helpful to agriculture and industry while liberating ordinary men and women from superstition and credulous religious beliefs. The British goal for education was more narrow: " ... dissemination of the colonial ideology and utility for administrative needs were the main objectives of the educational policy of the British government ... The alien rule was maintained not simply with the help of police and the army but also by an illusion created by ideological influences. In creating the illusion, education, which could help project British institutions and values as the idea, was conceived as an effective medium" (9). A second major parting of the ways was British insistence on the primacy of English over Indian languages, which was for administration of the empire and not renewal of India. The religious issue was Christianity versus India's traditional religions.

The vision of intellectuals was doomed from the start. They could not implement liberal Western ideology (democracy, industrialism, rationalism, individualism, humanism, self-determination) under the thumb a colonial ideology for which control, exploitation, profit were on behalf of bourgeois values that ignored the masses of India. At the same time, there was "an awareness of the inadequacy of traditional institutions to cope with the new situation created by colonial intrusion" (58). Even promising reforms in that sphere were ultimately blocked by colonial ideology and policy.

Panikkar is a valuable figure in historiography for his secular outlook and insistence that history stay with verifiable facts untainted by mythology. He represents a credible, scholarly, fair-minded example of Marxist historiography applied to understanding India's encounter with colonialism.

Works by Panikkar

Against Lord and State: Religion and Uprisings in Malabar, 1836–1921 (New Delhi: Oxford University Press, 2002).

Colonialism, Culture, and Resistance (New Delhi: Oxford University Press, 2007).

Culture, Ideology, Hegemony: Intellectuals and Social Consciousness in Colonial India (London: Anthem Press, 2002). First published in 1995.

31. ELEMENTARY ASPECTS OF PEASANT INSURGENCY IN COLONIAL INDIA (RANAJIT GUHA, 1922–)

Guha is founder and most distinguished representative of Subaltern historiography, which studies the subordination of Indian peasants to British rule during the colonial period. Subaltern studies focus on uncovering a historiography of those subordinated to the dominant power of elites both Indian and British. A more general meaning is the study of people assigned lesser status because of gender, ethnicity, religion, class, or sexual orientation. A considerable literature has accumulated that aims to turn the interpretation of Indian history in the nineteenth century upside down in favor of the subordinate Indian masses rather than the highly visible and powerful elites who governed them.

Guha's work is indebted to Marxian ideas of alienation, class consciousness, and struggle between classes for power. He appeals to works of the British Marxists E.H. Hobsbawn and Christopher Hill (see essay 44 in this volume). His use of symbolism and the function of signs to explain insurgent behavior relies on the linguist Ferdinand Saussure. There is no specific reference to the Annales School, but Guha is obviously digging into history for the "mentalities" of ordinary people in rural India. He refers frequently to peasant disturbances in the West and China for comparative purposes. A comprehensive account of uprisings in detail is disclaimed, but there is nevertheless close analysis of many insurgencies to illustrate general points, which he delivers with absorbing detail, a wealth of references, and a helpful glossary of terms.

Setting aside British and Indian rural elites (landlords and money lenders), the vast majority of Indians in the nineteenth century were illiterate farmers working small plots in the countryside, many of them on land owned by someone else. Famine, indebtedness, mistreatment, and other hardships aroused resentment and desperation that resulted in frequent uprisings. A major worry of the British East Company was this sea of potential peasant discontent: "They were concerned to stop their newly acquired dominions from disintegrating like the moribund empire of the Mughals under the impact of peasant insurrections. For agrarian disturbances ... were endemic throughout the first three quarters of British rule until the very end of the nineteenth century" (1).

Colonialism and insurgency were India's twin realities. The British kept scrupulous records of confrontations with the insurgent "other." Administrative accounts of peasant insurgency emerged as a form of Western historiography and a narrative of self-conscious power. The narrative was always from the perspective British interests: "By making security of the state into the central problematic of peasant insurgency, it assimilated the latter as merely an element in the career of colonialism ... the peasant was denied recognition as a subject of history in his own right ... " (3). No matter who did the writing, an official or a private party, the perspective was never that of the peasant, who was denied consciousness of his place in history.

A consequence of usurping historical narrative was an elitist claim that uprisings were spontaneous, formless outbursts, "elitist because it makes the mobilization of the peasantry altogether contingent on the intervention of charismatic leaders, advanced political organizations or upper classes" (4). The result was for elitist historiography to view peasant insurgency as the unconscious prehistory of the organized

Indian freedom movement under the Congress Party and Gandhi rather than as a concrete expression of peasant consciousness. The error is to suppose that whatever is conscious means conscious leadership and political organization like that of the British, although Guha wants to argue that peasant movements were not without leadership and organization, however weak because of "localism, sectarianism, and ethnicity" (10).

His objective is to focus on "consciousness as our central theme" and to "depict this struggle not as a series of specific encounters but in its general form" (11). The stages to full consciousness occupies six of the eight chapters—negation, ambiguity, modality, solidarity, and transmission. The phrase "elementary aspects" refers to recurrent general ideas and practices in agrarian uprisings. The time span for recovering historical evidence is the 117 years between 1783 and 1900. The evidence is predominantly elitist—various kinds of records from police, army, and administrative sources, as well as private diaries and mémoires.

Folklore and oral accounts might add something here and there but are not sufficient either in quantity or quality. Getting at insurgent consciousness through elite sources works because "counter-insurgency, which derives directly from insurgency ... can hardly afford a discourse that is not fully and compulsively involved with the rebel and his activities" (15). It turns out that elite sources are full of direct and indirect references to peasant behavior and attitudes, as they had to be as reports on uprisings. But care is needed not to be captive of the "subjectivity of the guardians of the law and order ... " (106).

The consciousness of a peasant was stimulated by awareness of his distance from those wielding power. Self-knowledge through negation and inversion, or turning things upside down, were points of departure to full consciousness of class status: "It was this fight for prestige which was at the very heart of insurgency. Inversion was its principal modality. It was a political struggle in which the rebel appropriated and/or destroyed the insignia of his enemy's power, and hoped thus to abolish marks of his own subalternity" (75). The insignia taken over during an uprising included clothing, conveyances (horses), and customs of language that were marks of the rural elite. Taboos of distance between classes were ignored: "He spoke thus in a 'borrowed language'—that of his enemy, for he knew no other" (Ibid.).

Inversions of language were accompanied by specific acts of demolition: "There was hardly a peasant uprising ... that did not cause the destruction of large quantities of written or printed material including rent rolls, deeds and bonds, and public records of all kinds ... popular violence was often astutely selective about all written evidence of peasant debts" (51). Since religion favored the rural elite, peasants sought either to appropriate or destroy it. Peasants were denied access to temples, major symbols of Hinduism reserved for the elite, so desecration usually resulted from an uprising.

Inversion as a means of upsetting the status quo was the beginning of peasant consciousness. A transition from negations to the stage of ambiguity has to do with perceptions of criminality that usually preceded an uprising. Two codes clashed, one for upright defenders of laws that kept them in power, and a second for "criminals" who flouted the laws out of anger and deprivation. Ambiguity emerged as criminals were sometimes successful enough, like Robin Hood, to shed their notoriety and enjoy high status with "custodians of order" (79). This unexpected interplay of two codes obscured the unchallenged authority of established law.

Insurgencies condemned by authorities have common features that distinguish them from individual criminal acts: "The mass, communal aspect of rebel violence follows thus from its open and public character and differentiates it from the typically individualistic or small-group operations of crime" (115). Peasant rebellion is not the same as rural crime: " ... insurgency soon extricates itself from the placenta of common crime in which it may be initially enmeshed and establishes its own identity as a violence which is *public, collective*, destructive and *total* in its modalities ... opposition between the two types of violence may be represented as a series of binary contrasts thus—public/secretive, collective/ individualistic ... " (109).

Interaction of modalities unfolds into the next stage:

> From the insurgent's point of view perhaps the most essential aspect of the phenomenon often described as contagion by his foes, is solidarity. This is an important signifier of consciousness in two ways. First, it represents the rebel's consciousness of his own activity; solidarity is, in other words, a figure of his self-consciousness. Secondly, it separates his own consciousness of this activity completely and unequivocally from its cognition by his enemies ... What is regarded by one side as a symptom of disease, immorality and negation of reason is to the other a positive sign of health and spiritual rejuvenation based on the unquestionable right of the oppressed to resist.
>
> (168–69)

The identification of resistance as a disease was evident during the sepoy–peasant rebellion of 1857–58, when British officials described it as a "contagion" or "infection" of "epidemic" proportions (220–21).

With the emergence of solidarity in a peasant movement, consciousness within the group is clear about who is a true supporter and who is an enemy, collaborator, or traitor: "The insurgents' defence of their solidarity assumed its most dramatic expression in their violence against active collaborators of all kinds. In this respect the peasant rebels of India were no different from those of any other country" (214). The weak consciousness of fence sitters and recalcitrants who resist solidarity within the community was addressed by "pressing," a combination of "intimidation and persuasion," also common to insurgencies everywhere (195).

The step from community solidarity to transmission of an insurgency in a preliterate culture was achieved more by spoken than by written means, but aural and visual signs and signals might be used as well, like beating of drums and dancing: "For in rebellion, as in other circumstances of real life, human communication operates eclectically by a mixture of signs" (227). Failure of British authority to grasp the meaning of signs used by insurgents demonstrated the failure "of alien authority fully to understand, hence control, the native population under its rule" (230). A key means of transmission and communication that confounded the rulers was rumor: " … it is … by virtue of its character as a type of speech that rumour serves as the most 'natural' and indeed indispensable vehicle of insurgency" (256). The dynamic of rumor is that once heard the hearer wants to pass it on to affect other people's behavior and their perceptions about what is going on.

Transmission had as its goals a successful insurgency and control of territory viewed as a homeland. Territoriality "as a positive factor of rebel mobilization" is best illustrated by the "mutiny" of 1857. Formerly peaceful peasants in dozens of villages revolted out of a sense of place against both rural and British elites. Geographical and social space coincided as many ethnic groups, Rajputs, Mewatis, Gujars, rose to recover usurped territory: "In some of the revolts involving these ethnic masses the political motivation could hardly be missed. They took up arms in order to recover what they believed to have been their ancestral domains" (318).

Guha has attempted an analysis of consciousness and its reform that explains the behavior of subaltern masses in colonial India who tried to turn the "rural world upside down" (337). Some critics have suggested that he attempts too much with too little suitable evidence.

On the other hand, with richness of exposition, an instructive conceptual framework, careful sifting of available sources, and ready acknowledgment of limitations, he has done his best and added a valuable dimension to historiography.

Works by Guha

An Indian Historiography of India: A Nineteenth Century Agenda & Its Implications (Calcutta: K.P. Bagchi and Co., 1988).

Dominance Without Hegemony: History and Power in Colonial India (Cambridge, Massachusetts: Harvard University Press, 1998).

Elementary Aspects of Peasant Insurgency in Colonial India (New Delhi: Oxford, 1983).

Works about Guha

Amin, Shahid and Gautam Badra, *Subaltern Studies: Writings on South Asian History and Society*, 10 vols. (New Delhi; Oxford: Oxford University Press, 1994–99). Volume VIII contains a biography of Guha.

Sathyamuthy, T.V., "Indian Peasant Historiography: A Critical Perspective on Ranajit Guha's Work", *Journal of Peasant Studies*, 18:1 (October, 1990): 93–141.

Useful references

Guha, Ranajit and Gayatri Chakravorty Spivak (eds.), *Selected Subaltern Studies* (New York: Oxford University Press, 1988).

AFRICA

Themes 2 (non-Western historiography), 3 (issues of critical historiography), 4 (genres of history), 5 (breadth of inquiry)

Africa is perhaps the most difficult of all places to bring into historical focus because of its teeming array of peoples, cultures, and kingdoms. A British historian once proposed that Africa has no history, a view now antiquated. But there are problems. In addition to numerous ethnic groups, there are currently some 50 countries to take into account on a continent three times the size of the USA. A second obstacle to historical understanding is the relative absence of written materials before the colonial period. Historians glean what they can from a skeletal record but must have recourse to linguistics, archeology, art, comparative linguistics, oral history, anthropology, and geography to fill out a picture. The historian who tries to encompass Africa as a whole needs far more elaborate equipment for research and assessment than a historian of Europe.

For our purposes, African history can be divided into several phases: long centuries when peoples and cultures of Africa flourished and were virtually unknown to Europeans south of the Sahara and the Sudan; the transatlantic slave trade that brought Europeans into contact with Africans along the western coastal regions and resulted in a mass involuntary transportation of Africans to Latin America, the Caribbean, and America; the period of direct colonial occupation and exploitation after 1870; and decolonization and state independence after 1960, which has included an active Pan-African movement. Specialized studies abound in all these areas. The challenge for African historiography is how to organize and integrate this historical and cultural multiplicity from a wide angle perspective.

32. THE AFRICAN EXPERIENCE (VINCENT KHAPOYA, 1944–)

Khapoya was born in Kenya and educated initially in Catholic mission schools. He came to the USA for higher education and took a

Bachelor's degree in mathematics and political science at Oregon State University, a Master's degree in international studies at the University of Denver, and went on at the same institution to finish a doctorate in political science. He has taught at the universities of Nairobi, Denver, and Wayne State. His specialties are African politics and foreign policy. He is the author of numerous articles on African affairs. He is currently professor of political science at Oakland University in Rochester, Michigan. *The African Experience* is based on a college course, Introduction to Africa, he has taught for many years. It attempts a very difficult task.

The "history" of Africa does not lend itself to readily coherent exposition. In Khapoya's account, the more than 50 countries presently comprising Africa, including island satellites like Madagascar, occupy a continent 5000 miles in length and 3000 miles in width. The topographical variety includes the world's largest desert, the Sahara, the world's longest river, the Nile, a mountain higher than any in the USA, Kilimanjaro, an immense rainforest in Congo, the world's second largest fresh water lake, Victoria, and hundreds of square miles of open savanna, some of which still has abundant wild life. Inhabiting the land is a bewildering variety of ethnic groups speaking up to 800 different languages in four major language families. Languages are so plentiful in many nations, up to a half dozen in one country, that European tongues are declared "official," mostly English, French, Portuguese, and Spanish, to head off disruptive claims and debate about what native language should be official. Amidst this kaleidoscope of cultural diversity, the problem for Khapoya is to find a coherent center around which lesser details can be gathered.

Roughly a third of his work is on African culture before colonial intrusions, a second third on policies and effects of the colonial period, and the final third on African nationalism and problems after the departure of colonial powers around 1960, including a long chapter on South Africa, which "in some peculiar way until now represented the failure of African nationalism and a brazen humiliation of Africans purely on account of their race and color" (xiv). We must be content to sample what he offers, with South Africa left out altogether.

Khapoya aims to "overcome the temptation to present Africa as though only its politics, or history, or language matters and nothing else. Africa needs to be understood in its totality" (xiii). This totality has a historical dimension, but Khapoya wishes to suggest the unfolding and consolidation of an African "experience" that rises above a multitude of particulars. In seeking that end, his work undertakes to tame the diversity. The question raised for historiography is how Africa's immensity and the profusion of its languages and cultures and the complexity of its history can be focused as an "experience."

The methodology and use of sources is interdisciplinary by necessity:

> Africa needs to be presented comprehensively: in its physical attributes, its history, its social structure and culture. The accumulation of evidence about African history in pre-colonial times has been remarkable and opened wide vistas once obscure: ' ... new kinds of historical techniques and data made it possible for Africans and Africanists ... to seriously begin reclaiming the rich African past ... linguists developed techniques for indicating ancient historical connections between different African language families, and historians ... developed increasingly rigorous techniques for collecting, transcribing and evaluating different kinds of oral traditions from medieval African kingdoms.'
> (69–70)

He clears away some verbal underbrush. Certain words used to talk about Africa are best left aside, notably "tribe" and "race." The idea of tribalism was a colonial legacy: "Not only do many Africans regard the connotation of the word 'tribe' along with words like 'primitive,' 'superstitious,' and 'natives,' as derogatory, but most Africanist scholars have also come to regard the denotation of the word 'tribe' as both imprecise and misleading" (13). Better to speak of societies, clans, ethnicities, classes, or just the name of a people, like the Yoruba in Nigeria, even though more than a few African nations still use tribal designations for administrative purposes, another inheritance from colonialists. The idea of "race" associated with skin color is equally vague and unhelpful. The most fruitful criterion is language: "Language differences ... have indeed become the Africanist's primary tool in trying to differentiate, classify, or compare and contrast the various cultures and peoples of Africa" (15).

Race may not be a key to African cultures and history, but it does have something to do with identity and common "experience," as Khapoya illustrates with an anecdote about unexpected recognition, likeness, and empathy:

> One afternoon many years ago, while strolling downtown Ayr on the west coast of Scotland, I saw a black man waving wildly at

me from across the street. I stopped. When he crossed the street and walked over to me, he said he could just tell from a distance that I was an African. He said there were no other Africans in Ayr and he was dying to talk to 'brother.' The gentleman was from Nigeria. We talked as though we had known each other for years.

(28)

Thus the color black brought together a Kenyan from East Africa and a Nigerian from West Africa in, of all places, a small town in Scotland.

Despite linguistic and ethnic diversity Khapoya notes shared African values and practices, small and large, which underlie a common experience. Greetings are more formal and extended than in the West. Older people are more revered for their experience and wisdom. In obvious contrast to the West, the individual is subordinated to the group: "African societies are collectivist societies. The group is paramount, and the group's interests clearly supersede those of the individual. A person defines his identity in terms of belonging to a group" (44). Bad behavior reflects on the group as well as the individual. Social groups have much in common with respect kinship and marriage. In matters of religion, despite variations on the theme of divinity, Africans are highly spiritual and accept belief in a Supreme Being who created the world. There is a shared belief in spirits that inhabit the natural world, including ancestral spirits.

Although descent in a family may take place several ways, including matriarchy, or through the mother's line, the most common arrangement is patriarchal, or through the father's line. Descent "determines such matters as inheritance, identity, the identity of a child born into a marriage (or outside a marriage for that matter), and even the location of a new house for a new couple" (31). Throughout Africa, marriage is about the security and stability of extended families rather than desires and hopes of individuals. Marriage involves a transfer of wealth, called "bridewealth," usually in the form of cattle, goats, and sheep, which, among other things, compensates the bride's family for losing the value of her labor.

Polygamy (taking more than one wife or husband) "is found virtually in all African societies" (34). The common form is polygyny, or a man taking a second wife, or maybe even a third. Among reasons for the practice are more premature deaths of male children than of females, leaving more women than men when everyone is expected to marry; having many children as a "hedge" against infant deaths;

and providing hands to work the fields and perform other valuable economic tasks. In the absence of male prospects, there is even a custom in some places of women marrying women and delegating impregnation to a male relative.

Pre-colonial Africa fostered two kinds of political systems: " ... states and 'stateless' societies. States were organized structurally in much the same way as modern states ... The 'stateless' societies ... were politically decentralized entities, had no bureaucracies to speak of, and tended to be based on kinship (i.e., lineage systems and extended families)" (61). Before the coming of Europeans, most Africans lived in stateless societies, but there were African leaders who "succeeded in building effective large-scale governments ... " (70). An example is the medieval (1000–1600) empire of Songhay, which flourished in the fifteenth and sixteenth centuries with a famed university in Timbuktu. Furthermore: "Medieval civilizations 'rose and fell' throughout the tropical rain forests and savanna woodlands of West Africa's coasts and hinterlands ... " (89).

A new setting for African experience was the international slave trade (1440–1870) that eventually carried off twelve million West Africans and several million from other places. Mass bondage contributed to the commercial and industrial development of Europe while Africa receded into relative underdevelopment. In the first half of the nineteenth century, the slave trade continued to disrupt African development. In the second half of the century, usurped African territories were helpless against modern European weapons (96). Effects are well known: "Even as nineteenth-century Africans were building more productive economies and broader national identities, European colonization ended such trends and interrupted the ongoing continuities in African political development" (110). By 1900 virtually the whole of Africa minus four percent was under the dominion of European powers, mostly the British and French with about 70 percent, Belgium, Germany, Italy, Portugal, accounting for the rest. Khapoya summarizes motives of European states and charts the political, economic, and social course taken by colonization.

The shared experience of colonialism has more than one side. For many academics and Africans colonialism is Western civilization's original sin, but others are ambivalent about losses and gains. Khapoya' judgment is even handed. On the negative side:

> There was massive exploitation of Africa in terms of resource depletion, labor exploitation, unfair taxation, lack of industrialization, the prohibition of inter-African trade, and the introduction of

> fragile dependent one-crop economies ... The exacerbation of ethnic rivalries ... The alienation and undermining of traditional African authority patterns through the use of chiefs for colonial duties ... The destruction of African culture and values through the imposition of alien religions ...
>
> (144)

On the positive side of the colonial experience, five benefits are cited:

> One is the introduction of Western medicine ... Second, the introduction of formal education ... to unlock the hidden potential of the African people ... Nearly all leaders who emerged from World War II to lead African colonies toward independence acquired their rhetorical and organizational skills from colonial education ... Third, the small infrastructure that colonial authorities established [roads, harbors, water systems, railroads, etc.] became the foundation upon which the new African leaders built their new national institutions ... Fourth, the introduction of Islam and Christianity ... greatly simplified African spirituality ... Fifth, by imposing arbitrary boundaries ... countries were created with the stroke of a pen. Colonization may have shortened considerably the process of state-formation.
>
> (144–46)

With the end of colonial rule, African nationalism arose in a spirit of optimism, which Khapoya argues existed generically in pre-colonial times:

> It is worth stressing that African nationalism, like nationalism elsewhere in the world, is not new. It is as old as ancient times. In fact, in Africa, contrary to a common view in Western scholarship of Africa, African nationalism predates colonialism ... one finds coherent, organized African communities with a very strong sense of identity, prepared to defend their territories and cultural integrity against those who would want to undermine or destroy them.
>
> (150)

Recent African nationalism is mirrored in the subsequent history of peoples subdued by the now defunct Soviet Empire: "What binds all these groups is a common heritage, based on religion, language, and historical experience. The historical experience of living under foreign hegemony or being governed by political parties thought to be manipulated by an outside power has been a potent driving force behind national secessionist attempts in Eastern Europe as well as in modern Africa" (Ibid.).

Where African nationalism differed from that of Europeans was in the absence of states with fixed boundaries, but if political nationalism was rare, cultural nationalism was not: "There are ... many African groups with strong historical and social identities comparable to the ethnic and national groups of Europe ... In political terms, African nationalism began to assert itself primarily after the Second World War" (169). In the African experience, freedom had to be demanded, for colonial powers were not prepared to offer it (176).

Failure of Africans to make progress hoped for after independence is an experience in part of political instability, which hindered the creation of strong states and stalled improvement of material well being for ordinary people: "Many African nationalist leaders, not having been exposed to the 'democratic traditions' of their pre-colonial heritage, or of the European metropoles, were determined not to share power or let anyone challenge them ... African leaders often saw themselves as participants in a 'zero-sum' game of politics in which gains by one side are always made at the expense of the opposition" (189). Military coups proliferated, wars over arbitrary boundaries were disruptive, economies stagnated for want of intelligent planning, ethnic conflict surfaced, irresponsibility in government was rife: "Bad economic and political choices and decisions, economic mismanagement, corruption, lack of vision on the part of leaders, lack of open political discourse, and accountability, explain Africa's sad story" (212).

Khapoya balances this dismal side of African experience with a few success stories of economic growth, education, improved health care, and political reform, but much work lies ahead: "Africans themselves are going to have to take the lead in changing systems and improving their lives. They cannot sit on the sidelines and be spectators. Years of sympathetic words from the West ... and decades of expert advice from expatriates have not lifted Africans out of poverty" (217).

Amidst a host of books on African history and culture, few have attempted an overview of the world's second largest continent, its history and cultures, in a single volume. Khapoya's work is reasonably successful with this vast subject and has the advantage of being written by a born African. Obviously all the material, explanations, and judgments that would satisfy specialists could not be included, but at least the historiography of Africa has been provided with a respectable scholarly base for more detailed study, which is assisted by varied references at the end of each chapter and a concluding bibliography.

Works by Khapoya

The African Experience (2nd ed.: Upper Saddle River, New Jersey: Prentice Hall, 1998).
The Politics of Decision: A Comparative Study of AfricanPolicy Toward the Liberation Movements (Denver: University of Denver, 1975).

Useful references

Gates, Henry Louis and Kwame Anthony Appiah (eds.), *Africana: The Encyclopedia of the African and African-American Experience* (New York: Basic Civitas Books, 1999).
Maquet, Jacques, *Africanity: The Cultural Unity of Black Africa* (New York: Oxford University Press, 1972).
Oliver, Roland, *The African Experience: From Olduvai Gorge to the 21st Century* (rev. ed.; London: Weidenfeld and Nicolson, 1999).

33. PAN-AFRICAN HISTORY: POLITICAL FIGURES FROM AFRICA AND THE DIASPORA SINCE 1787 (HAKIM ADI AND MARIKA SHERWOOD)

Adi took his doctorate at London University and is a senior scholar at Middlesex University in London where he teaches history of Africa and the African Diaspora. He co-founded the Black and Asian Studies Association (BASA) which he chaired for a number of years. In addition to his scholarship on the African Diaspora, he has written several history books for children and appeared prominently in television documentaries. Sherwood is a senior fellow at the Institute of Commonwealth Studies, University of London. She is also a co-founder of BASA and serves as its secretary.

An explanation is needed for the choice of *Pan-African History* as a "key work" among the 50 surveyed in this volume. It consists of 40 mini-biographies or "profiles" of men and women connected with "Pan-Africanism" and the "African Diaspora." There is an immense literature of books and articles on the history of Africa, the slave trade, racism, and the dispersion of blacks around the world. The value of this brief *Pan-African History* is its panorama of personalities, leaders, rebels, and thinkers, a reminder that individuals make a difference in the broader currents of history, as Henri Pirenne believed (see essay 20 in this volume).

"Pan-African" refers to a long pursued, much diffused agenda for some form of African political and economic unity that includes people of African descent. Part of that effort has been an issue of identity to foster collective African consciousness apart from individuals in particular states, societies, or non-African environments. "Diaspora" refers to the movement of Africans by the millions, over several centuries, to North America, South America, the Caribbean, the Middle East, and Europe. An overwhelming majority of these people were unwilling migrants snatched up and transported in the European and Arab slave trade.

Much scholarship, commentary, and a host of conferences have sought to establish a coherent, working connection between Pan-African ideals and black people embedded in other cultures around the world. Thus the "pan" suffix has been extended beyond the continent of Africa to include Africans everywhere by a single criterion, whatever their assorted views and doings: "What underlies their manifold visions and approaches is the belief in some form of unity or of common purpose among the peoples of Africa and the African diaspora" (vii).

Many of the 40 men and women discussed in this work knew each other, worked for the same organizations, or attended the same conferences. As it turns out, however, Pan-Africanism did not come out of Africa: "Before 1945 many of the leading figures in Pan-African history lived and worked in the diaspora rather than in Africa itself. Indeed for a time Europe might be seen as the center of the Pan-African world" (ix).

An institutional framework for a global approach to African unity in Africa and abroad has been the Pan-African Conference. The first was held in 1900 with others to follow. Conference objectives were: " ... to bring into closer touch with each other the Peoples of African descent throughout the world, to inaugurate plans to bring about more friendly relations between Caucasian and African races, to start a movement to secure to all African races living in civilized countries their full rights and to promote their business interests" (Quoted: 191). At a more local or national level, many additional organizations have been founded, supported by books, manifestos, journals, and newsletters.

Many of the "leading figures" are well known, such as Toussaint L'Overture, Frederick Douglas, Martin Luther King, Jr., and Nelson Mandela. Others are more obscure, even if important from a Pan-African perspective, such as Nathaniel Fadipe, George Padmore, Amy Garvey, Martin Delaney, and James Horton. Assembled are journalists, historians, activists, and politicians, but there is no visible convergence on strategy, methods, or even a developed philosophy to unite people of African descent in a consistent vision of how their lives might be improved by mutual help and cooperation. Some of this variety and the clash of views within it can be sampled. A major parting of the ways among Pan-Africanists is how to achieve concrete objectives. Violence is defended by Frantz Fanon and Malcolm X, while nonviolence is the path chosen by Nelson Mandela and Martin Luther King, Jr.

The earliest figure is Quobna Ottobah Cugoano, born in 1757 in Ghana, sold into slavery at age 13, shipped to Granada, and after two years as a slave was taken by his owner to England. In some unknown way he became free, a status that was reinforced by baptism. He went to work as a servant to some well-known artists. Soon he was associated with Sons of Africa, a black abolitionist organization. He was the first black author in print denouncing the slave trade. *Thoughts and Sentiments on the Evil and Wicked Traffic of the Slavery and Commerce of the Human Species*, published in 1787, "demolishes the principle pro-slavery arguments which questioned the humanity of Africans or preached benevolence of the trade" (27). He sought to mobilize Africans on behalf of their own interest, and charged that everyone in Britain was responsible for slavery unless actively opposed to it. He advocated anti-slavery patrols along the coast of Africa and called for normal trade relations with Africans, ideas already afloat among abolitionists, which became the substance of British policy two decades later.

Edward Blyden (1832–1912) "has been seen as one of the key thinkers in the development of Pan-African ideas" (11). He was born in the Virgin Islands of free parents. After being rejected by several American colleges because of color, he turned to the American Colonization Society whose goal was to ship American Negroes to Liberia in West Africa. Blyden continued his education and career in Liberia, and came to believe Liberia would be the salvation of all oppressed black people, but especially by Christian Negroes from America, who would bring civilization with them.

His views often conflicted with Pan-Africanism. He rejected race mixture and wanted to keep the "mulatto" out of Liberia. He argued that Africans need an educational system suited to their needs and culture, but insisted on study of Latin, Greek, and the Bible. On colonialism, "Blyden began to believe that British imperialism might play a more important civilizing role in West Africa than migrants from the USA or the Caribbean ... He supported British imperialism not only in West Africa but elsewhere too, welcoming the invasion of Egypt in 1882. He believed that Britain was the colonial power that would best protect the interests of Africans ... " (13–14). He even favored European partition of Africa as best for Africans. He defies any simple idea of what a Pan-Africanist might believe and want, but is still important: " ... Blyden was one of the key contributors to the ideologies of Pan-Africanism and West African nationalism, and one of the first to articulate a notion of 'African personality' and the uniqueness of the 'African race'" (14).

W.E.B Du Bois (1868–1963), called the "father of 'Pan-Africanism,'" has been seen as "the most influential African-American intellectual of the twentieth century" (48). At the 1900 Pan-African Conference, "he chaired the committee charged with drafting its appeal 'To the Nations of the World.' It was in this appeal that the famous phrase 'The problem of the twentieth century is the problem of the colour line' first appeared." (Ibid.). He planned four future congresses held in various European capitals and in New York: "The four congresses established the idea of Pan-Africanism and drew together activities and delegates from the USA, Ethiopia, Liberia, Haiti, and the colonies ... but few anti-colonial activities from the African continent itself were represented, there was little support from African-American organizations and no permanent organization or organizing center was established" (50).

Frantz Fanon (1925–61) analyzed "the effects of colonization on people and nations ... Writing from his own experience in the Algerian struggle for independence, he sought solutions, promoted violent struggle, and extolled the necessity for African unity" (64). He believed the paramount danger for Africa was the absence of coherent ideology. Nothing would happen to bring Africans together in common cause if one half opposed colonialism and the other half collaborated with it: "Fanon now began to define what he meant by 'unity', which could take many forms—for example, the economic cooperation being attempted by Nigeria and Liberia ... " (67). He argued for reparations from Europe to the Third World to repair the damage of colonialism and rejected peaceful means of reform: "Fanon also argued against Gandhian non-violence ... Violence was a cleansing force, freeing the native from his inferiority complex and from his despair and inaction" (Ibid.).

Pan-African History is strong in detailed biographical-historical essays (each accompanied by a brief bibliography) that reached across two centuries. For the historiography of singular black people in or out of Africa, there is nothing quite like it. The weakness is absence of integration, a pulling together of themes, a summary of agreements, disputes, and ambiguities, which the Preface does not provide, so the forest can be viewed beyond the trees. A question left mostly unanswered is the extent to which enough "unity" has been achieved so Kenyans or Congolese at least feel conscious kinship with blacks in Jamaica, Britain, and America. The idea of "unity" still remains tantalizing and vague in this example of Pan-African historiography.

Works by Adi and Sherwood

Adi and Sherwood, *The 1945 Manchester Pan-African Congress Revisited*, ed. by George Padmore (London: New Beacon Books, 1995).

Adi, West *Africans in Britain, 1900–1960: Nationalism, Pan-Africanism, and Communism* (London: Lawrence and Wishart, 1998).

Pan-African History: Political Figures from African and the Diaspora since 1787 (London: Routledge, 2003).

Sherwood, *After Abolition: Britain and the Slave Trade since 1807* (London: I.B. Taurus, 2007).

Sherwood, *Kwama Nkrumah: The Years Abroad, 1935–1947* (Legon, Ghana: Freedom Publications, 1996).

Useful references

Esedebe, P.O., *Pan-Africanism—the Idea and the Movement, 1776–1963* (Washington, D.C.: Howard University Press, 1982).

Harris, J.E. (ed.), *Global Dimensions of the African Diaspora* (2nd ed.; Washington, D.C.: Howard University Press, 1993). See the chapter by J.E. Harris.

Jalloh, A. and S.E. Maizlish (eds.), *The African Diaspora* (Texas: A & M University Press, 1996). See the chapter by G. Shepperson.

Walters, Ronald W., *Pan-Africanism in the African Diaspora: An Analysis of Modern Afrocentric Political Movements* (Detroit, Michigan: Wayne State University Press, 1997).

TWENTIETH-CENTURY EUROPE AND AMERICA

Themes 3 (issues of critical historiography), 4 (genres of history), 5 (breadth of inquiry), 6 (problematic historiography)

The flood of historical writing from the nineteenth century spilled into the twentieth century and rushes on unimpeded. The range of topics embraced by historians has multiplied to include historical sociology, the history of ideas, history of mentalities, women's history, intellectual history, psychohistory, history of technology, cross-cultural history, history of science, African and Afro-American history, and much besides, such as histories of art, literature, architecture, and language. The history of art tradition established in part by Burckhardt now encompasses every society. It seems as works pour from the presses that every subject in every age under the sun has found a historian.

The critical apparatus developed in the nineteenth century and before has been firmly institutionalized and widely adopted. Mostly its canons of evidence, such as citation of sources, are taken for granted and a historian who departs from them can expect to be chastised. Historians have diversified methods and sources by making use of economics, sociology, anthropology, and psychology to examine and coordinate every aspect of human experience. Some historians still dream of breaking history to the harness of statistics, an aspiration that has been eased somewhat by computer technology since the 1970s. The computer revolution has indeed provided a huge array of databases that can be accessed almost instantly for the most obscure factual material.

This section aims to illustrate selectively the varied interests and approaches of historians in the past century working in Europe and the USA. Works have appeared increasingly with broad focus and bold interpretations. A number of "schools" have emerged allied to conceptual schemes and methods inspired by Marx, Freud, French *Annales*, retrospective sociology and anthropology, gender studies, postcolonialism, and postmodernism. The latter category has to do with recent works unfolding doubts about the viability of historical knowledge, although such doubts were on the table as early as the 1920s and 1930s. They contrast sharply with the nineteenth confidence that history is a viable and special kind of knowledge. The twentieth century is represented also by non-Western works included earlier for India, China, Japan, and Africa. We began with works by classical historians. We shall conclude with a work that does history by analyzing a Greek epic using mature resources for inquiry.

34. THE PROTESTANT ETHIC AND THE SPIRIT OF CAPITALISM[1] (MAX WEBER, 1864–1920)

Weber is considered a prodigy among classical sociologists, whose influence on historians, economists, philosophers, and sociologists, even if they disagree, is unabated. His work has breadth, systematization, analytical rigor, and insight which is difficult to ignore. Starting off with law and economics, he broadened into religion, art, morality, politics, and technology. He wrote also about China, Hindu and Buddhist India, and Judaism with a view to examining connections between religious systems, social relations, and economic behavior. This range of knowledge and curiosity is reflected in *The Protestant Ethic*.

Legal studies were pursued at the University of Heidelberg in 1882 and continued at Berlin and Göttingen. His 1889 doctoral thesis, "Development of the Principle of Joint Liability and a Separate Fund of the General Partnership out of the Household Communities and Commercial Associations in Italian Cities," was included in his first book, *History of Commercial Partnerships in the Middle Ages*, which is available in English. To compete for a professorship in Germany, a doctorate was not enough. Required was a second professional thesis on top of the doctoral research dissertation at a higher level of scholarship defended before a committee. Success at this level earned the title *Privatdozent* (private docent), which authorized him to teach students privately for fees but without salary or rank at the university.

Weber's second thesis was *Roman Agrarian History and its Significance for Public and Private Law*, which established him as an authority on agrarian economics. By 1891 he was drawn to social policy and the influence of economics on society and religion, and shortly thereafter secured a professorship at Freiburg and then at Heidelberg. In 1897 he began to suffer insomnia and had a nervous collapse that made teaching difficult and blocked scholarly output for four years. After time in a sanitarium, he resigned his academic post to become a private scholar, helped along financially by an inheritance in 1907. He died prematurely in 1920 of pneumonia.

He stood apart from the French positivist school of sociology and rejected the Marxist view that social and economic phenomena arise exclusively from material conditions of life. In his scholarly works, he remained aloof from ideology by taking a position of "value neutrality," which holds that science cannot judge the validity of conflicting belief systems, secular or religious. All science can do is assess their internal coherence, the effectiveness of their means to achieve goals, and consequences of their choices. In this spirit, his analyses of society in its various dimensions interpenetrate—for example, politics with science, religion with economics, art with morality, and so on.

He aimed to develop a systematic "interpretive method" for the explanation and understanding of social relations by comparative study, tempered with quantitative data where available, and clarified by an arsenal of concepts—for example, rationalization, ideal type—to untangle complexities of historical reality (43–44). History is always a moving target. Human activity, he argued, evolves continually with changing circumstances, which distinguishes social relations as objects of study from those in the natural world. Those arising from human activity embody meanings and motives to be interpreted. Phenomena in nature do not.

The Protestant Ethic and the Spirit of Capitalism (*Die protestantische Ethik und der Geist des Kapitalismus*) examines historical and causal relationships between religious belief and concrete economic practice. It is a relatively short work, about 200 pages, written in 1904–5 and revised in 1920, dense in exposition, close in argument, and weighty in scholarship. It continues to be one of the most provocative examples of historical sociology. The extent and variety of his reading are remarkable. He seems to have left no relevant source unused.

He means by the "spirit of capitalism" the pursuit of economic gain for its own sake, which he distinguishes from traditional economics (11). The purpose of accumulating wealth is not merely to satisfy material needs of life: "Instead, the '*summum bonum*' of the ethic is the *making of money* and yet more money, coupled with a strict avoidance of all uninhibited enjoyment" (12; Weber's emphasis unless otherwise indicated). This spirit of modern capitalism cannot be explained within capitalism itself. An outside element was introduced to create the system of production, exchange, and consumption later called economic rationalism.

Although capital accumulation by calculation of expense against income was commonplace, custom and tradition rather than pressures of the market governed relations between workers and business owners. The traditional work ethic that prevailed until recently did not elevate work above other aspects of life, such as family, hobbies, friends, and pleasures of the table. Higher pay in traditional piecework, putting out industries to increase production did not succeed in squeezing further profits from a business. Workers took the pay and withheld more output because they would not organize their lives around work even if rewarded to do so. Therefore the spirit of capitalism, unlike the traditional work ethic, involves "an *irrational* element ... whereby a man exists for his business, not vice versa" (23).

In Weber's analysis, the group is more important than the individual in understanding this acquisitive "spirit." The existence of isolated, random entrepreneurs in every civilization is not sufficient to explain the development of capitalism into its modern form. Benjamin Franklin of Pennsylvania had the spirit with "almost classical purity," but his print shop was traditional and never became a capitalist enterprise (9–11). While the "drive" to pursue money "is as old as the story of humanity itself," it is not "the attitude from which the capitalist 'spirit' emerges as a *mass phenomenon* ... " (15). Capitalism could arise only through mass social action, "not just individuals, but as an attitude held in common by groups of people. The origin of this attitude is therefore what needs to be explained" (13). The group most at issue is the *bourgeois* middle class.

The Protestant Ethic has two objectives: first, to explain where and how the spirit originated; second, to explain its role in producing modern capitalism. Weber rejected Catholicism as an economic catalyst because there is no relationship between its means of salvation and a worldly vocation in which making money is "an end in itself ... " (25). Catholic lives were not organized methodically around secular work as a sacred duty. Luther approved a vocational "calling" but considered all callings equal, never challenged the traditional economic ethic, and did not believe in profit as the objective of a calling. Weber also rejected Werner Sombart's thesis in *The Jews and Modern Capitalism* that Jews were instrumental in capitalist development. They were too marginalized socially and their economic activity, though extensive, was traditional. It was not rationalized methodically into a life of work dedicated to the glory of God.

The English Puritan idea of a "calling," a spiritual obligation to pursue work ascetically in the world as a duty, is treated by Weber as "a single phenomenon" in Protestantism amidst differences between radical Calvinists, Methodists, Baptists, Quakers, and Mennonites (105). Attention to concept formation is pursued by an exhaustive historical and philological analysis of "calling," *Beruf* in German (52–61). Meanings and uses of the term are discussed from Greek, Roman, medieval Christian, Danish, Spanish, German, and other sources. The issue is how an insecurity focused on salvation among Protestants was transmuted into a duty to acquire wealth untainted by worldly gratifications. The transition is traced to Calvinism: "Historically, Calvinism was undoubtedly one of the providers of training in the 'capitalist spirit'" (51).

Protestant reformers elevated faith above Catholic means of salvation through an apostolically consecrated Church and its sacramental system, especially rejecting "works" of confession and penance. After discarding the Catholic mechanism for securing grace, other assurances of salvation were pursued with consequences for economic relations. Calvin highlighted predestination in his theological system, the doctrine that God had decided on a few to be saved while most would be damned. Luther chose to put the doctrine on a back shelf.

To head off anguish and fatalism among the faithful, Calvinism taught that election to salvation might be detected in those who prospered materially while preserving simplicity, discipline, and holiness in worldly service of God. Business success was viewed as a divine favor, and indirectly a mark of election. Absence of self-confidence that profit was a sign of election suggested the opposite fate—damnation. Thus "inner worldly Protestant asceticism works with all its force against the uninhibited *enjoyment* of possessions; it discourages *consumption*, especially the consumption of luxuries" (115). This explanation of the inner ethic focuses on the individual who wants proof of grace for himself. In his essay on "The Protestant Sects and the Spirit of Capitalism," Weber introduces an explanation that shifts the need for assurances of grace from the individual to the congregation of a sect, which insists on daily evidence that an individual has qualities indicative of divine election. On this premise, predestination ceases to be an issue.

Weber's analyses rely heavily on the concept of "ideal type," which is not a value judgment. A "type" can be abstracted from popes or prostitutes. In *The Protestant Ethic*, an ideal type identifies what is distinctive in all modern capitalists with respect to self-image and social action. The ascetic Protestant is an ideal type, distilled from many examples, committed to business as a religious calling. Sermons of the Puritan divine Richard Baxter, who modified Calvin's harsh theology to make room for selfless material accumulation, are prime examples.

In Weber's discussion of how "good works," including selfless business enterprise, might serve the faithful, he cautions that using an ideal type to find common ground amidst differences "to some extent ... does violence to the historical reality. Without it, the amount of qualifications necessary would make any clear formulation impossible" (145).

For Baxter and his followers, work was a commandment of God to glorify him and enrich his kingdom: "According to God's unambiguously revealed will, it is *only* action, not idleness and indulgence, that serves to increase his glory. Wasting time is therefore the first and most serious of all sins. The span of life is infinitely short and precious, and must be used to 'secure' one's own calling" (106–7). This ethic supported capital growth and investment in a mode of capitalism devoted to single-minded accumulation of wealth as an end to please God. This is the element missing in other civilizations that otherwise had a foundation for modern capitalism in population growth, technology, industries, raw materials, and money economies, China being a dramatic example. A Protestant ethic that entailed an imperative to organize life rationally was not an exclusive cause of modern capitalist development. Weber rejects mono-causality and assumes several at work—religious, economic, legal, technological—that cannot be pinned down definitively. Nevertheless, the Puritan work ethic was pivotal.

Major historical change was a consequence of the Protestant ethic:

> "The Puritans *wanted* to be men of the calling—we, on the other hand, *must be*. For when asceticism moved out the monastic cells and into working life, and began to dominate innerworldly morality, it helped to build that mighty cosmos of the modern economic order which is bound to the technical and economic conditions of mechanical and machine production. Today this mighty cosmos determines, with overwhelming coercion, the style of life not only of those directly involved in business but of every individual who is born into this mechanism, and may well continue to do so until the day that the last ton of fossil fuel has been consumed."
>
> (120–21)

Works by Weber

Economy and Society, edited by Guenther Roth and Claus Wittich (Berkeley, California: University of California Press, 1978).

General Economic History, trans. by Frank H. Knight (New York: Collier Books, 1961). See Chapters 22 and 30.
The Protestant Ethic and the Spirit of Capitalism, intro. and trans. by Stephen Kalberg (3rd ed.; Los Angeles, California, 2002). The introduction is a lengthy 81 pages. The volume includes "The Protestant Sects and the Spirit of Capitalism," trans. by H.H. Gerth and C. Wright Mills.
The Protestant Ethic and the Spirit of Capitalism, trans. by Peter Baehr and Gordon C. Wells (New York: Penguin Books, 2002).

Works about Weber

Lehmann, Hartmut and Guenther Roth (eds.), *Weber's Protestant Ethic: Origins, Evidence, Contexts* (Cambridge: Cambridge University Press, 1993).
Marshall, Gordon, *In Search of the Spirit of Capitalism: An Essay on Max Weber's Protestant Ethic Thesis* (London: Hutchinson, 1982).
Oaks, Guy, "Four Questions Concerning the Protestant Ethic," *Telos*, 81 (Fall 1989), 77–86.
Scaff, Lawrence A., *Fleeing the Iron Cage: Politics and Modernity in the Thought of Max Weber* (Berkley, California: University of California Press, 1989).
Schlucter, Wolfgang, *Rationalism, Religion, and Domination: A Weberian Perspective*, trans. by Neil Solomon (Berkeley, California: University of California Press, 1989).

Useful references

Kalberg, Stephen, *Max Weber's Comparative-Historical Sociology* (Chicago, Illinois: Chicago University Press, 1994).
Tawney, R.H., *Religion and the Rise of Capitalism* (New York: Harcourt, Brace and Co., 1926).
Turner, Stephen P. (ed.), *The Cambridge Companion to Weber* (Cambridge: Cambridge University Press, 2000).

35. THE GREAT CHAIN OF BEING: A STUDY OF THE HISTORY OF AN IDEA (ARTHUR O. LOVEJOY, 1873–1962)

Lovejoy was born in Berlin, Germany. His mother died of a pill overdose when he was 18 months old. His father responded by giving up medicine to become a minister. The son was encouraged to follow his example but preferred philosophy and comparative religion, which he studied at the University of California. On the side of religion, he leaned toward Unitarianism. He taught briefly at Stanford University, was turned down by Harvard because the president suspected he was a campus agitator, and ended up at Johns Hopkins

University in 1910, where he stayed on for the next 28 years as a preeminent student of ideas. He never married and lived in modest bachelor quarters, a second floor apartment, whose chief distinction was a horde of books.

He was known for vast learning, analytical power, and a prickly style of criticism that could arouse discomfort in the unwary and deliver a serious sting. He believed ideas have layers of meaning accumulated across time and require excavation. His method was to cut through the layers in search of a rock bottom unit idea upon which all its variations depended. A public demonstration occurred when he was questioned by the Maryland State Senate for a position on the state's educational board of regents. When asked if he believed in God, Lovejoy expounded 33 meanings of "God," while smoking 15 or so cigarettes, and asked the legislator which meaning he intended. There were no further questions and his nomination was confirmed.

Lovejoy's approach to ideas in *The Great Chain of Being* has three premises. First, history of ideas is not just one of many disciplines. Multiple fields of knowledge are needed to isolate and extract unit ideas from their historical developments and uses. Ideas are indifferent to disciplinary compartments and may overlap with science, theology, philosophy, art, and literature. Lovejoy's writings are a major illustration and model for interdisciplinary inquiry: "The history of ideas is therefore no subject for highly departmentalized minds; and it is pursued with some difficulty in an age of departmentalized minds" (22).

Second, with ideas, a point in history is reached where little that is fundamentally new has been said. What may appear to be a novel idea is merely a recombination and reworking of older ideas: "But the truth is that the number of essentially distinct philosophical ideas … is … decidedly limited … The seeming novelty of many a system is due solely to the novelty of the application or arrangement of the old elements which enter into it. When this is realized, the history as whole should look a much more manageable thing" (4).

Third, ideas assembled in history by recombination are reducible to their basic units. While units undergo transformations in larger-scale ideas, at bottom they remain the same and can be teased out. Various "isms" like Rationalism and Romanticism are not units, but rather elaborate conglomerates built up over time that can be broken down into simpler components. So it is with the Chain of Being and its three constituent parts. In classical Greece, Plato originated a distinction between an ultimate Good independent of the world which was also linked to the world and its contents, high and low, good and evil. He raised two questions: why is there a world of becoming, and what determines the kinds of things in it and their relationships? The questions were answered with three ideas—plenitude, continuity, and gradation. The first came from Plato, the other two from Aristotle, although plenitude implied both. The three ideas were organized into a world system later by Plotinus and Neoplatonists like Augustine, and visualized still later in an astronomical framework borrowed from the Greeks. A model of the creation extended from God in the Empyrean to the center of the earth, with fixed stars, seven planets, and the four elements (earth, air, fire, and water) arranged in between—the familiar three-tiered universe of heaven, earth, and hell.

Plenitude means the otherworldly Good must overflow into the sensible world to complete itself. Continuity means there can be no gaps in the universe, that all possibilities must be realized. The world must be full to the brim or the goodness of its author would be doubtful. Gradation means all existing beings and things are not the same and are arranged in a cosmic hierarchy of relative potentiality to assure maximum diversity.

> The result was the conception of the plan and structure of the world, which through the Middle Ages and down to the late eighteenth century, many philosophers, most men of science, and, indeed, most educated men, were to accept without question—the conception of the universe as a 'Great Chain of Being,' composed of an immense ... number of links ranging in hierarchical order from the meagerest kind of existence ... through every possible grade ... to the highest kind of creature ... every one of them differing from that immediately above and that immediately below it by the 'least possible' degree of difference."
> (59)

This arrangement of the universe as the major framework for thought raised difficulties for hundreds of years.

A dual conception of the highest Good had a long run in Western thought. On one side, its perfection depends on separation from the messy, changing world of experience. On the other side, perfection requires attention to the world of change: " ... Two-Gods-in-One, of a divine completion which was not yet complete in itself, since it could not be itself without the existence of beings other than itself ... an Immutability which required, and expressed itself in, Change" (50). This dual identity was codified in the Chain of Being, a synthesis of the three-unit ideas that shaped western attitudes, preferences, beliefs, and expectations from antiquity into the nineteenth century.

It "has been one the half-dozen most potent and persistent presuppositions in Western Thought. It was ... until not much more than a century ago, probably the most widely familiar conception of the general *scheme* of things, of the constitutive pattern of the universe; and as such it necessarily predetermined current ideas on many other matters" (viii). The Great Chain was expounded and interpreted in myriad ways by the best minds in theology, politics, philosophy, ethics, poetry, and science.

The problem for medieval thinkers was how God could be almighty and do whatever He liked while obliged by plenitude, continuity, and gradation to create everything just as it was with no imaginable alternative. The issue was between necessity and choice. Both points of view held their own in an uneasy relationship:

> But through the Middle Ages there was kept alive, in an age of which the official doctrine was predominantly otherworldly, certain roots of an essentially 'this-worldly' philosophy: the assumption that there is a true and intrinsic multiplicity in the divine nature ... indeed, the very essence of the good consists in the maximum actualization of variety; and that the world of temporal and sensible experience is thus good, and the supreme manifestation of the divine.
>
> (97–98)

Lovejoy explains the tortuous, logical dilemmas posed for scholastics like Abelard and Thomas Aquinas, neither of whom could unravel the problem of God viewed as a remote One involved with worldly Many at the same time. If some possible things have been denied existence, then God cannot be wholly Good. In a human world stained by sin the necessity of a material world implied a perverse optimism with respect to the existence of evil and imperfection. Apparently both are part of a necessary scheme of fullness through which God expresses His infinite goodness.

In the sixteenth and seventeenth centuries, the Great Chain sparked belief in multiple inhabited worlds in boundless space, an idea more radical than the heliocentrism of Copernicus and Kepler: "The theory of the plurality of inhabited worlds tended to raise difficulties, not merely about the minor details of the history included in Christian belief, but about its central dogmas" (108). Earth lost its uniqueness possibly along with the Christian drama of Sin, Redemption, and Resurrection. The argument that an infinite number of worlds and stars exist made the universe shapeless without a center: "The change from a geocentric to a heliocentric system was far less momentous than the change from a heliocentric to an acentric one" (109).

Turning to the eighteenth century, "there has been no period in which writers of all sorts—men of science and philosophers, poets and popular essayists, deists and orthodox divines—talked so much about the Chain of Being, or accepted more implicitly the general scheme of ideas connected with it ... " (183). Most conspicuous were attempts to show that various evils, natural and moral, are sources of progress and perfection: "So far from asserting the unreality of evils, the philosophical optimist ... was chiefly occupied in demonstrating their necessity. To assert that this is the best of possible worlds implies nothing as to the absolute goodness of this world; it implies only that any other world would be worse" (208).

Perfection did not mean parts of the Chain were fully good: "On the contrary, the fundamental and characteristic premise of the usual proof of optimism was the proposition that the perfection of the whole depends upon ... the existence of every degree of imperfection in the parts" (211). All kinds and conditions of existence must be represented in the Chain. Optimists viewed defects in every creature as a necessity that contributed to the highest good: "Man cannot ... rationally complain because he lacks many endowments and means of enjoyment which might conceivably have been granted him" (216). Progress in scientific inquiry was viewed in part as a search for unobserved links in the chain, which included the "missing link" between man and ape.

Two further developments reached into the nineteenth century and beyond. The first was the introduction of process into the Chain, which "came to be conceived by some, not as the inventory but as the program of nature, which is being carried out gradually and exceedingly slowly in the cosmic history ... It is only of the universe in its entire temporal span that the principle of plenitude holds good" (244). Instead of a static hierarchy with a fixed content, the Chain was redefined as a dynamic source of novelty, becoming rather than being, a prelude to the climate of opinion that favored cosmic change and biological evolution. The second was the Romantic premise that individuality counts more than uniformity: "If the world is the better the more variety it contains, the more adequately it manifests the possibilities of differentness in human nature, the duty of the individual ... was to cherish and intensify his own differentness from other men. Diversitarianism thus led also to a conscious pursuit of idiosyncrasies, personal, racial, national ... " (307). Plenitude says no possibility of existence should be neglected, which was interpreted to mean no standardization of type and cultivation of all peculiarities. Embedded in the Great Chain was the world view of Johann Herder (see essay 17 in this volume) and his glorification of difference.

Lovejoy cites eighteenth-century critics of the Great Chain who saw clearly the Achilles heel of plenitude. Thus Samuel Johnson and Voltaire observed that so-called intermediate stages in the chain would have to be infinite on the premise of plenitude, which violates both logic and experience, but they had no influence. Had such criticisms found a wide audience, the doctrine of optimism derived from the principle of plenitude would have collapsed. In an ironic shift, the fixed chain began to give way to a dynamic chain subject to development and improvement in time: "The static and permanently complete Chain of Being broke down largely from its own weight" (245). Emanuel Kant revised traditional meanings of plenitude and the Great Chain. For him, "continuous development and progressive diversification is the supreme law of nature, not only for the universe as whole but for every component of it, from solar systems to individual living beings" (268).

Lovejoy put ideas on the map of historiography. The feat was accomplished not only by subtle scholarship. He also founded an institution, the Hopkins History of Ideas Club, and co-founded a medium, *Journal of the History of Ideas*, that brought interested parties together in a fresh historical conversation about the nature and role of ideas. Some critics have denied the existence of "unit ideas." Lovejoy's method seems to them a reductive approach to complex movements of thought. While such criticism may be just, it always needs to be fleshed out with detail complementary to Lovejoy's. Meanwhile, it is doubtful that his specific case for the great Chain of Being and its unit ideas has been refuted as a pervasive theme in Western thought. His method has explanatory power and clarifies what many thoughtful people have believed for centuries about the universe and themselves, and why they believed it.

Works by Lovejoy

Essays in the History of Ideas (Baltimore: Johns Hopkins University Press, 1948).

The Great Chain of Being: A Study of the History of an Idea (Cambridge, Massachusetts: Harvard University Press, 1936). Reprinted by Harper and Row in paperback.

The Revolt Against Dualism: An Inquiry Concerning the Existence of Ideas (n.p.; Whitefish, Montana: Kessinger Publishing, 2007).

Works about Lovejoy

"Arthur O. Lovejoy": Biographical Essay from Gale's *Dictionary of Literary Biography*, Vol. 270 (code 17, digital: 24 October 2003).
Kieger, Dale, "Tussling with the Idea Man," *Johns Hopkins Magazine* (April, 2000).
Wilson, Daniel J., *Arthur O. Lovejoy and the Quest for Intelligibility* (Chapel Hill, North Carolina: University of North Carolina Press, 1980).

Useful references

Bynum, William F., "The Great Chain of Being After Forty Years: An Appraisal," *History of Science*, 13 (1975): 1–28.

36. TECHNICS AND CIVILIZATION (LEWIS MUMFORD, 1895–1990)

Mumford was a prolific author for over 70 years, architectural critic and urban theorist, historian of technology and cities, intellectual generalist in a half dozen fields, biographer and man of letters, social activist and moral philosopher, and long-term watchdog over the condition and prospects of Western civilization. He authored 30 books (most still in print and translated into multiple languages), and some 700 articles. *The City in History* won the American National Book Award. His last book was published at age 84. All of his writing is infused with moral intensity.

Although awarded the three American national medals for art, freedom, and literature, he never graduated from college (too much "tick-tock," he said). For many years he wrote an influential column on architecture for the *New Yorker*. He knew just about everyone of intellectual distinction in and out of the country. For some five decades, he lived with his family (his son was lost in the war) in a humble wood frame house in rural Amenia, New York, carried on a voluminous correspondence, and was an activist against nuclear weapons, urban sprawl, self-indulgent architecture, environmental disruption, and other excesses of modern civilization.

Writing about the history and meaning of technology was an innovative choice that expanded historical inquiry. It was also a virtuoso performance, since Mumford never claimed to be a specialist in anything. As a generalist who used the work of specialists, he had no qualms about taking a subject by storm. Historical perspective is the foundation, for emergence of the modern machine age is unintelligible without plunging into history. Readers are cautioned to take deep breaths. The influence of mechanistic values over life and its choices began in medieval times, not with James Watt and the steam engine or the Industrial Revolution. Only a long view can adjust our vision enough to understand conditions under which the machine might better serve wider human interests than power and mastery of nature.

Technics and Civilization is divided into eight chapters that address 90 different topics, one of which, "The Monastery and the Clock," is especially notable and widely cited. The clock and not the steam-engine was the key machine of the modern industrial age. Benedictine monasteries measured time to structure hours of prayer and work and thereby "helped to give human enterprise the regular collective beat and rhythm of the machine; for the clock is not merely a means of keeping track of the hours but of synchronizing the actions of men." In due course, "time-keeping passed into time-serving and time-accounting and time-reckoning ... Eternity ceased gradually to serve as the measure and focus of human actions" (14). Organic time keeping, modulated by the sun, moon, and alternation of the seasons, gave way to mechanical time keeping, which marks the onset of modern man's infatuation with machines and their powers.

There are numerous carefully chosen illustrations accompanied by explanatory captions, from "The Genesis of the Machine" to "The New Environment." The page on "Aesthetic Assimilation" (XIV) comments on how machine aesthetics moved practical structures like a grain elevator toward "elementary forms" and art toward "impersonality." Nine pages list a host of inventions from the tenth century (water clock) to 1933 (aerodynamic motor car). Twenty-seven pages of annotated bibliography indicate his sources. There are no footnotes, which he regarded as baggage of academic pedantry, infallible signs of narrow specialization directed at the few. Declaring himself "anti-professor," he wished to address the many. His method was to develop a frame of reference, ask the right questions, read widely, assimilate knowledge, and serve it up in readable prose. In short, scholarship was integrated with the text to convey an impression of spontaneous thought.

His procedure is historical exposition and analysis with frequent applications to the present: "To understand the dominating role played by technics in modern civilization, one must explore in detail the preliminary period of ideological and social preparation. Not merely must one explain the existence of the new mechanical instruments: one must explain the culture that was ready to use them and profit by them so extensively" (4). The relations of humanity with the machine are a "result of human choices and aptitudes and strivings, deliberate as well as unconscious, often irrational when they are most objective and scientific" (6). Throughout Mumford expresses moral unease for the effects of technology on society and the individual.

"Technics" refers broadly to artifacts and tools useful to humans since their emergence as a species. Processes like basket making, distilling, brewing, and tanning (all likely developed by women) are technics as well as more familiar instruments like microscope, telescope, printing press, clock, sailing ship, steam engine, and telephone. The machine he defines more narrowly as " ... knowledge and skills and arts derived from industry or implicated in the new technics, and will include various forms of tool, instrument, apparatus and utility as well as machines proper" (12). Modern technology he calls "megatechnics" because the machine's status in human life has become exaggerated and domineering.

The difference between traditional and modern technics is that the former served life purposes without usurping them. Modern technology has far more dramatic effects on human and natural environments with a potential for corrupting human well being. For Mumford, the machine is good if humans control them, bad if they do not. They can enrich human life with significance or diminish it. In modern times, enrichment has gotten the short end of the stick. Technics in the wide sense is less fundamental to understanding human nature than myth, art, and language, though all are essential to a balanced life. In effect, humans are more symbol-using than tool-using creatures. Mastery of self came before mastery of physical nature. *Homo symbolicus* rather than *homo faber* is the foundation of human development and fulfillment.

The transformation of consciousness that revolutionized technics and society was a shift from qualitative to quantitative judgment in most departments of life, a preference for numerical order modeled on measurements of time and space: "The new attitude toward time and space infected the workshop and the countinghouse, the army and the city. The tempo became faster: the magnitude became greater ... In time-keeping, in trading, in fighting men counted numbers; and finally, as the habit grew, only numbers counted" (22). This quantification of human life arose during the scientific revolution of the sixteenth and seventeenth centuries and accelerated thereafter. But technological determinism is rejected. The machine is not independent of human will and purpose. Mechanistic, quantitative tendencies of the modern age came from a change of mind. Organic values of informality, autonomy, intuition, and feeling gave way to mechanical values of organization, regularity, control, and standardization. That change can be reversed or revised by another act of human will: "Technics and civilization as a whole are the result of human choices and aptitudes and strivings, deliberate as well as unconscious, often irrational when apparently they are most objective and scientific ... The machine itself makes no demands and holds out no promises: it is the human spirit that makes demands and keeps promises" (6).

While technics has altered nature and transformed the material basis of life in the West, Mumford places its origin, growth, and influence in human wishes, desires, beliefs, and ideals: "Men had become mechanical before they perfected complicated machines to express their new bent and interest; and the will to order had appeared once more in the monastery and army and the counting house before it finally manifested itself in the factory" (3). Over the past thousand years, he identifies three waves of technology—eotechnic, paleotechnic, neotechnic—that still exist, overlap, and interpenetrate. The anticipated next stage is a biotechnic society that serves a vital standard for balanced human development in a life economy at peace with the environment. The successive waves are distinguished by sources of energy, materials exploited, types of artifacts produced, kinds of labor demanded, and values implied for society and the individual.

From medieval times to about 1750, the **eotechnic** wave relied on wind and water, used wood and glass, and was marked by the clock, the printing press, mining, and textile manufacture. Craftsmanship had a place despite invention of the factory, human dignity mattered, and the organic integrity of nature and life were not seriously violated: "The goal of eotechnic civilization as a whole until it reached the decadence of the eighteenth century was not more power alone but a greater intensification of life: color, perfume, images, music, sexual ecstasy, as well as daring exploits in arms and thought and exploration" (149). This eotechnic age is much underrated compared to nineteenth century industrial Europe, which thought itself in the vanguard of progress. In truth, medieval cities were "far brighter and cleaner and better ordered than the new Victorian towns," and "in many parts of Europe the medieval worker had demonstrably a far higher standard of living than the paleotechnic drudge" (183).

The **paleotechnic** wave flourished from the early eighteenth century to around 1870. It relied on steam for power, coal, and iron for raw materials, and revolved around the steam engine, railroad, the mechanized textile mill, the iron ship, and debased factory towns filled with stupefied wage earners: "This second revolution multiplied, vulgarized, and spread the methods of and goods produced by the first" (151). This age was narrow, greedy, destructive, and predatory: "There was a sharp shift in interest from life values to pecuniary values ... It was no longer sufficient for industry to provide a livelihood: it must create an independent fortune: work was no longer a necessary part of living: it became an all-important end" (153). Profits and prices in an abstract free market governed natural and human relationships: " ... the environment itself, like most of human existence, was treated as an abstraction. Air and sunlight, because of their deplorable lack of value in exchange, had no reality at all" (168). Whole regions were diminished and debased by the new factory towns, and "human beings were dealt with in the same spirit of brutality as the landscape: labor was a resource to be exploited, to be mined, to be exhausted, and finally to be discarded" (172). The whole period functioned as a dismal bridge, still to be burned behind us, between the eotechnics that came before and the neotechnics age that followed.

The third wave, **neotechnics**, is powered by electricity. Chemistry supplies new materials like aluminum and synthetics. The internal combustion engine appears. Telephone and telegraph shrink time and space. In short, science and technics joined hands. The neotechnic age has been characterized above all by automatic machinery. The paleotechnic era "was marked by an orgy of uncontrolled production and equally uncontrolled reproduction: machine-fodder and cannon-fodder ... In the neotechnic phase the whole emphasis begins to change ... with better opportunities for healthy living and healthy parenthood, untainted by ill-health, preventable diseases, and poverty" (263).

Yet the promise of neotechnics has not been fully realized. Worthy tendencies such as new scientific discoveries, inventions, and techniques have infiltrated old structures without entirely coming into their own: "We have merely used our new machines and energies to further processes which were begun under the auspices of capitalist and military enterprise: we have not yet utilized them to conquer these forms of enterprise and subdue them to more vital and humane purposes" (265). Neotechnic means are applied to paleotechnic ends: "The real significance of the machine ... does not consist either in the multiplication of goods or the multiplication of wants, real or illusory."

Significance lies in more energy through increased conversion of resources, "through efficient production, through balanced consumption, and through socialized creation ... the important factors here are not quantities but ratios: ratios of mechanical effort to social and cultural results." How energy is converted and used defines the health of a society and its members: "A society in which production and consumption completely cancel out the gains of conversion ... would remain socially inefficient, even if the entire population were constantly employed, and adequately fed, clothed and sheltered" (378).

The machine can serve life rather than life serving it, but a machine-based civilization can also undo itself by misdirection and misuse that lead to energy conversion for the sake of limitless consumption with few returns for body, mind, or personality. Writing in the Great Depression, of all times, Mumford argues that economic arrangements and technics should not function to supply an aimless expansion of consumption but to provide for "vital needs." At a glutted level where acquiring more of the latest goods is the prevalent activity of men and women, consumerism blocks the flow and growth of human life, wastes resources, and diminishes the environment. He ends his trek across the centuries on an optimistic note with a musical metaphor. The notation, instruments, and musicians have been assembled to make fine music, but so far the sounds are uncoordinated and discordant: " ... we will have to rewrite the music in the act of playing it ... Impossible? No: for however far modern science and technics have fallen short of their inherent possibilities, they have taught mankind at least one lesson: Nothing is impossible" (435).

Works by Mumford

Interpretations and Forecasts: 1922–1972 (New York: Harcourt Brace Jovanovich, 1979). An anthology selected by Mumford and organized around several themes.

Technics and Civilization (New York: Harcourt, Brace and Company, 1934).

The Future of Technics and Civilization (London: Freedom Press, 1986). This convenient volume is the second half of Technics and Civilization. It is cited because it may be more accessible to some readers than the 1934 volume.

The Myth of the Machine: I. Technics and Human Development (New York: Harcourt, Brace and World, 1967).

Works about Mumford

Novak, Frank, "Lewis Mumford and the Reclamation of Human History," *Clio*, 16:2 (1987): 164–65.

Stunkel, Kenneth R., *Understanding Lewis Mumford: A Guide for the Perplexed* (Lewiston, New York: The Edwin Mellen Press, 2004), Chapters 9 and 14.

Useful references

Hughes, Thomas P. and Agatha C. Hughes (eds.), *Lewis Mumford: Public Intellectual* (New York: Oxford University Press, 1990).

Miller, Donald L., *Lewis Mumford: A Life* (New York: Weidenfeld & Nicolson, 1989).

37. RELIGION AND THE DECLINE OF MAGIC: STUDIES IN POPULAR BELIEFS IN SIXTEENTH- AND SEVENTEENTH CENTURY ENGLAND (KEITH THOMAS, 1933–)

Thomas's academic career was pursued in colleges of Oxford University. He graduated from Balliol College and was subsequently elected Fellow of All Souls College and Fellow of St. John's College. In 1986 he became president of Corpus Christi College. Until his retirement at age 67 in 2000, he was Professor of Modern History at Oxford. Thomas has received no less that ten honorary degrees in acknowledgment of his scholarship and many services to the profession of history. He is known by former students and colleagues as a man of exceptional learning, wit, and integrity. A voracious reader, despite severe near sightedness, he is reputedly able to "gut" a book in record time. He is one of several early pioneers to make use of social anthropology in his research and to argue for a collaboration of anthropological and historical methods.

His book asks why the English at all levels of society believed in magic and its many offshoots several hundred years ago:

> This book began as an attempt to make sense of the systems of belief which were current in sixteenth- and seventeenth-century England, but which no longer enjoy much recognition today. Astrology, witchcraft, magical healing, divination, ancient prophecies, ghosts and fairies, are now all rightly disdained by intelligent persons. But they were taken seriously by equally intelligent

persons in the past, and it is the historian's business to explain why this is so.

(ix)

This formidable inquiry unfolds in six hefty sections, preceded by a comment on England's physical and social environment. Beliefs addressed include ritual church magic; magical healing; astrology; prophecy; witchcraft; ghosts, fairies, and omens. He argues that magic declined in part because Reformation reformers rejected its presence in rituals of the medieval church. Thomas provides a wealth of examples and cases supported by profuse documentation of the rarest kind. He marshals an ocean of scholarship to explain beliefs that made life bearable for two centuries, and does so in a style consistently lucid and unpretentious.

Life in England was short while beleaguered by disease, pain, and suffering irrespective of social class. The primitive state of medical knowledge and institutions afforded little or no help and often made things worse: " ... medical science was helpless before most contemporary hazards to health" (8). The two greatest fears were bubonic plague and fires, against which human effort was helpless. In the midst of unremitting insecurity, relieved a bit by alcohol and tobacco, men and women sought understanding and protection wherever they could find it. The beliefs they held "were all concerned to explain misfortune and so mitigate its rigour" (21).

A second function of supernatural and magical belief was to reinforce and preserve community solidarity in the face of persistent, often divisive afflictions and threats. Plague and suspected witches could demoralize whole communities. In line with the title of his book, Thomas undertakes to explain why a belief in magic and witchcraft eventually declined while religion forged on. The struggle of Protestantism with beliefs and practices of the medieval church was a key to the puzzle, both of which were "a system of explanation, a source of moral injunction, a symbol of social order, or a route to immortality" (25). On doctrinal grounds, however, Protestants rejected the entire paraphernalia of ritualized magic and miracle.

The Church was a "repository of supernatural power which could be dispensed to the faithful to help them in their daily problems" (32). The instruments of miraculous assistance, many originating in Greco-Roman paganism and modified by the medieval church, were shrines, consecrated church yards, holy water, prayers, sign of the cross, relics of saints, and sacraments of the Church, especially the Mass, in which physical objects, bread and wine, were invested with supernatural power, which fed the "popular belief in the material effects of ecclesiastical ritual" (39).

Thomas's first 150 pages explain the magical functions of medieval church ritual, the reaction of Protestant reformers, and why divine providence, prayer, and prophecy persisted after magic was diminished; "Even after the Reformation ... organized religion continued to help men cope with the practical problems of daily life by providing an explanation for misfortune and a source of guidance in times of uncertainty." The other stimulus to religion was social, for "religious worship emphasized the unity of society as well as its social divisions." The rest of the book addresses the question of why people turned to "non-religious systems of belief" like astrology and popular magic (151–52).

Several kinds of secular magic were recognized even by scientists and philosophers:

> The cosmos was an organic unity in which every part bore a sympathetic relationship to the rest. Even colours, letters, and numbers were endowed with magical properties ... three types of magical activity thus lay open: *natural magic*, concerned to exploit occult properties of the elemental world; *celestial magic*, involving the influence of the stars; and *ceremonial magic*, an appeal for aid to spiritual beings. Charms, amulets, incantations, potions, conjuring, rituals, fortune telling, and other magical aids proliferated to exploit these cosmic domains, which might include Christian prayers and biblical readings.

Such options lacked institutions, theology, and moral teachings of organized religion but were nevertheless competitive. Many people lacked piety, avoided church attendance, or knew nothing about Church teachings: " ... many of the poorest classes never became regular church-goers ... Even when they did put in a reluctant appearance, the conduct of many church-goers left so much to be desired as to turn the service into a travesty of what was intended" (160–61). Religious unorthodoxy among dissenters might shade into skepticism. Auricular confession was rejected by Protestants while many people still needed advice. Lost property had to be recovered and thieves detected. Disease or injury required all the help one could get, whether from petitionary prayer, wizards, or the "royal touch" that reputedly cured plague. A wizard was a "cunning man," who sought to achieve supernatural effects without God's help, which put him in league with dark powers, but he did a brisk business anyway.

Nearly everyone believed the stars influence human life. Astrologers claimed comprehensive powers of explanation: "Astrology was thus less a separate discipline than an aspect of a generally accepted world picture ... It was not a coterie doctrine, but an essential aspect of the intellectual framework in which men were educated" (285). Astrologers supplied *predictions* about epidemics, crops, politics, and war, horoscopes, or *nativities* based on birth date, for individuals, *elections* for the right time for an action, or answered *horary* questions on the spot by matching the heavens with when a question was asked. Possibilities for explanation were limitless. Cities and countries as well as men can have horoscopes, disease can be predicted, and so on. Astrology declined as its explanations became less convincing: "The intellectual pretensions of astrological theory were irreparably shattered by the astronomical revolution initiated by Copernicus and consummated by Newton" (349). On the religious side, astrology was rejected because it threatened "free will and moral autonomy." Medical and agricultural predictions were acceptable, but not predictions about "human behavior" (361).

Witchcraft in England was viewed as an "anti-social crime" and not heresy or devil-worship: "For most men 'witchcraft' remained essentially the power to harm others" (448). Belief in witchcraft exercised by occult means persisted until the last quarter of the seventeenth century. An accused witch holding a "grudge" explained any misfortune befalling an individual. Witches had to be detected, a task for wizards: "The methods by which the wizard purported to diagnose the witchcraft were diverse. He might use a technique ... such as boiling the victim's urine, or burning a piece of thatch from the suspected witch's house to see whether this brought her running to the scene" (186). Protestants rejected folk magic as well as magic of the Church: "For those Protestants who believed that the age of Christian miracles was over, all supernatural effects necessarily sprang from either fraudulent illusion or the workings of the Devil" (256). The result was a dilemma: " ... Protestantism forced its adherents into the intolerable position of asserting the reality of witchcraft, yet denying the existence of an effective and legitimate form of protection or cure" (494–95).

Thomas's place in historiography is his success in showing how history and anthropology can work together. Thomas distinguishes history from anthropology on the principle of access to a society. A historian must "visit" a past society by means of documents and archeological remains. The anthropologist either lived in or at one time visited a society under study.

A second difference is a matter of style. Historians commonly write rhetorically and impressionistically, and are prone to indulge broad generalizations. Anthropologists, in line with a tradition that their discipline is a "science," are more austere, cautious about generalization, and stay close to data yielded by fieldwork, which is usually more complete than evidence available to historians: "The task of the historian is thus infinitely harder than that of the social anthropologist, studying a small homogeneous community in which all inhabitants share the same beliefs, and where few of those beliefs are borrowed from other societies" (5).

While anthropologists connect facts with a social system viewed as a whole, historians specialize in chunks of society, whether economic, technological, social, or political. Consequences for "explanation" are different. A student of seventeenth-century agriculture is not likely to say much about religion or relate them to one another or to the wider society even though all major activities and beliefs of a society are interconnected. For improved understanding, their relations must be seen against the background of the whole society, a task the anthropologist better exemplifies than the historian. An ideal shared perspective of history and anthropology is a holistic approach to myriad facts and various levels of society—how customs, traditions, beliefs, and institutions connect with and influence one another.

In Thomas's work, beliefs in a pre-industrial society are examined and understood not for their own sake, or as examples of superstition displaced by advances of critical reason, but for their wider "social and intellectual implications" (Ibid.). It is socially and intellectually significant that many beliefs Thomas explores continue to have followers in the modern world despite advances in science and medical knowledge. Arthur Conan Doyle, for example, believed in fairies at the end the nineteenth century. Astrology and miracle healing still have their champions. Thomas's explanations of belief in the sixteenth and seventeenth centuries still resonate in the present.

Works by Thomas

"History and Anthropology," *Past and Present* 24 (1963): 3–24.

"The Tools and the Job," *Times Literary Supplement* (April 7, 1966): 275–276.

Man and the Natural World: Changing Attitudes in England, 1500–1800 (London: Allen Lane, 1983).

Religion and the Decline of Magic: Studies in Popular Beliefs in Sixteenth and Seventeenth Century England (London: Weidenfeld and Nicolson, 1971).

The Ends of Life: Roads to Fulfillment in Early Modern England (Oxford: Oxford University Press, 2009).

38. THE HEAVENLY CITY OF THE EIGHTEENTH CENTURY PHILOSOPHERS (CARL LOTUS BECKER, 1873–1945)

In the opening pages of Becker's elegant, disconcerting book on eighteenth-century thought, he evokes St Thomas Aquinas and Dante and points out how difficult, if not impossible, it would be to have a discussion with the former about natural law and with the latter about a League of Nations, general ideas still in currency. After summarizing their views, he points out their strangeness and even unintelligibility: "What renders Dante's argument or St. Thomas' definition meaningless to us is not bad logic or want of intelligence, but the medieval climate of opinion—those instinctively held preconceptions in the broad sense, that *Weltanschuung* or world pattern— which imposed upon Dante and St. Thomas a peculiar use of intelligence and special type of logic" (5).

Thus does Becker initiate a succinct meditation on the nature and limitations of history while unfolding a subtle interpretation of the eighteenth-century Enlightenment in four compact chapters: Climates of Opinion, The Laws of Nature and Nature's God, The New History: Philosophy Teaching by Example, and The Uses of Posterity. His contemporary, Charles A. Beard, judged it the best book written by an American historian. It is a signature work epitomizing Becker's strengths. In it he united scrupulous, varied scholarship, stylish writing, provocative ideas, and an often world-weary skepticism about what and how much we can know about the past. Early on as an undergraduate he decided to write history instead of novels and to understand what people thought about themselves and their world, what they had done, why they did it, and why they believed it was worth doing. The era of particular books, he said, can be verified readily enough; the important questions are why authors wrote them in the first place and in what kind of world.

He was skeptical about possibilities of literal historical truth with universal implications. Ranke's view fell by the wayside. The past is not knowable with detachment as "it actually happened" by isolating and confirming facts through external and internal criticism (see essay 18 of this volume). Past time, he argued, is not a thing in itself immediately accessible to perception. Since facts reside in the minds of historians, history is not what happened, but our memory of it, which depends on a record left by someone. Facts by themselves mean very little until placed in the context of larger historical patterns, and seemingly simple facts, like the great Lisbon earthquake that inspired Voltaire's *Candide*, are comprised of innumerable subsidiary facts unknown to us. The whole must be reconstructed and the gaps filled in by acts of imagination, which is interpretation that takes place in a specific *climate of opinion*. Prediction and control of nature are the goals of science. The goal of history is self-awareness and self-knowledge. By reanimating what others have done and thought in the past, humans have a better sense of what they do in the present and what they may want to do in the future. History is one with science because it is about *knowledge* rather than practical, esthetic, and moral issues.

Without a framework of ideas history is little more than a dry heap of facts best displayed in a catalogue. But frameworks of ideas are not invariable. Evidence for a climate of opinion is the pervasive language of an era for discussing nature, man, and society: "In the thirteenth century the key words would no doubt be God, sin, grace, salvation, heaven, and the like; in the nineteenth century, matter, fact, matter-of-fact, evolution, progress; in the twentieth century, relativity, process, adjustment, function, complex. In the eighteenth century the words without which no enlightened person could reach a restful conclusion were nature, natural law, first cause, reason, sentiment, humanity, perfectibility ... " (47). In each case, the world addressed by those separate clumps of words is different. Representatives from each in a debate would talk past one another and perhaps express open bewilderment. In short, what their respective vocabularies indicate are contrary world views.

The Heavenly City proceeds to unravel ways of thinking in these identifiable climates of opinion (the phrase comes from philosopher-mathematician Alfred North Whitehead)—the Middle Ages, the Enlightenment, and the Modern Age. The main argument is that philosophers of the eighteenth century, with all their confidence in seemingly modern ideas like reason, nature, nature's laws, and natural rights, and all their apparent skepticism about God and Providence, had more in common with the thirteenth century than with the twentieth century. For medieval people life was a cosmic drama with well-defined acts (Creation, Incarnation, Day of Judgment) on a theme of redemption: "The duty of man was to accept the drama as written, since he could not alter it; his function, to play the role assigned ... The function of intelligence was therefore to demonstrate the truth of revealed knowledge ... " (7).

Reason had the power to demonstrate faith and was at its best in theology, the queen of the sciences. For the eighteenth-century *philosophes* reason had as much prestige as in the age of Thomas

Aquinas, but was associated with the world system of Isaac Newton, which provided the cosmic basis for reform and progress. Reason was at its best in science and philosophy. St. Thomas and Voltaire were not that far apart: "What they had in common was a profound conviction that their beliefs could be reasonably demonstrated. In a very real sense it may be said of the eighteenth century that it was age of faith as well as reason, and of the thirteenth century that it was an age of reason as well as faith" (8).

Whatever the climate of opinion, it has consequences for assessing facts. The modern climate of opinion, for example, grounded in scientific knowledge, automatically sorts out testimony historians accept as evidence. Testimony about events that violate known laws of nature, most obviously about miracles, are rejected no matter how many testimonials are available, which was not the case in medieval times. The eighteenth-century philosophers were hostile to organized religion and traditional theology, including miracles, but still accepted, with a few exceptions, a divinely ordered world on quasi-scientific principles. They did not accept existence of a deity for the same reasons Thomas Aquinas did, yet both claimed to be following the guidance of reason, but to different ends. St. Thomas subordinated reason to faith, the philosophers subordinated faith to reason, but in each case both were retained.

For Becker, this relativism was qualified. Knowledge properly understood is attainable through critical methods, but its extraction from sources is indirect and has objectivity limited by one's involuntary presence in a time and place. The common need for history as memory of what was said and done is rooted in human nature, an instinct to remember that supplies bearings in the present and anticipation of the future. Then we have critical history, "the instinctive and necessary exercise of memory, but of memory tested and fortified by reliable sources. The facts may be determined with accuracy, but the 'interpretation' will always be shaped by the prejudices, biases, needs, of the individual and these in turn will depend on the age in which he lives" (quoted in Smith, 85).

Climate of opinion always restricts the reach of critical methods. Historians have no choice but to study the past through lenses provided by their own time: " ... all historical writing, even the most honest, is unconsciously subjective, since every age is bound, in spite of itself, to make the dead perform whatever tricks it finds necessary for its own piece of mind" (44). This last observation about playing tricks on the dead is from Voltaire (see essay 15 of this volume), whowas referring only to fraudulent historians. Becker extends the idea of playing tricks in an ironic but offsetting sense to all historians, even honest ones, because they are unavoidable hostages to various climates of opinion and their own unconscious subjectivity.

Bias for St. Thomas was conditioned by the prospect of heaven beyond this world. Bias for the eighteenth-century philosophers was focused on this world, but leaned toward the future rather than the past. A fixation on posterity guided their historical ventures and judgments, even Montesquieu, who was the most empirical of the lot: " ... the eighteenth-century Philosophers were not primarily interested in stabilizing society, but changing it ... What difference does it make, they seem to be saying, how society came to be what it is? There it is for all men to see, obviously irrational, oppressive, unjust, obviously contrary to the essential nature of man, obviously needing to be set right, and that speedily" (97–98). Claims of posterity were more imperative than those of the past, a clear rejection of historicism favored in the nineteenth century. Posterity was for a Voltaire what heaven was for a St. Thomas. Voltaire was the author of a "new history" in his *Essay on Customs*, but so was St. Augustine in his *City of God*, each tailored to needs of the time: "The 'new history' is an old story. Since history is not an objective reality, but only an imaginative reconstruction of vanished events, the patter that appears useful and agreeable to one generation is never entirely so to the next" (88).

Becker lived through two destructive world wars and a traumatic economic depression, experiences which confirmed pessimism about the human condition. In his darker view, the only tangible gain made by humanity is undeniable, continuous lordship over nature. The modern climate of opinion, shaped by findings of physical and biological science after the passage of eight centuries of intellectual history, tells us this power will be short lived. Enlightenment optimism about a brighter future has its parallel in medieval optimism that salvation waits at the end of the road. The faith of the Enlightenment was expressed in its purest form by Marquis de Condorcet in 1793, that science and technology will undergird the ultimate perfectibility of man.

The climate of opinion in modern times is indebted to advances in science that have detached human values and self-consciousness from empirical fact and natural law: "Man is but a foundling in the cosmos, abandoned by the forces that created him. Unparented, unassisted and undirected by omniscient or benevolent authority, he must fend for himself, and with the aid of his own limited intelligence find his way about in an indifferent universe. Such is the world pattern that determines the character and direction of modern thinking" (15).

A cosmos indifferent to humans means it is "quite impossible for us to regard man as a child of God for whom the earth was created" (14). In effect, Zeus has been dethroned by history. People, thoughtful or not, may still believe in Zeus, but that is a private matter, not a guiding world view: "No serious scholar would now postulate the existence and goodness of God as a point of departure for explaining quantum theory or the French Revolution"(16). Our climate of opinion will not permit it. In this phase of history, we start with the premise of Aristophanes that "Whirl is King" and we are obliged to make the best of it.

Becker's skepticism about facts being identical with historical reality and his argument that all historical understanding takes place in climates of opinion are in the mainstream of contemporary historiography. Rather than being taken as a brief against historical objectivity, his views have strengthened rather than demolished it. After all, Becker shed light on the past from a modern climate of opinion by identifying and explaining two other climates of opinion and demonstrating their relationships. He selected facts relevant to his questions and proposed an interpretation that often rings true. *The Heavenly City* is still considered a masterpiece of historical writing despite reservations that Becker overdid his comparison of medieval and Enlightenment thought.

Yet, whatever the residue of Christian ideas found among the philosophers, their secularism and confidence in critical reason and its practical applications was a departure from medieval ideals. A major response to Becker's claim that the Enlightenment built its own "heavenly city," is Peter Gay's reinterpretation. He argues that the *philosophes* were modern pagans, inspired by ancient Rome, who self-consciously jettisoned Christian baggage and embraced science to improve the estate of mankind. When Becker says "the task of the Philosophers was to present another interpretation of the past, the present, and the future state of mankind," he means to say they were merely updating the Christian worldview. For Gay, their interpretations were a fundamental break with the past that led circuitously, for better or worse, to our modern world.

Works by Becker

"What are Historical Facts?" *The Western Political Quarterly*, VIII (September, 1955): 327–340.

"What is Historiography?" *American Historical Review*, XLIV (October, 1938): 20–28.

Detachment and the Writing of History, in *Essays and Letters of Carl L. Becker*, ed. Phil. L. Snyder (Ithaca, New York, 1958). First published in *Atlantic Monthly*, CVI (October, 1910).

Everyman His Own Historian: Essays on History and Politics (New York: F. S. Crofts and Company, 1935).

The Heavenly City of the Eighteenth Century Philosophers (New Haven, Connecticut: Yale University Press, 1932).

Works about Becker

Beard, Charles A., Review of *The Heavenly City*, *American Historical Review*, 38 (April, 1933): 590–91.

Krutch, Joseph Wood, "The Doctrine of Recurrence," Review of *The Heavenly City of the Eighteenth Century Philosophers*, *New York Herald Tribune Books* (December 18, 1932).

Smith, Charlotte W., *Carl Becker: On History and the Climate of Opinion* (Ithaca, New York: Cornell University Press, 1956).

Useful references

Strout, Cushing, *The Pragmatic Revolt in American History: Carl Becker and Charles Beard* (New Haven, Connecticut: Yale University Press, 1958).

Wilkins, Burleigh T., *Carl Becker: A Biographical Study in American Intellectual History* (Cambridge, Massachusetts: M.I.T. Press and Harvard University Press, 1961).

39. THE GRAND TITRATION: SCIENCE AND SOCIETY IN EAST AND WEST (JOSEPH NEEDHAM, 1900–1995)

Needham was trained as a biochemist and received a doctorate from Cambridge University at the age of 25. As an intellectual prodigy on track for a conventional, successful career, his life suddenly changed. With the help of Lu Gwei-djen, a woman scientist who came to work with him in 1936, he mastered notorious difficulties of the Chinese language. She became his lover, confidant, and some 50 years later his wife. For three years in the 1940s he traveled extensively in parts of China to collect data and artifacts relating to ancient and medieval science, visiting nearly 300 college libraries and research centers. He met two brilliant young men, Wang Ling and Huang Tsing Tsung, who became helpers and guides. With their steady collaboration, and that of Lu Gwei-djen, he devoted subsequent years to documenting and explaining the astonishing history of Chinese science and technology.

The result was *Science and Civilization in China*, arguably the greatest work of scholarship in the twentieth century. The project now amounts to some 25 published volumes, with others in preparation since Needham's death. Fifteen of those formidable books were written by Needham and Wang Ling. Thereafter others took over as Needham's strength waned in his eighties. One of the most remarkable and daunting volumes is the third on "Mathematics and the Sciences of the Heavens and the Earth" (1959). Extensively illustrated and footnoted, it comprises 874 pages. Three bibliographies total 109 pages. The first, Chinese books before +1800, takes up 30 pages.

In recognition of unprecedented achievement, Needham collected many honorary degrees and was elected to the Royal Society, the British Academy, and awarded a Companionship of Honour by the Queen, the only living person to receive all three distinctions. He also served a few years as president of Caius College at Cambridge. These honors were accumulated despite a publically unconventional life and immersion in left wing politics that made him sympathetic to the communist regime in China.

Along the way he wrote other books about Chinese science and technology before the modern era. He shows indisputably that Chinese ideas about nature and its operations, as well as numerous technical inventions, long preceded similar developments in the West. His writings are haunted by the "Needham question"—a grand historical issue touching the course and destinies of two civilizations. If Chinese science was so sophisticated, why did it lose steam and languish in later times? In Needham's words: "Why did modern science, the mathematization of hypotheses about Nature, with all its implications for advanced technology, take its meteoric rise *only* in the West at the time of Galileo?" (16). He asked this big question before visiting China: "When I first formed the idea, about 1938, of writing a systematic, objective, and authoritative treatise on the history science, scientific thought, and technology in the Chinese culture-area, I regarded the essential problem as that of why modern science had not developed in Chinese civilization (or Indian) but only in Europe?" (190).

The question is explored in *The Grand Titration*, a collection of papers and essays that "titrate" two civilizations, a chemical term referring to a compound encountering a second one that changes the character of the first and results in a third. The eight chapters in 330 pages, with Needham's unfailing brio and learning, address "poverties and triumphs" of Chinese science, China's global influence, science and social change, science and society in China, social relations in imperial China, a comparison of science and society east and west, the Chinese idea of time and its significance, and Chinese tension between human law and laws of nature. The basis for his puzzlement lies in the scope and priority in time of Chinese discoveries and inventions. The magnetic compass, gunpowder, paper, and movable-type printing are the merest tip of a colossal iceberg of scientific and technological achievements. A vast body of such accomplishments in ancient and medieval times preceded their counterparts in other societies by centuries.

Non-optical astronomy was advanced and included star maps with coordinates: " ... the Chinese were the most persistent and accurate observers of celestial phenomena anywhere before the Renaissance" (17). In a civilization dominated by literary values, mathematics was complex. Algebraic work included decimal place-value and a blank space for zero. The hexagonal property of snow flake crystals was recognized. Physics excelled at the study of optics, acoustics, and magnetism.

Engineering produced the first mechanical clockwork and elaborate hydraulic projects to control water ways. Other inventions and techniques were the segmental arch bridge, a seismograph, the umbrella, deep drilling for wells, knowledge of chemical affinity, the wheel barrow, the breast-strap harness for draft animals, quantitative cartography, cast iron, canal locks, the mould board for ploughs, barrel guns and cannon, the stern post rudder, porcelain, a chain drive for irrigation pumps, inoculation, and use of mineral remedies for illness. So skilled were the Chinese at so many things, they were in demand by foreigners: "People were always asking for Chinese technicians ... in A.D. 1126 when Chin Tartars besieged the Sung capital at Khaifêng, all kinds of craftsmen were asked for as hostages ... " (25).

Chinese nautical technology was the world's most advanced in the early Ming Dynasty (1368–1644). In the early fifteenth century fleets of huge ships traveled as far as Africa in open water, a generation before tiny Portuguese vessels crawled down the west coast of Africa looking for a route to India. Before the expeditions (seven of them) were discontinued and the fleets destroyed, China was in a position to establish a commercial and military empire in the very territories and sea lanes later dominated by Europeans.

Chinese work was not only technical but included naturalistic theorizing. Later borrowers, Indian, Arabic, and Western, were attracted to practical uses rather than theoretical inquiry (62–63). But given the practice of theory in ancient China, what accounts for failure to follow through with coherent methods of discovery and demonstration like those achieved by Galileo and Newton? Needham proposes suggestive explanations without being definitive. Social, economic, and intellectual factors inhibited or encouraged ongoing scientific inquiry and technological innovation

Chinese and European feudalism had different outcomes. After 221 B.C., when separate states were unified into an empire, there was one "lord" in China, the emperor or Son of Heaven, who ruled a single kingdom through a non-hereditary bureaucracy chosen predominantly on merit. The standard for appointment was performance in state examinations. The subject matter was literary classics focused on ethics, ideals of government, and skill at calligraphy. Science and technology were considered irrelevant to self-cultivation in knowledge of what is morally right. The dominant body of ideas was state Confucianism, whose economic theory stressed agriculture over commerce and unspecialized moral knowledge over any kind of technical specialization. Technology and science were needed only for building and maintaining water works, irrigation systems, and canals to exploit agricultural potential of the land.

Action was in the countryside where peasants, most of the population, were taxed on produce and supplied seasonal labor for public works (195–96). There were no cities with charters guaranteeing rights and autonomy where invention and commerce could flourish. With degree-holding literary men in charge, who monopolized the revered written language, artisans and merchants were marginalized as non-productive elements of society: " … the merchant guilds in China never achieved anything approaching the status and power of the merchant guilds of the city-states of European civilization" (197).

Knowledge was not sought and valued by the ruling mandarins from all quarters: "Nature is no respecter of persons. If someone takes the floor before an audience of scientific men and women, wishing to speak of observations made, experiments carried out, hypotheses formed, or calculations finished, the status of this person as to age, sex, colour, creed, or race, is absolutely irrelevant. Only his or her professional competence as observer, experimenter, or computer is relevant" (139). In China, there was little public sympathy for the Royal Society's motto, *Nullius in verba* (take no one's word for it). In China, "the best magistrate was he who intervened least in society's affairs … " (210). Judicious non-intervention was policy toward nature as well.

The loosening of Europe's feudal order left a hereditary military-aristocracy in charge of independent states competitive with one another for territory, wealth, and glory. Scientific inquiry and technical innovation were embraced as sources of power and prestige. Science was supported by state institutions. Artisans were valued for their usefulness and enjoyed high status. Merchants were influential. Central to European ideas of efficiency was the development of clock technology, which became essential to business, military planning, navigation, and science (83). The dominant metaphor for nature in the seventeenth century was the clockwork universe. The Chinese invented the first mechanical clock, but nothing ever came of it. For Europe, it was a major catalyst of economic and intellectual change.

The competitive state system stimulated intense commercial activity and the emergence of proto-capitalism in the Renaissance. Religious controversies connected with issues of state power led to the Reformation. Instead of harmony, the ultimate goal of Chinese civilization, Europeans were continually in a state of tension and conflict. Aggressiveness in politics and economics was extended to nature—it was there to be mastered: "The built-in instability of European society must therefore be contrasted with a homoeostatic equilibrium in China" (214).

The ideal of equilibrium is associated with a view of nature that was organic, that is, whatever happened was related to everything else governed by two principles, the complementary, oscillating yin and yang (female and male principles), and the cyclical five elements (fire, water, earth, metal, wood). The contents of "nature" were sorted out in fives according to the latter principle. The idea of linear causation, the basis of Western "laws of nature," may have existed but was not central to Chinese cosmology: "In this philosophy of organism all things in the universe are included: Heaven, Earth, and Man ... " (325).

Maintaining harmony between elements of this triad was the role of the emperor and his virtuous Confucian bureaucracy, not discovery of natural law by means of experiment and mathematical reasoning. Such a universe is not designed to be measured. It has nothing in common with the mechanical world view that reached maturity in the physics of Isaac Newton. Chinese thought did not favor a creator god as celestial law giver, whose decrees could be deciphered by reason. In Europe there was "the idea that to the earthly lawgiver there corresponded in heaven a celestial one, whose writ ran wherever there were material things" (Ibid.). In due time, however, the West dropped its law giver and retained laws of nature.

The chief criticism of Needham's big question is that it should not have been asked at all because it is unhistorical. It makes sense, so the argument goes, to ask why something happened but no sense to ask why something did not happen. There was no historical reason for the Chinese to develop modern science, so why should they? They had uses for empirical, theoretical, and technical knowledge already nicely integrated into the fabric of their civilization. To develop modern science their institutions and way of thinking had to been different, in short, more like those of the West.

On the other hand, in response to this criticism, a comparison of China and the West is informative about conditions under which a mathematical-experimental approach to phenomena in search of regular laws might appear, and what unfavorable conditions might block its development (327–30).

Works by Needham

Chinese Science: Explorations of an Ancient Tradition (Cambridge, Massachusetts: MIT Press, 1973).

Science and Civilization in China (Cambridge: Cambridge University Press, 1954 –). Twenty-five volumes to date.

Science in Traditional China: A Comparative Perspective (Cambridge, Massachusetts: Harvard University Press, 1982).

The Grand Titration: Science and Society in East and West (Toronto: University of Toronto Press, 1969).

The Shorter Science and Civilization in China, abridged by Colin A. Ronan (Cambridge: Cambridge University Press, 1978 –).

Within the Four Seas: The Dialogue of East and West (London: Allen and Unwin, 1969).

Works about Needham

Spence, Jonathan, "The Passions of Joseph Needham," *New York Review of Books* (August 2008). An extended review of Winchester's book.

Winchester, Simon, *The Man Who Loved China: The Fantastic Story of the Eccentric Scientist Who Unlocked the Mysteries of the Middle Kingdom* (New York: Harper and Row, 2008).

Useful references

Stunkel, Kenneth R., "Technology and Values in Traditional China and the West," *Comparative Civilizations Review* (in two installments: Fall 1990 and Spring 1991).

Temple, Robert K. G., *The Genius of China: 3,000 Years of Science, Discovery, and Invention*, introduced by Joseph Needham (London: Prion, 1991).

40. THE MAJORITY FINDS ITS PAST: PLACING WOMEN IN HISTORY (GERDA LERNER, 1920–)

Gerda Kronstein Lerner was born in Austria to a Jewish pharmacist father and an artist mother, both of whom were assimilated Austrians and politically liberal. The family was financially well off. Lerner's upbringing included a good secondary school education. Her feminist instincts were first aroused by the partial exclusion of women from Jewish temple services. She refused to participate and declared herself an unbeliever. When the Nazis marched into Austria in 1938, her father escaped. Lerner and her mother were imprisoned for six weeks as the Nazis connived to take over the family property. Lerner's imprisonment was a brutal and threatening experience forced upon her as she reached her eighteenth birthday. Facing death toughened her for survival and provided material for later works of fiction like *The Prisoners*, published in 1941.

In 1939, an expedient marriage secured a visa for Lerner and a way out of Austria to the USA. While learning English she worked as sales girl, waitress, and X-ray technician. She divorced the first husband and married the screen writer and film maker Carl Lerner. After bearing and raising two children, she began higher education in her forties. A baccalaureate degree in 1963 from the New School for Social Research was followed by a doctorate in 1966 from Columbia University, where she began to pursue women's history, not without support from colleagues but in an atmosphere of skepticism about the worth of her "exotic specialty." On completion of her degree, she was advised for pragmatic reasons to identify herself as a social historian rather than a women's historian, advice that was declined. She believed women's history could not be folded into social history.

From 1963 to 1979 she established an academic foundation for women's studies. She taught probably the first course ever in women's history at the New School for Social Research. At Sarah Lawrence College she founded the first graduate program in women's studies. She was co-founder of a Seminar on Women at Columbia University. After 1980 she became Robinson Edwards Professor of History at the University of Wisconsin, Madison, where she developed a doctoral program in women's history.

Lerner's achievements include many scholarly books, works of fiction, three screen plays, a musical drama, and social activism on several fronts. She has long been active in the movement to expand civil rights for blacks as a race and women as a group. She is persuaded that the historical lot of women cannot be understood apart from race and class. Her analysis of patriarchy relies in part on the Marxist idea of class consciousness that connects male domination of women with male power over the means of production. Lerner also pursued economic and social reform for women in the Congress of American Women. In 1969 she became co-president of the caucus of women historians. She has received many honors for her thought, scholarship, and activism on behalf of women. Notable are a prize from the Austrian Ministry of Women's Affairs and the Austrian Cross of Honor for Science and Art, the highest award from the Austrian state.

As an overview of Lerner's thought and writing, the text under discussion is a good introduction. The 12 chapters, preceded by Autobiographical Notes that explain what motivated each essay, address methodology, assumptions, and interpretations in women's history, issues of class and race, how feminism as a social and political battle for rights and emancipation should be understood in relation to the scholarship of women's history (the two are not the same), the changing objectives of feminism, interaction of black with white women, the experience of black women in America, both contemporary and during the anti-slavery movement, the culture of the housewife, women's history and traditional historiography, and much besides. She decided that "oppression" of women, although historical fact, is of limited use to understanding the consciousness and lives of women at all levels of society: "More important are questions like: What were women doing? How were they doing it? What was their own understanding of their place in the world?" (xxv). On these and other matters, Lerner writes with intelligence, learning, clarity, and a grasp of distinctions in women's history that further and deepen possibilities of discovery.

A recurrent theme in her work is the historic prevalence of patriarchy, which she views as a universal form of consciousness that defined for millennia who and what women are, what they can and must do, and how they should behave: "All conceptual models of history hitherto developed have only limited usefulness for women's history, since all are based on the assumptions of a patriarchal ordering of values" (157). The emergence of women's consciousness in the historical record has been slow. Women's history has passed through several stages. The first was to identify outstanding women "missing from history," to fill in the gaps: "The resulting history of 'notable women' does not tell one much about those activities in which most women engaged, nor does it tell us about the significance of women's activities to society as a whole" (145). Exceptional women do not encompass the majority of women and their varied experiences in a world that is patriarchal wherever one looks.

The second level concentrated on women's contributions in a "male-defined society." What have women added to various social, economic, and political movements in American history, from Progressivism to the New Deal? Always the movement was in the forefront, not the women making a contribution, although they are now included. But standards for judging the worth of any contribution came from men: "Margaret Sanger is seen merely as the founder of the birth-control movement, not as a woman raising a revolutionary challenge to the centuries old practice by which bodies and lives of women are determined and ruled by man-made laws" (147). "Contribution history" is not unimportant, but remains in the confines of traditional historiography: "When all is said and done, what we have ... is ... what men in the past told women to do and what men in the past thought women should be" (149).

The third level looks to the actual experience of women, which entails a fundamental shift in assumptions: "The most advanced conceptual level by which women's history can now be defined must include an account of the female experience as it changes over time and should include the development of feminist consciousness as an essential aspect of women's historical past" (161). The key issue for women is not liberation from patriarchal control through legal equality and rights, although such changes are essential, but achievement of autonomy: "Autonomy means women defining themselves and the values by which they will live, and beginning to think of institutional arrangements that will order their environment in line with their needs" (Ibid.).

Implications are considerable for historical time frames. Periodization schemes of traditional history based on political and military events reflect a patriarchal bias:

> Traditional history is periodized according to wars, conquests, revolutions, and/or vast cultural and religious shifts. All of these categories are appropriate to the major activities of men, especially political men. What historians of women's history have learned is that such periodization distorts out understanding of the history of women. Events that advance the position of men in society, adding to their economic opportunities, their liberties and their social standing, frequently have the *opposite* effect on women.
>
> (175)

What seems important to men in the past may have no relevance whatever for women, especially in the spheres of politics and military affairs.

If autonomy is the goal for women beyond various mechanisms of emancipation, who and what women are and what they can do cannot be judged by the roles as housewife and homemaker in the family. Women are an unbroken thread in the history of the family, but the family does not exhaust the history of women. From pre-industrial America to the present, the family has been an institutional arrangement encircling women with patriarchal definitions of their meaning and status: "The confinement of women to the sex-linked housewife-breeder-feeder role has been the key element in her subordination in all her other societal roles" (144).

Socialist and utopian attempts to create a model to replace the patriarchal family mostly failed, which suggests the "breeder-feeder" role of women is hard to undo and redefine, although reforms in Sweden suggest that significant change is within reach with strong government support. The solution in most Western countries will be more radical than "work-sharing and redefinition of gender-roles in work assignments." The housewife image, function, and status are "major social and political problems, which demand large-scale societal solutions" (143). In many non-Western societies the subordinate role of women is even more entrenched and reinforced by patriarchy, tradition, and religion.

Women are not a single unified group to which adjectives like "oppressed" can be applied. Women have not been victimized everywhere in the same way, nor have their responses been uniform. Black women in nineteenth-century America and before had two burdens—the oppression of a patriarchal culture and de facto slavery. Since the abolition of slavery, patriarchy has rolled on undiminished in the company of racial discrimination and prejudice. Lerner elaborates that black and white women have not been disadvantaged in the same way. Among white women, there is a world of difference between a rich woman and her servant girl, even though both are governed by ideals of patriarchy.

Lerner has influenced historiography by expanding its breadth and conceptual framework. She has drawn attention to experiences of at least half the human race. As she points out, women are not a "minority" but probably now in the majority. In theory and practice, she developed women's history as a legitimate field that can no longer be ignored. The result has been fresh, unexpected perspectives that enrich the fabric and texture of history: "When the historian adopts such a stance, even as a temporary strategy, the darkness of history lifts and the historical experience of women becomes visible, different from that of men and yet integrally part of it. Different life cycles, different turning points, different expectations, different opportunities, even different consciousness of self and others" (178).

She distinguished feminist activities from women's history. They are not the same thing. Writings of the former are commonly ahistorical, as with Betty Friedan's *The Feminine Mystique* (38n). Feminists want rights, or civil liberties, and emancipation from "restrictions imposed by sex" (49). Apart from securing rights, protections, opportunities, and freedom enjoyed by men, a key target of feminists is the patriarchal family that assumes women belong in the home to provide sexual, reproductive, and housekeeping services. A second target is sexual relations based on male dominance rather than mutual respect and satisfaction. The main thrust of activity is reform rather than historical research to understand experiences of women in the past.

Lerner cautions that women's history is not a splendid, isolated island, or a special category. The ideal is integration with mainstream history: "What is needed is a new universal history, a holistic history which will be a synthesis of traditional history and women's history. It will be based on close comparative study of given periods in which historical experiences of men are compared with those of women, their interactions being as much the subject of study as their differences and tensions" (180).

Works by Lerner

The Creation of Feminist Consciousness: From the Middle Ages to Eighteen-Seventy (New York: Oxford University Press, 1993).
The Creation of Patriarchy (New York: Oxford University Press, 1986).
The Female Experience: An American Documentary (Indianapolis, Indiana: Bobbs Merrill Educational Publications, 1977).
The Majority Finds Its Past: Placing Women in History (New York: Oxford University Press, 1979).
The Women in American History (Mento Park, California: Addison-Wesley Publishers, 1971).

Works about Lerner

Antler, Joyce, *The Journey Home: Jewish Women and the American Century* (New York: The Free Press, 1997).
Lerner, Gerda, *Profiles* (History Department, University of Wisconsin, Madison, n.d.).

41. THE AMERICAN POLITICAL TRADITION AND THE MEN WHO MADE IT (RICHARD HOFSTADTER, 1916–1970)

Hofstadter was an admired and widely read American historian. Most of his academic career was spent at Columbia University. His doctoral dissertation and first book, *Social Darwinism in American Thought*, remains a standard work on the subject. The book on America's political tradition was begun in 1943 when he was 27 years old and completed four years later. He called it a "young man's book," but its depth of scholarship and maturity of thought belie the modest characterization.

He won the Pulitzer Prize twice, first for *The Age of Reform* and then for *Anti-Intellectualism in American Life*. Premature death of leukemia at age 54 was lamented by the historical profession as an irreplaceable loss. He had no illusions that history is a science capable of supplying proofs about the past. What matters are usable insights. He did no archival work. Although he used mainly printed materials in the public domain, his mastery in that respect was wide and deep, suggested by informative bibliographical essays on each chapter, 37 pages of text, which were used to write his book.

The American Political Tradition discusses historical patterns, events, trends, and personalities marking successive phases of American history from the Founders to Franklin Delano Roosevelt. The account of Lincoln's career, for example, includes political, social, and ideological currents of the age he grappled with, and explains persuasively transformations of the slavery issue in his mind and its tangled connections with his goal to preserve the Union. This interplay of personality with events is organized into 12 chapters of 349 pages focused on Thomas Jefferson, Andrew Jackson, John C. Calhoun, Abraham Lincoln, Wendell Phillips (the abolitionist), William Jennings Bryan, Theodore Roosevelt, Woodrow Wilson, Herbert Hoover, and Franklin Roosevelt. Two chapters are collective portraits of the Founding Fathers and Robber Barons of the Gilded Age. Every chapter marshals telling quotations from players in each historical era, colorful portraits of leading figures, and an abundance of instructive notes.

Within this panorama of presidents, politicians, businessmen, and social activists he follows the ups and downs of a political tradition that dominated American history from its beginnings to at least the 1930s: "The sanctity of private property, the right of the individual to dispose of and invest it, the value of opportunity, and the natural evolution of self-interest and self-assertion, within broad legal limits, into a beneficent social order have been staple tenets of the central faith of American ideologies" (viii). This was the broad outlook of every president, most politicians, and the general public until the election of Franklin Roosevelt in 1933, when the "common man" was down and out and government was compelled to intervene aggressively in economic affairs during the Great Depression. The tension for more than a century was between special interests and the aspirations of ordinary people to better themselves without obstruction. Hovering in the background was a government obliged in theory to provide nothing more than conditions of fairness and justice.

Hofstadter traces this "faith" through the nation's history, explaining when and how it flourished, however imperfectly, when it served as a hypocritical mask to excuse or justify economic and political abuse, or when it simply degenerated into a pious myth. The faith was intact with Jefferson, Jackson, and Lincoln, dominated the post-Civil War era until the 1893 recession, and picked up steam again until the crash of 1929 and the end of Herbert Hoover's administration: " ... the keynote of Hoover's public career remained the same—a return to the conditions, real or imagined, of the past. Free trade, free enterprise, competition, open markets, open opportunities—this was the logic ... projected on a larger scale. The future would be just like the past, but more so" (312). Franklin Roosevelt initially affirmed Hooverism but soon decided it was a dead end, defied his own privileged class, and embraced welfare of the masses: "He became an individual sounding-board for the grievances and remedies of the nation" (328).

Meanwhile, whatever the grim realities of politics and economy, few dissented from the core tradition or favored revolutionary options. They were a small minority with little enduring influence on practical politics. While politicians might be sharply divided during campaigns for office, after an election they usually shared a rough framework of ideas centered on personal achievement and open enterprise: "In these pages I have tried, without neglecting significant conflicts, to keep sight of the central faith and to trace its adaptation to varying times and various interests" (ix).

Viewed as an ideal type, the tradition's hero was the common man who lifted himself to wealth, power, and status through hard work, frugality, and ingenuity in a political system that ideally encouraged opportunity and protected success. The role of government was to provide fairness and justice. For much of the American experience, especially following the Civil War, after advancement through land ownership and craftsmanship had its day, the economic setting for personal advancement was industrial capitalism. The evil staved off by aggressive individualism was perceived as fixed class relationships impeding opportunities for advancement—the specter of aristocracy: "Failure to rise in the economic scale was generally viewed as a fault in the individual, not in society. It was the outward sign of an inward lack of grace—of idleness, indulgence, waste, or incapacity ... It was the belief not only of those who had arrived but also of those who were pushing their way to the top" (104).

This "Protestant ethic" revered the self-made man, whose strength lay in self-help in a competitive system seconded by divine Providence (see essay 34 in this volume): "Jefferson rejected from his political philosophy the idea that one man has any intrinsic superiority over another, but he implicitly took it back again when he accepted competitive *laissez-faire* economics with its assumption that, so long as men were equal in law, and government played no favorites, wealth would be distributed in accordance with 'industry and skill'" (39). Jackson was fully attuned to this philosophy of merit versus privilege: "He understood the old Jeffersonian bias against overgrown government machinery, The Westerner's resentment of the entrenched East, the new politician's dislike of the old bureaucracy, and the aspiring citizen's hatred of privilege" (59).

Lincoln thought of himself as a common man. The issue for him was entrenched privilege and its contempt for men at the lower end of the social scale. In due time, black labor and white labor were seen resting on the same principles: " ... the equality of man [before the law], the dignity of labor, and the right to move upward in the social scale. It [privilege] defied the beliefs of millions of free men in the North who, like Lincoln, were ambitious to move forward and believed that the most sacred thing free society could do was to give the common man freedom and opportunity to make his own way" (119). Despite much waffling and reluctance, these principles were extended by Lincoln to negroes on behalf of free labor and not just to win a war by destroying the South's labor system.

The Robber Barons who dominated the American scene between 1865 and the end of the century illustrate a one-sided adaptation of the faith:

> They directed the proliferation of the country's wealth, they seized its opportunities, they managed its corruption, and from them the era took its tone and color. In business and politics the

captains of industry did their work boldly, blandly, and cynically. Exploiting workers and milking farmers, bribing Congressmen, buying legislatures, spying upon competitors, hiring armed guards, dynamiting property, using threats and intrigues and force, they made a mockery of the ideals of the simple gentry who imagined that the nation's development could take place with dignity and restraint under the regime of *laissez-faire*.
(164–65)

They believed a higher good was being created: "If they could buy Congressmen without making an apology, even to themselves, it was because they operated—or so they thought—on behalf of a benign transformation of tremendous magnitude. Because the abiding significance of their deeds would be so great and so good, they did not need to fret about their day-to-day knaveries." In the end they were mostly self-made men pursuing the American dream of unregulated self-betterment. Any one of them was "expressing his passionate American conviction that he had every honest right to come into his own ... " (165).

The political result of such uninhibited *laissez-faire* was to galvanize fitful, uneven reform in the Square Deal of Theodore Roosevelt, the New Freedom of Woodrow Wilson, and the two phases of Franklin Roosevelt's New Deal. The ideal of self-made men wore thin after the frontier closed in the 1890s, half the population moved from land to cities, and a small body of corporate powers dominated resources and production. An example of unsuccessful adaptation, and an instance of Hofstadter's shrewd historical overview, is Wilson's quest for world peace at Versailles after the Great War:

> No matter how historians may dramatize Wilson's struggle with Clemenceau and Lloyd George, it was not a struggle between an Old Order and a New Order, but merely a quarrel as to how the Old Order should settle its affairs.
>
> In this attempt to organize and regulate a failing system of competitive forces the theme of Wilson's domestic leadership was repeated on a world scale. Just as the New Freedom had been, under the idealistic crusade for the rights and opportunities of the small man, an effort to restore the archaic conditions of nineteenth century competition, so the treaty and the League Covenant were an attempt, in the language of democracy, peace, and self-determination to retain the competitive national state system of the nineteenth century without removing the admitted

source of its rivalries and animosities. It had always been Wilson's aim to preserve the essentials of the *status quo* by reforming it; but failing essentially to reform, he was unable in the end to preserve. (276–77)

Hofstadter relentlessly demythologizes American history, showing at every stage how it has been falsified and distorted. In the case of a revered Founder: "The mythology that has grown up around Thomas Jefferson is as massive and imposing as any in American history ... The issues of his time have been overdramatized, and Jefferson has been overdramatized with them" (18). Writing at a time when fascism had ravaged a good part of the world, his book is a caution against using the past as an ideological weapon. He deflates individuals while chiding their irresponsible hero worshipers. No figures are more vulnerable to mythical treatment and ideological exploitation, both friendly and unfriendly, than American presidents and high-level political officials. He quashes belief that the Founders, Jefferson, Jackson, Lincoln, Wilson, and Franklin Roosevelt were unalloyed liberal democrats, exposes their less than democratic convictions and tendencies, and demonstrates a mostly stable consensus around the "faith" of ordinary men rising to success in a *laissez-faire* environment.

But underlying the "faith" was a distrust of the masses by those in power. The Founders were not champions of the people: "They did not believe in man, but they did believe in the power of a good political constitution to control him ... this distrust of man was first and foremost a distrust of the common man and democratic rule" (3). Why the distrust? "Modern American folklore assumes that democracy and liberty are all but identical ... But the Founding Fathers thought that the liberty with which they were most concerned was menaced by democracy. In their minds liberty was linked not to democracy but to property" (10). The irony is that controlling the masses meant also controlling the reach of government to escape tyranny, so power was divided and apportioned in such a way that decisive, collaborative government action was hard to come by, a legacy that haunts the present.

Hofstadter was a force in American progressive and liberal historiography as observer, critic, activist, and scholar. Philosophically he was associated with a "consensus school" of American historiography, which held that whatever the upheavals in American political thought and institutions, they eventually returned to a state of pragmatic agreement and stability, unlike the often destructive, chaotic political experiences of Europe. Within this general scheme of conflict alternating with consensus, he applied social-psychological ideas to historical structure and dynamics, teased out unconscious psychological motives of his subjects, laid bare their irrational hostilities, explained political conflict as partly a result of "status anxiety," and isolated symptoms of political paranoia that stifle reason and hinder social progress.

Works by Hofstadter

Anti-Intellectualism in American Life (New York: Knopf, 1963).
"History and the Social Sciences," in Fritz Stern (ed.), *The Varieties of History* (New York: Vintage, 1972).
Social Darwinism in American Thought (rev. ed.; New York: Braziller, 1959).
The Age of Reform From Bryan to F.D.R. (New York: Knopf, 1955).
The American Political Tradition (New York: Knopf, 1948). Reprinted as a Vintage paperback.
The Paranoid Style in American Politics, and Other Essays (New York: Knopf, 1965).

Works about Hofstadter

Brown, David S. and Richard Hofstadter: *An Intellectual Biography* (Chicago, Illinois: University of Chicago Press, 2006).
Elkins, Stanley and Eric McKitrick, *The Hofstadter Aegis. A Memorial* (New York: Alftred A. Knopf, 1974).
Schlesinger, Jr. Arthur M. and "Richard Hofstadter," in *Pastmasters: Some Essays on American Historians*, ed. by Marcus Cunliffe and Robin W. Winks (New York: Harper and Row, 1969).
Singal, Daniel J., "Beyond Consensus": Richard Hofstadter and American Historiography, *American Historical Review*, 89 (October 1984): 976–1004.

Useful references

Geary, Daniel, "Richard Hofstadter Reconsidered," *Reviews in American History*, 35:3 (September 2007): 425–431.
Greenberg, David, "Richard Hofstadter Reconsidered," *Raritan Review*, 27:2 (Fall 2007): 144–167.
Lasch, Christopher, "On Richard Hofstadter," *The New York Review of Books* (8 March 1973).

42. INVENTING HUMAN RIGHTS: A HISTORY (LYNN HUNT)

Born in Panama and brought up in St. Paul, Minnesota, Hunt was educated at Carleton College (B.A. in 1967) and Stanford University

(Ph.D. in 1973). Her specialty is the French Revolution, on which she has written authoritative books and articles. Hers is an articulate voice also on the nature, scope, and possibilities of the "new history," which embraces economic, social, and cultural history. She has written as well about gender in European history and historiography.

She taught at the University of Pennsylvania for 11 years and was a professor at the University of California, Berkeley and Stanford University before settling in at the University of California, Los Angeles as the Eugen Weber Professor of Modern European History. She has been visiting professor at the École des Haute Études in France, Beijing University, and the Universities of Utrecht and Amsterdam. Many honors have come her way. In 1991 she was named a Fellow of the American Academy of Arts and Letters, and in 2002 was elected president of the American Historical Association.

While the idea of human rights is known, even if resisted or neglected, nearly everywhere in the modern world, and is more or less taken for granted in the West, not much thought has been given to exactly where it came from and under what conditions it was formulated: "How did these men, living in societies built on slavery, subordination, and seemingly natural subservience ever come to imagine men not at all like them and, in some cases, women too, as equals? How did equality of rights become a 'self-evident' truth in such unlikely places?" (19). Those questions are addressed in five compact chapters supported by 30 crowded pages of notes and references, many in French. An appendix supplies the text of three documents— the American (1776), French (1789), and United Nations (1948) declarations of human rights.

A claim of self-evidence was itself a remarkable development in European and American history, since what is self-evident requires no argument or proof: "This claim of self-evidence, crucial to human rights even now, gives rise to a paradox: if equality of rights is so self-evident, then why did this assertion have to [be] made, and why was it only made in specific times and places?" (Ibid.). The usual explanation is that it originated as a rather amorphous, philosophically appealing notion in the Enlightenment of the eighteenth century and was nailed down to specifics by American and French revolutionaries in 1776 and 1789.

In France, England, and America the idea of rights in some form was in the air as "rights of mankind," "rights of humanity," "natural rights," "rights of our being." Familiar names associated with a discussion of rights were Rousseau, D'Holbach, Condorcet, Blackstone, Jefferson, and Paine. Hunt weaves an account of how these trial expressions finally came together as "human rights." The messiness of history with regard to the emergence of "rights" is resolved into clarity through the prism of high scholarship. The heart of this clarity was what human rights ultimately came to mean. They must be "*natural* (inherent in human beings); *equal* (the same for everyone); and *universal* (applicable everywhere)" (20).

For these meanings to take hold certain conditions had to be satisfied. The first was affirmation that individual humans are autonomous, that is, capable of making decisions based on knowledge of right and wrong: "To have human rights, people had to be perceived as separate individuals who were capable of exercising independent moral judgment" (27).

The second was empathy, an awareness and acceptance that others have autonomy or a potential for it, as with servants, slaves, and women, that all men and women have thoughts and feelings like us: "Human rights depend both on self-possession and on the recognition that all others are equally self-possessed. It is the incomplete development of the latter that gives rise to all the inequalities of rights that have preoccupied us throughout history" (29). Recognition that others were autonomous beings led to an insistence in politics on shared decision-making.

The third was growing awareness that everyone has a body worthy of respect, and that our physical being is sacred and must not be violated. Higher regard for the body arose from changing social sensibilities, like disgust with urination and defecation in public, distaste for spitting and blowing one's nose on clothes or in one's hand. Where whole families slept in the same bed in earlier times, the trend was toward separate beds for parents and children where possible. In the theater polite silence and attention replaced former noisy conversation and random wandering about during a performance.

This positive attitude toward other people's bodies was a necessary condition for the movement to abolish torture and cruel punishments, which proceeded unevenly from place to place. Hunt provides a graphic account of torture, like breaking on the wheel, and its public settings. Judicial torment to extract confessions and repay society came under fierce attack: "Torture ended because the traditional framework of pain and personhood fell apart, to be replaced, bit by bit, by a new framework, in which individuals owned their bodies, had rights to their separateness and to bodily inviolability, and recognized in other people the same passions, sentiments, and sympathies as in themselves" (112).

Empathy was articulated and dramatized in literature and works of art: "My argument will make much of the influence of new kinds of experiences, from viewing pictures in public exhibitions to reading the hugely popular epistolary novels about love and marriage. Such experiences helped spread the practices of autonomy and empathy" (32). Epistolary novels were written in the form of exchanged letters in the first person, which lent a more personal dimension to the characters than was the case with conventional third person narrative. The most celebrated empathetic novels were Rousseau's *Julie, or the New Héloise* and Richardson's *Pamela* and *Clarissa*.

Empathy was not invented in these works, but they did convey an overwhelming experience of "psychological identification" with the female characters. A wave of shared feelings and emotions stirred readers: "Human rights grew out of the seedbed sowed by these feelings. Human rights could only flourish when people learned to think of others as their equals, as like them in some fundamental fashion. They learned this equality, at least in part, by experiencing identification with ordinary characters who seemed dramatically present and familiar, even if ultimately fictional" (58).

If fictional women could arouse such empathetic responses, what about their rights? "Eighteenth-century people, like almost everyone in human history before them, viewed women as dependents destined for family status and thus by definition not fully capable of political autonomy ... They had rights, but not political ones" (67). In the French constitution of 1789, women were entitled to rights of a "passive citizen," which included protections of "person, property, and liberty," but not involvement in public affairs. Jefferson held the same view. The rising tides of empathy and recognition of autonomy had a limit at this historical juncture.

At first the rights discussed fixed narrowly on rights of colonists as British subjects, the traditional rights of Frenchmen, and so on. Soon a broader conception of rights emerged in the face of critics who argued that universal rights were an arbitrary invention and not at all self-evident: "Despite its critics, rights talk was gathering momentum after the 1760s" (125). The "climate of opinion" was right for key documents that consolidated the fruit of this talk—the American Declaration of Independence (1776) and the French Declaration of the Rights of Man and Citizen (1789).

French leaders decided that constitutional monarchy was not good enough. Colonists and their leaders decided that securing the "rights of Englishmen" was not good. Both settled on universal rights. "If monarchical authority simply needed repairs, then a declaration of the 'rights of man' could hardly be necessary. For those ... who agreed with Jefferson's diagnosis that the government had to be rebuilt from scratch, a declaration of rights was essential" (130).

Once declarations of universal rights had been made in America and France, the next step was implementation of principles to define civil as well as natural rights. There were no specifics about the status of women, children, religious minorities, foreigners, and slaves, or about property qualifications, tax status, and religious tests for participation in government: "In both the new United States and France, declarations of rights referred to 'men,' 'citizens,' 'people.' And 'society' without addressing differences in political standing" (148). In America, the first ten amendments of the Constitution, which came after the French declaration, enumerated freedoms and protections to limit powers of government over the individual. Most details were left to the states: "The thirteen colonies denied the vote to women, African-Americans, Native Americans, and the propertyless" (Ibid.). With a centralized national legislature at work in France, implementation of rights is easier to follow.

Hunt explains a dynamic set in motion: "The French Revolution, more than any other event, revealed that human rights have an inner logic. As the deputies face the need to turn their lofty ideals into specific laws, they inadvertently developed a kind of conceivability or thinkability scale. No one knew in advance which groups were going to come up for discussion, when they would come up, or what the resolution of their status would be" (150). Within a few years, the logic of rights conceded political equality to Protestants, Jews, and free blacks. Slaves were freed in 1794 before any other country. From France, the language of universal rights spread abroad and provoked reforms.

Despite inner logic, women did less well: "The Rights of women clearly ranked lower on the 'conceivability' scale than those of other groups ... women simply did not constitute a clearly separate and distinguishable *political* category before the Revolution" (168–69). Feeling the humanity of others was not enough: "Learning to empathize opened a path to human rights, but it did not ensure that everyone would be able to take that path" (64). On the other hand, "the philosophy of natural rights had an implacable logic, even if it had not yet worked itself out in the case of women, that other half of humanity" (175; see essay 40 in this volume). In due time, women in the West would come into their own.

In her last chapter, "the Soft Power of Humanity," Hunt reviews the ups and downs of human rights into the twentieth century.

Exclusion from rights came from several quarters: a battle between traditionalism and rights philosophy, a preference of the masses for equality over liberty, perverted biological arguments for inequality from evolution, and the pressure of nationalism to put self-determination ahead of rights. The cruel aberrations of totalitarianism—Nazi, Fascist, and Communist—canceled the rights of millions, but accelerated movement toward a United Nations Declaration of Human Rights after World War II: "Throughout the nineteenth and early twentieth centuries benevolent societies kept the flame of universal human rights burning as nations turned in on themselves" (205). But she explains that the call for rights has stirred a back lash, "the growth of new and sometimes fanatical ideologies of differences ..." The utterly dehumanizing crimes of the twentieth century only became conceivable once everyone could claim to be an equal member of the human family" (212).

The importance of Hunt's book for historiography is its subject and her treatment of it. The idea of human rights is explored in a wider domain of intellectual history fundamental to an understanding of Western civilization. If there is such a thing as shared values in the West, human rights are surely the centerpiece. Her perceptive use of literature, philosophy, art, and social history furthers the book's explanatory power, demonstrating that a multi-dimensional fix on history yields the best results, and that just such breadth is needed to understand an idea like human rights.

The word "invention" in the work's title is misleading, since Hunt's exposition makes clear that no single group, person, or country came up with the idea in its fullness and consequences. It emerged with many twists and turns in the most unexpected and complex ways. Identifying and unraveling those circumstances is the achievement of her book. Perhaps "discovering" universal human rights might have been a better word, mirroring Isaac Newton's discovery of universal gravitation and suggesting that human rights have an objective reality.

Finally, her explanation for the appearance and initial successes of human rights is persuasive. Her explanation for the failure of rights to become universal, and, indeed, to suffer monstrous setbacks, is less so. It is not clear how being a member of the "human family" makes genocide "conceivable." But she is right that consciousness of what is not acceptable has become pervasive: " ... you know the meaning of human rights because you feel distressed when they are violated" (214).

Works by Hunt

Appleby, Joyce, Lynn Hunt and Margaret Jacob, *Telling the Truth about History* (New York: W.W. Norton, 1994).
Beyond the Cultural Turn: New Directions in the Study of Society and Culture, ed. and intro. by Victoria E. Bonnell and Lynn Hunt, Afterword by Hayden White (Berkeley, California: University of California Press, 1999).
Inventing Human Rights: A History (New York: W.W. Norton, 2007).
Politics, Culture, and Class in the French Revolution (Berkeley, California: University of California Press, 1984).

Useful references

Hunt, Lynn (ed.), "History, Culture, and Text," in *The New Cultural History* (Berkeley, California: University of California Press, 1989).

43. THE HOUR OF OUR DEATH (PHILIPPE ARIÈS, 1914–1984)

Lucien Febvre, a founder of the French *Annales* school of historiography, complained that no one had written a history of death. The deficiency was corrected many years later by Ariès, a medieval historian. He attended the Sorbonne but failed a key examination that denied him an academic career. Thereafter he became a successful agronomist while pursuing social and cultural history as a sideline, with his wife's help on some projects. Ariès was politically conservative and described himself as a "right wing anarchist." Right wing sympathies included Action française, founded in the late nineteenth century as a counter-revolutionary monarchist organization. True to his "anarchism," however, he eventually decided the group and its outlook were too authoritarian for him. Although clearly influenced by *Annales*, he was never formally part of the movement.

Ariès wrote some 15 works. In 1960 he published the groundbreaking *Centuries of Childhood*, which argues that childhood was nonexistent in the Middle Ages and emerged only later as a social reality. His expansive work on death applied the idea of "mentalities," the collective beliefs and feelings of ordinary people manifested in daily life. In these two books he fixed attention on polarities, the bookends, of human life—childhood and death. His use of every kind of source to understand collective social behavior and belief is informed by historical and symbolic anthropology as well as ideas from psychoanalysis, especially "the collective unconscious" (298, and see essay 37 in this volume).

The book on death examines attitudes, practices, and artifacts relating to death over a thousand-year period. Why a thousand years?

> Changes in man's attitude toward death either take place very slowly or else occur between long periods of immobility. Contemporaries do not notice these changes because these periods of immobility span several generations and thus exceed the capacity of the collective memory. If the modern observer wishes to arrive at an understanding that eluded contemporaries, he must widen his field of vision. If he confines himself to too short a time span ... he runs the risk of attributing originality to phenomena that are much older.
>
> (xvi–xvii)

The work is not a chronological narrative but rather falls into a series of topics roughly chronological.

Ariès's method for spanning a thousand years is strongly intuitive: "The observer scans a chaotic mass of documents and tries to decipher, beyond the intentions of the writers or artists, the unconscious express of the sensibility of the age" (xvii). While preferring a "subjective" approach in the book, he makes some use of quantification, a signature technique pursued by historians in the *Annales* movement. Data collected on the social position of people, from nobles to unnamed commoners, buried in four parishes and a number of churches and their cemeteries, all in France, are presented in two pages of tables (84–85). Sixty to 70 percent of those buried in churches were

> merchants, tradesmen, skilled craftsmen, and their wives and children. The trades mentioned include master tailor, tapestry weaver, stained-glass painter, hosier, shoemaker, baker, weaver, apothecary, wigmaker, innkeeper, mason, dyer, brushman, cutler carpenter, chandler, cloth shearer, serge maker, and spurrier ... So we see that burials in churches seem to consist of almost all the nobles, members of the legal profession, and petty and high officials, as well as a large segment of the middle-class tradespeople.
>
> (88–89)

The social composition of cemeteries was about two-thirds common people and about a third from the middle group. About a quarter to a third were children under the age of one.

Ariès's survey of ten centuries is guided by a conceptual framework: "I turn and cast my eye over this thousand year landscape like an astronaut looking down at the distant earth. The vast space seems to me to be organized around the variations of four psychological themes." The themes are "awareness of the individual," "defense of society against untamed nature," "belief in an afterlife," and "belief in the existence of evil," which are applied to five models: "the tame death," "the death of the self," "remote and imminent death," the "death of the other," and "the invisible death" (603). Each model has its burial rituals, places of burial, types of markers (tombs, sarcophagi, stone effigies), and collective attitudes about confronting death, the afterlife, and the existence of evil. Following Ariès's analysis in this framework is not easy. He detours the reader through numerous byways thick with detail and jumps back and forth between centuries. The concluding chapter, however, conveniently reviews all the themes acting within the models with brevity and clarity.

Themes and the models they qualify are fleshed out by reference to clerical documents, tombs, sarcophagi, coffins, cemeteries, prayer books, churchyards, paintings, treatises, sculptures, wills, chapels, churches, village and town registers, poetry, and much more—Ariès's "chaotic mass" of evidence. The material comes from France, England, and America, although he alludes to other places. Forty-one rare illustrations are keyed to the text. The first shows Roman tombs on the Appian Way, the dead placed outside the city walls for distance from the living, the second a Christian necropolis, the dead placed close to the living for intimacy. The ninth image from 1402 shows a half-decomposed corpse to illustrate the macabre iconography of the fourteenth to the sixteenth centuries, when flesh was represented widely in decay between death and the naked skeleton.

Tame Death was encircled by ritual, processions, viewings, grievings, and other public displays that acknowledge and try to blunt the reality of personal destruction. Death removed a person from the community and weakened it by leaving a gap. For Ariès, civilization itself, with all its resources of government, religion, law, and community solidarity is a fortress to defend against savage, heartless nature. Death is the ultimate assault of nature and must be tamed by all the activities and institutions man can devise. Therefore a funeral could be festive, with lights and refreshments. The "vile and ugly death" is to be feared and avoided, "the secret death that is without witness or ceremony: the death of the traveler on the road, or the man who drowns in a river, or the stranger whose body is found at the edge of a field, to even a neighbor who is struck down for no reason" (11).

Death of the Self involved a change in eschatology, the doctrine of last things. Until 1150 the dead slept and were awakened by the Second Coming of Christ to be resurrected. There was an interval between death and renewal. No mention was made in texts or art of punishment or the damned. Thereafter the stress was on judgment and punishment, and in church sculpture both expectations were represented briefly during the transition (99). The threat to self was fear of immediate judgment replacing confidence in resurrection that followed an interval of rest and waiting:

> The drama no longer took place in the vast reaches of the beyond. It had come down to earth and was now enacted right in the bedroom of the sick person, around his bed ... The bedroom, however, was to take on new meaning in the iconography of death. It was no longer the scene of an event that was almost commonplace ... It became the arena of a drama in which the fate of the dying man was decided for the last time, in which his whole life and all his passions and attachments were called into question.
>
> (107–8)

No one in the bedroom was aware of the Trinity on one side of the bed and Satan on the other debating the sick person's fate. Within this model of physical death "at the actual moment," macabre representations of vivid bodily decomposition flourished. In a setting of immediate judgment the dying person's legal will was a sacred duty in an atmosphere obsessed with judgment and the reality of evil.

Remote and Imminent Death was a backing off after the sixteenth century from the moment of death to a lifetime of meditation on death, which resulted in "the good death, the beautiful and edifying death, which replaces the death ... in the bedroom invaded by the powers of heaven and hell, the memories of life, and the feverish fantasies of the devil" (310). Melancholy reflection on death is aided by "vanities," "pictures and objects that evoked the passage of time, the illusions of this world, and even the tedium of life" (327). The macabre was sanitized as skull and the skeleton, "clean and gleaming," presentable to polite company and even children, replaced "the naked cadaver being eaten by worms and bitten by snakes and toads ... " (328). Fresh corpses or the nearly dead even take on an erotic aura inviting expressions and acts of necrophilia (374).

The Death of the Other was a sensibility that emerged from Romanticism and was a revolution in feeling. Before the nineteenth century two ideas of the individual had alternated: the common lot of all and a personal biography. Community and individualism were replaced by privacy focused on the family and its members grieving, not death of the person, but his or her separation from the living. A sense of evil and belief in hell retreated and death became a source of beauty: "Death was no longer familiar and tame ... but neither was it absolutely wild. It had become moving and beautiful like ... the immensity of nature ... " (610). Belief in an afterlife persisted because of reluctance to give up the loved one altogether. Less beautiful was a crisis of cemeteries and their location as they filled up and became suspect because of public health. The wildness of death amidst the savagery of nature was blunted by science, technology, and industrialization.

The Invisible Death of the twentieth century is denial that anything has happened. Disappearance of an individual no longer ruptures continuity of the community: "Everything in town goes on as if nobody died anymore" (560). Remoteness from death was initially a Victorian distaste for dirt and bad smells: "A new image of death is forming: the ugly and hidden death, hidden because it is ugly and dirty" (569). Death met with revulsion "leads to the hidden death of the hospital, which began very discreetly in the 1930s and '40s and became widespread after 1950." The public face of death was masked and "eliminated its character of public ceremony, and made it a private act. At first this act was reserved for intimates, but eventually even the family was excluded as the hospitalization of the terminally ill became widespread" (575).

Cremation became more desirable than burial, which means the role of the cemetery as a place of memory and visitation receded. Public mourning has gone into decline: "Society refuses to participate in the emotion of the bereaved. This is a way of denying the presence of death ... " (580). The dying person can now be kept alive for long periods by medical intervention with drugs and tubes in the body, even if in a coma, and is denied "control of the end of his life, and of his death ... Death has ceased to be accepted as a natural, necessary phenomenon" (586). In short, the ugly, graceless death has become the norm: "This is always the death of a patient who knows" (587).

In historiography, Ariès reflects the ideals of *Annales* with a commitment to problem-oriented history rather than traditional narrative, attention to varied aspects of ordinary life, and an interdisciplinary style of research that ignores the isolation of separate disciplines. These ideals include isolation of collective mentalities along with techniques of historical anthropology and its descriptive approach to community life. He generalizes broadly from the evidence at hand. With respect to burials in English churches, "it would appear that burial in church was reserved always for a smaller number of privileged persons, the families of lords, a few laborers and inhabitants living in the middle class manner, and also priests ... We may assume that the situation was not very different in the other countries of western Europe ... " (91).

Despite the "models," Ariès's work on death does not stand as a coherent whole, which is not surprising given "the formless mass of documentation" he coped with (602). It is episodic and discursive in a way that often invites browsing and skipping about. Description and exposition without narrative, although quite "thick" in the anthropological sense, dominates the stage rather than explanation. In short, the overall focus is both wide and blurred, but as a resource on humanity and death in Europe for a long haul, it is irreplaceable.

Works by Ariès

Centuries of Childhood: A Social History of Family Life, trans. from French by Robert Baldick, with new introduction by Adam Phillips (London: Pimlico, 1996). French title: *Enfant et la vie familiale sous l'Ancien Régime.*

The Hour of Our Death, trans. from French by Helen Weaver (New York: Oxford University Press, 1991). French title: *Homme devant la morte.*

Works about Ariès

Burke, Peter, *The French Historical Revolution: The Annales School, 1929–89* (Cambridge: Polity Press, 1990).

Hutton, Patrick H., *Philippe Ariès and the Politics of French Cultural History* (Amherst: University of Massachusetts Press, 2004).

Useful references

Dosse, Francoise, *New History in France: The Triumph of the Annales,* trans. from French by Peter V. Conroy, Jr. (Chicago, Illinois: University of Chicago Press, 1978).

Hunt, Lynn, "French History in the Last Twenty Years: The Rise and Fall of the Annales Paradigm," *Journal of Contemporary History,* 21:2 (April, 1986): 209–224.

Iggers, Georg G. and Q. Edward Wang, *A Global History of Modern Historiography* (Edinburgh Gate, United Kingdom: Pearson Longman, 2008).

Stoianovich, Traian, *French Historical Method* (Ithaca, New York: Cornell University Press, 1976).

44. INTELLECTUAL ORIGINS OF THE ENGLISH REVOLUTION (CHRISTOPHER HILL, 1912–2003)

Born into a prosperous middle class family in York, Hill attended well-known St. Peter's School. While studying there, his intellectual talent came to the attention of faculty at Balliol College at Oxford University. He went to Oxford and in 1932 took a degree with first class honors. While at Balliol, he was converted to Marxism. In 1935 he went to the Soviet Union, learned Russian, and studied Soviet historiography. On returning he accepted a position at Cardiff University. When war broke out in 1940, he became a private in the British army and was later commissioned as an officer. About that time he began to publish articles about seventeenth-century England.

In 1946 he joined the Communist Party of Great Britain in the company of other notable historians like E.P. Thompson and Eric Hobsbawn. British Marxist historians formed the Communist Party Historians Group. After the abortive Hungarian Revolution in 1956, Hill pulled out of the Communist Party, which he found too undemocratic, but retained his Marxist leanings with qualifications. Marxism in its pure form is deterministic. As a result of class struggle, sparked and driven by what social group controls economic life, a direction is set in history that unfolds toward a definite end. The final outcome, a classless society, is inevitable. Hill was uncomfortable with determinism and preferred a compromise.

The rigidity of dialectical materialism as a law (thesis, antithesis, synthesis) governing historical change was abandoned or soft pedaled while the role of class relations and economic forces in historical change was retained, with more elbow room for subjectivity and choice. From this perspective, ideas are not merely superstructure rationalizing and justifying a mode of production: " … a sociological approach to intellectual history carries its own risks. Marx himself did not fall into the error of thinking men's ideas were merely a pale reflection of their economic needs, with no history of their own" (3). On the other hand, as Hill stresses, Marx was right that ideas are not solely a result of their internal logic nor do they appear and function in a social-economic vacuum.

Hill's "English Revolution" is the period of civil war, execution of Charles I, and the Commonwealth under Cromwell from 1640 to 1660, not the Glorious Revolution of 1688 when the Stuart king James II was replaced peacefully and a constitutional monarchy was established. Prominent changes brought about by the first Revolution were less power for the King and more for Parliament, an imperialist foreign policy, growth of economic liberalism, more equitable taxation, a surge of religious toleration, and "the triumph of modern science" (132).

Hill's erudition and scholarly apparatus are imposing. Pages are heavy with names, events, books, and ideas supported by notes that may occupy a half or a third of a page. Rather than digging in archives, his sources are printed works from the Bodleian and other libraries. It seems there is no book, pamphlet, or treatise from the sixteenth and seventeenth centuries he overlooked. His style is disarmingly casual amidst dense thickets of exposition, analysis, and references. The search for ideas that underlay the first English Revolution reaches from cellar to attic as obscure people in religion, law, literature, and other pursuits share the stage with celebrated writers, scientists, and thinkers.

What is the issue? "The problem I want to discuss is so obvious that we are apt to overlook it. For as long as history recorded there had been kings, lords, and bishops in England ... Yet, within less than a decade, successful war was levied against King; bishops and the House of Lords were abolished; and Charles I was executed in the name of his people. How did men get the nerve to do such unheard of things ... Medieval kings in plenty had been assassinated ... but the sanctity that hedged in a king had never before been publically breached" (5). The ideas in men's heads are part of the explanation: "The history of ideas necessarily deals with trends to which there are individual exceptions. I shall argue that on the whole the ideas of the scientists favoured the Puritan and Parliamentarian cause" (4–5).

A revolutionary climate of opinion emerged from several quarters. A source of irreverence for authority was men who "subverted the doctrine of degree by preaching the equality of man and advocating a career open to talents" (267). Individual virtue was held to trump birth and inheritance, a legacy of the Renaissance. It was such virtuousness that permeated the New Model Army of the Puritans. A second kind of resistance was "feudal doctrines of contract" influenced by "new commercial and legal ideas" (268). The agent of that influence was "Puritan contract theology," which held that contracts were sacred and not to be violated, a blow aimed at royal interference with business. A third was the notion widely shared that the world was about to end, which was indirectly "a stimulus to direct revolutionary action ... " (269). Outside of England the major influence was the nearby example of Dutch prosperity, enlightened government, and freedom of inquiry.

Hill's guiding premise is that middle class types—merchants, artisans, craftsmen—were most receptive to scientific inquiry and discovery, and that science rather than religion had the deepest impact on the climate of opinion that erupted into civil war. His approach to intellectual origins is to use prominent Englishmen—Francis Bacon, Walter Ralegh (sic), and Edward Coke—as points of reference and reach out from them to other sources of ideas that laid a ground work for the Revolution:

> None of our three was a wholly original thinker, not even Bacon: their function was to state clearly what other men were groping towards, which is the definition of an historical great man ... Bacon, Ralegh, and Coke shared common enemies with the Puritans—the dissolute, shallow, increasingly pro-papist court; the pro-Spanish and bribed section of the aristocracy; lack of government interest or support for educational projects or for overseas expansion; use of historical research to free the government from Parliament and common law; interference with free enterprise ...
>
> (289)

Other common interests of the three were science and "an optimistic belief in progress and Parliamentarianism" (Ibid.). These interests were embraced by Puritans, artisans, and men of commerce who resisted subservience to a conservative status quo. The "great man" being groped after was to be Oliver Cromwell.

Bacon (1561–1626) was long near the center of political power until his disgrace for bribery as Lord Chancellor. He was a prolific author, tireless critic of Aristotelian-Scholastic science and philosophy, champion of consulting nature rather than books, and pragmatist and optimist about the power of knowledge to improve the human condition despite original sin: "His theories suggested that reality could be changed by human effort ... Mere intellectual activity divorced from practice is a form of laziness and escapism ... Here again the parallel with the Puritan effort to realize God's kingdom on earth is valid" (110). Although his ideas about science and improvement were not much heeded in his time, they "became widely influential during what used to be called the Puritan Revolution" (111). Overall impact of his thought was to encourage the secularization of society contrary to interests of the throne: "In many respects, Bacon's ideas are closer to those of the Parliamentarians than those of the kings whom he served" (96). Hill cites 25 "influential thinkers" influenced by Bacon's empiricism and experimentalism by the 1640s (115–16).

Ralegh (1552–1618) was explorer, soldier, poet, scientist, founder of the first English colony in America, a favorite in Elizabeth's court, and author of a *History of the World*. With some likeminded colleagues, he planned to found a teaching and research academy in London, which "would bring modern and practical subjects to royal wards and other sons of nobles and gentlemen—mathematics, cosmography, astronomy, naval and military training, navigation, shipbuilding, engineering, medicine, cartography languages, and above all history" (138). In a treatise on royal power, Ralegh "makes out a case for political opposition to the crown—even violent opposition ... " His purpose "is to convince James [King James I] that Parliament *cannot* be wished out of existence, because those whom it represents cannot be wished out of existence" (152–53).

Ralegh elevated history to a major field of study and instruction. He "illustrates the intimate connexion between early science and historical studies" (173). The connexion also held in politics: "In a sense, the Parliamentary opposition's case against the first two Stuarts was wholly based on history, even if the history was not always very accurate" (178). "History had an exalted role: ... though history is for Ralegh ... the theater of God's judgments, it is much more that that. God represents the principle of law in history" (180). No wonder James I tried to suppress *The History of the World*, and Cromwell recommended it to his son. History taught that "precedents were not to be followed simply because they were old ... historical evidence was the raw material for political judgment, for adjusting institutions to suit changing circumstances ... " (199).

Coke (1552–1634) was a jurist, member of Parliament, Elizabeth's attorney general, and author of works on common law authoritative for 150 years:

> To grasp Coke's significance we must recall what had been happening to English law. During the Tudor century decisive changes were taking place in society. The Church was completely subordinated to the secular power; the House of Commons rose to a position of new importance; there were sweeping economic changes. Peace and internal order, the end of feudal violence, the dissolution the monasteries, and increased prosperity ... had 'set lawyers a-work.'

(227)

Bacon attempted unsuccessfully to modernize the code by compiling 300 legal maxims. Coke took up the task and succeeded in 13 volumes of *Reports*. Coke undertook to protect property, abolish the hold of guilds on employment, and increase the power of Parliament. Coke's reform forbade torture. Thus he "systematized English law and ... continued and extended the process of liberalizing it, of adapting it to the needs of a commercial society" (256). He also fostered a myth about the English constitution and its precedents as "monuments to the eternal vigilance with which God's Englishmen had defended their liberties" (257). The effect on revolutionaries was to bend their heads toward parliament and common law rather than the king for justice.

Critics of Hill have argued that he overdoes the connection between Puritanism and science, and that his view of science ignores important developments on the continent. Perhaps the most nettlesome doubts concern his use of evidence, that he is guilty of "source-mining," that is, selecting evidence that supports his case and assembling it to fit an already articulate pattern. But Hill acknowledges the traps he can fall into, and he is cautious about the impact of his three notable men: "I do not want to claim too much: Jericho was not overthrown by trumpet blasts. But Bacon, Ralegh, and Coke together with many lesser figures whom we have studied in this book, helped to undermine men's traditional belief in the eternity of the old order in Church and state ... without the successful accomplishment of which there could have been no political revolution" (291).

Works by Hill

Intellectual Origins of the English Revolution (Oxford: Oxford University Press, 1965; rev. ed. 1997).

Puritanism and Revolution: Studies in Interpretation of the English Revolution of the 17th Century (New York: Schocken Books, 1964).

The Century of Revolution, 1603–1714 (Edinburgh: T. Nelson, 1961).

The World Turned Upside Down: Radical Ideas During the English Revolution (New York: Viking Press, 1973).

Works about Hill

Eley, Gioff and William Hunt (eds.), *Reviving the English Revolution: Reflections and Elaborations on the Work of Christopher Hill* (London: Verso, 1988).

Kaye, Harvey J., *The British Marxist Historians: An Introductory Analysis* (Cambridge: Polity Press, 1984), Chapter 4.

Useful references

Richardson, R.C., *The Debate on the English Revolution Revisited* (London: Methuen, 1977).

Samuel, Raphael, "British Marxists Historians, 1880–1980," *New Left Review*, 120 (March–April, 1980): 21–96.

45. FROM SLAVERY TO FREEDOM: A HISTORY OF AFRICAN AMERICANS (JOHN HOPE FRANKLIN 1915–2009)

Franklin was born in Rentiesville, Oklahoma and graduated from Booker T. Washington High School in Tulsa. His baccalaureate degree was from Fisk University in 1935. At the age of 26 he took a doctorate in history at Harvard University. A man of high intelligence and tireless industry, his imposing work on the history of negroes in America was published in 1947 and has sold millions of copies. His intention was to correct the absence or neglect of black history in the mainstream of American history. Few doubt that he succeeded.

Despite a superior education, he was subjected to humiliating experiences in a country rife with prejudice and segregation. The tendrils of racism enveloped him during attempts to volunteer his services in World War II. When he applied to serve as a clerical worker with the navy, he was informed by a recruiter that his qualifications were fine except for color. The War Department, for the same reason, would not take him on for a history project. When he obeyed the draft requirement for a blood test, the physician refused him access to the office. Thereafter he sidestepped the draft on grounds that his country had no use for him because of his color. In the early 1950s he worked with a team under Thurgood Marshall to prepare background for the case known as Brown *v.* Board of Education, which led in 1954 to the Supreme Court decision that ended segregation in public schools.

After holding a number of teaching positions, he was hired by Brooklyn College to become the first black person to chair a history department. In 1964 he was recruited by the University of Chicago, occupied an endowed chair until 1982, and chaired the university's history department for three years. In 1985 he became a professor of legal history for seven years in the Duke University Law School. In contrast to wartime snubs, he was honored in many ways, which included presidencies of the Southern Historical Association (1970), Organization of American Historians (1975), and the American

Historical Association (1979). He was appointed to a number of national commissions. In 1976 the National Endowment for the Humanities tapped him to deliver the prestigious Jefferson Lecture. In 1995 he received the Presidential Medal of Freedom.

From Slavery to Freedom has a monumental quality about it, equipped with an arsenal of detail rendered coherent by plain writing and engaging narrative. The scope in time and space is immense, from the sixteenth to the twentieth century. Interacting themes in the sordid drama of slavery and oppression are the struggle for identity and liberty, successes and failures, advances and setbacks, great figures and anonymous masses. The impressive range of topics is structured in 25 well-proportioned chapters: African cultural background, African and domestic slave trade, slavery in the Caribbean (where slaves were "seasoned" for shipment to the mainland), slavery in colonial America, and Latin America, negroes in the American Revolution and aftermath to the Civil War, the work of anti-slavery groups, free and "quasi-free" Negroes, the plantation system in the South (the "peculiar institution"), Negroes in westward expansion in the Civil War, white supremacy and corruptions of Reconstruction, Negroes in World War I, the Harlem Renaissance, Negroes and the New Deal, Negroes in World War II, the movement toward "revolution" in post-war years, the results of success and "illusions of equality, and American Negro impact on the world." Meantime, everywhere in the text, dozens of notable black men and women are given their due.

The "selected" and annotated bibliography of primary and secondary sources occupies 39 pages. Appendices provide key documents: The Emancipation Proclamation, the Brown *v.* Board of Education decision, the Fair Employment Executive Order, and John F. Kennedy's Message to the Congress on Civil Rights. There are supporting maps and many illustrations. The work is in every respect a major one. This sweeping history of Negroes in the Americas can only be sampled here to illustrate the range of Franklin's knowledge, the quality of his judgment, and his modest style.

On the slave trade:

> Upon arrival at a trading post in Africa the trader was ready to establish his contacts both with officials at the post and with the local Africans who assisted in securing the desired slaves ... In addition to the various courtesy visits and negotiations that protocol required and that the traders were inclined to in order to keep the local leaders in good humor, it was often difficult to find enough 'likely' slaves to fill a ship of considerable size ...

The Africans offered stiff resistance to their capture, sale, and transportation to the unknown New World. Fierce wars broke out between tribes when the members of one sought to capture members of another to sell them to the traders.

(40)

On the "one way" passage: "The voyage to the Americas ... was a veritable nightmare ... There was hardly standing, lying, or sitting room. Chained together by twos, hands and feet, the slaves had no room in which to move about and no freedom to exercise their bodies even in the slightest" (41). While the death rate was enormous, it is estimated that nearly ten million were transported between 1451 and 1870: "It is more difficult to measure the effect of such activity on African life ... The expatriation of millions of Africans in less than four centuries constitutes one of the most far reaching and drastic social revolutions in the annals of history" (42–43). In effect, the flower of West African manhood was spirited away.

On the response of colonists to criticism of the British slave trade in a draft of Jefferson's Declaration of Independence: "Those who favored slavery at all realized that if Jefferson's views prevailed ... , there would be no justification for the institution once the ties to England were completely cut. It would be better ... to reject the strong language in which the complete responsibility was laid at the door of George III" (84; see essay 42 in this volume).

On Negroes in the Revolutionary War: "The British bid for Negroes during the war had the effect of liberalizing the policy of colonists toward blacks. Not only did Washington order the enlistment of some free Negroes, but most of the states [except for Georgia and South Carolina] ... began to enlist both slaves and free Negroes ... Of the 300,000 soldiers who served the cause of independence, approximately 5,000 were Negroes" (88).

On the slave's perception of his status:

> Owners of slaves almost always sought to convey the impression that their human chattel were docile, tractable, and happy ... There is no reason to conclude that the personality of the slave was permanently impaired by his engaging in duplicity in the slave-master relationship ... Any understanding of his reaction to his status must be approached with the realization that the Negro at times possessed a dual personality: he was one person at one time and quite a different person at another time.

(149)

On the significance of Lincoln's proclamation of Negro freedom:

"If the Emancipation Proclamation was essentially a war measure, it had the desired effect of creating confusion in the South and depriving the Confederacy of much of its valuable laboring force. If it was a diplomatic document, it succeeded in rallying to the Northern cause thousands of English and European laborers who were anxious to see workers gain freedom throughout the world. If it was a humanitarian document, it gave hope to millions of Negroes that a better day lay ahead, and it renewed the faith of thousands of crusaders who had fought long to win freedom in America."

(215)

On the strategy of post-Civil War white supremacy:

When it became evident that white factions would compete with one another for the Negro vote, and thus frequently give the Negro balance of power, it was time for the complete disenfranchisement of the Negro, the Fifteenth Amendment to the contrary not withstanding. On this most southern whites were agreed ... There were problems that had to be solved by state constitutional conventions when they undertook to write into their fundamental law a guarantee of white supremacy. It was in Mississippi, where a majority of the population were Negroes, that the problem was first faced and solved.

(263)

On the battle for civil rights after 1964: "Although there was a notable decline in discrimination in some fields, the period following the passage of the Civil Rights Act of 1964 was marked by strong resistance to its enforcement and ... considerable violence in some places ... In the North it manifested itself in the actions of whites who discovered their prejudices for the first time or who resented direct action protests to eliminate discrimination in their own communities" (474).

On black radicalism: "Even before his death Martin Luther King had been criticized by militant, action-oriented blacks who insisted that whites would not respond to black demands on the basis of Christian charity, good will, or even peaceful demonstrations. Some also felt that whites would never concede complete equality to blacks" (485).

The power of Franklin's work as a black historian derives in large part not just from massive scholarship but from an unwavering spirit of calm objectivity. His narrative, analysis, and conclusions are free of ideological or partisan lapses. His serene even handedness with a large-scale subject weighted down for centuries with cruelty, rancor, and prejudice is a singular achievement.

Works by Franklin

From Slavery to Freedom: A History of Negro Americans (5th ed.; New York: Knopf, 1980).

Mirror to America: The Autobiography of Jon Hope Franklin (New York: Ferrar, Strauss, and Giroux, 2005).

Racial Equality in America (Columbia, Missouri: University of Missouri Press, 1993).

Reconstruction after the Civil War (Chicago, Illinois: University of Chicago Press, 1961).

The Militant South, 1800–1861 (Cambridge, Massachusetts: Harvard University Press, 1956).

Works about Franklin

Finkelman, Paul, "John Hope Franklin," in Robert Allen Rutled (ed.), *Clio's Favorites: Leading Historians of the United States, 1945–2000* (Columbia, Missouri: University of Missouri Press, 2000).

Useful references

Black Leaders of the Twentieth Century, ed. by John Hope Franklin and August Meier (Urbana, Illinois: University of Illinois Press, 1982).

46. ORIENTALISM: WESTERN CONCEPTIONS OF THE ORIENT (EDWARD W. SAID, 1935–2003)

Edward Said was not a historian, although he made extensive use of historical literature and perspectives. As University Professor of English and Comparative Literature at Columbia University, his standing came chiefly from literary and cultural criticism. He took a doctorate at Harvard and was fluent in Arabic and French as well as English. As a Palestinian-American, or as he put it, "a Christian wrapped in a Muslim culture," he was an ardent defender of Palestinian rights and supported a two-state solution to the Palestinian–Israeli stand-off. A news photo has activist Said tossing a stone over a barrier from Lebanon into Israel as a symbolic gesture. He also worked for reconciliation. A notable example was collaboration with conductor-pianist Daniel Barenboim to organize the East–West Divan Orchestra, an ensemble of young musicians from various Middle East countries, including Palestinians and Israelis.

Orientalism is his most influential work. Even critics admit the book swept across the spectrum of Middle Eastern studies in the USA and elsewhere. It runs 350 pages, including 21 pages of notes and an introduction of 28 pages that explains his thesis and methods of analysis. Whether his thesis is persuasive or not, the work is distinguished by varied erudition, acute intelligence, and stylistic authority. It quickly assumed command as a core text of postcolonial thought and activism focused on countries once under Western imperial rule.

Postcolonial theory and writing seeks to clarify the cultural legacy, either direct or indirect, of former colonial powers and the responses of subject peoples, especially intellectuals, after liberation in the post-World War II era. Postcolonial thought claims that Western political and military hegemonies left behind widespread, enervating cultural influences that soaked in after decades of occupation, and that in some cases, as in South Africa, the foreigners never left. At best, the result everywhere was compromised independence and ongoing struggles to recover and clarify repressed or confused identities. For Said, oriental scholarship and thought in the West have been intimately associated with attitudes of superiority and policies of domination for some two centuries and even before.

His intellectual reach transcended postcolonial theory, but his book belongs to that genre while casting a wider net for bigger fish. Yet he acknowledges its limits and knows many authors have been left out, but explains that an encyclopedic approach was not his purpose. He understands also that the complexity of Western–Orient relations is evident as a process of self-Orientalization as Middle East countries seek a path to modernization.

He distinguishes three meanings of Orientalism. First, there are doctrines, claims, and interpretations of professional academics— historians, sociologists, anthropologists, philologists, etc.—who study and write about the Orient, by which he means Arab-Muslim countries, or the Middle East. Second, it is "a style of thought based on ... distinctions made between 'the Orient' and (most of the time) 'the Occident'." This broader group includes not only literary figures and philosophers but economists and imperial bureaucrats. What the diverse assemblage shares in common is acceptance of "the basic distinction between East and West as the starting point for elaborate theories, epics, novels, social descriptions and political accounts concerning the Orient, its people, customs, 'mind,' destiny, and so on." These two meanings of Orientalism interpenetrate and reinforce one another. The third meaning, with its inception in the late eighteenth century, is Orientalism as a "discourse" (a term borrowed from Michel Foucault), "a corporate institution for dealing with the Orient ... by making statements about it, authorizing views of it, describing it, by teaching it, settling it, ruling over it" (2–3). But one must be careful at this point, for Orientalism is "more formidable than a mere collection of lies ... not an airy European fantasy ... but a created body of theory and practice in which, for many generations, there has been a considerable material investment ... a system of knowledge about the Orient, an accepted grid for filtering through the Orient into Western consciousness ... " (6).

The impact of Orientalism embodied in these meanings has been to corrupt, obscure, and delimit ideas and policy directed at the Orient. Said aims to show that in the West, imaginative writing, institutions, speculations, and scholarship blended as Orientalism drove a wedge, consciously or otherwise, between East and West and, at its worst, vindicated colonialism. His views struck an immediate and resonant chord in postcolonial intellectuals. They absorbed the view that colonial domination of materially weaker countries and peoples was accompanied by a fudging of differences between them by Orientalists, whose outcome was a monolithic, simplistic portrayal of the Other.

For Said, Orientalism is specifically a complex structure of false, misleading representations of Arab-Muslim countries that amounts to a creation of the Orient. Western writing about the Middle East are "discourses of power, ideological fictions—mind forg'd manacles" (328). The appeal of Said to Arab-Islamic intellectuals and public officials is immense, but he also collected followers among Western academics and writers who view imperialism as the original sin of Western civilization, about which nothing good can be said. Because of it, they believe, no former imperial power can be trusted to produce objective scholarship that truly represents an abused Other. Although *Orientalism* is about Western scholarship and the Middle East, the system's structure can be adapted to the study of any non-Western culture or civilization.

The flaw of Western scholarship and commentary about the Orient is essentialism, the idea that Arab-Muslim societies have a core that is changeless and stagnant, thus dulling a feel for gradations of tone and nuance. Such stereotyping has encouraged prejudice, racism, and justification for Western domination of the Other. Misrepresentation is unconscious as well as conscious, deriving ultimately from an underlying drive for power, a type of postmodern analysis owed to Foucault. The chief offenders, the agents of Orientalism, are Britain and France from the beginning of the nineteenth century until the close of World War II. America picks up the thread in the postwar era. Russian, Spanish, Portuguese, and German Orientalism are omitted because those peoples were not a presence in the Orient like the British and the French. As for Germans, theirs was "almost exclusively a scholarly, or at least a classical Orient ... ," but dependent on materials provided by Britain and France (18–19).

The book divides into three sections: "The Scope of Orientalism," "Orientalist Structures and Restructures," and "Orientalism Now." His methodological framework is

> *strategic location*, which is a way of describing the author's position in a text with regard to the Oriental material he writes about, and *strategic formation*, which is a way of analyzing the relationships between texts and the way in which groups of texts, even textual genres, acquire mass, density, and referential power among themselves and thereafter in the culture at large.
>
> (20)

In the first section, Orientalism is explained as an attitude of superiority over Arab-Islamic culture. Condescension to the Other means haughtiness expressed as a stereotype, a view of Middle Easterners as irrational, sensual, and backward, as peas in a single pod. The posture of Orientalists in their "discourses" is one of intrinsic, deserved ascendancy over inferior peoples. A key document for the nineteenth century was the *Description de l'Égypte* in 23 volumes published between 1809 and 1828, an outcome of Napoleon's attempt to occupy Egypt in 1799: "The *Description* became the master type of all further efforts to bring the Orient closer to Europe ... to cancel, or at least subdue and reduce, its strangeness and, in the case of Islam, its hostility. For the Islamic Orient would appear as a category denoting the Orientalists' power and not the Islamic people as humans nor their history as history" (87).

The second section explains the foundation and structure of Orientalism as a discourse, a "system of thought." It arises in political and military dominance, spreads from one country, political leader, and bureaucrat to another, and finally settles into various forms of authorship. Domination of East by West is more than 2000 years old, dramatized in Aeschylus's tragedy *The Persians* in the fifth century B.C. Modern roots of Orientalist discourse are in the eighteenth century, whose branches spread in the nineteenth century with explorers and writers like Richard Burton (translator of *The Arabian Nights*) and Edward Lane (author of *Manners and Customs of the Modern Egyptians*), both of whom were fluent in Arabic.

Europeans not only occupied countries but took over their languages and literatures to "construct," consciously or otherwise, biased histories of the Orient useful to Europeans. The discourse of Orientalism seeped into the work of authors and teaching in educational institutions until it permeated Western civilization. A binary picture of masculine versus feminine was set in stone, on one side, a strong, rational West, on the other side, a weak, irrational Orient. Moreover, because of this binary opposition, the twain can never meet as equals or attain mutual understanding.

The achievement of Richard Burton is instructive, for "he took the assertion of personal, authentic, sympathetic, and humanistic knowledge of the Orient as far as it would go ... " (187). His knowledge of Arabic and mastery of rules that governed life in the Orient enabled him to blend with the people and even succeed in a pilgrimage to Mecca. No scholar or traveler in Europe could rival him. Nevertheless, his preeminent knowledge and quasi-anthropological attunement were forms of mastery over the Other that anticipated political, economic, and military control: " ... what is never far from the surface of Burton's prose is ... a sense of assertion and domination over all the complexities of Oriental life" (196).

In the third section, Said reviews the career of Orientalism in recent history up to 1978. At this point, he raises questions about trans-cultural study and understanding that intersect with postmodern doubts about the viability of historical judgment and objectivity: "How does one represent other cultures? What is another culture? Is the notion of a distinct culture (of race, or religion, or civilization) a useful one, or does it always involve either in self-congratulation (when one discusses one's own) or hostility and aggression (when one discusses the 'other')" (325). The first two questions ask a historian to explain the what, how, and why of writing a non-Western history, which is reasonable enough. If an answer to the second part of the last question is yes, then historical inquiry outside one's own cultural framework is doomed to failure no matter how much scholars want to be fair and objective.

Is that Said's position? Apparently the answer is no. His rejection is directed not at historical knowledge as such but at *systems of thought* like Orientalism: "My contention is that without examining Orientalism as a discourse one cannot possibly understand the enormously systematic discipline by which European culture was able to manage—and even produce—the Orient politically, sociologically, militarily, ideologically, scientifically, and imaginatively during the post-Enlightenment period" (3). Said is not afflicted with postmodern skepticism about a real past and objective knowledge about it. He concedes that good scholarship and authentic understanding of the Orient is possible in the West if scholars stay close to their disciplines and avoid enclosure by the corporate *system* of Orientalism: "The methodological failures of Orientalism cannot be accounted for by saying the *real* Orient is different from Orientalist portraits of it, or by saying that since Orientalists are Westerners for the most part, they cannot be expected to have an inner sense of what the Orient is all about. Both of these propositions are false" (322).

Some reservations can be mentioned here from a considerable literature critical of *Orientalism*. Said has been faulted for addressing broadly "the Orient" while leaving out China, Japan, Southeast Asia, and saying little about India while confining himself to the Middle East. Are Sinologists and Indologists included in his indictment of Orientalists? His inclination to find racism and ethnocentrism among all Orientalists throughout Western history has been challenged as ungenerous exaggeration. Orientalists were defending both the Orient and Islam long before postcolonialism became fashionable in the academy. Moreover, Said's thesis has more to do with identity politics than scholarship and for that reason is hard to refute decisively.

If it is true that no Western scholar can really know the Orient, the reservation must apply as well to Harvard-educated Said, whose field of study was not the Middle East. As the factual scaffolding of his book was undone by critics, he confessed inability to know the *true* Middle East and Islam. It is historical naïveté to ignore the double edged sword of cultural exchanges in history. While the West has influenced the Orient, so has the Orient left its imprint on the West. Stereotyping cuts both ways. History is not a one way street. Saddling Orientalists with a charge of essentialism without admitting that Arab-Muslim perceptions of the West amount to a biased counterpart—Occidentalism—amounts to an Occident "constructed" by the Orient. At some points in history, what the West has done to the East has been reciprocated. An unhappy side effect of *Orientalism* has been a politicization of literary and Middle Eastern studies, a consequence that must have caused Said discomfort as a wide-ranging literary critic.

Finally, Said's thesis appears to be self-contradictory. He wants to say that Western Orientalism, with its essentialist bias, has been an effective consulting tool for imperialist domination of the Other, but also claims that Orientalism as a system of knowledge about Arab-Muslim ways is a failure. If Western knowledge is a misleading or a false "construction," then how could imperialists make use of it in real life situations? At bottom, his position that truth is culturally relative makes futile any effort, including his own, to study an Other with good will and objectivity.

Works by Said

Culture and Imperialism (New York: Knopf, 1993).
Orientalism: Western Conceptions of the Orient (New York: Pantheon Books, 1978).
The Edward Said Reader, ed. Moustafa Bayoumi and Andrew Rubin (New York: Vintage Books, 2000).
The World, the Text, and the Critic (Cambridge, Massachusetts: Harvard University Press, 1983).

Works about Said

Ibn Warraq, *Defending the West: A Critique of Edward Said's Orientalism* (Amherst, New York: Prometheus Books, 2007).
Irwin, Robert, *For Lust of Knowing: The Orientalists and Their Enemies* (London: Allen Lane, 2006). Published in the United States as *Dangerous Knowledge: Orientalism and Its Discontents*.
Windschuttle, Keith, "Edward Said's *Orientalism* Revisited," *The New Criterion* (17 January 1993).

Useful references

Gellner, Earnest, "The Mightier Pen? Edward Said and the Double Standards of Inside-out Colonialism," review of *Culture and Imperialism*, by Edward Said, *Times Literary Supplement* (19 February 1993).
Green, Anna Green and Kathleen Troup, *The Houses of History: A Critical Reader in Twentieth Century History and Theory* (New York: New York University Press, 1999), Chapter 11.
Tibawa, A.L., "English-Speaking Orientalists: A Critique of their Approach to Islam and Arab Nationalism," *Islamic Quarterly*, 8 (1964): 25–45.

47. THE HISTORY OF SEXUALITY, VOLUME 1: AN INTRODUCTION[2] (MICHEL FOUCAULT, 1926–1984)

Foucault was born into a prominent French provincial family. His father was a respected surgeon who failed to recruit him into the same profession. Early education was in a Jesuit college, which prepared him for the École Normale Supérieur, a launching platform for students in humanities. At this school, he fell into depression, sought psychiatric care, and as a side effect turned to the study of psychology. The outcome was two degrees—one in philosophy, the other in psychology. He took a doctorate in 1961 after, according to French custom, submitting a major and a secondary thesis.

Possessed of a sharp, original intelligence, he taught at a string of universities until finally elected professor at the most prestigious of them all—the Collège de France. He also lectured in Germany, Poland, Tunis, and the USA. He was politically active on behalf of homosexuals, co-founded an organization to help prison inmates make public complaints, and participated in student protests. Initially attracted to existentialism and Marxism, he soon gave up both as his way of viewing human experience and the past matured. For a couple of years he was an indifferent, skeptical member of the Communist Party. Foucault was an early victim of AIDS, which killed him: "Sex is worth dying for" (156). In a relatively short life, he became an influential French thinker and author. His ideas diffused abroad to make him one of the most frequently cited philosopher-psychologist-historian of the twentieth century.

Foucault's major works have a common aim—a critique of claims to knowledge by means of historical knowledge. Since history has been a frequent target of skeptics, it is ironic that an arch skeptic of conscious rationality like Foucault would turn to history as his medium. Yet he is not easily pigeonholed. The usual attempts connect him with structuralism (language as a closed system of signs), post-structuralism (language creates reality), and post-modernism, labels he rejected. He also denied classification as historian, philosopher, or psychologist, thinking of himself as a mind in motion. He did confess kinship with Friedrich Nietzsche, whose idea that morals are not absolute but have a genealogy, a lineage or a history, Foucault uses in his later work.

The History of Sexuality examines and rejects the "repressive hypothesis," which says that freedom and openness about sex in the seventeenth century retreated before a wall of negative discourses and gave way to shame and secrecy, accompanied paradoxically by endless talk about sex:

> Why has sexuality been so widely discussed, and what has been said about it? What were the effects of power generated by what was said? What are the links between these discourses, effects of power, and the pleasures that were invested by them ... The object, in short, is to define the regime of power-knowledge-pleasure that sustains the discourse on human sexuality in our part of the world.
>
> (11)

Foucault concludes that multiplication of discourses about sex since the seventeenth century made power relations surrounding it more abundant and complex, although some repression was part of the larger picture. Sex flourishes behind numerous discourses masking sexuality.

The usual setting for his works is historical, but he marshals and applies ideas both psychological and philosophical, and uses art and literature as well. His main conceptual tools for historical analysis are "discourse," "power," "deployment of alliances," and "deployment of sexuality." With respect to sex, there is what people actually do, say, think, and desire. In a historical period, sex is translated into discourses—that is, classifications, theories, judgments, social norms, standards of right and wrong, or even a "science" of sexuality—which in turn generate power relations between individuals, groups, and institutions: " ... at issue ... is the over-all 'discursive fact.' The way in which sex is 'put into discourse' ... my main concern will be to locate the forms of power, the channels it takes, and the discourses it permeates in order to reach the most tenuous and individual modes of behavior ... " (11).

His idea of power departs from conventional meanings. He does not mean "institutions and mechanisms that ensure the subservience of the citizens of a given state ... a mode of subjugation ... a general system of domination exerted by one group over another ... power must be understood in the first instance as a multiplicity of force relations immanent in the sphere in which they operate and which constitute their own organization" (92). Two kinds of "deployment" are:

> The deployment of alliance is built around a system of rules defining the permitted and the forbidden, the licit and the illicit,

whereas the deployment of sexuality operates according to mobile, polymorphous, and contingent techniques of power. The deployment of alliance has as one of its chief objectives to reproduce the interplay of relations and maintain the law that governs them; the deployment of sexuality ... engenders a continual extension of areas and forms of control.

(106)

Discourse conceals sex: "Until Freud at least, the discourse on sex—the discourse of scholars and theoreticians—never ceased to hide the thing it was speaking about. We can take all these things that were said ... as so many procedures meant to evade the unbearable" (53). In the nineteenth century the truth of sex was reduced to two discourses—reproductive biology and medicine. He distinguishes sex from sexuality, the latter being a center from which many tendrils of power branch out: " ... we must not refer a history of sexuality to the agency of sex, but rather show how 'sex' is historically subordinate to sexuality ... sexuality is a very real historical formation; it is what gave rise to the notion of sex ... " (157).

Foucault argues that every culture, society, or historical period has an unconscious substratum of meanings and truths that shape particular discourses and ensuing forms of power. For example, only in Western civilization has a discourse of sex as science developed that involves concealment, whereas in other civilizations the discourse has been an art of sex in the open guided by the wisdom of a "master." Foucault investigates substrata in his earlier works, such as *Madness and Civilization*, by "excavation" from surface discourses allegedly to their source. In *The History of Sexuality* this archeological program goes on. The problem of substrata isolated from one another in time is addressed by genealogy, which supplies connecting links, say between eighteenth and nineteenth centuries, that are results of contingency, or unpredictable chance.

Discourses can become sources of power that impose prohibitions on sex, which he illustrates in the Catholic sacraments of confession and penance in which details about sexuality are suppressed from the seventeenth century onwards: "One avoided entering into that degree of detail ... for a long time believed indispensable for the confession to be complete: descriptions of the respective positions of the partners, the postures assumed, gestures, places touched, caresses, the precise moments of pleasure—an entire painstaking review of the sexual act in its very unfolding" (18–19; see also 61–67). A translation of explicit, unadorned sex into discourse became general in the eighteenth century: " ... there emerged a political, economic, and technical incitement to talk about sex ... This need to take sex 'into account,' to pronounce a discourse on sex that would not derive from morality alone but from rationality as well ... " (23–24).

Multiplication of discourses about sex "called for management procedures; it had to be taken charge of by analytical discourses ... sex became a 'police' matter ... " (24). This intensification of scrutiny focused on children: " ... the sex of the schoolboy became in the course of the eighteenth century ... a public problem ... Around the schoolboy and his sex there proliferated a whole literature of precepts, opinions, observations, medical advice, clinical cases, outlines for reform, and plans for ideal institutions" (28).

Foucault's *History of Sexuality* is difficult, eclectic in form and content, and not at all like history generally understood. Why, then, is it included among 50 key works of historiography? There are three reasons.

First, Foucault believes he is doing history within a time span of some 200 years, although his "narrative" is heavily infused with philosophical flights, psychological analysis, and much space is given to defining idiosyncratic terminology.

Second, the work embodies radical transformations that have overtaken historiography in the past 50 years, usually characterized as the "post-modern challenge" (see the Introduction to this volume). Turning Foucault's pages, one asks in puzzlement what history has become.

Third, if he appears everywhere in footnotes and bibliographies, as indeed he does, it is likely that his work has some fruits for historical understanding. What these amount to are mostly warnings not to look for overall meaning or essences in the past, or to suppose a contemporary activity like sex has anything in common with its historical antecedents. Otherwise he seems to be saying that discourses about knowledge come from processes of social control and that "objectivity" about the past is determined by power relationships and their discourses.

There are many obscurities unrelieved by a frequently opaque style, his discussions of power perhaps being the best example of confused ambiguity (94–95). Sources to support generalizations are sparse, so there is much pulling of rabbits from a hat (110). He is unclear how a transition is made genealogically from one social sphere to another and how it might be verified, which leaves clumps of "discourses" isolated from one another with no continuity, influence, or development (119). If discourses emerge from a substratum shared *unconsciously* by everyone in a society, a connection between the two, causal or otherwise, which would make explanation possible, seems unattainable. Just as seriously, history would be helpless to test its assumptions against a host of rules governing unconscious cultural formations.

Works by Foucault

Discipline and Punish: The Birth of the Prison, trans. by Alan Sheridan (New York: Pantheon, 1977).

History of Sexuality, 3 vols.: Introduction, The Uses of Pleasure, and Care of the Self, trans. from the French by Robert Hurley (New York: Vintage Books, 1988–90). The original title of the "The Introduction" was The Will to Knowledge (*La volonté de savoir*).

Madness and Civilization, trans. by Richard Howard (New York: Pantheon, 1965).

The Archeology of Knowledge, trans. from the French by A. Sheridan Smith (New York: Harper and Row, 1972).

Works about Foucault

Han, Béatrice, *Foucault's Critical Project* (Stanford, California: Stanford University Press, 2002).

Macey, David, *The Lives of Michel Foucault* (New York: Pantheon, 1994).

Useful references

Green, Anna and Kathleen Troup, *The Houses of History: A Critical Reader in Twentieth Century History and Theory* (Washington Square, New York: New York University Press, 1999).

Gutting, Gary (ed.), *The Cambridge Companion to Foucault* (2nd ed.; Cambridge: Cambridge University Press, 2005).

48. YOUNG MAN LUTHER: A STUDY IN PSYCHOANALYSIS AND HISTORY (ERIK H. ERIKSON, 1902–1994)

Erikson was born in Frankfort, Germany, the outcome of an extramarital affair. His Danish mother belonged to a Jewish family from Copenhagen. The biological father is unknown and the mother later married a Jewish pediatrician who adopted Erikson. Facts about his illegitimate origin were concealed in childhood, an obvious source of his later attention as analyst and writer to issues of identity. He coined the phrase "identity crisis" that he later applied to the study of Luther. He was raised as a Jew and was taunted in temple as "Nordic" and in grammar school as "a Jew," which intensified further insecurities of identity.

He became a private school teacher in Vienna and met Sigmund Freud's daughter Anna. With her encouragement, he underwent analysis and decided to become an analyst. After graduating from the Vienna Psychoanalytic Institute in 1933 he moved to Denmark and then to the USA where he held prominent positions as a child psychologist in Massachusetts, including the Harvard Medical School, and acquired a distinguished reputation for clinical work. He moved on to teach for while in the medical school at Yale University, then to the University of California at Berkeley, which he left in protest at being required to sign a loyalty oath.

For a decade he was at the Austin Riggs Center, a psychiatric treatment center in Stockbridge, Massachusetts, and then returned to Harvard as a professor of human development until retirement in 1970. Erikson received many honors. In 1973 the National Endowment of the Humanities selected him to deliver its prestigious Jefferson Lecture, which was titled "Dimensions of a New Identity." His book *Gandhi's Truth* won a Pulitzer Prize and the National Book Award.

Erikson was a Neo-Freudian, which means he accepted with amendments Freud's view of human psychology and his therapeutic technique of psychoanalysis. He expanded the function of Ego in Freud's model of the human psyche (Id as instinctual needs such as sexual life, Superego as self-criticism and demands of society expressed as conscience, and Ego between the two as mediator, censor, and source of repression) to include for the Ego a role of creative independence. Throughout the study of Luther, Freudian categories of analysis and explanation are employed—for example, conscious and unconscious minds, Oedipus complex (hostility to the father as a rival for the mother), repression and its defense mechanisms: regression, rationalization, and anxiety.

Freud outlined five stages of psychosexual development for the individual. Erikson proposed eight stages from birth to death. Like Freud, Erikson believed these psychological stages of human development apply in all historical periods and cultures. He argued that each stage of psychosocial development involves a conflict that must be resolved. The resolution can be either negative or positive, but whatever the outcome the meaning and direction of a person's life are likely to change.

Erikson notes that most historians are amateur psychologists when assessing motives and causes of behavior in historical figures. They do so, however, without a self-conscious theoretical framework to guide judgments. Consequently,

> we cannot leave history entirely to nonclinical observers and professional historians who often all too nobly immerse themselves into the very disguises, rationalizations, and idealizations of the historical process from which it should be their business to separate themselves. Only when the relation of historical forces to the basic functions and stages of the mind has been jointly charted and understood can we begin a psychoanalytic critique of society as such without falling back into mystical or moralistic philosophizing. (20–21)

His work on Luther sets out to do history as well as psychology: "I intend to take my subtitle seriously. This 'Study in Psychoanalysis and History' will re-evaluate a segment of history (here the youth of a great reformer) by using psychoanalysis as a historical tool; but it will also, here and there, throw light on psychoanalysis as a tool of history" (16). What to look for in his book is how we come to understand Luther as a youth from the perspectives of depth psychology and history. With Luther the focus is not on his childhood experiences, where Freud would have looked for root causes in the unconscious of anxiety, conflict, and neurosis, nor on his mature manhood, whose achievements have been raked over by conventional scholarship, but on his youth, ages 22 to 30. Erikson's notes and references to Luther scholarship in the text indicate a wide, sophisticated knowledge of historical sources, including more personal writings of Luther that shed light on his psychological history. His critics acknowledge that he knows the literature.

The complex richness of Erikson's analysis in eight instructive chapters can only be suggested here. Terrified by a thunderstorm, Luther left the University of Erfurt without his harsh father's permission in 1505: "Before the thunderstorm he had rapidly been freezing into a melancholy paralysis which made it impossible for him to continue his studies and to contemplate marriage as his father urged him to do. In the thunderstorm, he had felt immense anxiety ... he felt a sudden constriction of his whole life space, and could see only one way out: the abandonment of all his previous life ... " (39–40). Removal from the father was a necessity and a dilemma: "Faced with a father who made questionable use of his brute authority ... a father to whom he could not get close and from whom he could not get away ... how was he going to submit without being emasculated, or rebel without emasculating the father?" (67).

At age 21 he entered the strict, austere confines of an Augustinian monastery, an answer to his dilemma and a choice, in Erikson's view, that could be interpreted as regression to a mother's care in infancy. He had just received a Master of Arts degree with honors and was expected by his self-sacrificing parent to study law and succeed in administration or politics. Instead: "Before him lay long years of the most intense inner conflicts and frequently morbid religious scruples; these eventually led to his abandonment of monasticism and to his assumption of spiritual leadership in a widespread revolt against the medieval papacy" (24). Erikson sees the monastic period not as regression but as a "moratorium," a period of "marking time," while pieces of a new identity came together and were forged into Luther the theologian and preacher who stood against traditions and teachings of a Church 1000 years old.

This was the phase of life in between, the "young great man" who underwent an "identity crisis." When he declared "Here I stand" at the Diet of Worms in 1521, he was ready to defy papal authority and initiated change in the religious and secular character of Western civilization: "I will not be ashamed then, even as I analyze what is analyzable, to display sympathy and empathy with a young man who (by no means lovable all the time) faced problems of human *existence* in the most forward terms of his era" (22). Erikson is careful not to entangle himself with theological issues that occupied Luther when he emerged from his moratorium to take on the Church, but he understands the magnitude of his thought and writing: "His basic contribution was a living reformulation of faith. This marks him as a theologian of the first order; it also indicates his struggle with the ... most basic problems of life. He saw as his life's work a new delineation of faith and will, of religion and law ... " (257).

On Luther's psychosexual side, he discovered that sexual urges could not be surmounted by most men and women, an insight from his monastic days. Marriage was the solution, though for Luther sexual release was not the only issue: " ... one finds in his remarks references to a kind of eliminative sexuality, a need to get rid of bodily discharge which one could ascribe to a persistent preoccupation with the body's waste products" (237).

Chapter VI is a discussion of the theological and philosophical background of Luther's faith and the influence of his lectures on the Psalms: " ... at about the age of thirty—an important age for gifted people with a delayed identity crisis—the wholeness of Luther's theology first emerges from the fragments of his totalistic reevaluation" (201). During this time, the retentive inhibitions fostered by "lifelong constipation and urine retention" receded: " ... his power of speech was freed from its infantile and juvenile captivity, he changed from a highly restrained and retentive individual into an explosive person; he had found an unexpected release of self-expression, and with it, of the many-sided power of his personality" (205). No longer pent up, he began that astonishing career as an author that made him the preeminent writer in German of his time, and resulted in a translation of the Bible that put the German language itself on the map: "The importance of Luther's early lectures lies in the fact that they bear witness not only to the recovery of his ego, but also to a new theology conceived long before he suddenly became famous as a pamphleteer in the controversy over indulgences" (223).

Chapter VII contains a blend of straightforward historical exposition and Luther's newly revealed or released personality traits that crystallize the aspirations, tensions, and conflicts of an age: "At Worms Luther faced ostracism and death ... because of *personal* convictions, derived from inner conflict and still subject to further conflict ... Luther's emphasis on individual conscience prepared the way for the series of concepts of equality, representation, and self-determination which became in successive secular revolutions and wars the foundation not of the dignity of some, but of the liberty of all" (231).

The most obvious criticism of Erikson is that he does not have Luther on the couch for questions and answers that can coax to the surface repressions and anxiety buried in the unconscious mind. The test of psychoanalysis as a therapy is relief of symptoms in a live patient. With a dead "patient" the application of theory and results from live case histories can only be suggestively indirect. A more troubling problem is the projection backward into a vanished age of a complex psychological theory that has been attacked as unverifiable by behavioral empiricists. Erikson's response is that anyone displeased with the Freudian option needs to come forward with a credible systematic alternative that explains the psychological basis of family, society, and the individual. Meanwhile, he provided a useful if controversial demonstration of how psychohistory might be done as historiography's "next assignment."

Works by Erikson

Childhood and Society (New York: W.W. Norton, 1950).
Gandhi's Truth: On the Origin of Militant Nonviolence (New York: W.W. Norton, 1969).

Insight and Responsibility: Lectures on the Ethical Implications of Psychoanalytic Insight (New York: W.W. Norton, 1964).
Young Man Luther: A Study in Psychoanalysis and History (New York: W.W. Norton, 1958).

Works about Erikson

Albin, Mel (ed.), *New Directions in Psychohistory; the Adelphi Papers in Honor of Eric H. Erikson* (Lexington, Massachusetts: Lexington Books, 1980).
Green, Anna and Kathleen Troup, *The Houses of History: A Critical Reader in Twentieth Century History and Theory* (New York: New York University Press, 1999). See Chapter 3.
Mazlish, Bruce (ed.), *Psychoanalysis and History* (Englewood Cliffs, New Jersey: Prentice Hall, 1963). See the last essay by Donald Meyer.

Useful references

Bainton, Roland, *Here I Stand: A Life of Martin Luther* (New York: A Mentor Book, 1950).
Barzun, Jacques, *Clio and the Doctors: Psycho-History, Quanto-History & History* (Chicago, Illinois: Chicago University Press, 1974). The most ferocious attack on psycho-history.
Gay, Peter, *Freud for Historians* (New York: Oxford University Press, 1985).
Kren, George M. and Leon H. Rappoport (eds.), *Varieties of Psychohistory* (New York: Springer Publishing, 1976).
Langer, William H., "The Next Assignment," *American Historical Review*, LXIII (1958): 283–304. Langer's presidential address to the American Historical Association urging more attention to psychological and psychoanalytic approaches to historical interpretation.
Smith, Preserved, "Luther's Early Development in Light of Psychoanalysis," *Journal of Psychology*, XXIV (1913): 360–377.

49. METAHISTORY: THE HISTORICAL IMAGINATION IN NINETEENTH-CENTURY EUROPE (HAYDEN WHITE, 1928–)

White is professor emeritus at The University of California, Santa Cruz, and has retired as professor of comparative literature at Stanford University. As an undergraduate at Wayne State University he studied history. He took a doctorate at the University of Michigan in 1956. He is not a practicing, published historian. Rather his connection with history is through literary theory, techniques, and analysis. His work merits a place in this book because it best represents what has been called the postmodern "challenge" to any and all claims to reliable historical knowledge.

White rejects the view that history is a "science" and denies also that it occupies middle ground between art and science. Relativism in history results in part from the inability of historians to agree on what they are doing and how it is done:

> Historiographical disputes on the level of 'interpretation' are in reality disputes over the 'true' nature of the historian's enterprise. History remains in the state of conceptual anarchy in which the natural sciences existed in the sixteenth century, when there were many different conceptions of the 'scientific enterprise' as there were metaphysical positions ... disputes over what 'history' ought to be reflect similarly varied conceptions of what a proper historical explanation ought to consist of and different conceptions ... of the historian's task.
>
> (13)

What is his purpose in this difficult book? "One of my principal aims, over and above that of identifying and interpreting the main forms of historical consciousness in nineteenth-century Europe, has been to establish the uniquely poetic elements in historiography and philosophy of history in whatever age they were practiced" (x). His task then is not to discuss history as a science, but history as an art, "to establish the ineluctably poetic nature of historical work ... " (xi). He wishes to show that poetic language prefigures and shapes the "science," or the "theoretical concepts" by which historians seek to explain what happened in the past. To that end he wishes to explain historical thinking. What should be kept in mind is a preoccupation with language that leads unavoidably to historical relativism.

Levels of historical explanation and interpretation are four modes of consciousness understood as "tropological" strategies. Tropes are used to analyze poetic and figurative language to distinguish "objects in different kinds of indirect, or figurative, discourse" (34). They are metaphor, metonymy, synodoche, and irony: " ... it is my view that the dominant tropological mode and its attendant linguistic protocol comprise the irreducibly 'metahistorical' basis of every historical work. And I maintain that this metahistorical element in the works of the master historians of the nineteenth-century constitutes the 'philosophies of history' which implicitly sustain their works and without which they could not have produced the kinds of works they did" (xi).

Metaphor expresses the similarity or difference of objects from one another and is representational. Metonymy occurs when a part of a whole is used to represent the whole and is reductionist. Synedoche is similar to metonymy but differs in that the part taken from the whole to represent it is a quality and is integrative. Irony reverses or denies what is literally viewed or affirmed and is negational. Historical styles are governed by one of these tropes.

All historical works exhibit one of several conceptual levels: chronicle, story, emplotment, argument, and ideology. A chronicle arranges events in a temporal sequence whose beginning and end are open and arbitrary. A story has definite structure with chosen motifs that provide a distinct beginning, middle, and end. Emplotment is a form of explanation with four modes—romance (triumph over the world of experience and its changing fortunes), tragedy (a provisional threat of irreparable upheavals and division), comedy (hope for reconciliation and unity of opposing forces), and satire (denial of the other three, and belief that history cannot help the present): "These four archetypal story forms provide us with a means of characterizing the different kinds of explanatory effects a historian can strive for ... " (10). If a historian chooses the plot structure of comedy, the past is explained one way; if he chooses satire, it is explained another way.

Argument is an attempt to formulate laws of history to explain events. Marx's causal relationship between material base and ideological superstructure is White's example (when the material base changes, ideas in the superstructure change). Argument as the road to explanation can be formist, organicist, mechanistic, and contextualist.

Formism is explanation when unique objects "in the historical field" have been properly identified and classified. *Organicism* explains individual objects by placing them in a whole greater than its parts, the goal of synthesis for all historical processes. *Mechanistic* explanation "turns upon the search for the causal laws that determine the outcomes of processes discovered in the historical field" (17). *Contextualism* as explanation means relating events or objects in the historical field to one another. The historian is limited to two of these options: " ... for professional historians, Formism and Contextualism have represented the limits of choice among the possible forms that an explanation of a peculiarly 'historical' sort may take" (20). Mechanism and organicism have been kept at arm's length.

Ideological explanation means "the ethical element of a historian's assumption of a particular position on the question of the nature of historical knowledge and the implications that can be drawn from the study of past events for the understanding of present ones" (22). The ideological positions are anarchism, conservatism, radicalism, and liberalism.

The historians chosen to illustrate four "styles" are Jules Michelet (romance), Leopold von Ranke (comedy), Alexis de Toqueville (tragedy), and Jacob Burckhardt (satire). The philosophers of history are G.W.F Hegel, Karl Marx, Friedrich Nietzsche, and Benedetto Croce. What the former had in common is modes of language determining how they would do history. What the latter shared was some awareness of linguistic determinism: " ... it is undeniable ... that all of them [the philosophers] understood the essential point I have tried to make: that in any field of study not yet reduced (or elevated) to the status of a genuine science, thought remains captive of the linguistic mode in which it seeks to grasp the outline of objects inhabiting its field of perception" (xi). In this essay we shall confine ourselves briefly to Ranke and Burckhardt, both of whom appear in this volume (see essays 18 and 20).

Ranke's narrative plot is comedy and his tropological strategy of explanation is synecdoche:

> The ternary movement of Comedy, from a condition of apparent peace, through the revelation of conflict, to the resolution of the conflict in the establishment of a genuinely peaceful order, permitted Ranke to delineate, self-confidently and convincingly, the main units of time into which the gross historical process can be divided ... But the characterization of a given context—such as that of the 'Middle Ages' ... —provides the reader with a sense of a succession of formal coherencies through which the action moves in such a way as to suggest the integration of the parts with the larger historical whole ...
>
> (177)

Ranke's ideology is conservatism.

Burckhardt's narrative plot is satire and his tropological strategy of explanation is irony: "The enthusiasm of Romance, the optimism of Comedy, and the resignation of Tragic apprehension of the world were not for him. Burckhardt surveyed a world in which virtue was usually betrayed, talent perverted, and power turned to the service of a baser cause" (234). His satirical approach to history was to divest it of any significance for the problems of his time, so he dealt with the Renaissance as an isolated "work of art." Burckhardt's ideology is liberalism.

White denies, perhaps with irony he would appreciate, being a relativist or a postmodernist. His conceptual apparatus is hard to digest, which he admits: "The terminology I used to characterize the different levels on which a historical account unfolds and to construct a typology of historiographical styles may prove mystifying" (ix–x). This admission is not lightly taken. A critic of historical knowledge must be understood before he can be answered. While White is rough going when laying out his conceptual framework, he is more accessible and straightforward in discussions of the four historians and their philosophical counterparts.

It is not unfair to point out that the conceptual scheme and its supporting arguments are vulnerable to the self-excepting fallacy. Historical inferences are declared relative to this or that mythos that encapsulates historians, but White's inferences from his conceptual scheme apparently are not. His argument that unconscious linguistic modes generate incompatible historical interpretations is seemingly a universal "truth" for historiography. If historical interpretation is understood as moral and poetic subjectivity and not as verifiable knowledge, there is a question about the status of White's interpretations, which must also be moral, poetic, and relative. A daring response to this criticism is to accept contradiction on grounds that historical relativism itself is relative, although how that leap, which White does not consciously take, might improve the validity of his arguments is not clear.

White's view of historical explanation and thinking sidelines discovery, evaluation, and logical uses of evidence. His theoretical framework does not allow that historical knowledge has empirical supports that reach across historical "styles." His position is clear: " ... the best grounds for choosing one perspective of history rather than another are ultimately aesthetic or moral rather than epistemological" (xii). Evidence and logic from this point of view are not a common denominator for romantics and satirists. Incompatible linguistic strategies rather than evidence determine explanations and interpretations in history. White dodges strict relativism by suggesting that one style may be translatable, like written languages, into one another, but the result of that option would still be poetry, not empirically verifiable historical knowledge.

Works by White

"The Burden of History," *History and Theory*, 5:2 (1966): 127.
Metahistory: The Historical Imagination in Nineteenth-Century Europe (Baltimore, Maryland: Johns Hopkins University Press, 1973).

The Content of the Form: Narrative Discourse and Historical Representation (Baltimore, Maryland: Johns Hopkins University Press, 1987).

Works about White

Canary, Robert and Henry Kozicki (eds.), *The Writing of History: Literary Form and Historical Understanding* (Madison, Wisconsin: University of Wisconsin Press, 1978).

Kansteiner, Wolf, "Hayden White's Critique of the Writing of History," *History and Theory*, 32:3 (October 1993): 273–295.

Kellner, Hans, *Language and Historical Representation* (Madison, Wisconsin: University of Wisconsin Press, 1989), pp. 221–225. He explains White's conceptual framework in *Metahistory*.

Konstan, David, "The Function of Narrative in Hayden White's *Metahistory*," *Clio*, 11 (1981).

Useful references

Burke, Peter, "History of Events and the Revival of Narrative," in Peter Burke (ed.), *New Perspectives on Historical Writing* (Cambridge: Cambridge University Press, 1991).

Gardner, Patrick, *The Nature of Historical Explanation* (London and New York: Oxford University Press, 1961).

Stone, Lawrence, "The Revival of Narrative: Reflections on a New Old History," *Past and Present*, 85 (1979): 3–24.

50. THE WORLD OF ODYSSEUS (M. I. FINLEY, 1912–1986)

Moses Israel Finley had duel national roots. He was born in New York City and died a British citizen. Higher schooling was at Syracuse University and Columbia University. A master's degree was taken in public law and a doctorate in ancient history. He taught at Columbia University and at City University of New York before taking a post at Rutgers University, from which he was dismissed during the communist witch hunt of the early 1950s. He took the Fifth Amendment when asked by a Senate Committee if he was or had been a member of the Communist Party. Unable to find a teaching job thereafter he moved to Britain in 1955 and taught classical studies at Cambridge University. He became Professor of History in 1970, Master of Darwin College in 1976, a Fellow of the British Academy in 1971, and a knight of the realm in 1979. He wrote extensively on social and economic issues in the classical world.

The World of Odysseus explores how people lived in the tenth and ninth centuries B.C. This short but densely packed account of the Greek "dark ages" uses the Homeric poems as historical documents: "I am a historian; my professional interest in the *Iliad* and *Odyssey* is in their usefulness as tools, as documents, for the study of the Bronze Age" (142). A lack of other documentation is addressed with the help of anthropology, oral traditions, philology, and archeology. There are two appendices: "The World of Odysseus Revisited" updates his research, and a second, "Schliemann's Troy—One hundred Years After," discusses and summarizes what we know, or rather, what we do not know, about the Trojan War. Finley is blunt about the relationship between Heinrich Schliemann's famous excavations at "Troy" in Asia Minor and the Trojan War of Homer's epics: "Nor can it be reiterated enough that the excavations at Hissarlik have not produced a jot of evidence to support the tales" (152). A bibliographical essay concludes the volume.

Finley explains his task:

> The serious problem for the historian is to determine whether, and to what extent, there is anything in the poems that relates to social and historical reality: how much, in other words, the world of Odysseus existed only in the poet's head and how much outside, in space and time. The prior question to be considered is whence the poet took his picture of that world and his stories of its wars and its heroes' private lives.
>
> (29)

With respect to social institutions and values identifiable in the poems, he assembles a descriptive and explanatory model: "A model can be constructed, imperfect, incomplete, untidy, yet tying together the fundamentals of political and social structure with an appropriate value system in a way that stands up to comparative analysis, the only control available to us in the absence of external documentation" (153). Four categories of evidence are marshaled to support the "model": manufactured objects, narrative, institutions, and values. For comparative purposes he turns to sources like Tamil heroic poetry and culture of the Trobriand Islands.

The "prior question" is answered by pointing out that Greek heroic epic, unlike Virgil's *Aeneid*, a literary epic, was composed and transmitted orally, usually by illiterate bards, built up from a vast repertory of materials passed along: "It has been calculated that there are some twenty-five formulaic expressions, or fragments of formulas, in the first twenty-five lines of the *Iliad* alone" (29). Bards composed and chanted tales in front of an audience using stock formulas of metaphor (e.g., "wine dark sea," "rosy fingered dawn"), events (the Trojan War), and people ("city-sacking" Achilles has 36 epithets). They did so in a dialect no one spoke, known as Homeric Greek:

> The genius of the Iliad and Odyssey does not lie primarily in the individual pieces, or even in the language, for that was all a common stock of materials available to any bard in quantity ... the greater the mass of accumulated materials, the greater the poet's freedom ... a Homer could create a remarkably coherent world, on the one hand different in details, and even in some essentials, from what older bards had passed on to him, and on the other hand still within the fixed path of bardic tradition, retaining a large part of the traditional world.
>
> (34–35)

The two poems, however, "look to a departed era, and their substance is unmistakably old" (33). The departed era is the tenth and ninth centuries, the age of Greek beginnings that followed the collapse of Mycenaean civilization toward the end of the thirteenth century. While the *Iliad* belongs to the second half of the eighth century and the *Odyssey* comes a generation or two later in the seventh, neither mentions the *polis* (city state) which was emerging in their time as the premier form of political organization, a decisive indication that their narrative materials belong to an earlier age. The poems no doubt underwent some modification in the process of transmission once they were set down in writing: "One thing seems sure: there was no excessive tampering with substance." The poems were too well known throughout the Greek world to be meddled with: "None of this is decisive ... but it permits the historian to work with his *Iliad* and his *Odyssey*, cautiously and always with suspicion, yet with a reasonable assurance that basically he is working with a fair approximation of eighth- or seventh-century poems" (39).

The chronological setting of the *Odyssey* is a base line for understanding life in Odysseus's kingdom of Ithaca:

> The world of Odysseus was not the Mycenaean age five or six or seven hundred years earlier, but neither was it the world of the eighth or seventh centuries B.C. The list of exclusions of contemporary institutions and practices is very long and very fundamental—no Ionia, no Dorians to speak of, no writing, no

iron weapons, no cavalry in battle scenes, no colonization, no Greek traders, no communities without kings. If ... the world of Odysseus is to be placed in time, as everything we know from the comparative study of heroic poetry says it must, the most likely centuries seem to be the tenth and ninth.

(48)

The destruction of Mycenaean culture erased detailed memories except for a vague recollection of palaces, chariots, and heroes preserved in later epic poetry. Military uses for chariots, for example, were forgotten. Homer's heroes use them as transportation to the battlefield and then dismount to fight on foot.

Social values and material culture of the poems bear no resemblance to the Mycenaean civilization distilled from thousands of tablets inscribed with Linear B, an early form of Greek, a writing system that disappeared along with Mycenaeans:

> The very existence of the tablets is decisive: not only was the Homeric world without writing or record keeping, but it was one in which the social system was too simple and the operations too restricted, too small in scale, to require either the inventories or the controls recorded on the tablets ... Homer, we too easily forget, had no notion of a Mycenaean Age, or of the sharp break between it and the new age that followed its destruction.

(45)

The world of Ithaca, island kingdom of Odysseus, was not contemporary with the *Odyssey*. The poem preserves memories of land, family, community, and beliefs from the tenth to the sixth century when the poem was committed to writing in its unique dialect. It is a lens through which outlines of a vanished society come into focus. Ithaca is a small place, about 45 square miles, the rocky land suitable mostly to pasture cattle, sheep, and goats. Life was defined by the *oikos*, class, and kin. The *oikos* comprised territorial possessions, family, slaves, retainers, and "guest-friends." The latter form of "friendship" was an institution for bonding between rulers and aristocrats outside of marriage through mutual hospitality, support, feasting, and gift-giving. The center of the *oikos* was the storeroom where metal, fabrics, gold, and wine were secured, a further sign of status: "Odysseus's Ithaca was more household- and kinship-bound, less integrally a civic community, than many a civilized centre of earlier centuries" (79).

Class had a neat horizontal cleavage—aristocrats, who unequally controlled power and wealth on top, and everyone else below. Homer ignores the common people: "Whatever the conflicts or cleavages among the noble households and families, they were always in accord that there could be no crossing of the great line which separated the *aristoi* [aristocrats] from the many, the heroes from the non-heroes" (107). For those outside the hero or warrior class, merit and achievement mattered not at all: " ... the main theme of warrior culture is constructed on two notes—prowess and honour. The one is the hero's essential attribute, the other is his essential aim. Every value, every judgment, every action, all skills and talents have the function of either defining honor or realizing it" (113). Prowess was demonstrated on the battlefield or in competitive games. Honor was achieved through distribution of spoils from raids and gift-giving: "No single detail in the life of the heroes receives so much attention in the *Iliad* and the *Odyssey* as gift-giving, and always there is a frank reference to adequacy, appropriateness, recompense" (65). The gift treasured above all was metal, usually in the form of tripods and cauldrons; next came gold, horses, and women: " ... the heroic world was unable to visualize any achievement or relationship except in concrete terms ... The emotions and feelings were located in specific organs of the body, even the soul was materialized" (123).

Thought and action were enclosed and governed by kinship: " ... kinship thinking permeated everything" (83). Finley relies on anthropology for evidence that kinship is a universal shaper of human behavior. Family was the focus of judgment. In Odysseus's time there was no sense of public responsibility for a crime. Indeed, "crime" had no meaning. A murder, theft, or other offense had to be dealt with within a kinship network or not at all. When Odysseus killed all the suitors for his wife's hand, any reprisal was up to their families.

Anthropomorphized divinities, as opposed to formless nature spirits or gods half animal, half human, were a major accomplishment of Odysseus's culture. Olympian deities, led by Zeus, differed from humans only in their superior powers and immortality:

> God was created in men's image with a skill and genius that must be ranked with man's greatest intellectual feats. The whole of heroic society was reproduced on Olympus ... The world of the gods was a social world in every respect, with a past and a present, with a history ... The gods came to power on Olympus as men came to power in Ithaca or Sparta or Troy, through struggle or family inheritance.
>
> (132)

Self-knowledge was a consequence of Homer turning gods into men.

Finley's contribution to historiography in this subtle work is to show how literature in the absence of other documentation can be used for historical analysis with the aid of archeology and anthropology. While scholars may dispute details, his overall view of Odysseus's world and its location in time is persuasive.

Works by Finley

Ancient History: Evidence and Models (New York: Viking Press, 1986).
Ancient Slavery and Modern Ideology, ed. Brent Shaw (expanded edition; Princeton, New Jersey: Markus Wiener Publishers, 1998). First published in 1980.
Economy and Society in Ancient Greece, ed. and intro. Brent Shaw and Richard Saller (New York: Viking Press, 1983). First published in 1953.
The Use and Abuse of History (London: Chatto and Windus, 1975).
The World of Odysseus (rev. ed.; New York: Viking Press, 1965). First published in 1954.

Works about Finley

Watson, George, "The Man from Syracuse: Moses Finley (1912–86)," *Sewanee Review*, 112:1 (2004): 131–137.

Useful references

Cartledge, Paul, "The Greeks and Anthropology," *Anthropology Today*, 10:3 (1994): 4.
Hornblower, Simon, "A Gift from Whom," *Times Literary Supplement* (December 24, 2004). A review of *The World of Odysseus*.

Section Notes

1 This essay uses the translation by Baehr and Wells.
2 Three volumes of Foucault's *The History of Sexuality* cannot be explained coherently in a short essay. Volume 1 is difficult enough and within it are ideas contained also in volumes 2 and 3, which deal with sexuality in classical Greece and Rome. I do not pretend to understand all that Foucault says, but an effort to catch the gist of it has been made.

INDEX

Please note that page numbers relating to Notes will have the letter 'n' following the page number. The prefix 'al' is ignored in filing order. Names beginning with Ibn are sorted under Ibn, whereas the letters 'al' are ignored.

abbeys, 50, 51, 76, 77
Abelard, Peter, 200
accuracy in historical sources *see* truth, in reporting/testimony
Action française, 241
Acton, John Dalberg, 133–37
Adherbal, 20, 21, 22
Adi, Hakim, 186–90
Aeneid (Virgil), 278
Aeschylus, 260
Africa, xiv, 179–90
African Experience, The (Khapoya), 180–86
Age of Constantine the Great, The (Burckhardt), 113
Age of Louis XIV, The (Voltaire), 83–88
Age of Reform, The (Hofstadter), 230
Alaric the Goth, 31–32, 33, 50
Alberti, Leon Battista, 117
Alcibiades, 9
Alexander VI, 117
Alfonso V, court of, 60
Alfred the Great, 50, 51, 52
algebra, 221
alienation, 174
Allah, 45, 46, 47, 111
American Civil War, 232
American Declaration of Independence (1776), 238, 254
American Dream, 233
The American Political Tradition and the Men Who Made It (Hofstadter), 230–41

anarchism, 241
Ancient Greece, 1–13, 149, 199;
 World of Odysseus (Finley), 278–82
Ancient Rome *see* Roman Empire
Anecdota (Procopius), 37
anecdotal reporting, 85–86
Anglo-Saxon Chronicle, xxiii, 49–54
Ankersmit, Frank, xxiv
Annales School, 174
annals, xv, xvi, 49–50, 51, 166, 242
Annals of Italy (Muratori), 92
Annals of the Benedictine Order (Mabillon), 76
anthropology, 212–13
Anti-Intellectualism in American Life (Hofstadter), 230
Antiphon, 7
antiquarians, 92
Antonina, 39
apologetics, xxi
Aquinas, Thomas, 200, 214, 215–16, 217
Arabian historiography, 44, 45
Arabic language and literature, 45
Arab-Muslim societies, 258–59
Aramaic language, 25
archaeology, xv, 29; Assyrian, 118
archival materials, 15, 104
argument, 274
Ariès, Philippe, xxiii, 241–46
Aristophanes, 218
Aristotle, 199
Arminius, 139
asceticism, 195

283

INDEX

Assyria, 118, 119
astrology, 212, 213
astronomy, 221
Athenian Empire, war with Sparta (431–404 BC), 1, 7–12
Atwater, Richard, 37, 41, 42
Augustine of Hippo, xxiii, 24, 30–35, 97, 199, 217; dualism of, 31
Augustus, 15, 16, 139–40
Aurelius, Marcus, 90
Austin Riggs Center, US, 268
authenticity, 70, 76, 77, 79, 104; *see also* truth, in reporting/testimony
autonomy, 228, 237
avant garde philosophy, xx

Babylon, 119
Bacon, Francis, 249–50, 251
Baghdad, Mongol invasion (1258), 43
Baptism, 195
barbarians, 3, 4, 36, 37, 109, 110, 111
Barenboim, Daniel, 257
Barnes, Harry Elmer, xxii
Barthes, Roland, xx, xxiii
Battle of Hastings (1066), 53
Bauer, Ferdinand, 129
Baxter, Richard, 195, 196
Bayeaux Tapestry, 53
Bayle, Pierre, 70, 71–76, 77, 91–92; on error, 71, 72, 73, 74, 78
Beard, Charles A., xix, 214
Beck, R. N., xxiii
Becker, Carl Lotus, xix, xxiii, 214–19
Bede (Venerable Bede), 51, 53
Belisarius, 36, 38, 39
Benedictine saints, 76
Beowulf, 50
bias, xiii, xx, 70, 82, 87, 217
biblical schedule of creation, 34
biography, 15, 16, 43, 46
Bismarck, Otto von, 138
Black, J.B., xxiv
Black and Asian Studies Association (BASA), 186
Black Sea, 110
Blyden, Edward, 188–89
Bodin, Jean, 59, 64–69, 126
Boia, Lucien, xxi
bondage, 183
Borgia, Cesare, 117

Bourne, Frank, 99
bridewealth, 182
British East India Company, 169, 174
British Museum, 119
Bronze Age, 278
Brown vs Board of Education case, US, 252
Bryan, William Jennings, 230
Buckle, Thomas, 157, 158
Buddhism, 146, 147, 159
Buildings of Justinian (Procopius), 40
Bultmann, Rudolph, 128
Bummeiron no gairyaku (Fukuzawa), 155
Burckhardt, Jacob, 113–18, 166, 275
burial, 245
Burton, Richard (writer), 260
Bury, J. B., xv, xxii
Byzantine Empire, 36–42, 90, 112

Caesar, Julius, 16, 17, 19, 138; assassination, 15, 20; *Commentaries*, 22
calendar, Ancient Greece, 11–12
Calhoun, John C., 230
Caligula, 15, 16, 17, 18
"calling," a, 194–95, 196
Calvinism, 74, 195; *see also* Huguenots (French Calvinists)
Cambridge Modern History, 134
Cannon, John, xxi
capitalism, 194, 196; proto-capitalism, 223
Carlyle, Thomas, 134, 187
Carr, E. H., xix, xxii
Carthage, 20, 110
Carthaginians, 18
Castiglione, Baldassare, 117
Catholicism, 57, 65, 70, 74, 77, 85; and Weber, 194, 195
causation, 223
celestial magic, 211
cemeteries, 242
Centuries of Childhood (Ariès), 241
ceremonial magic, 211
Chain of Being (Lovejoy), 198–202
Chang Hsüeh-ch'eng, 153
Charlemagne, 50, 79, 112
Charles I, King of England, 247, 248
Charles V, King of France, 55

Charles XII, King of Sweden, 83
Chen, Ann-ping, 153
Chiang Kai-shek, 149
Chichiba District uprising, Japan (1884), 164
Chi'en Mu, xvii, xxiii, 148–53
childhood, 241
chin shih (degree status), 144
China, xiv, xvii, 85, 143–53, 196; dynasties, 145, 150, 152–53, 221; governments/government appointments, 149–50, 151–52; and Japan, 155, 158, 160; language, 219; Needham on, 219, 220–22; sequential historical development absent in historical works, 145
Ch'ing Dynasty, China, 143, 145, 148, 150, 152–53
Christianity/Christians: and Byzantium period, 38, 41; chronological systems, 46; and eighteenth-century Europe, 85; and medieval Europe, 50, 55, 56; New Testament, 60, 128, 129, 130; and Renaissance Europe, 63; rise of, 90–91, 113; and Roman Empire, 25, 30–34; Roman persecution of Christians, 91; *see also* Catholicism; Protestantism
Christina, Swedish Queen, 107
chronicle, tradition of, 22, 49, 50, 51, 84; *see also* Anglo-Saxon Chronicle
chronography (sequential dating of events and people), 46
chronology, 34, 43, 46, 51–52
Chu Hsi, 147
Cicero, Marcus Tullius, 2, 19, 61
The Cicerone: A Guide to Works of Art in Italy (Burckhardt), 114
City in History, The (Mumford), 203
City of God, The (Augustine of Hippo), 30–35, 217
Civil Rights Act 1964, US, 255
Civilization of the Renaissance in Italy (Burckhardt), 114–18
class consciousness, 174, 226
Claudius, 15, 16, 17, 18
Cleopatra, 15
climate of opinion, 215, 216, 217, 218, 238

Clio (muse of history), 2
clock, 204, 223
Coke, Edward, 249, 250, 251
Coleman, Christopher, 69
colonialism, 171, 174, 183–84, 188–89, 189
Columbia University, 225
comedy, 275
Commodus, 90
Communist Party of Great Britain, 247
Complete Library of the Four Treasuries, 145, 146
Conditions in the West (Fukuzawa), 157
Condottiere, 116–17
confession, 265
Confessions (Augustine of Hippo), 30
Confucianism, 143–47, 149, 152, 154, 157, 158, 159, 160, 222
Congress of American Women, 226
consciousness, 175, 177, 205
Conspiracy of Catiline, 20
Constantine, Emperor, 60, 129
Constantinople, 36, 37, 38, 62, 89, 90; fall to Ottoman Turks (1453), 61
Contextualism, 274
continuity, 199
contribution history, 227
Copernicus, 118, 200, 212
Corcyra, 11
Corpus of Latin Inscriptions (Mommsen), 138, 139
Cortigiano (courtier), 117
Council of Trent (1564), 59
Counter Reformation, 77, 106
Court Gentlemen, China, 151–52
craftsmanship, 206
credibility *see* truth, in reporting/testimony
cremation, 245
critical historiography, xiv–xvi, xxiii, 70, 77
criticism, 129; literary, xx; postmodern, xviii–xxi, xxiii
Croce, Benedetto, 275
Cromwell, Oliver, 247, 249
Crusades/Crusaders, 44, 46, 54, 56, 57, 90
Cugoano, Quobna Ottobah, 188
cultural anthropology, xx

INDEX

Culture, Ideology, Hegemony: Intellectuals and Social Consciousness in Colonial India (Panikkar), 170–71
Culture of the Meji Era, The (Irokawa), 161–66
cuneiform (script type), 119
custom, 4

Dagobert (Merovingian king), 79
Damietta (port city), 56, 57
Dante, 214
death, Ariès on, 241–46; Death of the Other, 244–45; images of death, 243; Invisible Death, 245; Remote and Imminent Death, 244; Self, death of, 244; Tame Death, 243
Decline and Fall of the Roman Empire, The (Gibbon), 88–93; Great Books edition, 89–90, 99
Delaney, Martin, 188
Demaratus, 6
demonism, 41, 68
deployment, 264–65
Derrida, Jacques, xix, xx, xxiii
Descartes, René, 66, 72, 73, 74
descent (in families), 182
despotic rulers, 116, 117
development, 96
Devil, 40
dialectical materialism, 247
diaspora, 186, 187
Dictionary, Historical and Critical (Bayle), 71–76
Diderot, Denis, 72
Diocletion, 140
Dionysius of Halicarnassus, 8
discourse, 258, 264, 265
Discourse on the Forgery of the Alleged Donation of Constantine (Valla), 59–64, 129
diversitarianism, 201
divine, as history type, 67
divine dispensation, notion of, 171
documentation, 15, 74, 77, 78–79; and criticism, 129; primary, 103; truth in *see* truth, in reporting/testimony
Döllinger, Ignaz von, 133
Domitian, 15, 17

Donation of Constantine, as forgery, 59–64, 129
doubt, 73, 74, 135
Douglas, David, 58
Douglas, Frederick, 187
Doyle, Arthur Conan, 213
Du Bois, W. E. B., 189
dyarchy, 139–40

East-West Divan Orchestra, 257
Ecclesiastical Annals, 70
Ecclesiastical History (Venerable Bede), 51, 53
Edict of Nantes (1598), 71, 85
Ego (Freud), 268
Egypt, 4, 56
Eichhorn, Johann, 129
eighteenth-century Europe, 82–100
Elegancies of the Latin Language (Valla), 61
Elementary Aspects of Peasant Insurgency in Colonial India (Guha), 174–78
empathy, 237, 238
emperor system, 154, 161–62, 166
Encouragement of Learning, An (Fukuzawa), 157
engineering, 221
English Historical Review, 134
English historiography, 53
Enlightenment, 72, 82, 83, 84, 86, 96, 214, 217, 218; French, 94; *see also* reason
eotechnic wave, 206
Epicurus, 61
Erasmus of Rotterdam, 61
Erikson, Erik H., 267–72; Freud compared, 268
error, 71, 72, 73, 74, 78
erudition, 77
Essay on Customs (Voltaire), 83, 89, 217
Essay on the Study of Literature (Gibbon), 89
Essenes, 28
essentialism, 258–59, 261
ethnography, 5
Etruscans, 18
Europe: medieval, 49–58; Renaissance, 3, 31, 59–69, 105, 114–15, 117–18; Reformation, 3,

59, 70–81, 77, 117, 118, 210, 211, 223; eighteenth-century, 82–100; nineteenth-century, 101–42; twentieth-century, 191–282; Old Regime, 72, 83; and Roman Empire, 84
Eusebius, 38
Evans, Richard J., xxii
evidence, 7, 10, 22, 71, 82, 87, 91, 147, 242; *see also* truth, in reporting/testimony
Explorations in Words and Meanings in Mencius (Meng Tzu tsu-I shu cheng), 144–48
eyewitness accounts, 49, 52, 57–58, 102

facts, xv–xvi, 10, 74, 75, 84, 102; rejection of, 86–87, 214–15, 218; *see also* truth, in reporting/testimony
Fadipe, Nathaniel, 188
fairies, 213
faith, 215, 216
falsehood, 43, 74
famine, 51
Fanon, Frantz, 188, 189
Fate, 39
Febvre, Lucien, 241
female characters in fiction, 238
Feminine Mystique, The (Friedan), 229
feminism, and women's history, 229
feudalism, 116, 222
Fifth Amendment, 277
Finley, John H., 13
Finley, Moses Israel, 277–82
First World War, 109
Fitzsimmons, Matthew, xxii
Five Elements, 146, 223
Flavian Dynasty, 15
Florentines, 114
folk magic, 212
footnotes, 16
forgery, 79; Donation of Constantine as, 59–64, 129
Formism, 274
Fortune, 39
Foucault, Michel, xvii, xx, xxiii, 258, 263–67, 282
Founding Fathers, 230, 234

"four monarchies" theory, 67
Fourth Crusade, 90
France, 65
Franklin, Benjamin, 194
Franklin, John Hope, 252–56
Franks, the, 47, 111–12
Freeman, Mansfield, 153
French Declaration of the Rights of Man and Citizen (1789), 238
French Revolution, 236, 239
Freud, Anna, 268
Freud, Sigmund, 265, 268
Friedan, Betty, 229
From Slavery to Freedom: A History of African Americans (Franklin), 253–56
Fukuzawa Yukichi, xxiii, 154, 155–61, 162, 163

Gaius Julius, 51
Galba, 15, 16, 18
Galilee, 29
Galileo, 66, 74, 118, 222
Gandhi's Truth (Erikson), 268
Garvey, Amy, 188
Gaul, 111
Gay, Peter, 218
genres of history, xvi–xvii
Gibbon, Edward, 42, 82, 84, 88–93, 99, 109, 114
Glanville, Joseph, 125
God, 33, 39, 47, 48, 55–57, 65, 73, 129–30, 182, 196, 200; *see also* Christianity/Christians; Hinduism; Islam; Judaism
Goethe, Wolfgang, 94
Good, 199, 200
good and bad history, 67
"good works," 196
Gospels, 128, 129, 130, 131–32
Goths, 38, 50; *see also* Alaric the Goth
gradation, 199
The Grand Titration: Science and Society in East and West (Needham), 220–24
Graves, Robert, 23
The Great Chain of Being: A Study of the History of an Idea (Lovejoy), 198–202
Great Depression, 231

Greco-Roman historiography, 31, 32, 33, 34, 45, 59
Greece, Ancient, 1–13, 149, 199; *World of Odysseus* (Finley), 278–82
Greek literature, 38
Greek Paleography (Montfaucon), 91
Greene, Anna, xxii
Gregory XIII, King, 105
groups/communities, 96, 97
Guha, Ranajit, 168, 173–78
Guizot, Françoise, 157, 158

Haack, Susan, xxiv
Hadas, Moses, 99
hadith (Mohammed's actions and deeds), 44, 45
Hadrian, Emperor, 14–15
Hagia Sophia (Holy Wisdom), 38–39
Halicarnassus, Asia Minor, 2
Halley's Comet, 53
Hamann, Johann, 98
Han Dynasty, China, 143, 145, 150, 151
Harold, King, 53
Hassan, Ihad, xxiii
Hattin, Battle of (1187), 47
Heavenly City of the Eighteenth-Century Philosophers (Becker), 215–18
Hegel, Georg Wilhelm Friedrich, 96, 129, 275
heliocentrism, 200, 201
Hellenistic historiography, 22, 26, 29
Henry IV, King of France, 71
Henry of Huntingdon, 53
Herder, Johann Gottfried von, xvii, xxiii, 83, 94–99, 108, 202
Herod, King, 25, 26, 27
Herodotus, xxiii, 1–6, 33, 38; Thucydides compared, 2, 5, 7, 9, 11
heroic epic, Greek, 278, 280, 281
Hiempsal, 20, 21
Higher Criticism, 129
Hill, Christopher, 174, 247–52
Hinduism, 168, 169, 170, 176
Hippocratic School, 10
historical eras, periodization, 34
historiography: African, 179, 190; Arabian phase, 44, 45; breadth of, xvii; and Christianity, 32; Confucian, 158; critical, xiv–xvi, xxiii, 70, 77; defined, xi; English, 53; and footnotes, 16; genres of history, xvi–xvii; Greco-Roman, 31, 32, 33, 34, 45, 59; growth of historical writing, xviii; Hellenistic, 22, 26, 29; Indian, 168; Japanese, 154, 158; justification for the fifty "key" works, xii–xiii; Marxist, 170, 173; medieval, 49, 66; non-Western perspectives, xiv; pioneer works, xiv; postmodernism, xviii–xxi; problematic works, xvii–xviii; *see also specific periods in history*
Historische Zeitschrift, xv
history: ages in, 84; vs anthropology, 212–13; critical method, 70; defined, xi; genres of, xvi–xvii; laws of, 274; as memory, 214, 216; "new," 217; and science, xv–xvi, 78, 82, 86, 95, 135, 215, 230; types, 67; women in, 226–29; *see also* historiography
History of Calvinism (Maimbourg), 74
History of Civilization in England (Buckle), 157
History of Civilization in Europe (Guizot), 157
History of Coinage (Mommsen), 139
History of Commercial Partnerships in the Middle Ages (Weber), 192
History of Europe (Pirenne), 109
History of Latin and Teutonic Nations, A (von Ranke), 102
History of Rome (Mommsen), 138
History of Sexuality, The (Foucault), 263–67, 282
History of the Ancient Jews (Josephus), 25
History of the Popes: Their Church and State (Ranke), 103–7
History of the Rise and Influence of the Spirit of Rationalism in Europe (Lecky), 123, 124–26
History of the World (Ralegh), 250
Hobsbawn, E. H., 174, 247
Hofstadter, Richard, xxiii, 230–41
Homer, 2, 97, 278, 279, 280, 282
Hoover, Herbert, 230, 231
Hopkins History of Ideas Club, 202
Horton, James, 188

Hour of Our Death, The (Ariès), 242–46
Huang Tsing Tsung, 219
Hughes, H. Stuart, xxii
Huguenots (French Calvinists), 65, 71, 85
human affairs, as history type, 67
human rights, 236–40
humanism, 61, 64–65, 66
Hume, David, xix, 72, 92
Hunt, Lynn, 235–41

Ibn Khaldun, 43
Ibn Shaddad, Baha' al-din, xiv, xxiii, 43–48
Id (Freud), 268
ideal types, 195, 231
ideas, 198, 199, 201, 215; unit ideas, 199, 202
identity, cultural/national, 169
identity crisis, 268, 270
ideological explanation, 274–75
ideology, 169–70, 170, 172
Iggers, Georg G., xxii, xxiii
Iliad, 2, 278, 279, 281
imperialism, 168, 188–89
Inaugural Lecture on the Study of History (Acton), 134, 136–37
incompleteness, xxi
India, xiv, 168–78
individualism, 115, 116, 117–18
inner light, 73
inquiry, 2, 71, 82; scientific, 108, 222
insurgency, peasant, 174–75, 176, 177
Intellectual Origins of the English Revolution (Hill), 247–52
Intellectuals, 172
interpretive method (Weber), 193
Inventing Human Rights: A History (Hunt), 236–40
inversion, 175–76, 177
Ireland, 123, 124
Irokawa Daikichi, 154, 161–66
irony, 274
Islam, xiv, 43–48, 111, 112; Arab-Muslim societies, 258–59; "five pillars" of belief and practice, 44
Islamic historiography, 44, 45
isnad (chains of authority), 45

Italy, 59, 66, 114, 116, 123; cities, 115
Ithaca, Odysseus's kingdom of, 279–80

Jackson, Andrew, 230, 231, 232, 234
James II, 247
Jansenism, 85
Japan, xiv, 154–67
Jefferson, Thomas, 72, 230, 231, 232, 234, 239, 254
Jerome's Vulgate, 60
Jerusalem, 25, 27–28, 29, 44, 47, 141
Jesus Christ, 55, 56; *Life of Jesus Critically Examined* (Strauss), 127–32; as Messiah, 130, 131, 132; *see also* Christianity/Christians; Gospels; New Testament
Jewish Antiquities (Josephus), 25
Jewish Revolt against Rome, 67 AD, 24–30
Jewish War, The (Josephus), 18, 25–30
The Jews and Modern Capitalism (Sombart), 194
jisei (spirit of the times), 158
John of Worcester, 53
Johnson, Samuel, 202
Joinville, Jean de, 49, 54–58
Josephus, Flavius (Joseph ben Matthias), 16, 24–30
Jotapata city, 24, 25, 28
Journal of the History of Ideas, 202
journals, professional, xv
Judaea, 140–41
Judaism, 55–56
Judao-Christian tradition, 24–35
Judas Maccabeus, 26
Jugurtha, 20, 21, 22
Jugurthine War, The (Sallust), 20–23
Julio-Claudian Dynasty, 15
Julius II, 105
Justinian, Emperor, 36, 37, 38, 39, 40, 41

Kant, Immanuel, 202
keimo (Enlightenment), 155, 157
Kelley, Donald R., xxii, xxiii
Kepler, 118, 200
khabar (reports/accounts), 45
Khapoya, Vincent, 179–86
Kierkegaard, Sören, xix

INDEX

Kilimanjaro, 180
King, Martin Luther, Jr., 187, 188, 255
knowledge, 215, 216; by inquiry, 2; objectivity of, doubts concerning, xix, xx
Koran, 44, 45, 111
kultur vs *zivilization*, 114
Kyushu, Japan, 156, 163

La République (Bodin), 65
Lamprecht, Karl, 109
Lane, Edward, 260
language: African, 180, 182; Arabic, 45; Aramaic, 25; Chinese, 219; European, 180; Latin, 25, 50, 60, 61, 91, 111; of proof, 82; structuralism, 263
Latin language, 25, 50, 60, 61, 91, 111
laws of nature, 216, 221
Layard, Austen Henry, 118–23
Lazarus, 131
learning, historical, 134, 135
Lecky, William, 123–27
Lee, Dwight E., xxiii
legends, 130–31
Leibniz, Gottfried Wilhelm, 72
Leo X, Pope, 105
Lerner, Carl, 225
Lerner, Gerda Kronstein, xxiii, 225–29
Lévi-Strauss, Claude, xx
Liberia, 188
Life of Jesus Critically Examined (Strauss), 127–32
Life of Saint Louis (de Joinville), 54–58
Lincoln, Abraham, 230, 231, 232, 234, 255
Lindisfarne monastery, 49–50
linguistic determinism, 275
literary criticism, xx
Liu Chih-chi, 153
Lives of the Caesars (Suetonius), 15–19
Livy, 14, 25, 33, 87
Loeb Classical Library, 35, 36
logography (reporting of stories), 5
logos (things said), 5
Louis IX, King of France, 54–58
Louis X, King of France, 54

Louis XIV, King of France, 82, 83–88, 103
Louis XV, King of France, 86
Lovejoy, Arthur O., xvii, xxiii, 197–203
L'Overture, Toussaint, 187
Low, D. M., 99
Lower Criticism, 129
Lu Gwei-djen, 219
Luther, Martin, 102, 194, 195; Erikson on, 268–71
Lyman, Stanford, xxiii

Mabillon, Jean, xxiii, 70, 76–81, 91, 104
machine-based civilization, 208
machinery, automatic, 207
Madagascar, 180
Madness and Civilization (Foucault), 265
madrassa (mosque school), 44
Magdeburg Centuries, 70
magic, 124, 125, 209–13
Mahmud II, 90
Maimbourg, Pére, 74
The Majority Finds Its Past: Placing Women in History (Lerner), 226–29
Malabar Student Federation, India, 169
Malatesta, Sigismondo, 116
Malcolm X, 188
Mandela, Nelson, 187, 188
Manichaeism, 30
Manuel, Frank E., 96, 99
Marc Antony, 15
Marius, 21, 22
Marshall, Thurgood, 252
Marx, Karl/Marxism, 97, 154, 162, 174, 193, 226, 247, 274, 275; Marxist historiography, 170, 173
Masada siege, 25
Mass, 210–11
mathematics, 221
Maurists, 92
McHenry, Robert, 99
Mecca, pilgrimage to, 44
Mechanistic explanation, 274
mechanistic values, 204
medieval Europe, 49–58
Medina, Mohammed's flight to (622), 46

Mediterranean, 110, 111, 112
Meiji Restoration/period, Japan, 154, 155, 161–66
Melos, 8, 9
memoires, 49, 57
memory, history as, 214, 216
Mencius, 146, 147
Mennonites, 195
mentalities, 241
Mesopotamia, 119, 120, 121
Messalina, 18
Messiah, 130, 131, 132
Meta-History: The Historical Imagination in Nineteenth-Century Europe (White), 273–77
Metallus, 21
metaphor, 274
Method for the Easy Comprehension of History (Bodin), 66–68
Methodists, 195
Metternich, Prince Klemens von, 102, 105
Michelet, Jules, 275
Micipsa, King, 20
microcosm-macrocosm, 68
Middle Ages, 43, 112, 125, 126, 199, 241
Middle English, 51
Mill, John Stuart, 171
Ming Dynasty, China, 150, 152, 221
miracles, 124, 126, 131, 212, 213, 216
Mohammed and Charlemagne (Pirenne), 112
Molière (Jean-Baptiste Poquelin), 85
Mommsen, Theodor, xvii, xxiii, 137–41
monasteries, 204
monastic annals, 49–50
Mongols, 43
monograph, historical, 22
Montaigne, Michel de, 71, 126
Montesquieu, Baron de (Charles-Louis de Secondat), 89, 92, 217
Montfoucon, Bernard de, 77, 91
Mughals, 171, 174
Mukherjee, Supriya, xxii
multiculturalism, 98
Mumford, Lewis, xvii, xxiii, 203–9
Muratori, Ludovico, 92
Muses of Greek mythology, 2

Musil, Robert, xix
Mycenaean culture, 280
mythology, xi, 2, 130, 131, 132

Napoleon Bonaparte, 106
narrative, historical, 174
nationalism, 180, 184–85, 189
nations, 97, 105, 108
natural magic, 211
nature, 10, 223; laws of, 216, 221
Nazis, 225, 240
Needham, Joseph, xxiii, 219–24; on China, 219, 220–22
negroes, 253, 254, 255
nemesis, 39
Neo-Confucian tradition, 146, 147
neotechnic wave, 206, 207–8
Nero, 15, 16, 17, 18, 26
New Asia College, Hong Kong, 149
New Culture Movement, China, 149
New Deal, 233
New Freedom, 233
New School for Social Research, 225
New Testament, 60, 128, 129, 130
News of the Republic of Letters (Bayle), 74
Newton, Isaac, 3, 118, 212, 216, 222, 223
Nicholas V, Pope, 60
Nicias, 10
Niebuhr, Barthold, 102
Nietzsche, Friedrich, xix, 263, 275
Nile, 180
Nimrud, 119, 120, 121
nineteenth-century Europe, 101–42
Nineveh, 119
Numidia, kingdom of, 19, 20, 21

objectivity of knowledge, doubts concerning, xix, xx
Occidentalism, 261
oikos, 280
Old English, 50, 51
Old Regime, Europe, 72, 83
Old Testament, 128, 131
On Diplomatics (Mabillon), 91
On Pleasure (Valla), 61
On the Malice of Herodotus (Plutarch), 2
One More Philosophy of History (Herder), 94

INDEX

oppression, 226, 228
optimism, 201, 202
oral history, xv, 5, 9, 175
Order of Merit, 123
Organicism, 274
Orientalism: Western Conceptions of the Orient (Said), 257–62; meanings of Orientalism, 257–58; sections, 259–60
Other, Western domination of, 259
Otho, 15, 18
Ottoman Empire/Ottomans, 89, 90, 120
Outline of a Theory of Civilization, An (Fukuzawa), 155–61

Padmore, George, 188
paganism, 30, 32, 39, 92, 210
Paine, Thomas, 171
paleography, 77, 78, 91
paleotechnic wave, 206, 207
Pan African History: Political Figures from Africa and the Diaspora since 1787 (Adi and Sherwood), 186–90
Pan-African Conference, 187, 189
Pan-Africanism/Pan-African movement, 179, 186, 187, 188, 189
Panikkar, K. N., 168, 169–73
Papacy, 116, 117
papal history, Ranke on, 103–7
papal power, 60, 63–64, 70
Papal States, 103, 117
particulars, stressing, 107, 108
patriarchy, 226–27, 228
Paulus, Heinrich, 129
Peloponnesian War (431–404 BC), 7–12, 33
penance, 265
'people's history,' 162
perfection, 201
Pericles, funeral oration of, 8, 11
Perry, Commodore, 156, 158
Persian conquest, 45
Persian Wars, The (Herodotus), 1–6
Persians, The (Aeschylus), 260
Peter and Paul, 62–63
Peter the Great, of Russia, 83
Peterborough Abbey, 50, 51

Pharisees, 27, 28
Phillips, Wendall, 230
philological method, 59, 104, 144, 147
philosophes, 215–16, 218
philosophical history/historians, 82, 84, 91, 92–93
physical nature, as history type, 67
physics, 221
Pirenne, Henri, xxiii, 109–13, 187
Pius IV, 103–4
Pius VII, 106–7
plague, 51, 210
Plato, 97, 198–99
plenitude, 199, 201–2
Pliny the Younger, 14–15
Plotinus, 31, 199
pluralism, religious, 91
Plutarch, 2
poetry, 50, 278, 279, 280
Pollack, Martyn, 99
Polybius, 25, 38
polygamy, 182–83
polygny, 182
polytheism, Roman, 33
Popper, Karl, xxiii
Popular Account of Discoveries at Ninevah (Layard), 119–22
positivism, 193
postcolonial theory and writing, 257, 261
posterity, 217
postmodernism, xviii–xxi, xxiii, 191–92, 263, 276
post-structuralism, 263
power, Foucault on, 264
Praetorian Guard, 17–18
predestination, theology of, 85
problem-oriented history, 245
Procopius, xvii, xxiii, 8, 36–42
prognosis, 10
proof, common language of, 82
propaganda, xxi
prosopography (group biographies), 46
Protagoras, 7
The Protestant Ethic and the Spirit of Capitalism (Weber), 192–96; objectives, 194

Protestantism, 70, 71, 73, 74, 77, 106, 194–95, 196, 210, 211, 212, 232
proto-capitalism, 223
Providence, 34, 39, 107, 136, 232
Provinces of the Roman Empire from Caesar to Diocletian, The (Mommsen), 138–39, 140
psyche, Freudian model, 268
psychosocial development, 268
public histories, 38
Puritans, 194, 196, 248, 251
Pyrrhonism, 71

Quaestor, office of, 37–38
Quakers, 195
Quietism, 85

race, 181–82
Ralegh, Walter, 249, 250, 251
Rand, Calvin G., xxiii
Ranke, Leopold von, xxiii, 95, 96, 101–8, 113, 135, 136, 214, 275
Rare and Excellent History of Saladin, The (Ibn Shaddad), 44–48
rationalism, 125, 127, 198
Ravenna, Gothic capital of, 38
Rawlinson, George, 13
Rawlinson, Henry, 119
reason, 72, 73, 82, 83, 84, 86, 215–16; see also Enlightenment
Reflections on the Philosophy of Mankind (Herder), 94–99
Reformation Europe, 3, 59, 70–81, 77, 117, 118, 210, 211, 223
relativism, 216, 273, 276
reliability of historical sources see truth, in reporting/testimony
Religion and the Decline of Magic: Studies in Popular Beliefs in Sixteenth and Seventeenth Century England (Keith), 209–13
remembrance, xi
Renaissance Europe, 3, 31, 59–69, 105, 114–15, 117–18
repressive hypothesis, 263–64
resistance, 177
resources, conversion of, 208
respect, 237
Resurrection, 132, 244

Revue Historique, xv
Reynolds, Beatrice, 69
rhetoric, 71
Richard I, King (Richard the Lionheart), 47
rights, 236–37, 239
Rise of Rationalism, The (Lecky), 124
Robber Barons, 230, 232–33
Robinson, Chase F., xxiii
Roman Agrarian History and its Significance for Public and Private Law (Weber), 192
Roman Empire, xvii, 14–23, 109–10, 149; and Britain, 50–51; Eastern, 36, 37; and Europe, 84; invasion by Alaric the Goth (410), 31–32, 33, 50; Jewish Revolt against Rome, 67AD, 24–30; polytheism, 33; see also Byzantine Empire
Roman History (Niebuhr), 102
Roman law, codification, 38
Roman Peace, 15
Roman Public Law (Mommsen), 139–40
Romantic movement, 83, 96, 136, 244
Rome, city of, 89
Roosevelt, Franklin Delano, 230, 231, 233, 234
Roosevelt, Theodore, 230, 233
Rorty, Richard, xx
Roy, Rammohun, 171

Sadducees, 27, 28
Sahara desert, 180
Said, Edward W., xxiii, 256–62
Saladin, Sultan, biography of (Ibn Shaddad), 44–48
Sallust (Gaius Sallustius Crispis), xxiii, 14, 19–23; Suetonius compared, 22
samurai, Japan, 156, 160
Sanger, Margaret, 227
Saracens, 55, 56, 57
satire, 275
satraps, 63
Saunders, Dero, 99
Saussure, Ferdinand, 174
Scaliger, Johannes, 3
Schiller, Friedrich, 94
Schliemann, Heinrich, 278

INDEX

scholastic method, 73
Schweitzer, Albert, 128
science, 222–23; and anthropology, 213; and history, xv–xvi, 78, 82, 86, 95, 135, 215, 230; "new," 118, 126
Science and Civilization in China (Needham), 220
scientific attitude, xvi
scientific rationalism, 10
scribes, 52, 78
scripture, 46, 60
Scythians, 4
Second Temple, 25, 27, 141
secondary works, authors of, 102
Secret History (Procopius), 37–42, 42
secularization, 125–26
Self, death of, 244
self-betterment, 232, 233
self-evidence, 236
self-possession, 237
semeiology, 10
Senate House, Rome, 16, 17, 21
sensual beauty, 125
Sevenfold Conversation (Bodin), 65
Sextus Empiricus, 71
sexuality, Foucault on, 263–67
sharia (Muslim law), 44
Sherwood, Marika, 186–90
Shinto, 159
Shotwell, James T., xxii
Sixtus V, Pope, 89, 105
skepticism, 73, 211, 215, 218
slave trade, 183, 253–54
Smith, Caroline, 58
Social Darwinism in American Thought (Hofstadter), 230
solidarity, 177
Sombart, Werner, 194
Sons of Africa, 188
sources, historical, 28–29, 92–93, 114, 181; primary, 102; *see also* authenticity; evidence; truth, in reporting/testimony
sovereignty, 65
space, 200
Sparta, war with Athenian Empire (431–404 BC), 1, 7–12

Spencer, Herbert, 171
spirit of capitalism (Weber), 193, 194, 195
Spirit of Rationalism, The (Lecky), 123
Spitzer, Alan B., xxiv
Ssu Ma-ch'ien, 143
St. Bernard, 76
St. Peter's Basilica, 105
stars, 199, 212
Stern, Fritz, xxii
Stoics, 61
Strauss, David Friedrich, 127–33
structuralism, 263
studia humanitatis, 60
Stunkel, Kenneth R., xxiv
styles, historical, 274, 275, 276
subaltern studies, 168, 173, 175, 177
Suetonius (Gaius Suetonius Tranqullus), 14–19, 25; Sallust compared, 22
Sun Yat'sen, 153
Sung Dynasty, China, 146, 147, 150, 152
Superego (Freud), 268
supernaturalism, 26, 132, 210
superstition, 16
Supreme Being *see* God
Supreme Ultimate, 146–47
Sylvester II, Pope, 60
al Tabari, Muhammed, 43, 46

Tacitus, 14, 22, 25, 33
Tai Chen, 144–48
T'ang Dynasty, China, 150, 152
Taoism, 146, 147
Tartuffe (Molière), 85
Technics and Civilization (Mumford), 204–8; definitions, 205
technology, 203–9, 222; nautical (China), 221; waves of, 206–8
teleological cosmology, 118
territoriality, 177
testimony, 216
Theobald IV (Count of Champagne), 54
Theodora, 37, 39, 40, 41
theology, 47, 215, 216
Thirty Years War, 106
Thomas, Keith, xxiii, 209–13

Thompson, E. P., 247
Thompson, James Westfall, xxii
Thoughts and Sentiments on the Evil and Wicked Traffic of the Slavery and Commerce of the Human Species (Cugoano), 188
Thrace, 7
Thucydides, 1, 2, 5, 7–12, 22, 33, 38, 66; Herodotus compared, 2, 5, 7, 9, 11
Tiberius, 15, 16, 17
Tigris River, 119, 122
Tillemont, Louis-Sébastien Le Nain de, 92
time, measurement of, 204, 223
time frames, historical, 227
Titus, 15, 25, 26, 27–28, 29, 141
Tokugawa Sogunate, Japan, 154, 155, 156–57, 159, 165
Tolstoy, Leo, 138
Toqueville, Alexis de, 275
torture, 237
totalitarianism, 240
Traditional Government in Imperial China: A Critical Analysis (Ch'ien Mu), 148–53
traditional history, 227
travel, 5
Trevor-Roper, Hugh, 99
tribalism, 181
Trojan wars, 8, 278
tropes, 273, 274, 275
Troup, Kathleen, xxii
trustworthiness of documentation *see* truth, in reporting/testimony
truth, in reporting/testimony, 28–29, 43, 45–46, 73, 74, 76–78, 86, 87; *see also* documentation; evidence; facts; sources, historical
Tucker, Susan I., 58
Twain, Mark, 141
twentieth-century Europe and America, 191–282

uncertainty, xxi
uncritical history, 102
uniqueness, 108, 169
unit ideas, 199, 202
Unitarianism, 197

United Nations Declaration of Human Rights, 240
United States, twentieth-century, 203–9, 225–41, 252–56

Valla, Lorenzo, 3, 59–64, 78, 129, 147
value neutrality, 193
Vedas, 171
Vespasian, 15, 16, 26, 28
violence, 188
Virgil, 278
Virgin Mary, 56
Virtues of the Jihad, The (Ibn Shaddad), 44
Vitellius, 15, 18
Volk (historical identity), 96, 97, 98
volksgeist (distinctive spirit), 96, 98
Voltaire (Françoise-Marie Arouet), xviii, 12, 42, 72, 82, 83–88, 90, 92, 97, 101, 118, 202, 215, 216; *Essay on Customs*, 83, 89, 217

Waley, Arthur, xx
Wang, Q. Edward, xxii
Wang Ling, 219, 220
War of the Spanish Succession, 85
warfare, 116–17
Warrington, Marnie-Hughes, xxii
Wars of Justinian (Procopius), 39
Watt, James, 204
Weber, Max, 192–97
Western civilization, 155–61, 260
White, Hayden, xvii, xxii, xxiii, 272–77
Whitehead, Alfred North, 215
Whitelock, Dorothy, 50, 58
Wieland, Christoph, 94
William, Duke of Normandy (the Conqueror), 53
William of Malmesbury, 53
Williamson, G. A., 25, 35
Wilson, Woodrow, 230, 233, 234
Winchester chronicle (892), 51
witchcraft, 68–69, 124, 125, 126, 210, 212
witness reliability, 87; *see also* truth, in reporting/testimony
wizards, 211, 212
women, neglect of, 97, 122
women in history, 226–29

women's studies, 225
Woodman, A. J., 23
work ethic, 194
world history, 96
World of Odysseus (Finley), 278–82
worlds, infinite number of, 200–201

Xenophon, 91
Xerxes, 4, 6

yin-yang, 146, 223
Young Man Luther: A Study in Psychoanalysis and History (Erikson), 268–71
Yukichi, Fukuzawa, 149

Zealots, anti-Roman, 26–27
Zeus, 218, 281
Zoroastrianism, 30